Philosophy and Political Economy

T0295706

Classics in Economics Series
Warren J. Samuels, Series Editor

Economic Semantics,
   Fritz Machlup. With an introduction by Mark Perlman

The Economy as a System of Power,
   Edited by Marc R. Tool and Warren J. Samuels

Essays in Economics,
   Joseph A. Schumpeter. With an introduction by Richard Swedberg

Evolutionary Economics,
   David Hamilton. With a new introduction by the author

Institutional Economics,
   John Commons. With an introduction by Malcolm Rutherford

Inventors and Moneymakers,
   Frank W. Taussig. With an introduction by Warren J. Samuels

Main Currents in Modern Economics,
   Ben Seligman. With an introduction by E. Ray Canterbery

Methodology of Economic Thought,
   Edited by Marc R. Tool and Warren J. Samuels

Philosophy and Political Economy,
   James Bonar. With a new introdutcion by Warren J. Samuels

Political Element in Development of Economic Theory,
   Gunnar Myrdal. With an introduction by Richard Swedberg

State, Society, and Corporation Power,
   Edited by Marc R. Tool and Warren J. Samuels

Philosophy and Political Economy

James Bonar

With a New Introduction by
Warren J. Samuels

Routledge
Taylor & Francis Group

NEW YORK AND LONDON

This edition published 1992 by Transaction Publishers

First published in paperback 2018
by Routledge
711 Third Avenue, New York, NY 10017

and by Routledge
2 Park Square, Milton Park, Abingdon, Oxon OX14 4RN

Routledge is an imprint of the Taylor & Francis Group, an informa business

© 2018 Taylor & Francis

The right of James Bonar to be identified as author of this work has been asserted by him in accordance with sections 77 and 78 of the Copyright, Designs and Patents Act 1988.

First edition published by S. Sonnenschein 1893

Trademark notice: Product or corporate names may be trademarks or registered trademarks, and are used only for identification and explanation without intent to infringe.

Library of Congress Cataloging-in-Publication Data
Bonar, James, 1852–1941.
Philosophy and political economy/James Bonar; with a new introduction by Warren J. Samuels.
Includes index.
1. Economics–Moral and ethical aspects. 2. Economics–Philosophy.
I. Title
HB72.B65
330.1-dc20   91–8166

ISBN: 978-0-88738-438-7 (hbk)
ISBN: 978-1-4128-6527-2 (pbk)
ISBN: 978-1-351-31644-6 (ebk)

Typeset in Times New Roman
by Servis Filmsetting Ltd, Stockport, Cheshire

Contents

Book V   Modern Philosophy: Materialistic Economics and Evolution

Introduction to The Transaction Edition

James Bonar's *Philosophy and Political Economy in Some of Their Historical Relations* is one of the most remarkable if not unique books in the history of economic thought. Although Bonar tells his readers that "economics did not until modern times exist as a separate study" (p. 374), the principal significance of his book is the view that economics, even modern technical economic theory, necessarily has certain moral-philosophical assumptions. There are moral and philosophical questions on which any school of economics inevitably takes, largely implicitly, some position. The conclusions of economic theory, including those brought to bear on questions of policy, are channeled by, more or less specific to, and have meaning ultimately in terms of, moral and philosophical preconceptions, or larger system of philosophical thought, on the bases of which those conclusions are drawn.

More than philosophy as traditionally understood is involved: Bonar also stresses the psychological elements, preconceptions, and assumptions of economics. Writing at the end of the nineteenth century, Bonar also felt compelled to explore the implications for economics of the theory of evolution arising from the work of Charles Darwin and others.

In 1893 the discipline had not yet taken the name economics, with its emphasis on technical analysis–though nonetheless predicated on philosophical foundations. Bonar understands political economy as "the study of the relation of human society to its material wealth" and philosophy as "the study of first principles and ultimate issues." Both have to do with "men's thoughts about the world, and human life in general" (p. 3). This approach to the definition of economics is closer to that of Alfred Marshall, to whom it was the study of mankind in the ordinary business of life, namely, earning a living, rather than, for example, either the logic of choice or the allocation of limited resources that have alternative uses among multiple and unlimited objectives.

Bonar acknowledges that "Economical facts and practice ... as distinguished from theories about them, have, no doubt, had a still greater influence, both on economists and philosophers" (p. 3), but he is more interested in the influence that political economy and philosophy have had on each other, their *mutual* influence. It will not surprise the reader, however, that the precise relationships intended by Bonar are somewhat unclear. Bonar states that "the economical element is in Greek Philosophy subordinated to the political, and still more to the ethical," and that "In mediaeval and modern times (if we pass over the time when economic arrangements were forced into the rules of Canon Law), political economy grows out of political philosophy." He considers that "The mercantile theory was essentially political," and that "the theory of property, in which, as treated by Hobbes and Locke, economic considerations played a great part, was coloured by the politics of the day; and the question of origin was not sufficiently distinguished from the question of justification." As for Bernard Mandeville, Frances Hutcheson, David Hume, and Adam Smith, "modern political economy grew out of moral philosophy," although "it was hardly ethical so much as political in the hands of their contemporaries the French Economists," the Physiocrats. Political economy grew out of one or another branch of philosophy, including natural rights. Moreover, "modern socialism does no more than frankly combine what had in other quarters been tacitly combined, the economical and the philosophical problems" (pp. 5–6).

John Dewey, however, in his review of the book in *Political Science Quarterly* (1894), indicated that there may be something different here than one might expect. "What Mr. Bonar has *not* done," wrote Dewey, "is to show how the same fundamental problems and attitudes have underlain philosophic and economic thought from the outset, simply assuming different statements and outward garbs. He has not traced the reflection of philosophical conceptions over into the region of political economy, influencing and even controlling the economic writer without any consciousness on his part of the ideas of which he was the mouthpiece." "What Mr. Bonar *has* done," continues Dewey, "is to give a minute and solid account of the economic content to be found in many philosophic writers, for example Plato, Aristotle, Hobbes, Kant, Hegel; and of the immediate philosophic connections and leanings of such economists as Adam Smith, the Mills, Karl Marx and Lassalle."

Bonar's is, moreover, in Dewey's reading, a survey of ideas, a "continuous cataloguing." It is an analysis of neither "the persistence of some fundamental problems" nor "the chief crises through which the problem has passed, and the chief types which the solutions have assumed." The exception, according to Dewey, is Bonar's analysis in Book V of materialism and of evolution.

Dewey complains that both Comte and Rousseau are not given adequate treatment, and on this basis finds that the book "lacks a wide and commanding sweep." But, he concludes, the book "manifests a great sense of the immediate connections and the relevant historical implications of particular writers."

A glimpse at the contents will lead one to question Dewey's judgment as to sweep. Book I treats Ancient Philosophy, including Plato, Aristotle, the Stoics and Epicureans, and Christianity. Book II, on Modern Philosophy: Natural Law, treats Machiavelli, More, Grotius, Hobbes, Harrington, Locke, Hume, the Physiocrats, Smith, and "Natural Rights and Law of Nature." Book III, on Modern Philosophy: Utilitarian Economics, discusses Malthus, Bentham and James Mill, and John Stuart Mill. Book IV, on Modern Philosophy: Idealistic Economics, treats Kant, Fichte, K.C.F. Krause (now forgotten), and Hegel. Book V, on Modern Philosophy: Materialistic Economics and Evolution, centers on Marx, Engels, and Lassalle; treats the relation of economics to the theory of evolution as an epilogue; and concludes with a summary of the volume as a whole.

Dewey is entitled to his evaluations as to the relevant importance, and interpretations, assigned to individual writers. Two of the important considerations warranting the republication of this volume are, however, first, the variations of interpretive content and nuance given individual writers and, second, the variations of assessment of importance given individual writers, in comparison with positions taken by others, including Dewey himself.[1] Bonar treats Adam Smith, for example, under the aegis of Natural Law. But modern Smith scholarship is severely divided, with Smith being found to reside in supernaturalism, naturalism, empiricism, and/or utilitarianism, among other paradigms.

But what of Dewey's claim that the book incorporates no basic interpretive schema, that it identifies and analyzes no persistent fundamental problem? This, too, may not be the case. First, as this writer would insist, the central argument of the book is indeed the inexorable presence of the moral–political philosophical assumptions or preconceptions of economic theory. Such is much more important than the idea of mutual influences (or "connections") between philosophy and political economy, although both are ideas that run counter to the beliefs of some that economics has no connection at all with philosophy.[2]

Second, Bonar writes in his Introduction that "Perhaps the most striking phenomenon observed by all economists, is the apparently spontaneous organization of bodies of men for industrial work, an organization resulting without the deliberate intention of the separate members, at the bidding of economical motives" (pp. 4–5). (The doctrine of unintended consequences is central to both Adam Smith and Adam Ferguson. Ferguson's work is only noted in passing.) In the concluding pages of the book, Bonar argues that "The Darwinian theory is a particular form of the theory of development" (p. 393), that the Darwinian theory "provides us with no means of pronouncing a judgment as to the quality of the results of this evolution" (that is, it is not teleological), and that "economics, like Darwinism, gives us by itself no means of judging the results" (p. 394). Bonar also presents two conclusions, both bearing on the perennial relevance of philosophy.[3] The first is that the application of the Darwinian theory to society in general and to social change in particular requires that we "found our standard of judgment not on the Darwinian but on the philosophical notion of development" (p. 394). The second is that:

> It is not obvious that Darwinism would favour socialism, or indeed any particular plan of social reform. It explains, how, but not why,

certain occurrences have taken place, and leaves us still to deal with our old problems by the aid of conceptions outside the Darwinism itself. Darwinism is in keeping with the view that the industrial improvement and organization surrounding us have in great part grown up spontaneously, or tentatively, and that *laissez faire* does not necessarily mean chaos. The development of the individual members of society is the chief end of society itself, and of the State which is its articulate, representative head. To secure this end, the necessary outward conditions must be assured to each member of society; and, as long as human nature remains as it has been in all history, so long there will be need for a State to do this work. But, as each individual must himself use the opportunities, so assured to him, in his own way, there must be (in no narrow sense of the word) individual liberty secured to him. The future may bring with it changes in the statute laws of property, in order to bring it within reach of every one, as a condition of development. As long as there is room kept open for personal and moral freedom, originality, and every kind of individual valuation, the world of mankind will not be losers (pp. 394–395).

This view is essentially that of Carl Menger (also mentioned only in passing), writing in the tradition of Smith and Ferguson, that institutions that have developed spontaneously and organically, without either conscious design or teleological direction, must be subjected to deliberative critical inquiry–inquiry in which reasoned analysis, the domain of philosophy broadly comprehended, must be foremost. Thus, further apropos of economics in its relation to philosophy, writing about the phenomenon of spontaneous and unintended social organization of industrial life, Bonar adds that, "Such a phenomenon, in fact, has a much deeper meaning than economics can interpret; and parallel cases present themselves which show the need for a philosophical rather than a merely economical treatment of this part of the subject."

The irony is that, in the hands of many contemporary writers, the operative premise is that of self-interests giving effect to given individual preferences, rather than–as understood by Stuart Mill, Alfred Marshall, and Bonar and to which view philosophy is ultimately handmaiden–"the development of the individual members of society [as] the chief end of society itself, and of the State which is its articulate representative head." As Dewey would agree, there is need and room for both collective action by the state on behalf of the public and its problems, and spheres of meaningful individual autonomy and freedom. More fundamentally historically and analytically, Bonar was here seemingly giving effect to the conflict between the two central principles of Locke, that of the integrity of property (that is, of those interests given legal status and protection as private property), and that of the integrity of the legislature (and legislation) as the premier mode of governance–the conflict that focuses on the viability and direction of legal change of law as a mode of social change.

There is much in this volume that is more than survey, Dewey notwithstanding. There is interpretation, and much of it; indeed, perhaps it is all interpretation–or so says modern hermeneutics, which questions our ability to comprehend on their own terms and in their own ages the ideas of original writers, and also questions whether philosophy is a source of substantive analysis or a mode of discourse. And there is much that is controversial, for example, Bonar's view that modern political economy required as a precondition of its own rise, however paradoxically, the growth of the modern state and in particular the introduction of taxation in replacement of feudal obligations.[4] Absent, somewhat surprisingly, from the volume is any discussion of the *Methodenstreit*, the controversy over methodology, which was rampant during the period this book was written. This controversy had precisely to do with the proper methodological and philosophical foundations of economics as an intellectual discipline, and yet the book is silent. Moreover, although Pogson Smith concluded his review with the statement that "in some form or other the category of evolution–the principle of Hegel or the principle of Darwin–must leaven even the English economics is a prophecy which is already approaching verification," only five years after the publication of this volume Thorstein Veblen explored in the *Quarterly Journal of Economics* for 1898 the case for "Why Is Economics Not an Evolutionary Science?"–an argument that has been echoed to this day by economists in the diverse traditions of Veblen and Joseph Schumpeter.

We come to James Bonar himself. This volume on philosophy and political economy "in some of their historical relations" is all the more remarkable because of its particular author. James Bonar (1852–1941) came from a family of Scottish clergy. Eventually a leading authority on Adam Smith, and also on Thomas Robert Malthus, Bonar followed the much earlier trail of Smith from Glasgow University to Balliol College, Oxford, leaving the latter in 1877. Initially involved in the University Extension Movement in East London, Bonar became in 1881 a civil servant, with positions first in the Civil Service Commission and later in the Royal Mint, retiring in 1919.

Bonar numbered McKenzie King and Ramsay MacDonald–both prime ministers, the former of Canada and the latter of Great Britain–among a coterie of distinguished friends. Bonar was a founder and Vice President of the Royal Economic Society, a Vice President of the Royal Statistical Society, President of Section F (Economics and Statistics) of the British Association, and a Fellow of the British Academy. In addition to the present work (1893), Bonar earned a notable reputation for his *Malthus and His Work* (1885), and his *Catalogue of Adam Smith's Library* (1894). Altogether he published eleven books and numerous articles and reviews, many in the *Economic Journal* and in *Palgrave's Dictionary of Political Economy*. His seven Obituary Notices published in the *Economic Journal* included pieces on Friedrich Engels, Henry George, John Ruskin, Herbert Spencer, Eugen von Bohm-Bawerk, and Philip Wicksteed. Several of his writings introduced the work of the Austrian School to English-reading economists. His

scholarly career, largely as a historian of economics, was conducted contemporaneously with his work as a civil servant, as were those careers of
several other noteworthy economists, including James and John Stuart Mill,
R. G. Hawtrey, and John Maynard Keynes. The obituary of James Bonar
appeared in the April 1941 *Economic Journal,* written by G. Findlay Shirras
of University College, Exeter.

What is the view of the compass of economics held by such a man?
Consider, for example, Bonar's identification and treatment of the question
"whether the theory of Population belongs strictly to Political Economy at
all" (p. 211). Although his discussion directly involves but two paragraphs,
Bonar considers the relations of production and distribution and of wealth
and happiness, wherein Malthus agreed with Godwin (whose ideas in part
motivated Malthus to write his *Essay on Population* in the first place), and
wherein Malthus differed from Smith. It is over such matters that contro-
versies on the nature and scope of economics have been fought, and it is also
on such matters that, in part, the philosophical preconceptions of economics
derive their substance and make their appearance in the history of economic
thought, although often only implicitly.

Let us then return to the structure of the book and note some of what it
reveals, according to Bonar, about the "historical relations" of philosophy
and political economy. Book I's principal summaries of Plato and Aristotle
are divided into three sections: their conceptions of wealth, of production and
distribution, and of civil society; and its discussions of the Stoics, Epicureans,
and early Christianity explore the further complications introduced by these
bodies of thought, in part in regard to the functioning of the Church as social
control.

Book II's treatments of natural law demonstrate the fecundity of the con-
cept and its applications in the hands of Machiavelli, More, Bodin, Grotius,
Hobbes, Harrington, Locke, Hume, the Physiocrats, and Adam Smith, as
well as, less intensively, Rousseau, Burke, Bentham, and Paine, and the critique of the ideas of natural rights and natural law. Natural law is shown to
be both a mode or framework of discourse and an ontological position.

Book III considers Malthus, Bentham, and the two Mills, father and son,
under the rubric of utilitarianism, again demonstrating that quite different
bodies of substantive analysis can be articulated within a particular school
of philosophy.

Book IV covers so-called idealistic economics, writers now not so commonly associated with each other: Kant, Fichte, and Hegel, as well as the now
almost totally forgotten K.C.F. Krause (in only three pages). In each case, as
indeed is true of the other writers discussed by Bonar, our author identifies
and explores the philosophical topics on which the conduct of technical economic analysis (by the same writers or by others typically less philosophically
inclined or informed) makes assumptions. These include the nature of human
nature and of human wants; the nature and role of the state; the relation of
the individual to society; the nature and origin of property; the nature and

role of other institutions, such as money, church, and army; the role of ideals in socioeconomic life; and, *inter alia*, the question of class.

Finally, Book V's two chapters treat, first, Marx, Engels, and Lassalle as the progenitors of materialistic economics, and second, the relation of economics to the theory of evolution. In respect of both topics, the 1893 publication of the book necessarily means that Bonar was unable to consider either the Marxist revisionists or the non-Marxist or nonsocialist versions of evolutionism, for example, the ideas of Thorstein Veblen, for the simple reason that they had not yet blossomed. But even by 1893 diversity of formulation of materialism and of evolutionism suggests that these were both modes or frameworks of discourse and philosophical positions.

Let us return to Bonar's final paragraph, quoted in full above. Here he stresses that Darwinism need not "favour socialism, or indeed any particular plan of social reform." Darwinism is taken to signify comportment with the idea of spontaneous order, including the view that "*laissez faire* does not necessarily mean chaos." But Darwinism does not mean for Bonar the finessing of socioeconomic problems. It signifies for him that we are left "still to deal with our old problems by the aid of conceptions outside of Darwinism itself." We have created the received institutions, including the laws governing property, and "The Future may bring with it changes ... in order to bring it within reach of every one, as a condition of development" and "room kept open for personal and moral freedom, originality, and every kind of individual variation." These words have a saccharine quality to them but they also should indicate to the reader that at the heart of the relations of philosophy and political economy is the problem of order: the ongoing need to reconcile conflicts between freedom and control, continuity and change, and hierarchy and equality. The fundamental question to which philosophy and political economy are both brought to bear is that of changing the structure of power and opportunity in the social economy. It is in this regard that the philosophical assumptions on which political economy rests become so fundamentally operative and consequential.

Warren J. Samuels

Notes

1 See, for example, *Lectures by John Dewey: Moral and Political Philosophy*, edited by Warren J. Samuels and Donald F. Koch, *Research in the History of Economic Thought and Methodology*, Archival Supplement 1 (1989).
2 Another reviewer, W. Caldwell, writing in the *Journal of Political Economy* (1893), stressed that "there are others who, imbued with the spirit of specialization in science, instinctively fight shy of any connection that economics may have had with philosophy, and others still, like Dr. Ingram and the Comtists, who are ashamed of the philosophical origin of political economy, while still curiously at the same time desiring to merge it in a newer sort of philosophy." Whereas Dewey writes that Bonar "does hold that political economy sustains certain permanent relations to the philosophical sciences" and that "we might say that almost all the leading ideas of

political economy seem, according to this book, to have their roots in philosophy." Still another reviewer, W. R. Sorley, writing in the *International Journal of Ethics* (1893), agrees with the latter idea, saying that "economic facts ... form part of the material with which social philosophy is concerned; and systems of economics can be shown to be connected with philosophical views concerning human life and its position in the ultimate order of things" and "economic conceptions do not as yet stand by themselves, but are, as Mr. Bonar points out, subordinate to–indeed, form a part of–political and ethical conceptions."

3 Sorley takes exception to Bonar's use of the term "Darwinian development." Bonar is said to apply it, "for instance, to the survival of the mechanical inventions which best subserve the purposes of the industrial arts. The selection in this case is deliberate, made consciously by people who knew what they were about, and therefore chose the fit and rejected the unfit. What Darwin established was that a similar end was reached by natural causes without deliberation or consciousness of the end. To this only the term 'natural selection' should be applied. The former process is deliberate, or, as it is called, artificial. The survival of useful invention is as much due to artificial selection as the English racehorse."

4 The point is stressed by W. G. Pogson Smith in his review of the book in the *English History Review* (1894).

Introduction

Introduction

Political Economy, or the study of the relation of human society to its material wealth, and PHILOSOPHY, or the study of first principles and ultimate issues, have at various times exerted an influence on one another which the history of economics and philosophy makes very evident.

Economical facts and practice, the actual condition of national industries, wealth, and trade, as distinguished from theories about them, have, no doubt, had a still greater influence, both on economists and philosophers; and to estimate this effect of practice on theory would be a larger and perhaps a more important inquiry. Some writers have regarded this second inquiry as almost superseding the other, on the ground that the supreme force in human history is economical.[1] It is clear that we may at least go as far as Erdmann, who begins his chapters on Greek Philosophy with the remark that philosophy arises when the struggle for existence has given place to a life of leisure.[2]

But it is only the former question that can be considered here, namely, how far men's thoughts about the world, and human life in general, have affected their thoughts about the economical element of human life in particular, and how far this influence of thoughts upon thoughts may have been mutual. The subject cannot, in the limits of a single volume, be treated in full detail; but by the aid of the references the reader may supply this defect if he will.

As a separate study, Economics comes very late; and in our historical retrospect we shall be looking for answers to questions which have not always been consciously present to the authors embraced in our scrutiny. From the vantage ground of the comparatively complete and systematic economic doctrine of modern times, we shall be seeking in past philosophies for materials out of which to construct their answers to our questions.

In one sense, of course, no study is separate; no single study can deal exclusively and exhaustively with every aspect of a selected subject. Least of all can any claim to exhaustiveness and exclusiveness be made by a science dealing with so concrete a subject as the material wealth of human society. Modern writers, who pursue economics as a separate study, accept such data and such help from other special studies as they cannot refuse without lapsing into unreality; and the extent of this necessary debt is very considerable. At the

same time they are not merely borrowers; they are giving special consideration to subjects and aspects not specially considered by the studies that give
the data and the help, and they make a contribution of their own to human
knowledge.

The economist looks at the phenomena of human wants and the material means of satisfying them simply as given causes, while to Psychology,
Physiology, and Physics, the said phenomena are effects to be traced to
remoter causes. He considers, for example, that the conditions of distribution or the causes of a particular system of property in land, or in movable
goods, are subjects for History to investigate. More especially at the two
ends of economical inquiry,—at the beginning when dealing with wants
and the means of satisfying them, and at the end when dealing with the
economical aspects of the body politic, and of even larger groups of men,
economic science becomes conscious of its shortcomings. Its students are
forced to remember from how much, when merely economists, they have
abstracted; and they are compelled to seek light from other and complementary branches of the study of human society. Not only at the end and the
beginning, but even in the centre of their inquiries, they may well feel this
need. Perhaps the most striking phenomenon observed by all economists,
is the apparently spontaneous organization of bodies of men for industrial
work, an organization resulting without the deliberate intention of the separate members, at the bidding of economical motives. The presumably close
kinship of the social sciences with one another may be expected to lead
economists to gain light on such a phenomenon from biology, psychology,
ethics, and political philosophy.

Such a phenomenon, in fact, has a much deeper meaning than economics
can interpret; and parallel cases present themselves which show the need for
a philosophical rather than a merely economical treatment of this part of
the subject. Even writers like Plato, who have noticed that division of labour
seems to lead spontaneously to an organized society, have found it impossible
to suppose that society is a purely economical body. When economical ideas
were presented by Plato in the course of his ethical and political speculation,
it soon appeared that society and social growth were neither purely political
nor purely economical. Though Plato (with a purely ethical object) gives
to the State a purely economical origin, the result is by no means a purely
economical organization; and yet it was as little (at least in the *Laws*) the
deliberate contrivance of a governing body. Society must be distinguished
from State.[3]

Historically it is true that the economical element is in Greek Philosophy
subordinated to the political, and still more to the ethical. Such economical
doctrine as is traceable in the writings of the Greek philosophers grows out of
their moral and political philosophy.

In mediæval and modern times (if we pass over the time when economical arrangements were forced into the rules of Canon Law), political economy grows out of political philosophy. The mercantile theory was

essentially political. The theory of property, in which, as treated by Hobbes and Locke, economical considerations played a great part, was coloured by the politics of the day; and the question of origin was not sufficiently distinguished from the question of justification; still less were the two questions discussed with the calm indifference of science. Economical subjects were first brought prominently into ethical controversy by Mandeville; and the discussion of them in this connection by Hutcheson, Hume, and Adam Smith himself, has given countenance to the impression that modern political economy grew out of moral philosophy. But it was hardly ethical so much as political in the hands of their contemporaries the French Economists, who embodied it in their grandiose system of political and social philosophy, as a feature of first importance; and it was largely on the foundation of the physiocratic system that Adam Smith constructed his own. We owe to the physiocrats also the continuance of the discussion begun long before their time by Grotius, Hobbes, and Locke, about natural rights; and this abstract question of political philosophy has had a connection with political economy, which only the rigidly abstract student of the latter study can ever wish to ignore. The persistence of this question in conjunction with the comparatively new question of the rights of man has been a feature, not only of political, but of economical writings down to our own day; and modern socialism does no more than frankly combine what had in other quarters been tacitly combined, the economical and the philosophical problems.

The psychological element in economics has had less notice alike from philosophers and economists. For reasons given amply in other volumes of this series, psychology has come late in the history of philosophy. We shall find, however, even in ancient philosophy, that the materials for answering our questions under this head are not entirely absent.

As the subject considered is the historical relations of philosophy and political economy, no attempt has been made either to narrate the history of philosophy as a whole or to deal with the writings of authors who have happily not yet passed into history.

Debts to previous writers have, as far as possible, been acknowledged in the notes. There have been monographs on various parts of the subject, especially by German writers. Professor Hasbach's two books on Adam Smith[4] cover part of the ground much more fully than the present author could hope to cover the whole. Professor Espinas, in his *Histoire des doctrines économiques* (1892), has kept the connection of philosophy and economics in view; but the scope of his little volume is described by its title. The idea of the present book was suggested by a note of Professor Adolph Wagner, of Berlin.[5]

So far as the author knows, this is the first attempt to present a view of the relations of philosophy and economics through the whole of their history, and the absence of guiding models must be to some extent his excuse for the shortcomings of his work.

Notes

1 See below, Book V.
2 Erdmann, *Hist. of Philos.*, vol. i. p. 17, § 18.
3 For the distinction see below, pp. 24, 30, etc.
4 See below, Book II., ch. vii. Notes.
5 *Volkswirthschaftslehre, I*ster *Theil, Grundlegung*, 2nd ed., 1879, p. 413.

BOOK I
Ancient Philosophy

1   Plato (428–347 B.C.)

Economical ideas appear in relation to philosophical only when philosophy extends not only to outward nature, but to man, and not only to man, but to society.

We begin therefore neither with Thales, nor with Anaxagoras, nor even with Socrates, but with PLATO.

I. The conceptions of Wealth, Production, Distribution, and of the economical functions of State and Society are treated by Plato, some incidentally, others at length, but always in subordination to Ethics, and never as (even in theory) separable from ethical considerations.

This subordination is most evident in the case of the notion of wealth. When Socrates had become the founder of Moral Philosophy by definitely raising the question of man's chief end, the place of wealth among the ends of action could not fail to be discussed by any systematic philosophy proceeding on Socratic lines. Relating as they do to the main business of ordinary active life, the notion of wealth and the various definitions of what we now call economical ideas, offered a peculiarly suitable field for the practice of the Socratic method, in its three features, quest of an end, definition of general ideas, and induction from particular instances. Yet even in the early or Socratic dialogues of Plato he does not take hold of the notion of wealth or any other economical notion and sift it as he would have sifted a metaphysical idea.[1] We are told of its place in relation to man's chief end and among human concerns generally; but we are left to gather from scattered descriptions and classifications what Plato's definition of it might have been.

In the *Laws*,[2] for example, the Cretan constitution is praised as securing all blessings necessary to human happiness, the divine or spiritual blessings and the human or bodily and material. Wisdom, temperance, justice, and courage, are the divine; and, if a city possess them, the others are added to it; but wanting them, it will want the rest also. The rest, or human blessings, are health, beauty, strength, and wealth. Elsewhere in the *Laws*,[3] he says three things are of concern to men—mind, body, and estate ($\chi\rho\acute{\eta}\mu\alpha\tau\alpha$), and that is their order of importance. Wealth, therefore, though only in the third rank, is recognised by Plato as an element of real necessity and rationality in human life when it is intelligently and moderately used, and not blindly heaped up, without reference to the chief ends of life.[4]

The difficulty is that Plato does not directly define it, and therefore we have really to deal with wealth in two senses of the word; namely, outward goods and an excessive accumulation of them, or, in short, wealth and excessive wealth. The ambiguity is of perennial recurrence in the writings of moralists; but the emphasis on excess is characteristic of the Greek philosopher.

The former kind of wealth Plato recognises to be indispensable; and an assured competency is in his eyes *almost* a condition of goodness. He grants that poverty, ill-health, and wickedness are all evils, though not in the same degree.[5] In the first pages of the *Republic*, the old man Cephalus says that, if he had been poor instead of rich, he might possibly have lived less good a life, even as Themistocles, if he had not belonged to Athens, might not have become famous.[6] Cephalus no doubt is speaking for the old-fashioned Athenian morality, of which the Platonic Socrates proceeds to show the weakness. "Not only as soon as a man has a livelihood, but even before he has one," he should practise virtue.[7] Still, even in the first of the two ideal states of the *Republic*, though plain living and simplicity are at their highest point, the citizens are supposed to have the rude abundance of the golden age. To wealth in that sense Plato has no objection. But he far more commonly understands by wealth not this rude abundance, but the refined abundance of later times, the multifarious luxuries of sense, almost always associated by him with intemperance.[8] His description of the Oligarchical Man (in the 8th book of the *Republic*), is not inconsistent with this view. The Oligarchical Man is the money-maker, who devotes his whole energies to saving and accumulating wealth,[9] instead of spending it; and, since he consumes only what is absolutely necessary to satisfy the needs of his physical nature, he is described as devoting himself to the satisfaction of his "necessary wants" (τάς ἀναγκαίους ἐπιθυμίας), though, like all misers, he is really not pursuing satisfaction of any concrete wants at all, but an abstraction of the greatest possible quantity of the means of satisfaction generally. To Plato, his apparent temperance seems a kind of intemperance, for it does not spring from a regard to the real chief end of life; and it leads directly to the intemperance of other men who prey upon his savings as drones on the honey of the working bees, and who thereby satisfy all manner of artificial and unnecessary wants. Whether in the possessor of wealth himself or in other men, wealth and intemperance seem to Plato to go together. Hence he thinks it best for citizens of a good State to have neither poverty nor riches, for either extreme would be a temptation to sin in the individual and sedition in the State.

In the *Laws*, Plato speaks more than once of a fixed limit of wealth, which no one is to transgress under severe penalties. Human wants are limited by Nature or Reason; once allow personal enrichment a free course, and the wants of man become insatiable and illimitable in defiance of reason and nature. The notion of infinity is understood, as regards human wants, in a purely negative sense. It means absence of limit, and therefore lawlessness and irrationality. We could hardly expect to find the modern notion of an infinity of wants, conceived as an essential quality of human beings, and leading to a positive development of the spiritual nature of men. But we might have expected Plato to recognise that the unconscious influences of beautiful sights and sounds[10] require external appliances and imply an account of outward wealth not very easily fixed. His answer might have been that after all the City of Pigs was his first love, and, in that, a much simpler education than that of his Second Ideal would have been enough. Yet from the slight attention given to this simple State, we may conclude that Plato himself saw that human wants could not fail to grow beyond it and become luxurious. A more plausible answer might have been that, the guardians having no private property, the wealth that provides for their education is not their own but the public wealth. But, against this, we may take his own words in the *Laws*,[11] where he says it is no object even for the State to make itself as rich as possible; and there are reasons for supposing that he would have applied to States as well as to individuals his principle that "poverty results from increase of man's desires, not from diminution of his property."[12] Plato the artist and Plato the philosopher are not always in harmony with each other; and Plato the artist might take a different view of wealth from Plato the philosopher. The philosopher's view of wealth is the view that must rule our judgment of his economics; and on the whole his economic starting-point, his notion of wealth, is made by his philosophy less œsthetic than ascetic. The good man will have no wealth,[13] or, if you call his outward goods his wealth, it will be "such as to be in harmony with his inward wealth";[14] it will be small in quantity and of a fixed and determinate measure. He will be rich because, being wise, he will have few wants, knowing that the outside world, whether of men or of things, can do little or nothing for him.

II. Plato's conception of Production is in close connection with this view of Wealth. It is important not that men should have as many wants as possible, and satisfy them all,[15] but that they should find out what their special work is in the world and do it.[16] He illustrates this doctrine in various passages of the *Republic*, and especially in the clearest of his economic analyses, the account of Division of Labour in the Second Book.[17] A State, he there says, is formed because the individual is not able to supply all his wants by himself, but only when he makes common cause with other men, and devotes himself to one single industry for the common good, on the understanding that the rest are doing the same. Thus arise the separate trades of farming, building, weaving, and shoemaking; and this division of labour is best for the following reasons: Men and women are not all born alike, but with special powers fitting them for special work.[18] Second, by attention to one occupation alone men will do much better work than when attempting several. Third, because time is saved and opportunities (of season, etc.) are more promptly utilized. In this way articles are made in greater number, of better quality, and with greater ease, than when each man is a Jack-of-all-trades.

Industrial division of labour is thus described as the origin of the State. State, however, means in this case no more than City or Society; and it is in his second city[19] that we find a State in the sense of a central government.

In the *Laws* Plato gives the State a patriarchal origin.[20] In the *Republic*, with a purely ethical aim (the discovery of Justice) he gives it (as it would seem) a purely economical origin. Yet the principle of division of labour is not to Plato peculiar to industry. It is a general principle of human nature, with many applications. It is applied unreservedly to politics. The various classes in the State, the rulers and the ruled, whether men or women, are chosen from their birth because of their peculiar natural qualities—the gold, silver, or iron, in their nature, discovered by the Guardians. According to the metal of which they are made their work in life is prescribed for them. Once prescribed for them, it becomes their sole work. Versatility is no virtue. The "universal genius" (Hippias the Sophist, for example),[21] who can do and be anything, is to be escorted to the frontier. Actors, as trying to play more than one part in life, are to be excluded too.

It has been sometimes doubted whether industrial division of labour is illustrated by physiological division of functions and organs or is itself the source of the illustration.[22] Plato would not have discussed this question of priority. Industrial and physiological division of labour is only an example of a very wide philosophical principle. The claim of justice as such, its essence as a moral virtue, is that every man and woman, every class in the State, and every faculty in the soul, should have their own special work to do. So far as that claim of justice goes, there is no room for dispute about the analogy of the professions and arts to handicrafts, and of all of them to the spiritual life of men and its organs. Plato takes advantage of the obviousness of this particular analogy to assume a much closer general analogy than can perhaps be granted. The assumption was perhaps largely due to his sensitive regard for the reader's need of illustrations to help him in following a philosophical argument.[23] Plato has himself furnished reasons for doubting the completeness of the general analogy.

He tells us that the Philosopher should be a man of very varied powers,[24] that specialists, whether in arts or handicrafts or politics, are all of them narrowed by their exclusive concern with their one occupation,[25] one class of them indeed being marred and maimed by it in mind and body;[26] and finally, at least in his later years, he refused to apply his principle of the division of labour to international trade,[27] considering that each State, unlike each individual, should be as far as possible self-sufficient and independent of its neighbours. It might be added that in the second ideal at least it is by no means Plato's belief that every man should be the judge of his own capacities, and should freely take up an occupation and pursue it from the love of it. The Guardians, who are the governing body in his ideal State, are to ascertain each child's capacities and fix its career for it accordingly.[28] The philosopher indeed is a lover of work for its own sake; but that is not because he has chosen his own work for himself. His career is fixed for him, and he is allowed a certain freedom in his studies only because in the case of the intellect, compulsion is of no use, for nothing acquired under compulsion will remain in the mind.[29]

Compulsory division of labour therefore was to be universal, in the later Platonic State. The division of labour which created the first or simpler City (the "City of Pigs") is described as spontaneous; and it develops from agriculture into the simpler handicrafts, from them into inland trade with a common market and a currency, going on to a foreign commerce and a merchant navy.[30] Finally, we have the unskilled labourers, whose special power is simply their physical strength, and who are not slaves but hired servants. Plato professes to regard this as a complete picture of what a State might be, for he finds in it that for the sake of which he made the picture, namely Justice, written in the relations of the members one with another. He leaves this simpler ideal with genuine reluctance, but practically confesses that men are so constituted that they will never for any length of time confine their wants within such narrow bounds.

These narrow bounds are in any case sufficiently wide to contain a very great part of what have been called the "purely economical" as distinguished from the merely "legal" or "historical categories" of political economy.[31] The picture contains in it only such economical features as are independent of any particular legal institutions, such as those relating to property and contract.

Now it is quite true that there is a body of economical doctrines, such as those relating to the conceptions of wealth and of economy, and perhaps of value, which can be treated quite apart from any particular nation or even any particular age of the world's history. But the distinction seems less important to us when we consider how impossible it is for even such a simply organized State as Plato's first ideal to exist, except on a basis of customs, if not of laws, and of an understood, if not a formulated agreement as to the rules of the market-place, the conditions of sale and purchase, domestic and foreign, to say nothing of an agreement as to the currency that was and was not to pass,[32] and the terms of the hiring of labourers. Even from this point of view, the patriarchal origin of the State is prior to the economical. In the *Statesman*[33] Plato says there is no difference between a large household and a small State; and that the art of government may be called Politics or (Œconomics indifferently. Socrates (apud *Xenoph. Memtor.*, iii. 4) had substantially said the same thing before him; he thought the difference between the subjects of the two studies was only one of degree. This is only so far true that economy (in the sense of regard to greatest results, in the way of wealth, with least sacrifice) is possible both in the House and in the State; in every State there is an element analogous to that of housekeeping, and in every household an element analogous to that of government. Translating this into modern language, we might say that the government of a nation cannot be divorced from its industrial organization, and there can be no industrial organization without some kind of government.

Before passing, however, to questions of Political Philosophy, we may notice Plato's attempts to define and classify arts and handicrafts. We shall find the historical element forcing an entrance even into what seems a matter of colourless theoretical analysis. In the *Sophistes*, he divides all arts into (1) productive and (2) acquisitive. The former class include Agriculture, Manufacture,[34] and the Fine Arts. They produce something; they bring something new into existence. The second bring nothing new into existence, but help men to procure what is already there. They include all learning and science, and (coming down to the work-a-day world) they include the acquisition of worldly goods, in two sub-divisions—acquisition by exchange and acquisition by force. Exchange includes gift and sale; and sale may be either (*a*) of the seller's own productions or (*b*) of other people's. This last is either retail trade, between the members of one city, or commerce between city and city. In a passage of the *Laws*,[35] he adds that retail traders and general merchants are far from being necessarily bad, though so often associated with trickery and meanness; they do for the public a service very similar to that of money—"they equalize our needs and our possessions"; they furnish us with a common measure or standard by which to estimate what we have; and they enable things to go from where they are not wanted to where they are wanted.

To complete the analysis of productive industry, we may add the two remarks in the *Politicus* bearing directly on the subject. The first is that the work of every art is either to produce a good or to avert an evil;—it is either creative or preventive.[36] The second, that there is an order of precedence among arts, and those are subordinate and subsidiary which prepare the instruments for the principal. In the end, all the other arts are subsidiary to the statesman's,[37] which weaves the whole into one web.

From the above account it appears that Plato's economic analyses are only incidents in a larger philosophical investigation. In his division of the arts into productive and acquisitive, for example, he would rank together fishing and philosophy, under the latter heading. Now the notion of production itself, as the bringing into being of something new, could not in the Fine Arts, and need not in the handicrafts, mean anything more than change of form. Again, if production and acquisition are represented in Economics by production and distribution, we see how difficult it is felt, in the one case by the philosopher and in the other by the economist, to keep the two absolutely separate. It is impossible, for example, to separate the "acquisition" of knowledge by the artist or artisan from the "production" by either of them. And in the region of economics by itself, if we begin at a point anterior to the artisan's completed act of production, it is impossible to say that the persons whose help was indispensable to him are not in various degrees as truly productive as he; if we follow the finished product till the producer himself has got the fruits of it, this will involve, under any system of division of labour (*i.e.* under any organized society whatsoever), an inseparable association of distributors with producers. Even in Plato's City of Pigs the product would not be ready for the consumer till it was landed in the market; and it becomes difficult to refuse to retail dealers, and much more to wholesale, a certain title to the name productive. It would be difficult to say then at what point the economic categories pass into the historical. To construct a society on abstract principles is even harder than to do what the classical economists are supposed to have attempted—to construct an abstract individual man. Plato does his best to look at the matter in a dry light;[38] but he is forced to turn from the abstract to the concrete; and, relapsing into common prejudices, he tells us that, in the concrete, a freeman should consider retail trading to be beneath him.[39] Even the craftsmen who produce the articles afterwards retailed need surveillance in their work, or they will charge their customers above its value (ἀξία). What this value is, and how it is to be judged, Plato does not explain, but says that "they themselves know perfectly well what it is."[40] It is not enough for them to be honest (he adds), they must aim at good work and not simply at excelling their neighbours. Even when they obey all these rules they are still, in a sense, unprofitable servants, for their work spoils their body and cramps their mind; they can never be in the first rank of citizens or know the highest good. They are genuine producers of a definite and unquestioned good, whereas such a pretentious pursuit as Rhetoric can point to no definite product, and is therefore, in a bad sense, unproductive.[41] The artisan is from one point of view before the artist himself; he is one degree nearer to the reality.[42] But the artisan is as full of self-conceit as the most pretentious philosopher.[43] Plato has undoubtedly a prejudice against manual labour, more especially in its harder and coarser forms. Tolstoi and St. Paul, however like him in some important respects, have nothing in common with him in this matter.

No doubt there was here a general prejudice of Greek philosophers, due partly to the idea that an artisan's work unfitted him for military service, partly to the association of it with the labour of slaves, and partly to the fact that many of the industrial arts were introduced by foreigners. The same prejudice existed among the Persians, and has probably prevailed more or less among all warlike nations at a certain stage of development. Socrates, the son of an artisan,[44] rose above it, and it was perhaps dying out at Athens in Plato's time. It was a common taunt of the critics of democracy that democracies admitted artisans and shopkeepers to the government of the State. They never forgot that Cleon was a tanner, and Agoracritus a sausage-seller.[45]

In Plato, however, the prejudice against shopkeepers and merchants is much stronger than against the artisan. He grudgingly allows that division of labour seems to require them; but he thinks that, even on the strength of this principle, only the physically weakest men unable to do anything else should take up such work.[46] They were at the best a necessary evil. Their trades were under the strongest of temptations to the accumulation of wealth in private hands;[47] and gold and silver money, by facilitating trade, facilitated this accumulation.

Money-making as an end in itself is to Plato an unmixed evil. An art, especially of a high degree of skill, such as the physician's, ought (he thinks) to be practised disinterestedly from an eye to the ideal of the art itself, not from an eye to the fortune it may bring. It should lead to good work done for its own sake. To turn an art into a trade is, he says (in the first book of the *Republic*), to add to it the art of money-making. He condemns usury with equal emphasis; he excludes it, in the *Laws*, from the ideal city described there,[48] allowing only one exception in its favour, the case of a customer who does not promptly pay for work that has been duly executed to his order,[49] and who must after a certain time pay interest as well as the sum due.

Finally, he thinks he can prevent most of the abuses of money-making, money-lending, and trading by decreeing that gold and silver money shall never be private property, and the only currency shall be a small change of the nature of a token money.[50] He would be glad if he could to taboo private property also,[51] which he thinks to be one main root of the evil.[52] In his perfect ideal city (of the *Republic*) as distinguished from his practicable ideal (of the *Laws*), he had forbidden to the Guardians both private property in general, and gold and silver money in particular.[53]

Plato's Economics of Production may be thus summed up. Industrial Production is only one species of a genus Production which includes every kind of creation, mental or material, as distinguished from mere transfer or transformation of what is created; and industrial transfer is only one species of a genus Acquisition which includes every kind of transfer, material or mental, voluntary or involuntary. He attempts to draw something like a hard and fast line between the two genera, but only lands himself in the difficulty which all philosophers have experienced in separating the inseparable.

He comes near to anticipate the economic controversy as to the possibility of drawing a line between productive and unproductive labour. He leaves indications that he would have settled it by falling back on the common prejudice of Greek philosophers against "vulgar" trades and in favour of the "liberal" arts. He avoids the difficult questions of exchange and value, though he admits that even in his simplest Ideal State there must be commerce and a market, contracts, and therefore customs and laws. He thus suggests to us the conclusion that the simplest form of industrial society must rest on a basis of complex custom.

This appears more clearly when we consider in the third place Plato's conception of Civil Society and the State.

III. Plato professes to begin the foundation of his Ideal State by an act of abstraction. He proposes to make a clean sweep of things as they are, both in politics and in manners.[54] But he knows very well that his State is to be Hellenic, and not Barbarian;[55] and, though the surface is rubbed smooth, the material of the tablet remains. Even his strong imagination cannot body forth the form of a society of men with no character already stamped on them, and no habits already formed. He is deeply impressed with differences of race,[56] and we must not suppose him to mean that social as well as political institutions can be made and unmade by the lawgiver's fiat. It is a well-known fact that to most human beings even their political rulers seem, like the sun and the seasons, a matter beyond their control; and still more is it so in regard to social customs and rules, where there are no visible rulers, to be cashiered for misconduct, or made to govern differently. Though Plato occasionally speaks as if an absolute beginning could really be made, yet the current of his reasoning implies the contrary; we gather that the successful reformer is he who by instinct or intellect discovers the existing principle of the growth of a society, and grafts a new idea upon that principle. Human societies (as we now see more clearly than Plato), like animal organisms, do not owe their beginnings to the deliberate contrivance of their members; their union and their behaviour seem rather to be a matter of instinctive growth.

Even in the *Republic*, Plato has practically acknowledged this; and in the *Laws* he has expressed it un-mistakeably. Instead of trying to trace the origin of modern States from an absolutely first starting point, he begins with the simple shepherds who are supposed to have survived the primæval deluge.[57] In a passage near the beginning of the seventh book of the *Laws*,[58] after he has been discussing the nursing of children and its effects on the life of the adults, he says: "All such arrangements come under the head of what the common people call 'unwritten rules', and what they call 'laws of our fore-fathers,' are simply these several unwritten rules viewed as a whole. Our present description seems happy, for it implies that these rules should neither go without a name nor be mis-called 'laws.' They are the bonds that hold every State together, lying between all the written ordinances already in force and the ordinances that are to come. What is true of the ancestral rules is true of the rest. The ancestral and primæval rules, if rightly laid down (*i.e.* rightly worked into the people's habits), invest the primœval statutes with a shield of perfect security; but, if they go wrong, it is as with the main props of a building when they are off their centre; they bring down themselves and all dependent on them in one common ruin. We must keep this in mind, and bind your new city together for you throughout, leaving nothing out, if possible, great or small, that could be called a law or a custom or a practice; for by all such things a city is bound together, and, taken apart from each other, the several rules are not lasting. You must not be surprised then if rules and customs that seem at once many in number and trifling in importance come pouring in on us and make our laws a somewhat lengthy matter."

He seems to consider that written laws are only necessary from the weakness of human wills, which leads men away from the public interest to seek personal and private advantage. Public interest binds cities together, private interest divides and distracts them. Yet selfishness is shortsighted; the gain is greater both to the individual and to the commonweal when the common good is regarded and not the private advantage.[59] Laws are needed to bring the individual man to a sense of his duty and of his true interest. They are to regulate the details of private life from childhood upwards; and they are to creep between the folds of ancient custom and usage in order to share the veneration and permanence that attach to "what is grey with years." Even when they are innovations they must not seem so, for innovation, name and thing, must be made detestable to our citizens.

In such a community (as this of the *Laws*) there could be room for little else than historical categories. Agriculture, as a traditional object of honour, is prized above all other industries.[60] The Greek idea that cities are the limit of independence is closely preserved.[61] We are surprised to find that trade is to be left tolerably free between the home state and foreigners,[62] and there is to be no Alien Act as in Sparta.[63] But on the whole if Plato in his Ideal State is still a Greek, in his practicable State he is véry Greek indeed; and, with regard to industry in particular, his views are largely affected by his Greek prejudices.

It follows that, in the controversy introduced by Archelaus and Democritus and raised into public importance by the Sophists,[64] as to the relation between Custom and Nature, Plato stands logically in a middle position. In a society of men (he thinks) the customs which are a second nature have almost the authority of nature itself;[65] custom is always inspired.

But Plato is far from believing that whatever is is right. He is amazed that States contrive to live "in spite of bad rulers and bad laws";[66] and, like Socrates, he thinks that the virtue which consists simply in obeying the laws or traditions of the country is worth little or nothing. On the other hand, the virtue which is embraced with a clear consciousness of its rational principles is after all the same traditional virtue made clearer. The earlier part of the first book of the *Republic* is a long proof that Simonides and the ancients must have meant what Plato meant when they defined the virtue of justice in a particular way. Just as philosophy does not really mean lawlessness,[67] so the philosophy of society cannot be anti-social. The truth that we seek does not lie in the depths of our own mind, but is contained in the social scriptures, the actual moral rules of society, which we must therefore examine and interpret. The philosopher may not take them just as they stand, but he must not think himself above them,[68] still less must the ruler of the State.[69] They are like the spoken and written language of a people, which may often be inaccurate and defective, but is indispensable for human intercourse.

Plato is really following the same reasoning when he refutes Thrasymachus in the *Republic*[70] by pointing out that the spirit of grasping and overreaching cannot be made universal without destroying all union of men whatsoever— even a band of robbers must have some "justice" in them in order to hold together—and when he answers Glaucon's description of the original "war of all against all" by a rival description of the necessary dependence of men on each other, and the original growth of the State out of the consequent division of labour. He admits in the *Laws* that between State and State there is a perpetual war, and even within lesser circles, and within the individual man himself the same is in a sense beyond dispute.[71] But it is in a sense not irreconcilable with Plato's general view, as already expounded, and the survivors of the deluge are at peace with one another.[72] If every individual man were born with an aversion to every other, such a thing as education of habit and still more of precept would be impossible; and Plato's social philosophy, whether in the *Laws* or in the *Republic*, is essentially a system of education.

The difficulty of declaratory economics, as of declaratory ethics, is the risk of ratifying as permanent what is merely transient. As some economists have given the impression that their analysis of things as they are was also a construction of things as they ought to be, so a social philosophy that accepts the unconscious laws, under which a society has become what it is, may easily use language inconsistent with the possibility of any radical change for the better. For example, the fact that slavery existed in all communities in Plato's own day, is apparently a proof to him that slavery is a permanent factor in civilization, though there were theorists even then who questioned the reasonableness of the institution. He points out in the *Laws* what are the best kinds of slaves to have, and how they ought to be treated;[73] he does not vindicate the reasonableness of slavery as if that itself might be placed in question. The rhetoricians, who contended that the "natural right" of the strongest might fairly be used by the slaves as soon as they were *de facto* strongest, find no sympathizer in him.

From the absence of slaves in the City of Pigs, we may infer that he considered slavery to be the result of luxury and war; and he understands the dangers of the institution. The tyrant, he says, is like a rich slave-owner in the city who feels secure because the whole city is in league to protect itself against any rising; suppose him carried into a wilderness and set down among his slaves with no free man near, he will be in an agony of fear, and sink to any shifts to save his life; suppose him carried among a people who make war on all slave-holders, he will be in the midst of enemies, and in the last extremity of misery.[74] Yet Plato does not renounce slavery, he does not even clearly recognise that his own theory of the earth-born,[75] with their career determined from birth by their native gifts of intellect, amounted to a serious modification of the received theory and practice of slavery. He seems to adopt the view that foreigners conquered in war quite reasonably become slaves; and the most we can say for him is (1) that in his first or simplest ideal State there were no slaves;[76] (2) that slavery, in his second Ideal State, would seem to be not the hereditary fate of a whole race, but the lot of the incapable or the evil,[77] whoever their parents may have been; and (3) that in the State described in the *Laws* the condition of slaves is not to be one of extreme hardship.[78] The fact remains, however, that Plato's philosophy did not carry him entirely beyond the ideas of his age in this important matter; and the conservatism of his political principles was in this point inconsistent with reform. The remarkable reform he would introduce (in the *Republic*) in regard to the position of women,[79] placing them on a perfect equality with men as regards opportunities, is not fully carried out in the *Laws*. His principles had led him to a reform which he saw to be in present circumstances impracticable. Yet, of all his paradoxes, this is the one to which he clings most tenaciously; and even the changes of the *Laws* go beyond any known institutions of his own day in this particular.[80]

For judging of the importance of any thinker in the history of Economics, no matter is more important to us than the view he takes of the labouring population. In Plato's time these included freemen as well as slaves;

but his political philosophy prevented him from paying special regard to either class. Whether his psychology is rightly said to have been influenced (or coloured) by his political philosophy or not, it was clearly so with his economical views. His political philosophy led him to believe that the rulers of the best State must be philosophers; but the bulk of men (he considers) are not and cannot be philosophers, and, in proportion as they have little philosophy, they have little political importance in his eyes. He will allow them little political power, and they are of little account altogether. The unphilosophical Many should be ruled by the philosophical Few, and the many and conflicting appetites should be ruled by Reason. To suppose that any organization could be worked out by the people from below upwards would have seemed to him as strange as to suppose that the appetites might of themselves develop into something rational. His very anxiety to prevent the existence of extremes of wealth and poverty in the State is not founded on any sympathy with the sufferings of the poor.[81] With the religious ascetics of a later day, he considered that sin was the only real misfortune, and neither pain nor poverty was an evil. If the poor man had been "of golden metal," in other words of great powers of intellect, Plato's Guardians would have seized him at his birth and made him one of themselves; he would not have had wealth in the sense of extravagant profusion, but he would have possessed the means of developing his faculties; he might have fulfilled the promise and potency of his being. But to those of inferior metal Plato holds out no hope; he apparently thinks that the ordinary trade and commerce of his day and the unregenerate life of it are good enough for them; they are to be allowed, even in his *Republic*, to hold property and exchange it as people did in his own day, and he lays down no "national system of education" in which they should be included. The general principle of division of labour is so applied that the regenerate and unregenerate classes can never mingle, and the evils described by modern writers as flowing from industrial division of labour are not counteracted. It seems as if Plato had found by psychological analysis a principle of division of faculties which he transferred to politics and society, with too great a faith in the exactness of the analogy. In the present day we might doubt the correctness of the division of the faculties of the soul and their functions, and we should certainly doubt whether on the strength of the analogy it could be maintained that the separation of classes should be a fixed fate even for the individual's life-time. There are probably no modern theorists who would suggest that the State should destroy all openness of career, and itself undertake the determination of each man's work. Yet it is this kind of individual liberty which Plato disallows; he does not see the impossibility of an infallible State, and he does not see that there are reasons (quite apart from the fallibility of the State) why individual initiative should be left to all members of the State, and not confined to the philosophers.

If Plato grudges to admit the element of individual liberty in the sense of individual enterprise, industrial or otherwise, he does full justice to the dignity and value of the State as a function of society indispensable to human development. It is not the case that he identified State and Society, though he has no Greek word for the distinction. He refers to primitive societies that were not States (see *Laws*, III. 679), and he conceives (like Godwin and the Anarchists) that if all men were plain livers and high thinkers they would have no need of State or laws. Moreover, his recognition that the State is based on traditional custom implies that the custom itself is distinct from the State; it is what we would call social and not political; and he sees that the establishment of written laws and a constitution in accordance with that basis may be a slow and difficult achievement.[82]

Yet the two, Society and State, stood much nearer to one another in those days, when State was Church and University in one, and the whole spiritual life of the nation found expression in that one organ. Each citizen, too, felt his connection with the State to be very direct, for there was as yet no need for government by representatives, and he could take a personal part in all political action. If the large empires of modern times could ever be broken up into States of no larger size than the Hellenic, it would not be impossible then to have an action of government on individual and family life such as Plato designed, or Fichte after him. Society and State stand near to each other when the numbers are so small that all the citizens can take a direct part in government, and dispense with representatives. But there would be a difficulty in securing the desired isolation from other States, especially in trade; and, without that isolation, foreign influences would baffle the measures of the tiny home governments. Politics may be still the "architectonic art,"[83] but the architect has to work according to his materials and according to the purposes for which his building is wanted; and even in a small modern State the purposes are hard to secure, while in a large the materials are far from plastic. In regard to industry and wealth, a modern statesman might agree with Plato that inequality of property is bad, and even that the increase of national wealth is not the chief end of the State. But he would also recognise that the governing body could not impose changes without convincing the governed of the necessity of them, and certainly could not prescribe for the nation the ultimate or even the proximate ends to be pursued.

Note

The *Republic* was written about 381 B.C. Xenophon, in his *Cyropædia* (circa 362 B.C.) Book VIII. 2, shows us an even more "modern" Division of Labour and Separation of Trades in full operation. Dugald Stewart (*Pol. Econ.*, I. 328) recalled attention to this passage. It runs as follows: "As the other crafts (τέχναι) are carried out best of all in great cities, so the arrangements for meals are best managed in the king's household. In small cities, the man that makes beds may make doors, ploughs, and tables, and perhaps houses; he is glad if even so he can find customers enough to provide a living, and it is plainly impossible that a man practising many crafts can be good at them all. But in great cities, because there is a large demand for each article (διὰ τὸ πολλοὺς ἑκάστου δεῖσθαι), a single craft is enough for a living, or sometimes, indeed, no more than a single branch of a craft;—we find one man making men's boots only; and another, women's only; and another, cobbling or cutting out merely, for a livelihood; one man lives by cutting out garments, another by fitting together the pieces. The smaller the work the greater the skill in the craftsman (ἀνάγκη οὖν τὸν ἐν βραχυτάτω διατρίβοντα ἔργῳ τοῦτον καὶ ἄριστα διηναγκάσθαι τοῦτο ποιεῖν)."

Notes

1 The *Eryxias ἢ περὶ* πλούτον, is not genuine. It brings out at least the distinction of wealth from money.
2 *L.*, I. 631, B, C.
3 *L.*, V. 743, E; cf. IX. 870.
4 In the *Euthydemus*, 292, it is classed among those outward advantages which are in themselves neither good nor evil.
5 *Gorgias*, 477–78.
6 *Republ.*, I. 329–30.
7 *Republ.*, III. 407, A.
8 Cf. *Phaedo*, 66, C. We may perhaps consider the explicit distinction of luxuries and necessaries as first occurring in Plato.
9 πρὸς χρηματισμὸν τραπόμενος γλίσχρως καὶ κατὰ σμικρὸν Φειδόμενος καὶ ἐργαζόμενος χρήματα συλλέγεται.
10 *Republ.* III. 400–402. See Lewis Nettleship, in *Hellenica* (1880), art. "The Theory of Education in the *Republic* of Plato."
11 *L.*, V. 742.
12 *L.*, V. 736, E.
13 E.g. *Laws*, 743, A.
14 *Phædrus*, 279, C. ἔξωθεν δ᾽ ὅσα εἴχω, etc. Cf. *Sympos.* (Speech of Socrates).
15 Cf. *Gorgias*, §§ 491–494.
16 *Republ.*, II., cf. IV.
17 *Republ.*, II. 369, B. The account of Weaving in *Politicus* 279–80 is perhaps the best of his descriptions of industrial processes. For Xenophon's account of Division of Labour, see Note to this chapter.
18 This is a fact which Adam Smith (*Wealth of Nations*, Bk. I) did not *ignore*, but denied.
19 See below. Cf. Erdmann, *Hist. of Philos.*, vol. i. 122. Erdmann calls the first "the necessary," the second, the "organic or rational State."
20 *Laws*, III. 680.
21 *Republ.*, III. 398, A; cf. *Sophist*; 234, A.
22 See Herbert Spencer, *Study of Sociology*, ch. iii., "Nature of the Social Science".
23 Cf. *Politicus*, 277, D.
24 *Republ.*,VI. 503.
25 *Apology*, 21–23.
26 *Republ.*, VI. 495, D, E.
27 *Laws*, IV. Cf. *Republ.*, VI. 495, D, beginning. On the other hand he will have no taxation of imports and exports, VIII. 847, B.
28 *Republ.*, III. 414, 415.
29 *Republ.*, VII. 536, E.
30 *Ib.*, II. 370, E, 371, A; cf. *Laws*, V. 747, E.

31 The terms have become current under the influence of Rodbertus. See *e.g.* his book on *Kapital*, ed. Wagner and Kozak, 1884, pp. 226, 314. Sax, *Staatswirthschaft* (1887), p. 38 n. Compare Mill's distinction between the laws of production and the laws of distribution.
32 Beyond saying that money is a "token for the purpose of exchange," he gives no analysis of money. The ordinary terms for money-changers, etc., occur in the same connection as this definition.
33 *Politicus*, 259, B.
34 Compare *Soph.*, 219, A, B.
35 X. 919, B, C.
36 *Politicus*, 179, C.
37 *Ib.*, 281, D, E; cf. 287, D; 306, A.
38 As in the case of retail dealers, *Laws*, X. 919, B, C.
39 *Laws*, XI. 920, etc; cf. V. 741, E.
40 *Laws*, XI. 921.
41 *Gorgias*, 452, C.
42 *Republ.*, X. 596–598.
43 *Apology*, 22, D, E.
44 λιθονργοῦ, sculptor, stone-carver, or stone-mason. For his sentiments on the subject, see *Xen. Mem.*, I. ii. 56, ii. 7.
45 Aristoph., *Knights*.
46 *Republ.*, II. 371, C. On the other hand it is the common view of commercial men in England and the U.S. that only those take up professions who are not fit for business.
47 *Laws*, XI. 918, D, E.
48 V. 742, C. VIII. 842, D.
49 *Laws*, XI. 921, C, D. The mediaeval *usura punitoria*.
50 *Ib.*, V. 742, A.
51 *ib.*, V. 739.
52 *ib.*, VIII. 831, C.
53 *Republ.*, III. 416, 417.
54 Λαβόντες, ἦν δ' ἐγώ, ὥσπερ πίνακα πάλιν το καί ἤδη ἀνθρώπων, πρῶτον μὲν καθαρὰν ποιήσειαν ἄν [οί φιλόσοφοι]. *Republ.*, VI. 501, A.
55 οὐχ Ἑλληνὶς ἔσται; *Republ.*, V. 471.
56 *Republ.*, IV. 435, E., 436.
57 *Laws*, III. 677.
58 *Ib.*, VII. 793, A–D.
59 *Laws*, IX. 875, A–C.
60 *Lb.*, VIII. 842, C, D.
61 *E.g. ib.*, IV. 705, A.
62 *Ib.*, VIII. 847, B.
63 *Ib.*, XII. 950, B.
64 See Erdmann, *Hist. of Philos.*, vol i. pp. 60, 69, 76, 77.
65 So in *Gorgias*, 488 *seq.*, the argument seems to be:—There is νόμος everywhere, and it is the stronger.
66 *Politicus*, 302, A.
67 *Republ.*, VII. 538.
68 See *Crito*, 50, A, to end.
69 *Laws*, IV. 715, C, D; cf. VI. 751, C.
70 *Republ.*, I. 352.
71 *Laws*, I. 626, A–E.
72 III. 678, E *seq.*
73 *Gorgias*, 484, B.

74 *Republ.*, IX. 578.
75 *Ib.*, III 415.
76 *Ib.*, II. 371, etc.
77 *Ib.*, III. 415, A; *Polit.*, 309, A.
78 *Laws*, VI. 776, 777.
79 *Republ.*, V.
80 *Laws*, VII.
81 He does not seem to have found anything amiss in the judicial torture of slaves, which, as Mr. E. Poste reminds us (Aristotle's *Constitution of Athens*, 2nd ed., p. 139) took place in almost every action, criminal or civil, at Athens.
82 So Prévost Paradol complained that the Revolution had founded a society, but not a government.—*La France nouvelle*, p. 296 (see Lorimer, *Institutes of Law*, p. 549).
83 *Politicus*, 305, E.

2   Aristotle (384–322 B.C.)

Seeing among Aristotle's Works a treatise on *Œconomics*, we might be led to hope that here at least we should not need to depend on hints from scattered passages. But, in the first place, the treatise is not Aristotle's, and, in the second, even if it were, it is devoted to domestic economy, not to economics in the modern sense of the word.[1] We must gather Aristotle's views as we gathered Plato's; and we may take them for convenience under the same three heads, the view of Wealth, the view of Production and Distribution, and the view of Society and the State.

I. Wealth, says Aristotle, cannot be the chief end of man, for wealth is a collection of means to an end,[2] the end being the satisfaction of human desires. The principle of teleology is drawn from the obvious facts of human experience;—all human action and enterprise involve the pursuit of ends,[3] and some of the ends are subordinate to others, while all are subordinate to one chief end, which ethical and political philosophy must define and explain. His philosophy defines it as the realizing of the faculties that are distinctively human; and it is impossible (he allows) to realize these faculties without a sufficiency of outward goods and of leisure. A man must have the average worldly wealth of the average citizen before he can hope to attain to the highest good. "It is hard to be good without an income,"[4] or to be happy without maturity of manhood, health, and freedom from pain, or without friends.[5]

The highest ideal is the life of the philosopher, and this demands leisure. The next best life is that of perfect moral virtue as shown by the good citizen; and this is not possible without means and opportunities.[6] Still in either case, outward wealth is to happiness, as the lyre is to the tune; the music would not come without the musician.[7] Wealth is the instrument, and should never become the end. The proper amount of it is fixed by the end to which it is a means; "the wealth that is according to nature" is not unlimited, but has a very definite limit in each particular case; it ought to be no more than will enable a man to secure the chief ends of life.[8] It is only the wealth of the money-maker which is without limit.

The limit is drawn less narrowly by Aristotle than by Plato. The Guardians (of the *Republic*), who alone were to reach the highest good, were not to be allowed to have any wealth of their own. To Aristotle, on the contrary, personal property seems indispensable even for moral virtues. Certain virtues, such as Liberality and Magnificence (to say nothing of Temperance)[9] imply a considerable fortune, far beyond mere subsistence, and a man should have enough to live not only temperately (as Plato had it) but liberally.[10] It is quite true that Aristotle seems to allow that in proportion as a man draws near to the highest life of all, he needs wealth less and less, and the worse man he is the more wealth he needs.[11] Nevertheless leisure is indispensable, and leisure can only be secured by a certain amount of wealth.

The conception of life implied by this way of thinking is well described in the following passage of the seventh book of the *Politics*.[12] "Life is divided between business and leisure, war and peace, and actions are directed either to what is necessary and useful for us, or to what is noble. We have to decide between these on the same principles as between the [higher and lower] parts of the soul and the corresponding actions; the end of war is peace, the end of business leisure, the end of things necessary and useful is things fair and noble. A legislator must always keep this subordination in mind." The bearing of these principles on the question of the necessary education of a citizen is pointed out by Aristotle himself in the 8th book of the *Politics*; education must include the ancestral "music" or Art, for other elements, such as reading and writing and gymnastic, concern either the lower faculties or the lower aims of life.

It appears, then, that in the political philosophy of Aristotle, as of Plato, there is clear recognition that a certain amount of leisure and a certain distance from the cares of getting a livelihood are necessary to the full development of the highest human powers. In modern times the claim has been extended from a few privileged members of the community to all human beings everywhere;[13] the demand is made that extreme poverty shall cease, because the extremely poor can never develop their full powers of mind and body. Aristotle could not take so wide a view. He was too practical and too fully alive to the needs of human nature to be ascetic in his view of wealth; but he had no high estimate of human nature in the persons of his fellow-citizens: "Most men will the good, and choose the evil"; "most men delight in coarse pleasures"; "most men follow riches without limit"; "most men are neither very good nor very bad." And still farther below the level of ideal goodness lie the great multitude of slaves who "cannot be happy because they cannot have a citizen's career."[14] Aristotle would have counted it impossible as well as undesirable to provide for all men the means of reaching the highest good. To us it seems impossible, only if it means leisure without work instead of leisure and labour in alternation.

II. In regard to Production, Aristotle is undoubtedly clearer than Plato. It is no doubt true that his teleology, applied to economical subjects, is not substantially very different from Plato's division of labour; everything in Nature has its purpose, every living thing (and every faculty of every living thing) has its special function and work; and man's chief end is to fulfil his special function. Applied to the household, which is the industrial as well as the political unit, this principle means that the man and the woman play different and complementary parts in the household, the one acting as bread-winner and defender, the other watching over the children, and the indoor work.[15]

It may be added that not only does Aristotle thus apply the principle even farther than Plato, but he sees the limits of it more clearly than Plato. The free man may engage in manual arts up to a certain limit, but, if he devotes himself wholly to them, his mind is narrowed and his body enfeebled.[16] He becomes like a slave who is merely a "living tool." If we could only have shuttles throwing themselves, we should need no slaves,[17] and (we may infer) the industrial arts would not be degrading.

But, besides those general reflections, Aristotle gives us something like distinct economical analyses. He saw clearly that industrial production was specifically different from moral or political action, and that the old Socratic analogy (of which Plato availed himself, and which was in the main suggested by general Greek feeling) was misleading. Art (says Aristotle) has to do with production, ethics with action. In the former we demand not that the maker but that the work done shall be good.[18] It is true that, except accidentally, we cannot get good work without good workmen, men who produce on scientific principles, and are therefore said to possess the "art" of doing so.[19] But their act of production, unlike an ethical act, is not an end in itself; production in industry is strictly subordinate to an end outside itself.[20] The connection of producer and product ceases as soon as the product is launched on the world; and the producer's love of the work of his hands would not be returned by the latter, at least in equal intensity.[21] The subordination of the whole province of production to the lordship of ethics is unmistakeably indicated. The chief end of man is not products but actions, actions, which quite apart from any products, are ends in themselves.

To take the arts more in detail, each has its tools, and these are inanimate and animate; the latter including beasts of burden, slaves, and servants.[22] And the lifeless instrument as distinguished from the mere possession is that which is not used by the possessor, but is made a means of getting what the possessor means to use.[23] This is a near approach to the modern notion of Capital. Of the industries, Agriculture comes first and foremost by nature, rather benefitting than hurting the body, keeping man near to his mother earth, and benefitting him not at his neighbour's expense, but at hers alone. Then come the extractive industries like mining, which still keep near to earth.[24] The occupation, next, of Pastoral people who "till a living farm,"[25] involves little labour, and leaves them lazy in spite of their migrations. Then come Hunters, including pirates and fishermen, both depending not on mother earth, but on the sea. But agriculture is the industry of the great bulk of men. All these primitive kinds of industry agree in one thing: they make to use, not to exchange; and this is with Aristotle a point of great importance.[26] He seems to admire the simple happiness of their life, as Plato clings to his first City. In any given political society, strictly so called, we find (he tells us) four classes— farmers, artisans, traders, and labourers,[27] conveniently corresponding to four classes of fighting men: cavalry, heavy infantry, light infantry, navy. All are necessary, though the artizan class includes the makers of luxuries, who are plainly not necessary.[28] In speaking of the City of Pigs Plato had specified the weaver's, the farmer's, the shoemaker's, and the builder's as the necessary trades for the simplest of cities; but he adds the smith's, the herdsman's, the merchant's and the shopkeeper's. He should not (says Aristotle) have omitted an army to defend the State, and judges to settle disputes of these workmen and the citizens generally.[29] The political economy of the simplest State is, as Aristotle sees, inseparable from politics.

The subject of trade as distinguished from production is introduced by Aristotle (in the first book of the *Politics*), with the observation that both in the State and in the household there are natural and non-natural ways of acquiring wealth.[30] For the household the natural ways are the arts already mentioned; things are made by them for use in the household, and are used there. But there is another and non-natural mode of production: instead of making things for use we make them to exchange. Instead of wearing the shoes we make, we exchange them for other goods. In its first form even this exchange is not entirely unnatural so far as it results from an accidental surplus on the part of some individuals, and accidental deficiency on the part of others. As soon as the family has grown into the society, however, the excess will be intentional, and exchanges will become an established practice. In a simple and natural society such exchanges will be merely the bartering of one thing for another in kind, *e.g.* wine in exchange for corn; but barter without money will be found more and more difficult the larger the society becomes. Hence the invention of money.[31]

If I am in want of a certain product, when the producer for his part is in no such want of mine, I must bring him something that he will always be willing to accept; and the precious metals, guaranteed in weight and fineness by the stamp of the mint upon them, will always be accepted, and can thus serve as a common measure of value and common means of exchange.[32] By thus assisting the passage of goods from those that do not need them to those who do, money becomes a representative of the different and coincident needs of men in society, a reciprocity of needs which is the cause of all commerce. Yet money itself is only a piece of goods like the rest, and though tolerably constant is not absolutely invariable in its value. Moreover, it is an article of which the use is to exchange it; and, if it is for any reason not exchangeable, its possessor may die like Midas, surrounded by gold and silver, and without the means to live.[33]

It would seem from Aristotle's own account as if the use of money were as natural as Society itself, growing up by the same inevitable process of development. In this particular case Aristotle does not regard the development with favour, Like Plato, he thinks that the natural use of money is very closely connected with the abuse of it in money-making, where the object is not to get goods to use, but to accumulate money for the sake of the accumulation itself, quite apart from the use, the object being a boundless command over the means of satisfying boundless desires. Money-making in fact has excess for its beginning and excess for its end; and this, to a Greek philosopher who describes all moral virtue as lying in a mean between excess and defect, was a sufficient condemnation.[34]

Like later writers, Aristotle allows that profit may be made out of the growing of trees and the rearing of animals, without damage to one's neighbours, but shopkeeping and other forms of commerce he seems to regard as forms of cheating; in spite of his own concessions about division of labour, the gain of one man always seems to him the loss of another.[35] Most of all he thinks this true of Interest, an attempt to breed from barren metal, which is even farther from the proper use of money than is the use made by the ordinary moneymaker. After this, it is not surprising that he should count the spendthrift a better man than the miser. As miserliness in those days could only mean hoarding, Aristotle's position is excusable. The "rings and corners" of ancient Greece, in which even respectable philosophers, like Thales, had played a part,[36] are mentioned in a tone of contempt; but the serious treatises on such a subject as agriculture are barely mentioned; and Aristotle thinks it beneath the dignity of his discourse to give such subjects more than a cursory notice.[37]

Even general economic principles are not thought worthy of such full consideration as is bestowed on ethical or metaphysical principles. When Aristotle gives us a theory of exchanges, under the head of Particular Justice (or justice in the narrow sense of the word as distinguished from righteousness in general),[38] it is not an economic theory; and economic questions are touched very incidentally. Particular Justice is either (*a*) Distributive, or (*b*) Corrective. Distributive justice relates to distributions of honours or of wealth or of anything else that is portioned out among the members of a State. The distribution varies according as the privileges of citizenship depend on birth or on wealth or on personal attainments. The share is always to be determined by a uniform standard; it must be neither too little nor too much, according to that standard; but what that standard itself is depends on the constitution of each State. For example, if the standard were nobility of birth, it would be contrary to the principles of distributive justice that a *parvenu* should obtain the highest honours or get the largest grants; but in a democratic State it would be no violation of justice.

The second kind of Particular Justice is Corrective Justice, which redresses any infringements of equality, taking from him who has unfairly gained, and adding to the portion of him who has unfairly lost, that the balance may be restored.[39] This occurs in the case both of voluntary contracts and of involuntary (crime and punishment).

We may apply these principles positively by conjoining them with the old principle of "like for like."[40] If the builder and the shoemaker are to exchange on the principle of "like for like," the two artisans must first be brought into their proper relation as determined by the dignity or rank of their two several trades, and then after that adjustment[41] the relative goodness of their several wares must be reckoned. When these allowances have been made, then a certain number of shoes may be received by the builder from the shoemaker in exchange for a house, or (what is the same thing) the price of the shoes or of the house may be exchanged for the house or the shoes.[42]

We might make Aristotle's adjustments easier to understand if we supposed that the regard he insists on paying to the respective status of the producers was a regard paid to the respective skill and difficulty of their trade. But except in regard to money there is no clear analysis of economic facts in this much tortured passage. Aristotle is doing his best to find the principle of the Mean even in matters of trade, and to bring sense out of common sayings, by explaining them in the light of his philosophy. As the Mean essentially rests on a basis of popular belief, we could not expect to find any economical categories that were not largely if not wholly historical.[43] There seems no fair analogy between the ethical mean and the market value of an article,—except that the latter will sometimes be like the former in being a mean between two extreme estimates, a buyer's low one and a seller's high one.

III. Aristotle's conception of the State would in any case make it difficult to draw the line between historical and economical categories; it involves a justification by logic of the growth of the historical categories. A man is, as rational, social; his power of speech is sufficient presumption of it;[44] and other facts are present in abundance to confirm the presumption.

In the first place he is born able and usually willing to pair with another human being.[45] The family is a form of society that not only comes first in time but (in Aristotle's opinion) remains a permanent element in the larger forms of society. In the second place, after the family we have the village, which grows out of the family, and is as it were a family of families. But unlike the family it is not itself a permanent element; it gives place to the State, which grows out of the village.[46] Maine's aphorism that Society develops from the family to the tribe and from the tribe to the State is in substance Aristotle's. Now the last stage in this development, though last in time, is so far from being farther away from nature, that it alone represents the true nature of man. "Nature" is rather the full-grown organism than the undeveloped germ; and it is the State and not the family, still less the individual, that is the "limit of independence." The earlier forms of community come into being for simple preservation of bare life, but they develop into a community which serves not only that purpose but the higher ends of life. They, and especially the State, make it possible for man to show all that is in him.[47]

Aristotle makes therefore no attempt like Plato's to construct an ideal State from men in a state of nature, as they were in the City of Pigs. He recognises more expressly and consistently than Plato the necessity of a basis of unwritten law, a definite national character that has grown with many generations. The State is not a deliberate contrivance to suit a known purpose of usefulness; it results from one of those natural tendencies which insists on being satisfied whether useful or not.[48] Connected with this view (of the spontaneous growth of political institutions) is Aristotle's respect for the "fixed beliefs" of the vulgar. A belief that is universal must (he thinks) have some truth in it, whether in ethics or in politics. He seems to have been the first to formulate clearly the doctrine that the multitude have a collective wisdom not possessed by the individuals separately.[49] There is no nearer approach to this in Plato than the notion of binding customs (in the *Laws*) and the notion of principles dyed into a community, like colours into a web (in the *Republic*). Aristotle's case, however, is not strengthened by his illustrations. "As in a joint feast, every one contributes his portion of virtue and wisdom." "They become as one man, but a man with many organs of sense and understanding instead of few," and hence are a good judge, for example, of poetry and art in general. Taking the common judgment as represented in the current axioms of morality and politics, he professes a deep respect for it even in these regions.

This is plainly the case in his *Ethics*, for the definition of virtue makes it "a habit of choice lying in a middle [or regulated] state of the passions, a middle state relative to the agent concerned, and a habit fixed by reason in the way in which the ideally wise man would fix it."[50]

This is a re-statement in philosophical language of the thought which is common to the whole Greek world, that "measure is the best." Not that this notion is introduced into the ethics of Aristotle from without; it is Greek as the whole philosophy of Aristotle is Greek, because the philosopher was unconsciously formulating the thoughts of his own people and times. The Greek view of nature was in a sense artistic. The Greeks found in nature a number of elements and a principle that seemed to set them in order. This is exactly what Aristotle presents to us in his Metaphysics and Psychology and in his Economics (so far as we have traced it), and not least in his Ethics and Political Philosophy. In ethics if we ask what is to fix the limit or mean that brings order into the disorderly elements, in short, how reason is to limit passion, we are told that the limit is determined by the man of practical wisdom; and it is clear from what is said and not said about the latter that he performs his high function simply because he has been trained by the State in the traditional morality of his people and has a clearer view and a better grasp of their ideals than the average man who follows them unconsciously or unintelligently.

We see this view illustrated by the 10th book of the *Ethics*, in which Aristotle gives his view of the relation of Ethics to Politics.[51] There are three ways, he says, in which men become good; they are good by nature, or by precept, or by custom. The first is a happy chance that we cannot control; the second is uncertain unless the minds of the hearers have been prepared beforehand so that the seed is sown on good ground. Hence it is the last way, the way of custom, that must be used by the legislator. Nothing but a general and thorough system of moral education will give us a virtuous community. We must have laws for the whole of life from infancy upwards.[52] In other words, we must conquer human nature by obeying it and reform human society by adopting the very methods by which society has grown up to what it is, and using not only its written but its unwritten laws.[53]

The difficulty that meets Aristotle at this point is the difficulty that meets every one who tries to show that whatever is, is in a sense right. If Justice differs in different States, is it not in all equally conventional or equally natural? His answer is that there is one best form of government and the justice that prevails in that is the natural one, being that *for* which men are born and to which they ought to come.[54] While he allows that none of the existing States are perfect, he contends that the development of the State from family and village was quite natural. He distinguishes too the right sort of States (those in which the government aims at the public advantage) from the wrong (in which it seeks the advantage of individuals).[55] It is clear then that their laws and customs must, according to his own admissions, have a great deal of substantial truth in them; and accordingly his severest criticisms are directed against those who leave the path of history and experience and, like Plato, construct constitutions on abstract principles.

First and foremost he objects to Plato's *Republic* that it turns back the hands of the clock. It tries to perfect the unity of the State by destroying the variety in the life of its members. By abolishing the family it reduces the State itself to a family, and the next step would be to reduce it from a family to an individual.[56] Unity must not be uniformity. Though the criticism is not wholly justified, it is true that in his own Ideal State Aristotle not only preserves the historical elements which disappear in the Platonic State, or in its select circles, but finds a place for various social groups (including clubs and partnerships) ranked under the general head of "friendships," and serving as a bridge between the exclusiveness of the family and the comprehensiveness of the State.[57] There is no such continuity in Plato. The two books of Aristotle on Friendship (*Ethics*, VIII., IX.) are really a treatise on the different forms of social intercourse and communion, from the highest (the friendship between two good men) to mere attachments from pleasure and partnerships from utility.

He does not consider society by any means as *constituted* by this last class of associations, and the motive of self-advancement is never regarded by him as at all commendable, still less as worthy of dominating an entire society of human beings. Self-love, he says, is natural and in moderation pardonable,[58] but it is never admirable except in the good man, regarded as loving the goodness that is in himself, which he will value above all things else in the world.[59] A civil society, the dominant aim of whose members was commercial ambition, would be to him a degradation of the State. There is not even the notion that every man must earn his own livelihood by his own labour. His philosophy reduces the economical element in Society to a very humble place.

On the other hand he fully allows for human weakness. If all men were good, Society would have all its wants supplied.[60] It may be allowed, he says, that friendship dispenses with law,[61] yet true friendship is only between the good; the good are rare, and a friendship on the part of all citizens towards each other is inconceivable; the wider the circle the more "watery" is the feeling.[62]

His way is accordingly a *via media*. He has no notion of modern individualism; the individualism of his own day taught by the Cynics and Cyrenaics implied the hostility of the individual to Society, whereas modern individualism is distinctly a phase of social life. Aristotle sees that there is no salvation, physical or moral, for the individual outside of the State. Man is not only a social but a political animal; the expression in Greek implies on the whole far more of the latter than of the former. Man is born for the life of a citizen in a State, straitly regulated in all departments of his life by its laws and by the customs of his people, while at the same time he is allowed a family life of his own, property of his own, and free choice of a career in life. To have all things in common would mean to have nothing well cared for. So far the personal motives must have free course in regard to material wealth. Even if we suppressed them because they are often intemperate and therefore mischievous to the commonweal, we should not eradicate evil so long as the desires of pleasure and of worldly distinction remained.[63]

In his criticism of current socialistic theories, Aristotle no doubt uses what are sometimes considered strictly economical arguments; he would, for instance, demand from the socialists of his day that if they made all wealth common they should restrict population.[64] But he lays far more stress on his own positive argument that, if you direct men to their proper chief end, you secure the good of socialism without the evil; you equalize not the possessions but the desires of men; you make the possession private but the use public.[65] The modern notion of property as held in trust for the public good is foreshadowed.

The chief end of man, however, is not allowed to be the chief end of one large body of men, the slaves, who are mere "living tools." The slave is one who is "born to be dependent on another."[66] Nature has made some men to be slaves as it has made others to rule. As long as we have this notion that men as well as things can be mere instruments, we cannot have the notion of economics as now understood, in which the world of men stands over against the world of things as a world of ends to a world of means.

Perhaps the most remarkable feature in Aristotle's conception of the chief end of man, is that it is not directly social at all. The highest good is contemplation of truth, the next best is development of the virtues. The first involves seclusion from politics, and is the lot of a few highly gifted minds; it is the second that is open to the ordinary citizen. Aristotle was perhaps conscious that the Greek State was no longer to be the Alpha and Omega of civilized life. The history of his own country was making this painfully clear. When the State and Civil Society could no longer furnish a rule of life, some other guides must be sought; and they were sought in the individual rather than in the social nature of man.

Notes

1 As it is probably by a disciple of Aristotle, it has been used here occasionally in supplement of the known Aristotelian writings.
2 *Ethics*, I. 3, (5). *Pol.*, I. 3, (8): ὁ πλοῦτος ὀργάνων πλῆθος.
3 *Ethics*, I. 1.
4 *ib.*, I. (8), 15.
5 *ib.*, I. (9), 10; (10), 12, etc.; cf. VII, (13).
6 *Eth.*, I. 8, 15: καθάπερ δι' ὀργάνων, διὰ φίλων, etc.
7 *Pol.*, VII. 12.
8 *Pol.*, I. 3, (8).
9 *Eth.*, III and IV.
10 *Pol.*, II. 6 (al. 3): βελτίων ὅρος τὸ σωφρόνως καὶ ἐλευθερίως [ζῆν]. Cf. 5 (al. 2).
11 *Ethics*, X. 8, compared with *Pol.*, VII. 12.
12 VII. 13 (al. 14).
13 *E.g.* by Godwin, *Political Justice*. Cf. *Ethics*, X. 7.
14 *Ethics*, X. 6,8.
15 *Œcon.*, III.; cf. *Eth.*, IX. (12), 7: εὐθὺς γὰρ διῄρηται τὰ ἔργα, etc.
16 *Pol.*, VIII. 2; Cf. I. 2.
17 *Ib.*, I. 2.
18 *Eth.*, II. (4), 3.
19 *Eth.*, VI. (4), 3–6. The example is Building.
20 Cf. *Eth.*, I. 4.
21 *Eth.*, IX. (7), 3.
22 *Pol.*, I. 3; cf. I. I: βοῦς ἀντ' οἰκέτον τοῖς πένησιν. The ox is the poor man's domestic servant.
23 *Pol.*, I. 2.
24 *Œc.*, II.
25 ὥσπερ γεωργίαν ζῶ οταν γεωργοῦντες. *Pol.*, I. 3.
26 *Pol.*, I. 3.
27 *Pol.*, VI. 4 (al. 7). We think of Athens as a city of philosophers, but according to Socrates, *Mem.*, III. vn. 6, *traders* are the bulk of the ecclesia.
28 *Pol.*, IV. 3. Besides the mere superfluities there are the refinements necessary to good living.
29 *Pol.*, IV. 3.
30 *Pol.*, I. 3.
31 *Pol.*, I. 3. *Eth.*, V. (5), 13. Same example.
32 *Eth.*, V. (5), 11–16.
33 *Eth.*, V. (5). *Pol.*, I. (3).
34 *Pol.*, I. 3
35 *Eth.*, V. (5), 4,13, etc.
36 Thales foresaw a great harvest of olives, and he bought up olive, and he bought up olive presses in advance, with the greatest financial success. *Pol.*, I. 4.
37 *Pol.*, I. 4.
38 *Eth.*, V. (3).
39 *Eth.*, V. (4).
40 τὸ ἀντιπεπονθός *Eth.*, V. (5).
41 Cf. *Eth.*, VIII. (7).
42 *Eth.*, V. (5).
43 For a general account of the *Politics* see Erdmann, *Hist. of Philos.*, vol. i. § 89, and for a special account of the economical views of Aristotle, see Mr. D. G. Ritchie's article in Palgrave's *Dict. of Polit. Econ.*, and Prof. Elster's article in the *Handwörterbuch d. Staatswissenschaflen*. The latter gives the literature of the subject, such as it is.

44 *Pol.*, I. I. (The observation of modern doctors that madmen can seldom combine, and two warders can usually cope with twenty madmen, seems to show that it is reason and not speech that is essential.)
45 *Eth.*, IX. (12), 7. For the whole subject see "Aristotle's conception of the State," by Prof. A. C. Bradley in *Hellenica*, 181 *seq.*
46 In Rome we have the Municipality as a permanent element.
47 *Pol.*, I. 2; cf. *Eth.*, I. (7).
48 *Pol.*, I. 2, III. 6.
49 *Pol*, III. 6 τούς γάρ πολλούς ὧν ἕκαστός ἐστιν οὐ σπουδαῖος ἀνήρ, ὅμως ἐνδέχεται συνελθόντας εἶναι βελτίονς εκείνων, οὐχ ὡς ἕκαστον ἀλλ᾽ ὡς σύμπαντας.
50 *Eth.*, II. (6), 15.
51 X. (9).
52 *Eth.*, X. (9), 6–9.
53 *Pol.*, 14; cf. VIII. (13), 5.
54 *Eth.*, V. (7).
55 *Pol.*, III. 6, II.
56 *Pol.*, II. I: γινομένη τε μία μάλλον, οἰκία μὲν ἐκ πόλεως, ἄνθρωπος δ᾽ ἐξ οἰκίας ἔσται.
57 *Eth.*, VIII. (9) and (10). See Mr. E. Poste's note (p. 97 of his transl., 2nd. ed.) on Aristotle's Ἀ θηναίων πολιτεία, Section LII. [δίκαι] ἐρανικαὶ καὶ κοινωνικαὶ.
58 *Pol.*, II. 2. It is immoderate, he adds, when it means love of *money.*
59 *Eth.*, IX. 8.
60 IX. 8, 7.
61 VIII. 1.4.
62 *Pol*, II. 2.
63 *Pol.*, II. 4.
64 *Pol.*, II. 4, in relation to Phaleas of Chalcedon.
65 II. 2.
66 Compare *Rhet.*, I. 9, 27, ἐλενθέρον τὸ μὴ πρὸς ἄλλον ζῆν.

3 Stoics and Epicureans

In Plato and Aristotle we have seen that wealth does no more than furnish foothold and room for the practice of virtue and the perfect exercise of human faculties. A certain measure of material resources is no doubt held indispensable, but it is viewed as a fixed factor. The progressive increase of wealth in a people is regarded as an evil rather than a good. Anything beyond the necessaries of life is thought to tend to evil; and the necessaries of life are not conceived as expanding with spiritual needs, but (especially in Plato) as rather diminishing than increasing with the growth of extraordinary powers and gifts. This had probably been the teaching of Socrates himself, who practised plain living and high thinking, though on occasion he could share the pleasures of gay society.[1] He thought that to have few wants was godlike and therefore best for man. [2]

This independence, which was in the case of Socrates himself the independence of a citizen of a free State, was interpreted by some of his contemporaries and followers in an anti-political if not anti-social sense. Aristippus, the founder of the Cyrenaic Philosophy, which regarded the pleasure of the moment as the chief happiness and end of man, was by his own account a citizen of no State, but "a stranger everywhere." His independence consisted in making the best of the world as it stood, and getting the utmost enjoyment out of the good things of this life, without any regard even to scientific acquirements. It was the philosophical expression of the characteristically Greek joy of living. But this adapting of wants to circumstances was really a departure from the teachings of Socrates. Antisthenes and the Cynics were more truly Socratic, pursuing independence by subduing the feelings to the intellect and seeking after virtue rather than enjoyment; but the Cynics were unlike Socrates in trying to be independent of all other men and even of the Family and State; they were like the Cyrenaics, citizens of no State in particular but of the world in general. Their philosophy was the caricature, or *reductio ad absurdum*, of asceticism. If all men had tried to become "independent" by creating a "Sad vacuity," there would be an end first to civilization and then to the race itself. When new life was given to philosophical individualism by the extinction of the political independence of the Greek States, first under Philip (Chaeronea, 338 B.C.), then finally by the Romans (Corinth, 146 B.C.), the Cynic and Cyrenaic doctrines assumed a new phase; their extravagances were corrected; and a more plausible and rational expression was given to the same aspirations by Stoicism and Epicureanism.

The general doctrines of Epicurus concern us less than those of the Stoics,[3] at least in regard to their views of wealth and social relations. The chief end is conceived by Epicurus to be pleasure, not (as with the Cyrenaics) "gentle motion" and positive enjoyment, but absence of pain and disturbance;—or (positively) it is peace of mind, which Epicurus himself thought to be better secured by virtue and wisdom, plain living and high thinking, than by anything external or bodily, Real wealth is only gained by limitation of wants; and he who is not satisfied with little will not be satisfied at all.[4] But even by Epicurus opulence and comfort, though not held indispensable, are not forbidden; if there was not a doctrine of self-indulgence, there was at least no doctrine of asceticism, and though the ordinary forms of political and social life were ignored, the relation between man and man in friendship is highly valued. This is an unconscious testimony to the binding nature of the social union, disparaged in the case of the Family and the State. Aristotle had preceded Epicurus in the praise of friendship;[5] but with him friendship is always subordinated to citizenship. Zeller has noticed that, when current philosophy became again individualistic in the 18th century, the praises of friendship were again heard.[6] Similarly, too, Epicureanism and the later individualism both attributed the origin of the State to a deliberate convention made for natural protection and security.

> *"Net facile est placidam ac pacatam degere vitam,*
> *Qui violat factis communia foedera pacis."*[7]

The resolution of society as well as the general system of things into "atoms that swerve" brings us in thought nearer to certain modern ideas on which a political and economical system has been founded. In its ancient form the theory left at least as many difficulties as it seemed to solve. Epicureanism can hardly give materials for an economic theory, whatever be true of modern Utilitarianism.

It is otherwise with Stoicism. The opposition between nature and convention was, as we have seen, not new; but the interpretation of "nature" by the Stoics and their use of the maxim, "live according to nature," threw a new light on the matter.[8] Ethics, connected by Aristotle with politics, is connected by the Stoics with metaphysics. Even more than the Epicureans, they led the way to a clearer view of the relation of individuals to society, and showed how much there was in the individual that could not be explained by the State or made to depend wholly on institutions. They viewed men in their relation not to Civil Society or the State but to the whole human family, and they rose superior to the distinctions of race, property, and even of sex. Any human being who follows his reason and consciously acquiesces in the laws by which the world is governed becomes thereby wise, free, noble, and rich. No doubt men are "mostly fools"; but it is open to any one to be wise if he chooses, whether he be Jew or Greek, barbarian or Scythian, bond or free.

The first result of the acceptance of Stoicism was no doubt to provide for its chosen spirits a retreat from the political world into their own soul. The material world and external things, including wealth and power, were on principle indifferent to the Stoical wise man; and, like the Epicurean, he was rich because he had few wants. But it came to be recognised by the Stoics that their metaphysical principle of the reign of Reason or Nature was inconsistent with any mere hostility to the established institutions of Society. They accordingly recognised the naturalness or rationality of these institutions while holding paramount the laws of that larger society which is coextensive with humanity. That this recognition extended to the unconscious social growths as well as to the deliberately formed political organizations, appears from the fact that the Stoics instead of opposing the popular religion endeavoured to rationalize it. They recognised the truth that belief in cosmical and belief in social order are logically connected. At the same time they were perhaps the first to form a philosophical conception of individual personality. Subjectivity and personality had long been, *de facto*, recognised in the Roman as distinguished from the Greek conception of citizenship; and Stoicism in all probability owed no little of its popularity among educated Romans to this coincidence. But Stoic cosmopolitanism overtopped Roman citizenship as the Roman empire overtopped the old Latin and Italian State which was once identical with the Roman. Personality under Roman law and personality under the law of Nature or of the world were analogous but unlike conceptions. In fact Stoicism, like Christianity, was fatal to the old view of the supremacy of one particular earthly state. The rights of man were not the same as the rights of the Roman, still less of the Greek citizen. The eventual importance of these Stoical notions for economics will soon appear; but at present it must be said that in the hands of the Stoics they bore no fruits for economical theory. The Stoics did not even render the indirect service of clearing up the notion of civil society and the relation of its members to each other and to the State. In fact the distinction of civil Society and State was yet to be made; and the notion that the individual could be dependent on his fellow-citizens and on the State without losing his individuality was not yet understood.

Notes

1   Plato, *Sympos.*; cf. *Xen. Mem.*, I. III. 5., VI. I, etc., etc.
2   *Xen. Mem.*, I.VI. 10.
3   Professor Hashach has dwelt on the influence exerted by Epicureanism through Gassendi on modern philosophy and economics. *Allgemeine Philosophische Grundlagen d. polit. Oekon.* (1890), 7 *seq.* and 36 *seq.*
4   Zeller, *Stoics, Epicureans and Sceptics* (transl.), p. 459.

5 *Eth.*, VIII., IX.
6 *Stoics, Ep., and Scept.*, 468 n.
7 Lucretius, *De rerum nat.*, V. 1154–5.
8 Bishop Butler's second Sermon on Human Nature is an exposition of this maxim.

4 Christianity

What Stoicism began for the few, CHRISTIANITY accomplished for the many. It broke down the exclusive regard to State and citizenship. "We ought to obey God rather than man"; there is a higher law than that of the State and a higher order than that of politics or civil Society. As far as existing States were concerned, it was individualistic; but, like that of the Stoics, the individualism of Christianity was itself founded on the conception of a State,[1]—a State which was spiritual and owed nothing to the coercive force of armies and magistrates. The Church was a community which embraced men of all ranks and nationalities. It imposed on its members a law adopted by their own choice, and a law that was supposed to derive no support from the traditional morality or the old political institutions of Greece or Rome. It was first of all a mystical union in which the members were one in Christ Jesus, having their citizenship in the invisible world. It interfered with the earthly citizenship mainly by destroying its old identity with religion. Religion was no longer part and parcel of political citizenship.

But it was not long before the *visible* Church became a strongly organized body, claiming for itself all the claims of the invisible city. The treatise of Augustine *De Civitate Dei* was written[2] to defend the Christian religion against the charge of bringing down a curse on the city of Rome; and his answer is that Rome is falling by its own sins, but the City of God is coming down from heaven to earth, prepared as a bride adorned for Christ her husband, to take its place. This new organization was conceived by the theologians under the same figure as the Greek State was conceived by the Greek philosophers; it had, like the human body, one spirit and many members. The several Christians were the members, the Holy Ghost the one Spirit, or life in the whole.[3] The Church soon took to itself the external forms of a government; and its officers were not unlike the Guardians of Plato's republic, being distinguished (like them) from those who were indeed citizens but were not devoted body and soul to the service of the commonwealth. The Society so ruled was not constituted by any community of blood, but by an ignoring of nationality, tradition and custom, and (in the case at least of the early converts) at the cost of a deliberate breach with the whole past and present of the Greek and Roman and Provincial world. The early success of this effort seems to show that a complete social and political revolution, as opposed to a gradual development, is not at all an impossibility;—but the later history of the Church brings out the irrepressibility of the ignored traditions and national differences, and shows that the theology of the Church, as it shaped itself in her councils, was affected by the philosophies which it professed to supersede. The old secular nature was not revolutionized, and the Canon (or Ecclesiastical) Law, which gives us amongst other things the authoritative view of the Church on the economical relations of men, has substantially the old social problems to handle, and finds Greek philosophy helpful in the task. We are told indeed (in the *Corpus Juris Canonici*) that "by the law of nature" all things are common, and no less so by Divine law, for "the earth is the Lord's," and therefore no man can truly say "this field is mine," or "this house is mine." It is the corruption of human nature, the Fall of Man, that has destroyed natural community of goods. But canon law does not insist on literal obedience to this natural and Divine law except in the case of those who are in a very special sense the Lord's people, namely the Clergy, who, as individuals, forsake all for Him. The laity may have private property, though they should remember it is only the usufruct of the Lords freehold, and the duties belonging to it outweigh the rights. There is a dignity in labour, and the clergy may work for a livelihood like the apostles; but neither they nor the laity must allow wealth to become a main end of life. If possible, the slaves of the laity should be freed so soon as they (the slaves) become Christians. The slaves of the clergy are to remain slaves, for the clergy "having nothing of their own can give no liberty to another."[4] Hard bargaining and monopolizing are wrong;—"*turpe lucrum sequitur qui minus emit ut plus vendat.*" Still more wicked is usury, which is defined as "getting more than one has given", "*qui plus quam dederit accipit, usuras expetit*"; whether it be in money or in kind; and the usurer is simply a robber; "*rapinam facit qui usuram accipit.*" It is lawful only between enemies; "*ubi jus belli, ibi etiam jus usuræ.*" It is clear that the notion of wealth and even of the distribution of wealth remains substantially as it was to Plato and Aristotle. But there was a real progress, of importance both to economics and to politics, in the view of the relation of men to each other. There was recognised a spiritual bond that was not that of nationality or of the ancient Greek and Roman State, and yet was even more binding than these were. "The multitude of them that believed were of one heart and one soul." The individuals are essential to the union, but the united body is something far greater than the component members. Cosmopolitanism is made a popular notion; the utmost extension of the Christian Society (it was conceived) can only strengthen and never endanger it; the interests of the individual members are represented as inseparably connected with the interest of the whole body; and the demand was made that the opportunity should be given to every human being to enter on the spiritual inheritance open to him with all his fellow-men. The features in this ideal which come nearest to the features of the Platonic and Stoic and Aristotelian are superior to their Greek counterparts, partly in the wideness of their application and partly in their warmth of feeling and fulness of detail.

The literal realization of the Christian Society seemed rather to be hindered than hastened when, by the conversion of Constantine, Christianity came out of prison to rule, and had to deal with a temporal power as wide as her own and professedly under her own banner. As a separation was made between clergy and laity, so the temporal power was separated from the spiritual;—Rome had two Suns,[5] the Pope and the Emperor. By the separation of clergy from laity, the democratic and communistic element in Christianity ceased to have a universal application; the ideal life was no longer for all men, but for the few. And in the separation of the temporal from the spiritual power there was practically a confession that Christianity could not create a new political and social order. It might only control and guide the existing order, as the clergy the laity. Still the idea of one universal Christian government was dear to the Church, as an approach to her ideal; and deep was the disappointment when the temporal power was divided between East and West, when Islam disputed the whole ground, and when later the Carlomanian empire broke up into several kingdoms. Dante (*De Monarchia*) gave, if not the last, the most perfect expression to the aspiration. By his time the process of decentralizing had been accomplished; and, under the feudal system, the people of his own and of the other countries of continental Europe were exposed to constant wars at the will of petty rulers. As feudalism gave way to strong monarchies under national rulers, the growth of cities and the extension of production for sale as opposed to production for use made the retention of the principles of the ancient political economy impossible. As late as 1311 the Council of Vienne threatened usurers with excommunication, and new arguments were invented to buttress up the old prejudices. But it was impossible for the Church to succeed in resisting the universal practice of men. With the new monarchies we have the beginnings not only of new political but of new economical principles; and in the political philosophy of the later writers we find the Greek idea of a law of nature gaining precedence over ideas of a purely ecclesiastical system.[6] What an acquaintance with Aristotle had begun, even in the middle ages, was carried further at the Renaissance by an acquaintance with the whole range of classical authors. Even the Church writers had declared supreme power, whether imperial or ecclesiastical, to be limited by "*lex divina et lex naturalis.*"[7] When speculation was once devoted to the latter it was carried beyond the ideas of ancient and mediæval political philosophy.[8]

Notes

1   *Cf.* Plato, *Republ.*, IX. 592, and Dante, *Purgatorio*, XIII. 94: *"Cia-scuna [anima] è cittadina D'una vera città."*
2   413–426 A.D.
3   I *Corinth*, xii. 4–28. *Ephes. i.* 22, 23. *See* Gierke, *Staats- und Corporationslehre d. Alterthums* (1881), p. 106 *seq.*

4 *Corpus Juris Canon.*, I. *Distinctio*, LIV. *Palea*, c. XXII, Cf. II. *Causa*, XII., *Quæst.*, II. c. 39. The slaves might always become free by becoming priests.
5 Dante, *Purgatorio*, XVI. 106 *seq.*
6 See Gierke, *Staats- und Corporationslehre*, p. 512; cf. 561.
7 *Ib.*, 567. Compare "Papacy, Democracy, and Socialism." Anat. Leroy Beaulieu (Engl, transl.), 1892; p. 141 *seq.*
8 For the economics of the Middle Ages, see Endemann, *National-ökonomische Grundsätze d. Canonistischen Lehre* (1863), also Palgrave's *Dict. of Polit. Econ.*, art. "Canon Law."

BOOK II

Modern Philosophy (I)
Natural Law

1 Precursors of Grotius

Machiavelli.—More.—Bodin.

Modern Political Economy may be said to begin with the introduction of taxation as a means of supporting the State, in place of personal service, aids in kind, and revenues from crown property; and taxation begins with the absolute monarchy that superseded the feudal system. Thus Political Economy begins with the growth of States in their modern form. It grows out of the discussions about the relation of the revenue to the monarch, who received it, and who was anxious to find out the best ways of increasing it. Hence its early connection with questions of coinage, currency and debasement. It is connected at this middle stage of its history rather with finance and political philosophy than, as at first and afterwards, with moral philosophy. At the end of the middle ages any alteration in the view of wealth taken by speculative thinkers shows itself rather in sumptuary laws than in measures traceable to the "Mercantile Theory." Later, when there grew up a special branch of study roughly corresponding to our modern Political Economy, the said study was directed rather to the commercial relations between one nation and another than to the industrial order of one nation within itself, just as the study of natural law, so brilliantly revived by Grotius, was largely a study of international law.

As the notion of natural law, of all the notions of political philosophy, is perhaps the most important economically, we must look somewhat closely at the work of Grotius, and more cursorily at the work of his immediate predecessors in political philosophy—Machiavelli, Sir Thomas More, and Jean Bodin.

Machiavelli (1469–1527) has been said[1] to have "thrown ethics out of politics as Spinoza threw *ethics* out of ethics." This statement owes its plausibility to the emphasis which, from the needs of his own country, Machiavelli was forced to lay on the need of strength and cohesion in a State and worldly wisdom in the rulers. But, in his *Discourses on the First Ten Books of Livy*, and even in the *Prince*, there is proof that he recognized the complexity of the body politic and the presence of factors that were only indirectly of political importance. He would use the study of history as a means of discovering political truth. Human nature is the same, he says, in his day as it was in Livy's (*Discourses*, III. XLIII.); we can see, for example, that then, as now, the people were less fickle than the princes, and that both needed the restraint of laws and of customs.[2] He recognises the importance of the economical element in the national life. Money, he says, is not, as Quintus Curtius affirmed, the sinews of war, for it is useless without soldiers;[3] but well-governed and rich provinces are the sinews of a State; and political security is the sinews of agriculture and commerce on which the riches depend, for every man naturally likes to make what he can himself enjoy in his own person after it is made—private benefit thus securing public benefit. The wealth procured by commerce and industry is perhaps most durable of all.[4] Machiavelli recognises the power of self-interest as a motive to action, and the insatiableness of human desires. From his favourite notion that to be successful a man must be either perfectly good or perfectly bad,[5] we can hardly venture to draw economical conclusions where he certainly drew none. He sees in the perpetual failure of the Agrarian laws of Rome a sign that men's desires always outrun their powers of satisfying them.[6] When they cease to fight from necessity they fight for ambition. There are in such passages the beginnings of economic analysis, but it does not go very far. He praises the plain living of Cincinnatus;[7] a people may be rich if it reckons by its necessaries, not by the extent of its possessions, also if its money does not go forth of the country to buy foreign goods. Extravagance in a prince is a mischief if it leads to taxation, and public works are less important than a contented people. But idleness is the root of all evil. Christianity has praised humility at the expense of the active virtues.[8] Machiavelli, far from having the modern notion of progress, thinks[9] that there is a fixed quantity of happiness and unhappiness in the world at all times, but distributed differently at different times, so that a man may complain if he likes that he was born in Turkey and not in Italy, but not that he was born in one century and not in another. Such a notion reminds us of the belief of Adam Smith, that, on the whole, happiness was equally distributed among all classes of men.[10] But the latter, though it might weaken the zeal of reformers, could hardly allow one group of men to grieve at the prosperity of another group, whereas Machiavelli's dictum would mean that, in proportion to the wideness of the areas, the gain of one group would be the loss of another. Such a conclusion was indeed in keeping with the prejudices of Machiavelli's times. That in every bargain there is one party which gains and another which loses, or, as Bacon says in his *Essay on Seditions*, "whatsoever is somewhere gotten is somewhere lost," is the idea that probably first occurs to every man when he first gives any thought at all to such matters. It was the impression of the earliest economical thinkers; or, at least, it was a popular prejudice, which they were not entirely able to throw off. This problem contains the whole question of equitable exchange in miniature. Modern economists, while they reject the view that one party must necessarily be a loser, do not adopt *simpliciter* the opposite dictum that in a willing bargain both must equally gain. Such discussions, however, are not to be found at all in our author, and his political philosophy, on the whole, yields scanty gleaning for the economist.

As Machiavelli is driven into political theory by the pressing political problems of Italy in his day, **Sir Thomas More** (1478–1535) is driven into economics by the social problems of England in his day, which were not only calling
for attention, but, as a strong monarchy had already given political security,
were able to obtain it. When he wrote his *Utopia*, he was distressed about the
state of England as Plato, when he wrote his *Republic*, was distressed about
the state of Athens; but in More's case the social questions bulk far more
largely than the political, and the philosophy, such as it is, does not extend, as
in Plato's case, to the deepest problems of Metaphysics. The parallel between
the two authors is, however, so close, that we cannot consider the *Utopia* in a
clearer light than by taking its various themes in the order in which we have
taken them in the case of Plato, *i.e.*, taking first his conception of Wealth,
next, of Production and Distribution, and last, of Civil Society and the State.

"The whole island," or, in other words, the whole ideal commonwealth, is
regarded as one great family, and its economy is on the same lines as provision
for a large household. Wealth is represented as the abundance of necessaries
and commodities, as distinguished from superfluities and luxuries, whether
in the way of food, clothing, or other provision for the flesh, including ambition, ostentation, and covetousness. But (as in Plato) the natural pleasures
and the pleasures of the mind are distinguished from the false pleasures and
the bodily pleasures. No pleasure is forbidden that is not harmful and vicious.
The "necessaries and commodities" are those of a comfortable, healthy and
happy life, the life of men who, like the Athenians, are supposed to "cultivate
art without expense and philosophy without effeminacy". It is a picture not
unlike in many ways to the City of Pigs in the *Republic*, with this difference,
that there is universal communism. The range of wants, so far as they relate
to material goods, is confined, not in some but in all the citizens, within the
bounds of simplicity. There is no notion that money is in any special sense
wealth; it is, in fact, regarded as a hindrance to the diffusion of true wealth,
which is abundance.

Gold and silver in Utopia are degraded to base uses, that the citizens
may never be tempted into sin by "love of gold." Iron is prized much more
highly,[11] for (we are told) its usefulness is greater, and "Nature" has plainly
showed her preference by making iron, like air and water and earth, accessible to all, whereas gold and silver are valued because hard to come at. The
Utopian Commonwealth keeps a store of gold and silver for high political
purposes, and its foreign trade in surplus produce is useful in procuring these
metals for it; but in their every-day life its citizens despise them, and make
their meanest vessels of them.

Such is More's view of Wealth. His scheme of Production and Distribution
is as follows. Separate occupations are allowed, but besides his and her
separate occupation every man and woman must practise the one common
occupation of agriculture, which is to be restored to its ancient glory. They
first learn farming, and not till then may they take up one of the four or five
"sciences, crafts, and occupations"[12] above allowed on the island. They may

be weavers, smiths, carpenters, or masons, at choice. The Syphograuntes (or Guardians) must see to it that no one is either idle or over-worked.[13] As a rule the division of labour will be hereditary. The men will follow their fathers' crafts. The women will apply themselves to the easier handicrafts. There are to be six hours of labour a day;[14] three before noon, and, after two hours' interval, three again. Yet an ample supply of wealth will be furnished for all; and no one will be without leisure for study and literature, as well as amusement. The reduction of the time of labour will seem quite possible (he says) to any one who considers how many men and women, whether ecclesiastics or nobility, are now supported by the labour of others. If these were to do their share of work, the rest would not need to exhaust themselves as they now do. If every one worked a little, and only for what is necessary and natural for men to obtain, there would be no one who need work to excess; all might be healthy, wealthy, and wise. But that will never be till private property is abolished, and, like Plato's Guardians and the early Christians, the citizens have all things in common. This is the central political change prescribed in Utopia. It differs from Plato's communism, for (1) the family and family life are preserved (the family being indeed the political unit); and on the other hand, (2) it extends, not merely to the ruling class, but to all citizens in the State. The only "lower class" is the class of criminals who are bondsmen for their crimes.[15] In thus, as it were, throwing open Plato's ideal to all sorts and conditions of men, Sir Thomas More was taking a step of great theoretical as well as practical importance. He was introducing into the region of political theory the notion that there was a normal standard of outward comforts below which no human being could be allowed to fall without danger and disgrace to his country. The special economical development of this view was the work of a later time. It seems to be logically involved in every theory of communism, but, though a particular political or social theory may be generically the same as one a thousand years older, there is seldom more than a generic resemblance. The special reasons for its appearance at one particular epoch always give it a new aspect, and make its lessons appear entirely new. The communism of Sir Thomas More (like Plato's, in so far as material well-being is always subordinated to spiritual) is unlike Plato's, not only in its extent, but in its intention. To improve the condition of the poorer classes would seem to be More's first and last thought. With Plato it is a mere incident. More is impressed by the fact that in England "the sheep are devouring the men," covetous proprietors are throwing corn lands into pasture, and throwing men out of employment for the sake of gain. Agrarian difficulties were of course present to Plato's mind; but they were less important to him than the question of political government and political power. Plato's warriors are a class by themselves, and war (except against Greeks) has its honour. The Utopians abhor war; but, when they need to fight, all are warriors, even the women. Though More, like Plato, has no love for merchants, usury, and foreign trade, he has no hatred of foreigners. It might be doubted whether it was Plato's influence that widened More's

Christianity, or More's Christianity that widened his Platonism. He allows much greater room for individual enterprise and emulation, as well as much greater tolerance for differences of speculative belief, than Plato would have done, and his sympathy is wider. But, after saying that the Utopians incline most to the Christian religion, he gives one reason which is essentially in the spirit of Plato: they do so *because* "Christ instituted, among his, all things common, and the same community doth remain among the rightest Christian companies"; and he gives us to understand that the people of Utopia lived a good and happy life by means of their communism and before they heard of Christianity. As Machiavelli had separated politics, so More separates social reform from the Church, though not to the same extent. He does not assert that a mere change in the arrangements for the distribution of wealth will make and keep a people morally good, as if without moral goodness (to say nothing of science and wisdom) such a change could be either made or kept with success.[16] He is alive to the current objections against communism,[17] and he makes provision for the expansion of population by laying down a severe prohibition of waste land (as contrary to the "law of nature"), though diminution of population seems to him almost as likely an event as excessive increase. But he makes clear his opinion that the moral standard is most likely to be high among a people when every citizen (and not merely a solitary individual here and there) has a high standard of living, and therewith normal, but not excessive work, wealth, and leisure. If it is impossible in our own time for a political philosophy to leave out the economical element in the body politic without forfeiting all claim to be practicable, we owe this in some part to Sir Thomas More. His own scheme made no pretence to be practicable; it was too strongly opposed (he said) by two great enemies, "Lady Money and Princess Pride," one feature of the latter being that she measures her own wealth by the misery of others. He does not attempt (like Plato in the *Laws*) to show what legislation would make the new State practicable. Good men need few laws, he says, and good States few leagues. The bond of sentiment is better than a law, and institutions once established will gain strength by entering into the customs and traditions of the people. Spontaneous institutions would thus seem to bulk more largely in Utopia than legislative creations; but we have no clear account of the first genesis of the government of the Utopians itself. Whatever it is, it is not historical; and a more complete contrast to Machiavelli's writings than More's it would be hard to find.

It was not by accident that the first important English work on political philosophy in modern times had laid so strong an emphasis on the economical element in States. England had gained internal peace under a strong monarchy, and, self-preservation being assured, the question of self-development became important. When the stability of government is again insecure, we find the more strictly political questions displacing the social, in the philosophy of Hobbes, though in Harrington the latter reappear, and they are never afterwards wholly forgotten.

For our present purpose, in the interval of a century that elapsed between More and Hobbes, the interest shifts from England to the Continent. Bacon, "the father of Inductive Philosophy," gave no special attention to economic subjects, and his *New Atlantis*, though it touches incidentally on social reform, and its author seems frequently to have Sir Thomas More in view, is yet essentially an Ideal University rather than an Ideal Society. "Œconomics," in the great treatise on the *Advancement of Learning* (Bk. VIII. III init.) has its ancient sense of Domestic Economy, though it is hinted that we may use it analogically of the husbandry of the State. The economic observations of Bacon, sometimes in advance of his times—as on the whole on Usury and Colonies (Plantations),—sometimes on a par with current prejudices (as in dislike of foreign trade),[18] are given in the form of aphorisms; and we cannot speak of a philosophical treatment of the subject even in the matter of method. The Abstract or Geometrical Method and the Experimental are to him the only two possible in science. Whether he would have adopted the latter in Economics as in Physics we cannot say with certainty, for his only connected consideration of economic subjects is under the head of the Art of Government, and, even there, he takes us but a little way.[19]

Bodin (1530–97) (in his *République*, 1576) does not desire, like Plato and Sir Thomas More, to found an ideal State, but, like Machiavelli, to work out the rules of a practicable political philosophy. Machiavelli however, in Bodin's opinion, gave us the wrong political philosophy. Bodin tries to do the work over again.

All the three writers are still on the old classical ground so far as they do not begin with the individual human unit, but take human society for granted. Bodin not only agrees with More and Aristotle in regarding the Family as the political unit, but, like More, he conceives the State itself as a large family, and will not distinguish politics from "œconomy" (in its old sense). A State, he says, is in principle and origin an equitable government of several families together, and of what belongs to them all jointly, though this government, as time goes on, embraces the free associations of men outside of the family, formed for example for purposes of commerce. A national charac-ter[20] (he says) depends largely on geographical conditions. The peoples of the south are scientific; of the north industrious and mechanical; of the middle regions, commercial and judicial, law-giving and law-abiding. Dwellers in great towns or by the sea are likely to be enterprising and inquisitive, and, in trade, too cunning. A fertile soil will have indolent inhabitants. Historically, political changes have been often due to excessive wealth and poverty in a country, especially in ancient times when slavery and debt were serious evils. Seditions were aimed either at the cancelling of debts or the equalizing of property—both (in Bodin's opinion) impracticable. Bodin revives Aristotle's objection to communism, its effect on population. "Sir Thomas More would have families contain no less than ten and no more than sixteen children, as if he could make Nature obey his orders."[21] Rather than an absolute equality we should aim at such a distribution as would strengthen a Middle Class, neither very rich nor very poor. We should remove such causes of poverty as confiscations and excessive taxation, and such causes of opulence as the inter-marriage of the rich. In any case all progress must be gradual, for laws are respected in proportion to their antiquity, and we must imitate Nature, which perfects no life suddenly. The central government must be sovereign, and it must be strong, for there is no hope of growth within till there is protection against dangers outside. In a new colony, indeed, there may be an approach to a sudden creation of new conditions; and an approach to equality of pos-sessions is feasible there if anywhere. After military strength comes financial; there should be a census of goods and numbers, and the State, besides get-ting wealth from taxation, may get it from public lands and from colonies. Trade, which enriches the people, was once thought dishonourable, but was surely less so than robbery which was thought no disgrace. We may see, he adds, especially from a country like Portugal, how trade may make a country wealthy. As to gold and silver, abundance of them only serves to raise prices. The degradation of the coinage is mischievous to all parties.[22]

He inquires into the best form of government, and decides for monarchy as the "most in accordance with Nature." There is only one head in the body, one sun in the sky, and one God in the universe. Hence we see that, after all, Bodin's book is a pamphlet in favour of absolute monarchy even though in a purified and philosophical form.

The first modern product of strictly economical speculation, the Mercantile Theory, grew up out of the conditions of absolute monarchy. It was a stage through which all European governments have passed in the growth of their civilization; and in the writings of its advocates we have doctrines of fiscal finance that contain the germs of the mercantile theory even if these are not fully developed there. Even in the *Utopia* there is a reference to the idea that foreign trade is good because it brings gold and silver into the country. The absolute monarchs at first, however, concerned themselves about foreign trade rather as yielding them a revenue, and influencing the habits of their people, than with a view to a favourable Balance. A system of duties might be simply equivalent to a system of sumptuary laws, and this merely meant that the king had his own notion of what ought to constitute the wealth of his sub-jects and was trying to impose this notion upon them by law. The principles of the mercantile theory involved much more than this, as we shall presently learn. Meanwhile it is to be noted that Bodin's political philosophy, though full of illustration on points of detail, economical and political, does not (like that of Grotius) involve the discovery of any principle which was of great moment for latter speculation, political and economical. The notion that the Middle Class should be regarded as the most important is, perhaps, though it is not novel,[23] and is lightly touched on by our author, even economically the most interesting, from the part played by the Middle Class in modern indus-trial life and speculation. One of the leading questions of practical economics in our time is whether the Middle Class, after losing their political predomi-nance, will not also lose their domination over industry and commerce.[24]

Notes

1 By Knies, *Pol. Oekon. nach d. geschichtlichen Methode* (1853), p. 319.
2 *Discorst*, I. LVIII.; cf. LII. v.
3 *Discorsi*, II. x.
4 *Disc, on Livy*, II. II., etc.
5 *Ib.*, I. XXVI., etc.
6 *Ib.*, I. XXXVII.; cf. XLVI.
7 *Disc, on Livy*, III. xxv.
8 *Ib.*, II. II.
9 *Ib.*, II. I.
10 *Moral Sentiments.* A "fixed quantity of human life in the world " and "a station-ary total of animal and vegetable population" are remoter parallels. Cf. *Malthus and His Work*, p. 385.
11 Even where there is "no robbery," there may be different "Consumer's Rent." See Prof. Marshall, *Principles of Pol. Ec.*, Book III., ch. iv. (1st ed.).
12 *Quis non videt quam longe infra ferrum sunt? Lib. ii.*
13 *Artes* is his general word. The section is headed *De artificiis.*
14 In his own day, he says, artisans worked like oxen.
15 *Sex [horas] duntaxat operi deputant.* Ralph Robinson's translation is less clear on this point than the original.
16 Like convicts in our day.
17 *Utopia*, bk. II. 163, 164 (Pitt Press Transl.).
18 *Ib.*, bk. I. 63, 64 (Pitt Press Transl.), cf. 86.
19 See *Atlantis*, the essays on Riches, Seditions, Expense, True Greatness of Kingdoms, etc., and the famous passage on Enclosures near the beginning of the *Life of Henry VII.*
20 For an account of Bacon's economical views see W. Roscher, *Zur Geschichte d. Englischen Volkswirthschaftslehre* (1851), pp. 36–44. For an account of More from the economic point of view, Kautsky's *Thomas More und seme "Utopie"* (Stuttgart, 1888) is of interest; it presents a full statement of the historical context of our author's writings, though Kautsky, following Marx, is too inclined to refer all historical events to economical causes.
21 An idea followed out by Montesquieu, *Esprit des Lois*, more than a century later.
22 *Républ.* (ed. 1594), bk. V. p. 705.
23 Bodin was perhaps the first to point out the effect of the American discoveries of the precious metals on the value of the latter in Europe. *Réponses à M. de Malestroit*, 1568, 1578.
24 It is as old, perhaps, as the book of Proverbs ("Give me neither poverty nor riches"), and certainly as old as Aristotle.
25 For a full account of Bodin, see Baudrillart, *Jean Bodin et son temps*, 1853. Compare Prof. Espinas, *Doctrines écon.*, 1892, pp. 120–127. Prof. Flint, *Philos, of Hist.*, pp. 68 seq.

2 Grotius (1583–1645)

The work of GROTIUS on the *Laws of War and Peace* (*De jure belli et pads*, 1625) is not strictly political, like the writings of Machiavelli, nor social, like the *Utopia*, nor confined to the consideration of single States within themselves, like Bodin's *République*. Holland, unlike France, was nothing without its foreign trade and international connections; and the political philosophy of Hugo de Groot (Grotius) was appropriately devoted not to States within themselves, but to States in their relations with each other. But, in extending his view, like the Stoic philosophers, beyond the limits of the single State, Grotius drew attention to principles which bore not only on international but on civic relations, the relation of man to the State, and of man to man.

Historical events had prepared the way for this phase of political philosophy. The old international peacemaker, the Pope, had no longer universal authority; the unity of the Roman Empire was gone; the unifying influence of feudal ties had reached a very little way, and feudalism had yielded to absolutism. On the dethronement of the Church, Protestants found the need of providing another authority in sacred things; and on the discrediting of Papal mediation they had need to supply the like gap in secular government.[1]

Was there any authority left, to bind the nations of the world in their relations with one another? This is the question to which Grotius would furnish the answer.

In looking beyond the State to the world of States we might seem to be travelling farther away from the region of Economics. In reality we are being brought nearer both to Economics and to Ethics. We are brought face to face with the principles that have moulded economical theory more than all others in modern times, the principles of Natural Law and Natural Liberty.

It is true that in the history of natural law, whether as a legal or as a philosophical conception, Grotius is only one term of a long series.[2] But his propositions, from the immense currency they obtained and the influence they exerted, became a new point of departure for speculation.

He is attempting to show how a political philosophy (including an ethics and an economics, as yet undistinguished from one another) can be built up without the aid of theology.

Many, says Grotius, have regarded the law of nations as a mere empty phrase, and have supposed that outside the limits of a State the rule of the strongest is the only law,[3] and anything is just that is to the advantage of the strongest. Like Carneades of the New Academy, they say that men make laws by the standard of their own advantage merely (*pro utilitate*), and there is no law of nature. These theorists do not remember that man is a social animal, "*est* [*homini*] *appetitus societatis*"; and he desires not only companionship, but a quiet and well-ordered companionship with his like, as the Stoics perceived. Even animals are not guided only by individual advantage, but often by affection; and what is instinct with them is reason with men. This regard for society is the source of all binding laws; and, as all men are kindred in Adam, all are subject to natural law, first because of their common humanity,[4] next (and in a less degree) because advantage (*utilitas*) follows from obedience to it, and must always be presumed to do so. As civil laws are of advantage to citizens, international laws are of advantage to men as a body everywhere. No State is so strong that it does not in some way need the help of others, for example, in trade.

We infer a law of nature from the first principles of things, and an international law from the universal agreement of men. The former is independent of the deliberate will of men; the latter is a product of that will. "Unjust" in the first sense means conflicting with the existence and persistence of a society of reasonable beings, and tending to undermine it. God Himself cannot alter natural law, for He would then be making things to contradict the very Nature which He has given to them.[5] Natural law does not bind us to create particular institutions, but it binds us to adopt a certain course of conduct towards them when created.[6] It does not bind us to institute the modern tenure of property, but it binds us to respect it when created. It does not bind a nation never to go to war, but it binds the nation to certain conduct in its wars. All these and other positions are proved in the pages of Grotius by reasoning, by learned authorities, and by Scripture.

To look more especially at the institution of Property, there was at first a common right of all men to unappropriated things of the material world, as in the Garden of Eden. But soon (after the Deluge and Babel), the earth was divided, not only among nations, but among families. Things were divided by a tacit or by an expressed compact, whereby it was conceded that the first occupier should not be disturbed. The sea cannot be appropriated like the land, because it cannot be so occupied and devoted to separate human uses. Division of property follows, and does not precede occupation. Now this proprietorship is not subversive of the original law of Nature. In extreme need that law reasserts itself; self-preservation must overcome the rights of property, just as in a storm we may need to cut away the mast. But the need must be extreme to justify seizure of property, or forcible passage through another's territory, or the doing of damage to private individuals in war.

The law of nature is in favour of a right of passage for merchandise, for it is the interest of the human race generally that trade should go on, normal trade being a mutual gain to the two parties trading, and a loss to no one. The law of nature allows any nation to occupy land which is unoccupied by another nation. The law of nature does not absolutely condemn Slavery, for a necessity so extreme as to endanger life will give men a right to prefer slavery to death. Bodin and Grotius agree in giving slavery a relative or historical justification. No one is born free, or born a slave, but acquires the one condition or the other from subsequent fortune.

The law of Nations, as distinguished from the law of Nature, has to do with the relations of nations as jointly forming one society among themselves, in contrast both with the relations of individual men to individual men (under the law of nature) and with the relation of a single State to its citizens (by the civil law). The law of nations may often be in conflict with the law of nature, and the civil law of the State with both. A State is "an artificial body" or organism, whose identity remains though the component particles may change, as in an animal body.[7] Among the relations of citizens in a State to each other are the relations of contract and exchange.[8] Grotius at this point gives a good description of value, and cognate economical notions, drawing freely as usual on classical writers. The natural measure of value is, as Aristotle says, human needs (*indigentia*, χρεία), but there are desires of unneeded luxuries. Grotius takes account of cost in value, and makes a distinction very like that of Ricardo between the value of articles limited in supply, and the value of articles freely produced. The various commercial phenomena of monopolies and "corners," of usury, insurance, and commercial partnerships, are described at some length; and in all of them the principle is held that a bargain deliberately made is in those matters as binding and presumably as mutually beneficial as in any other contract. Like a true Dutchman, Grotius magnifies the importance of commerce, and gives historical facts in support of his contention, that commerce should be permitted, even during war.

The notion of contract plays a great part in Grotius. The first founders of a State are conceived as entering into the first of all contracts, which is the condition of all others within the State. This first contract, however, is simply declaratory of the law of nature; it is not an arbitrary act.[9] It is when we come to conventions like the League of Cambrai, or the Hanseatic League, and other unions for special purposes, that we find an *addition* to the law of nature. When once the first contract is entered into, the law of nature no longer permits and forbids all that it permitted and forbade before, in the "*primævus naturæ status*" before that contract. These references of Grotius to an original contract, and a *state* (as well as a law) of nature were of great influence on subsequent speculation. The good faith which respects all contracts from the first downwards is to him the necessary postulate of all union and communion of men, first on the large scale over the whole human society, then between nations, and finally between citizens within a nation. It is the breach of it that makes men unsocial, and leads to war. Not only Christianity, but "*humana utilitas*" itself bids us seek peace and ensue it.[10]

It must be clear from the foregoing statement that the doctrine of Grotius is by no means a mere revival of the doctrine of Aristotle that man is a social animal. To Aristotle the doctrine meant that man was born for life in a State, and that the State was the end, and a man, as an individual, was no end in himself. "Great Nature spake and it was done." The plan of the world included States, and men must be made to fulfil the end of Nature and become citizens. As Stahl truly says,[11] the emphasis is laid by Grotius not on "great Nature" but on human nature. Man has certain qualities which make him social, and hence he founds a State, while at the same time and for the same reason he belongs to other and often wider communities as well. This of course was implied, as we have seen,[12] in Christianity, but it had not been stated before so clearly, in a non-religious form and by a mere political philosopher. Moreover the very notion that the State begins in a species of contract conveys to us that in the mind of Grotius the individual men, not at first jointly, but severally, are the real starting-point. Without needing to represent original compact as a commercial bargain, we can readily understand the bearing of such a theory on economical speculation. By holding commercial bargains to be as innocent as all other contracts, Grotius was enabled to clear his mind of much of the current cant about usury and the wickedness of traders; and he did his part in making a dispassionate inquiry into economical subjects possible. But his importance in the history of the relations between Economics and Philosophy is mainly due to the influence of his Political Philosophy. From his epoch, if not from himself, we must date the increased interest in two lines of inquiry, both of which are in contact with Economics. The first is that assiduous study of the effects of foreign commerce which led to the Mercantile Theory. The other is the more abstract study of the first principles of politics and political philosophy, which we see in Hobbes, Spinoza, and Pufendorf. In our own Locke and Hume we have both studies pursued by the same individuals; but it is not till we come to the French Physiocrats that we find the principles of political philosophy and the practical principles of economic policy brought apparently into one channel, and made parts of one and the same system.

Note.—Richard Hooker (1553–1600)

Though Hooker's *Ecclesiastical Polity* (printed 1593 *seq.*) is (as the title shows) not a work on general jurisprudence, the author has really gone far along the path followed by Grotius in pursuit of the idea of a law of nature. The two men wrote independently, but with a similar motive, the one trying to vindicate Protestant Ethics, the other Protestant (or at least Anglican) Church government. The Church (says Hooker) is founded on the Scriptures, but the Scriptures are not in the barest literal sense the only rule to direct us, for the Scriptures themselves take for granted men as they are, placed by their physical and intellectual constitution under certain laws of nature, these including not only moral rules but a certain order of civil society and the rules thereof. Scripture gives all that is necessary to salvation, but assumes a human subject capable of understanding its teachings, as a teacher of elocution assumes that his pupil has a voice and knows grammar. Perhaps we might express this by saying that Christianity does not address itself to an abstract man, nor attempt the impossible task of beginning with a "tabula rasa." Similarly Augustine, *De Civitate Dei* (quoted by Dante, *De Monarchia,* III. p. 368, Fraticelli): *"Non sane omnia quæ gesta narrantur, etiam significare aliquid putanda sunt"* etc. *"Solo vomere terra proscinditur, sed ut hoc fieri possit etiam cætera aratri membra sunt necessaria."* For Hooker's influence on Locke, see *infra.*

Notes

1 Prof. Hasbach tries to show that the subsequent attempts to found a philosophical ethics were due to the discrediting of the religious sanction through the religious wars.
2 See *e.g.* Moritz Voigt, *Die Lehre vom Jus Naturale, etc d. Römer* (Leipzig, 1856), and Prof. Otto Gierke, *Johannes Althusius und die Entwickelung der naturrechtlichen Staatstheorien* (Breslau, 1880).
3 The doctrine of some of the Sophists. See Plato, *Gorgias,* and *Republic,* I. and II. Grotius, *De jure B. et P., Proleg.*
4 ὅσα κοινοῦ τινος μετέχει, πρὸς τὸ ὁμογενές σπεύδει, etc. Marcus Aurelius, *Meditations,* IX. 9.
5 *De Jure B.,* I. i. 4 and 5. So Hooker in his *Ecclesiastical Polity* (1593 *seq.*), makes the Law of Nature the necessary substratum of revealed religion.
6 *De Jure B.,* I. i. x., § 7. Cf. the statements of J. S. Mill about the "laws" of distribution.
7 *De Jure B.,* II. ix. § III., *"Corpora haec artificialia."*
8 *De Jure B.,* II. xii., *De Contractibus.*
9 *De Jure B.,* I. i., § iii., II. xv. § v. Compare III. iii. § ii.
10 *De Jure B.,* III. xxv., § iv.
11 *Rechtsphil.,* I. 174; cf. Bluntschli, *Staatslehre,* p. 70.
12 Above, p. 51.

3   Hobbes (1588–1679)

Thomas Hobbes (*De Cive*, 1642, *Leviathan*, 1651) wrote in the troubled times of the Civil War and the Commonwealth, when the need of a strong central government was more felt in England than the need of domestic reform or international mediation. He is the greatest modern apostle of the doctrine that Might is Right. He speaks like Grotius of a law of nature, and a state of nature, but conceives them very differently, and his writings may be read throughout as if controversial pamphlets against Grotius. What in the Dutch philosopher was only implied,—that the individual is the starting point of political philosophy,—is by the English made explicit and emphatic. In tracing State and Society to their first beginnings, we come (if we follow Hobbes) to individual men, by nature not social, but, "ad mutuam cœdem apti," selfish and anti-social, in a state of war with each other.[1] In this state of nature there are no laws, not even laws of nature. Every man is, roughly speaking, his fellow's equal in the balance of physical and intellectual gifts; every one has a claim to all things; his desires are boundless, and his will is only bounded by his power. It is the struggle for existence, with supremacy to the strongest, described in the 2nd book of Plato's *Republic*; and it is a struggle which ceases only when the combatants recognise that they are defeating their own ends by continuing it. The first law of nature is self-preservation, and that law bids them seek peace instead of war. They discover that the paths of gain and glory lead but to the grave. The voice of reason is first heard when passion finds out its own impotence. But to get peace they must make mutual concessions; each must give up his unlimited claims, on condition that the others do the same. Obeying the law of nature, they give up the state of nature, and found a political union, where the once independent individuals have surrendered their several wills to one sovereign authority. They do this by entering into a Contract, a contract on which all other contracts depend. The Sovereign may be a single man or may be a group, but in any case, represents their common self-denying ordinance, their common submission for Peace's sake. They then become one people instead of an aggregate of separate atoms.[2] To Hobbes, therefore (as to Grotius), the State is "an artificial body." "By art is created that great Leviathan called a Commonwealth or State, which is but an artificial man (though of greater stature and length than the natural man, for whose protection it was intended), and in which the sovereignty is an artificial soul giving life and motion to the whole body."[3]

Outside this State there can be no laws and no justice; particular States are to each other in a state of nature, which means a state of natural liberty and anarchy; of the laws themselves we can say they are good or bad, but not that they are just or unjust, for we have no other standard of justice but the laws themselves.[4] After departing from Greek notions by beginning with individual atoms having no bent for society in them, Hobbes goes on to make men depend on the State for their rules of life in a stricter way than the Greeks themselves. The State on which they so depend is, moreover, according to him, a contrivance of enlightened selfishness; and the source of all morality and justice is thus itself quite alien to either in any ordinary understanding of the terms. Political economy has been often understood to delight in a reign of law where the selfishness of many conduces to the benefit of all, but it has not claimed (as Hobbes claims for his State) that the fact of such conduciveness converts the selfish motive into a moral principle. Hobbes' immediate application of his theory was political: he inferred that no resistance to sovereign authority was ever lawful—to which the answer is, that the obligation which binds the action of man after the contract cannot be shown to rest on any other foundation than obligation before the contract; in other words, there is nothing, on Hobbes' own principles, to prevent a nation breaking this contract except their want of power to break it. If they have the power, they have all the justification, which, on the premises, is needed. It might be added that, if the assumption of such a contract is historically improbable, the assumption of its intentional unalterableness is still more so. In regard to Hobbes' theory, Professor Green says, very happily, and in the spirit of Grotius, that "where there is no recognition of a common good there can be no right in any other sense than power."[5]

But without at present dwelling on the political aspect of the theory, let us look a little at the economical. The injunction, "Seek peace and ensue it," applies to men as dealing with goods quite as much as to men in their other relations.[6] The two strongest motives for seeking peace are the fear of death and the desire of the comforts of life.[7] Outside of the State no one can be sure that he will reap the fruits of his labour, whereas (according to Hobbes) within the State every one can have that assurance. Without are fightings, but within are no fears; without are poverty, ignorance, and barbarism, within are the reign of reason, peace, security, wealth, refinement, and knowledge. Natural or absolute liberty and equality, however, are given up, and when we speak, for example, of equality in taxation we mean equality of burden, but not of payment (*equalitas non pecuniæ sed oneris*), for the burdens should be in proportion to the advantages gained by the citizens from the peace of the State, and these advantages are very unequal.

We see from the above that the connection of Hobbes' economical principles with his philosophical lies in the fact that the social compact is supposed to be necessary for economical growth, as well as for general security, culture, and happiness. To Hobbes himself economics is only one aspect of politics, and he does not include the former in his table of sciences. In many ways, however, he has prepared us for the view of economics as a separate study. He distinguishes the State from the household very sharply, and observes that public interests secure less active service than private. "To govern well a family and a kingdom," he says, "are not different degrees of prudence, but different sorts of business. ... A plain husbandman is more prudent in affairs of his own house than a philosopher in the affairs of another man."[8] Private interest is conceived as the real motive force in society; and human beings, he considers,[9] never "rest in the repose of a mind satisfied," but are continually advancing in their desires from one object to another; if there be any "highest good" at all, it is a never ending satisfaction of indefinitely increasing desires. It is true that this conception of insatiable human wants is not specially applied to wealth. Hobbes lays more stress on the resulting competition for power and praise, than for the comforts of life. But the latter, if subordinate, is still included; and, taking this notion (which anticipates the notion of Ricardo, that demand may be assumed to be constant and wants insatiable) as our starting point, we may proceed to gather up the other economical ideas of Hobbes as best we can from his fragmentary statements of them. The assumption that all men are by nature practically equal in ability,[10] is made by him deliberately, and adapted as a general political axiom. Here again we have a principle which of course applies to the economical relations of men amongst others; but, though here too we have an anticipation of a later economical hypothesis, we do not find it turned to special economic account by Hobbes himself. His general ideas on economics are most fully conveyed in the 24th chapter of the *Leviathan* (part II.), where he treats of the "Nutrition and Procreation of a Commonwealth."[11] The nutrition of it depends, he says, on the abundance of the materials of wealth, the fruits of land and sea, given by nature either freely or in exchange for labour, including the labour that purchases them from foreigners. It depends, also, on the distribution of those materials in accordance with the laws of property, without which no man can call the fruits of his toil his own. Thus the Greeks wisely used the same word νόμος, for law and for distribution or allotment.[12] There is, however, no right of property as against the Sovereign power, and the uniqueness of the position of that power should exclude it from the holding of domains as if it were an individual. For like reasons the Sovereign must control foreign trade, that men may not for private gain bring mischievous goods into the commonwealth. In the next place the nourishment of the commonwealth depends on the preparation or "concoction" of the said materials. They must be converted into goods that can be stored and transported, and exchanged for what can at all times be converted by the citizens into food. He explains that he is referring to the valuation of goods in money, and the exchange of them for money, money not only being prized for the sake of its material, all over the world, but being "bonorum cœterorum omnium mensura commodissima," the most convenient measure [of the value] of all other goods. By means of money a man can go to and fro, and always in a sense have his goods with him, in the shape of their equivalent, money. Money, circulating from man to man, is like blood in the physical body; and, as in the physical body the vitality is quickened by the passage of the blood from the extremities to the heart and back again from the heart to the extremities, so, when money is paid to the public treasury and again paid out on the public service, the State gains vitality by the process. From the fact that the material of money is itself of value, Hobbes infers the uselessness of attempts to profit by the debasement of the currency. He does not make any attempt to discuss the question of prices. He speaks, indeed, in one place of "the value or worth of a man being, like that of all other things, his price, that is to say, so much as would be given for the use of his power, and therefore not absolute, but dependent on the need and judgment of another," adding that: "As in other things, so in men, not the seller but the buyer determines the price. For let men, as most men do, rate themselves at the highest value they can, yet their true value is no more than it is esteemed by others."[13] "The value of all things contracted for is measured by the appetite of the contractors, and therefore the just value is that which they be contented to give," and therefore there is no injustice in selling dearer than we buy, or giving more to a man than he deserves.[14] It is clear that Hobbes, in speaking of what has since been called "value in exchange," has not distinguished it from "value in use." The latter sense influences his reasoning much more than the former, from the tendency of his mind to lay emphasis on the intensity of individual desire. The same tendency appears in his view of taxation. It must (as we have seen) mean equality of burdens; and, moreover, it must fall not on income, but on expenditure. We should tax what a man actually consumes on his own enjoyments, and then we are not only doing what is best in principle, but doing it in the way least unpleasant to the person taxed.[15] Taxation may also be a means of checking luxury and extravagant outlay on foreign goods; and, if we can tax the gains of mercantile companies, so much the better, for their aim is plainly private advantage, which is by no means necessarily coincident with public benefit.[16] Which ways of acquiring wealth are (in his view) of public benefit appears, to some extent, from his general description of the sources of wealth. The citizens of a State may grow rich, he says,[17] in three ways—by labour, by saving, and by the natural increase of their possessions. Some would add a fourth way, by war and plunder, but this is a lottery in which men as often lose as win. Only the two first are indispensable conditions of life and well-being; and only to the three first should the rulers give heed in their legislation. Their laws should favour good cultivation and fishing; they should discourage luxury, forbid idleness, and stimulate labour. They should honour the arts of navigation that are so useful to trade, the mechanical arts that are so productive, and the mathematical sciences that are so helpful to all the rest. But the laws, while they regulate the free action of men, must not discourage individual initiative, but steer a safe middle course, with the public good as the standard of action. In regard to those who through the accidents of life have fallen into penury, it belongs to the Sovereign power to see that the necessaries of life are supplied to them lest they be tempted to do violence or robbery; they ought not to be left to the uncertain charity of individual citizens. Such as are able-bodied should be set to labour in public works. Finally, he speaks of what he calls the procreation of a commonwealth. If the numbers of the people at home are growing too large, let them be transplanted to lands less fully peopled; this leads not to the extermination of the inhabitants already there, but to the better cultivation of their soil, though, in the end, if the earth is too strait for the feeding of its inhabitants, there is no resource but war.

From the above account of the economical views of Hobbes, it will be clear that, though not yet marked off even as a separate branch of political philosophy, economical inquiry was beginning to include nearly all the points now embraced in modern economics. It was not simply confined, as in the earlier Continental writings, to the Finance of a Monarchy. It included discussions of the causes of wealth, and even touched (however lightly) on the definition of economical terms, such as price and value, distribution and exchange; and it included a discussion of the social questions to which Sir Thomas More had attached so much importance. In this last matter, political philosophy was, perhaps, not much more than a commentary on contemporary legislation.

Political economy was thus growing up in England as an application of political philosophy. The philosophy of Hobbes, from its close resemblance on many points to the philosophy of Bentham, seems to furnish directly or indirectly many of the premises of what has been called the classical school of modern economics. He regards the world of men as a multitude of competing individuals, whose separate selfish actions lead to an unintended social benefit. But whether this involves the moral disintegration of Society or not, depends on the view taken of the competing individuals. If, like Hobbes, we regard them as anti-social by nature, and social only by a happy invention of farsighted selfishness, then the criticisms applied to Hobbes' political philosophy apply to modern political economy. But, if men are, as Grotius thought, in their nature not anti-social, but in the widest sense social, then their competition as individuals may result in a social benefit that is not against their will, even if not directly the effect of their wills. This result would be entirely analogous to other "*sponte acta*," of which we have heard already in Plato's *Laws* and elsewhere, though belief in spontaneous social products was logically impossible to any philosophers who regarded the individual man as the starting point, and supposed him to form societies by the union of his particular will with another in a formal contract. But it is, perhaps, one of the most searching objections to such an individualistic philosophy, that it conceives two parties, who have, by hypothesis, no common understanding already, to have enough of it to agree about the terms of a binding contract.[18] If there be any political economists who would deduce all intercourse, or even all commercial intercourse, from the deliberate initiative of individuals, living, till then, in absolute separation from each other, they must encounter the same objection.

It was, however, a service on the part of Hobbes to have laid emphasis on the important part played by the individual in the moulding of the world of men; and his logical difficulty in finding his way out of the individual into the Society is paralleled by the difficulty which metaphysical philosophy was then beginning to find, in getting out of the Ego into the world of things.

Note

Spinoza (1632–77), in his unfinished and posthumous *Tractatus Politicus* (written shortly before his death, and with full knowledge of the writings of Hobbes), shows us, indeed, how a theory identical in principle with that of Hobbes was modified when stated by a metaphysician of the first rank. For our present purpose we should gain nothing by entering into the views of Spinoza, as they neither bear on economical subjects, nor exert an influence on political philosophy apart from Hobbes. *Discrimen inter me et Hobbesium* (he says in a letter dated June, 1674, *Works*, ed. Bruder (Tauchnitz), vol. ii., Epistola 1. p. 298), *in hoc consistit quod ego naturale jus semper sartum tectum conservo, quodque supremo magistratui in qualibet urbe non plus in subditos juris quam juxta mensuram potestatis, quâ subditum superat, competere statuo,—quod in statu naturali semper locum habet.* See T. H. Green, *Philos. Works* (1886), vol. ii. p. 306, cf. 355–365.

For a very different reason we must pass over Samuel Pufendorf (1632–94), whose books *De jure Naturæ et Gentium* (1672), and *De Officio Hominis et Civis* (1673), found a wide circle of readers, and has preserved the fame of the writer for two centuries.[19] But he was the Martin Tupper of jurisprudence, *"vir parum jurisconsultus et minime philosophus"* (Leibnitz, *Epist.* vii., quoted by Lorimer, *Institutes of Law*, p. 293). He adopts a compromise between Grotius and Hobbes. Men's ruling motive is self-interest; but self-interest involves society and social sentiments; there is not only an immediate, but a wide and remote interest. The position bears a certain analogy to that of John Mill on Utilitarianism.

Pufendorf was the first of modern writers to give prominence to the distinction between duties of perfect obligation (the province of jurisprudence), and duties of imperfect obligation (the province of ethics). Kant has stated this doctrine in its most intelligible form; but the balance of opinion is certainly against it.

On the other hand, Pufendorf's ample economic discussions of money, price, and taxation in his treatise on *Natural Law* (bk. V.), would give him a place, though a humble one, in the history of economic theories; and the venerable economic historian, Prof. Roscher, has left on record his emphatic disagreement from the judgment of Leibnitz; he places Pufendorf among the most eminent of political and economical writers (*Geschichte d. Nat. Oekon. in Deutschland*, p. 305).

Notes

1 "Librum de Cive vidi. Placent quæ pro regibus dicit. Fundamenta tamen quibus suas sententias superstruit probare non possum. Putat inter homines omnes a natura esse bellum, et alia quædam habet nostris non congruentia" (namely, about Religion). Letter of Grotius to his brother, 11th April, 1643 (*Grotii Epistolæ*, Amsterd., 1687, pages 951, 952).

2 *De Cive*, ch. xii., 199, 200 (Elzevir, 1669). Compare Dante, *De Monarchia*, I. § v., Pax universalis is the final goal (ultimus finis) of man.

3 *Leviathan* (init.); cf. Grotius, *De Jure Belli et pacis*, II. ix. iii.

4 For concessions, see *Leviathan*, ch. xxiv., p. 122, and ch. xxx., ed. 1676. Kings (he allows) may sometimes act against their own interest and against the laws of nature.

5 T. H. Green, *Works*, vol. ii. p. 370 (*Principles of Political Obligation*).

6 *De Cive*, p. 161.

7 *Leviathan*, I. xiii. end.

8 *Leviathan*, ch. viii. In his English version, which is the earlier he says "privy councillor" instead of "philosopher."

9 *Ib.*, ch. ix.

10 *Ib.*, ch. xiii.

11 *De Civitatis facultate nutritiva et generativa.*

12 So Grotius reminds us that Ceres was "*legifera.*" *De Jure B. et P.*, II. ii. § 2.

13 *Leviathan*, ch. x.

14 *Leviathan*, ch. xv.

15 *De Cive*, pp. 218, 219. Roscher points out that the rise of the Middle Classes in the days of the Parliamentary Wars was the occasion of Excise and similar duties. *Englische Volkswirthschaftslehre*, p. 52.

16 *Leviathan*, ch. xxii.

17 *De Cive*, pp. 221, 222.

18 Society progresses not from contract to status, but from status to contract. See Maine, *Ancient Law*.

19 Readers of Fielding will remember the reference in *Tom Jones* (1749).

4 Harrington (1611–1677)

As More was to Machiavelli in the sixteenth century HARRINGTON is to Hobbes in the seventeenth. After a critical and cynical view of political philosophy, we have a political ideal. The prominence in Harrington's *Commonwealth of Oceana* (1658) of regulations for the establishment and good working of a satisfactory machinery of government is significant as reflecting the change in the English nation. Political self-government was, for the time, a more pressing question than social reform. At such a time "the errors of the people are occasioned by their governors."[1]

Harrington follows Grotius and Hooker in standing fast by the notion of a right reason, which is the law of nature, and which is not (as in Hobbes) identified with individual interest,[2] or the ruler's interest; but is identical with the "interest of mankind."

A popular government must be the ideal government, because a popular government comes nearest to secure the interest of mankind as distinguished from private gain; and the empire of laws as distinguished from that of men. The people must decide, for the people collectively are wiser than the individuals, while the opposite is true of an aristocracy;[3] but the few wise men must advise and must conduct researches, and make discoveries. *Oceana* is to have a Senate to debate, a popular assembly to resolve, and magistrates to carry out the resolutions. Elections are to be held, as in Venice, by ballot and rotation.

This ideal government will preserve a harmony of the two elements of all government—force and authority, the latter depending on the "goods of the mind," and the *choice* of those who obey it, the former operating by the "goods of fortune" (*Oceana*, p. 39).

It is the influence of the goods of fortune that Harrington represents in a new light. It is, no doubt, nothing new to say that wisdom, like courage, comes rather of necessity than inclination, and to point to the effect of circumstances on character (*Oceana*, 183). But the political empire (he says), or at least the domestic empire, as distinguished from rule over foreign dependencies, is founded on dominion or proprietorship. "Men are hung upon riches of necessity, and by the teeth; forasmuch as he who wants bread is his servant that will feed him. If a man thus feeds a whole people, they are under his empire."[4] He who owns the land is master of the people; *and the nature of a government is determined by the distribution of its landed property.* "Dominion" in money and moveables has great influence, and in the case of Genoa and Holland, may even overbalance the influence of property in land; but it is less stable ("lightly come, lightly go"), and in every large country, as distinguished from a mere city, land must dominate. Accordingly, one of the two "fundamental laws" of *Oceana*, stating what a man may call his own, is to be an Agrarian restriction, forbidding of man to hold property in land above what will yield £2,000 a year; and the other fundamental law (giving protection to the property so held) prescribes a government, or "empire." Peace is not possible (he considers) without government, nor a lasting government without the proper balance of property in land. A change in the balance of this property, such as was made under Henry VII. in England, may throw political power into new hands, and produce revolution. But, where there is the proper balance, it is no man's interest to overthrow the government,[5] and, where there is the proper (popular) constitution, there is no element of decay in the government itself (*Oceana*, p. 192). "The people never die, nor, as a political body, are subject to any other corruption than that which derives from their government"—a notion which might be well illustrated by a well-known poem of Lowell:—[6]

"The deacon's art
Had made it so like in every part,
That there wasn't a chance for one to start."

The "balance," moreover, is only in land. Harrington would not limit property in money, nor forbid usury. Usury, he says, was forbidden to the Jews, because fatal to small proprietors.[7] But England is the best of all commonwealths, a commonwealth of husbandmen.[8]

Harrington thinks that population increases slowly; even in his ideal State, in 41 years it only increases by a third (*Oceana*, p. 223). He would encourage it by giving exemption from taxes to a man who has ten children living, partial exemption (from half the amount) to the man who has five; and if he has been married three years, or be above twenty-five years of age, and has no child or children lawfully begotten, he shall pay double taxes.[9] He would institute a Council of Trade (described after Bacon as the "vena porta" of the nation), to arrive at an "understanding of those trades and mysteries that feed the veins of this commonwealth, and a true distinction of them from those that suck or exhaust the same," and to "acquaint the Senate with the conveniences and inconveniences to the end that encouragement may be applied to the one, and remedy to the other."[10] In these matters he writes in the spirit of the Mercantile Theory. On the other hand, he is before his time in advocating a free, national, and compulsory education.[11]

Oceana is important to us chiefly for the new principle that the economical element in a State will determine its government. Harrington, bound by the old prejudice in favour of agriculture, and not fully learning by the examples of Holland, Genoa, and Venice, confined his dictum to property in land. But the extension of it to property in general was too logical and obvious to escape the notice even of contemporary critics. He opposes this extension,[12] contending that, "though all riches have wings, those in land are most hooded and tied to the perch." The measure of truth that lies in such propositions will be discussed when their later statements come before us. It will be enough at present to remark that it was not by accident, or by his own mere reflection, that Harrington was led to give this importance to the economical factor in the State. Changes in political power, caused by changes in the distribution of wealth, were a feature of the epoch; and Harrington's political philosophy was (perhaps unconsciously) influenced by contemporary events quite as much as by Plato and Aristotle. He was able, indeed, even to remain outside of the great parties of the Commonwealth and Restoration, making, like Dante, a party by himself. His book was palateable neither to the Protector nor to the restored Charles. But, noble as it is in thought and language, it did not influence either economics or political philosophy so much as the writings of Locke, who is identified with a party, and who is ever in touch with the rough facts of his own time.[13]

Notes

1 *Oceana* (*Wks.*, ed. 1737, Millar), p. 76. Second Part of the Preliminaries. Compare p. 177.
2 Cf. *The Prerogative of Pop. Gov.* (*Wks.*, 1737), p. 252.
3 *Oceana* (*Wks.*, 1737), pp. 155, 158.
4 *Oceana* (*Wks.*, 1737, p. 39).
5 *Oceana* (*Wks.*, 1737, p. 52).
6 *Autocrat of the Breakfast Table*, ch. xl.
7 So Pufendorf, *De jure nat.*, bk. V. ch. vii. Harrington thought that a good cure for the ills of Ireland would be to colonize it with *Jews* (*Oceana*, Introd.).
8 Bright's *Hist. of Engl.*, p. 793, puts the country population at end of the seventeenth century as four millions, the town as one and a half. In 1891 the numbers were twenty in the town to eight in the rural districts (*Prel. Abstr. Census*). Hume says against Melun, that half the inhabitants of France, England, and most of Europe live in cities (*Essay on Commerce*, ed. 1768, vol. i. p. 288).
9 *Oceana* (Millar), p. 97.
10 *Ib.*, pp. 123, 127, 128.
11 *Ib.*, pp. 172–174, cf. 171, 177.
12 *Prerogative of Popular Government* (*Wks.*, 1737), pp. 243 *seq.*
13 For a good estimate of Harrington's political influence, see T. W Dwight in *Pol. Sci. Quart.*, ed. 1887, pp. 1 *seq.*

5   Locke (1632–1704)

Locke brings us perceptibly nearer to our own day by his conceptions of industry and society as well as by his general philosophy, on which the philosophy of the 18th century was founded. His conception of wealth may be gathered from his view of happiness—happiness depending on pleasure and pain as "the hinges on which our passions turn."[1] Man is placed in the world to procure "the happiness which this world is capable of, which is nothing else but plenty of all sorts of those things which can, with most ease, pleasure and variety, preserve him longest in it."[2] Pleasure and pain are "simple ideas"; that is to say, they are an immediate datum of experience. "Good" means what increases pleasure or diminishes pain; evil, what does the opposite. But pain rather than pleasure is described as the real cause of desire and therewith of action.[3]

Without "uneasiness" in the absence of a good thing there would be no "desire" for it, and there would be no work or effort to obtain it. Perfect contentment would be fatal to industry and action. God has given us the uneasiness of hunger and thirst and other "natural desires," returning at their seasons, in order to "move and determine our wills for the preservation of ourselves and continuation of our species." Bare contemplation of these as abstractly good and desirable would not have been enough. The object of desire is happiness, and happiness means "the utmost pleasure we are capable of"; but even things that are known to be assuredly the causes of happiness do not move the will unless they seem to the individual man to be part of his own happiness. Locke's language implies that he adopts an objective standard of what is really good as opposed to what seems so to the particular individual; but he takes no pains to be consistent. Elsewhere in the same chapter of the Essay (§ 58) he says that a man's judgment of his present good is always right, and then proceeds to impress on his readers that the government of our passions is within our power, and "the eternal law and nature of things must not be altered to comply with a man's ill-ordered choice." Men must school their palates and change disagreeable into agreeable things, that the true good which is remote may not escape them, "The remoter absent good" can compete with immediate good if the uneasiness of hunger and thirst and of the many other daily and vulgar wants has been allayed, and the mind has given itself fixedly to the contemplation of the greater object.[4] The obstacle to this contemplation is the perpetual recurrence of the lower wants. Locke speaks of human desires as, in a bad sense, irrepressible and innumerable in temporal matters (§ 46), but he does not seem to regard the desire of wealth as indefinitely expansive. The desire of "riches" is set down as a "fantastical uneasiness" alongside of the desire for honour and power, and "a thousand other irregular desires which custom has made natural to us."[5] The desire to have more than we need alters the intrinsic value of things.[6] When man has "all that this world can afford, he is still unsatisfied, uneasy, and far from happiness."[7]

A passage[8] of Locke's journal printed by Lord King in his *Life of Locke*, p. 84 *seq.* (*sub dato* Feb. 8th, 1677) gives us an idea of the way in which his thoughts worked on economical subjects, especially those afterwards handled in the early chapters of the *Wealth of Nations*. Amongst other things he describes "our stock of riches" as meaning "things useful for the conveniences of our life"; and his economical pamphlets show that he kept hold of the distinction between money and wealth. Even when he rather awkwardly speaks of wealth as consisting in plenty "of gold and silver," it is for the reason that these "command all the conveniences of life,"[9] and "commodities" are described as "moveables" that can be valued in money.[10] On the other hand, "it is with a kingdom as with a family"; spending less than your wares have fetched for you is the only way to be rich,[11] and "a kingdom becomes rich or poor just as a farmer doth and no otherwise," namely, by wise husbandry. His economic writings treat of the wealth of nations in the light of these analogies, and give us general principles of production and distribution more or less closely corresponding therewith.

The first of these principles is a truism. Without the uneasiness of unsatisfied wants there would be no industry; but more than this uneasiness is needed to cause industrial improvement. The "several arts conversant about [the] several parts of nature,"—as distinguished from ethics, which is the "proper science and business of mankind in general"—"are the lot and private talent of particular men for the common use of human life and their own particular subsistence in the world" (*Essay*, IV. xii., § 11). To these arts improvement is due. The natives of America are uncivilized, for example, because they remained ignorant of the use of iron. If we were to lose that knowledge, we should become as they are. "So that he who first made known the use of that contemptible mineral may be truly styled the father of arts and author of plenty" (*ib.*). But in the treatise on *Civil Government*, Locke speaks as if the main cause of the difference between a wealthy and a poor people were rather that the former are laborious and the latter idle; it is for this reason, he says (in language that may have suggested a celebrated passage in the *Wealth of Nations*), that "the king of a large and fruitful territory there [in North America] feeds, lodges, and is clad, worse than a day labourer in England"[12] (ed. 1740, vol. ii. p. 185). For the same reason he thinks that numbers of men are better for a nation than extent of territory, for where there are many hands there is much work done and much wealth created (*loc. cit.* and also *Considerations on Interest*, p. 33). Not science, but labour is all important.

"It is labour that puts the difference of value on everything" (*Civil Government*, p. 184), for it makes things more "useful to the life of man," and the "intrinsic value of things" depends entirely on that usefulness (*id.*, 183). He gives us no accurate analysis of value in use or value in exchange, if we may use these modern terms; and we are usually left to discover from the context which of the two is meant when he speaks of value. Money, he says, has little value except by consent, "being little useful to the life of man; but it came in lawfully enough by preference of men for what was lasting and did not spoil. Before it was introduced, and before possessions were heaped up by individuals, "all the world was America, and more so than that is now."[13] But the difference between civilized England and uncivilized America was due not to these secondary causes, but to the primary cause—industry. Locke fully understood the importance of the division of labour and separation of trades in producing the result. "An acre of land," he says, "that bears here twenty bushels of wheat, and another in America which, with the same husbandry, would do the like, are without doubt of the same natural intrinsic value; but yet the benefit mankind receives from the one in a year is worth £5, and from the other possibly not worth a penny, if all the profit an Indian received from it were to be valued and sold here; at least I may truly say, not 1/1000. It is labour, then, which puts the greatest part of value upon land, without which it would scarcely be worth anything; it is to that we owe the greatest part of all its useful products, for all that the straw, bran, bread of that acre of wheat is more worth than the product of an acre of as good land which lies waste, is all the effect of labour. For it is not barely the ploughman's pains, the reaper's and thresher's toil, and the baker's sweat, is to be counted into the bread we eat; the labour of those who broke the oxen, who digged and wrought the iron and stones, who felled and framed the timber employed about the plough, mill, oven, or any other utensils, which are a vast number, requisite to this corn, from its being seed to be sown to its being made bread, must all be charged on the account of labour and received as an effect of that. Nature and the earth furnished only the almost worthless materials, as in themselves. It would be a strange "catalogue of things that industry provided and made use of about every loaf of bread" before it came to our use, if we could trace them—iron, wood, leather, bark, timber, stone, bricks, coals, lime, cloth, dyeing, drugs, pitch, tar, masts, ropes, and all the materials made use of in the ship that brought any of the commodities made use of by any of the workmen to any part of the work, all which would be almost impossible, at least, too long, to reckon up" (*Civil Government*, ch. v. p. 185).

Locke is not like Plato, impressed with the social meaning of division of labour as a sign, symptom, or expression of the solidarity of the human race and the folly of isolation; he is looking almost entirely at the contrast between natural objects as "unassisted nature" gives them to man, and the same objects as modified by human labour. Accordingly, when he applies the above illustration to political philosophy, the application is not at all Platonic.

Economically, his first deduction is that it is labour that adds to the intrinsic value[14] of things, or makes them more useful to man. This is not a very deep analysis of "value in use"; but more unsatisfactory still is his employment of "value" in the sense of value in exchange, and his habit of styling either or both of them "natural" in different senses of the word natural. We hear of "natural value," "natural true value," "natural market value" (*Considerations on Interest, Wks.*, II. 51); and he says (*ib.*), "natural proportion or value I call that respective rate they [gold and silver] find anywhere without the prescription of law." This is, at least, definite and intelligible, though nature in this sense, while excluding the State, does not exclude Society. "By the constitution of Society" some men will need to borrow money at interest, and the "natural interest" will be that rate which the parties concerned will fix when the State does not interfere with them (*Considerations on Interest, Wks.*, II. 20, 24). So defined, the term "natural" might be applied to a market value that was double or treble the cost, so long as the "prescription of law" did not enter.

We see here an application to economics of the idea of a Law of Nature, but wholly on its negative side. It is something apart from deliberate human legislation, but there is no clear notion of any positive constructive activity working spontaneously in Society, as the law of nature was supposed, by Grotius and others, to be working itself out. Locke, up to a certain point, believed in the salutariness of "natural liberty" in economical matters; but he had no conception like Adam Smith's of its power to organize the industrial relations of Society under the motive force of uniform self-interest. Of the three chief classes in the commonwealth, "landlords, labourers, and brokers," the first (he says) is of most importance, as having most stability. Taxation, on whomsoever put in the first instance, falls in the end on the landowner, for the mercantile classes are always keen-witted enough to shift the burden, and the labourers, "just living from hand to mouth already" (*Wks.*, ii. 30, cf. 37), cannot bear any burden of taxation whatever. The consumer's interest, so far as the consumer is neither landlord, broker, nor labourer, is not worth regarding (16). Now (he argues) it is not for the advantage of the three classes mentioned, and least of all of the first of them, to carry out such a proposal as that of Lowndes and others[15] to keep interest on loans down to a low limit by law.

We see that the idea of "natural law" had carried Locke in the direction of what was afterwards called Physiocracy. The contact of economics and philosophy, however, appears even closer in his general theories of political society. He has left no general treatise economics, and his *Considerations of the Lowering of Interest* (published 1691), and *Raising the Value of Money* (1698), relate, of course, in the main to the subject of Currency, which touches Philosophy less closely than other economical subjects. It may simply be remarked that his description of the function of gold and silver is hardly consistent either with his philosophy or with his other economical definitions. "Mankind," he says, "have consented to put an imaginary value upon gold and silver"[16] by reason of their durableness, scarcity, and little liability to be counterfeited, and have made them "the common pledges whereby men are assured in exchange for them to receive equally valuable things to those they parted with for any quantity of these metals." Hence the intrinsic value of these metals came to be simply "the quantity which men give or receive of them." For they having as money no other value but as pledges to procure what one wants or desires, and they procuring what we want or desire only by their quantity, "tis evident that the intrinsic value of silver and gold used in commerce is nothing but their quantity" (*Consid.*, *Wks.*, ii. 12), and he speaks of "the intrinsic value which the universal consent of mankind has annexed to silver and gold" (*ib.* 13). If Locke understood that the precious metals had a value in use by virtue of certain specified qualities, he is not justified in giving this new meaning ("quantity") to "intrinsic value," for the usefulness of money to mankind depends no doubt on its exchangeability, but the exchangeability would not exist, in either great or small degree, without the "intrinsic value" of the qualities of the metals that compose it. Besides this economical criticism[17] there is the philosophical—that the estimate which a body of men find reason to attach to a given class of articles of a given quality no more deserves to be called "imaginary" or conventional than the estimate made by a single individual, unless we are to consider that nothing is "natural" but what is separate and singular, the act, feeling or thought of an individual by himself. We might even go further, and urge that by speaking of any estimate, joint or several, as "imaginary" we are assuming that there is a standard other than that of the several agents, by which we judge whether they are "following nature" or not. Locke, indeed, makes this assumption without hesitation. "My principles," he says, "have their foundation in nature";[18] and yet in his *Essay on the Human Understanding* we are told that the individual is the supreme judge in matters relating to his own happiness, and therefore implicitly in matters relating to the distribution of wealth.

These last difficulties are common to the whole Sensationalist and Utilitarian philosophy; and they will reappear in later writers. On the other hand, Locke's Political Philosophy is in some ways peculiar to himself. His aim, in writing his treatises on *Civil Government*, was "to establish the throne of our great restorer, King William," and to make good his title against the attacks of Sir Robert Filmer. Filmer[19] had advanced the Patriarchal theory of monarchy, in support of the dogma of the Divine Right of Kings and against the assertors of a "natural liberty of mankind," including not only English Whigs but "Papists" like Bellarmine and Suarez. All men (said Filmer) were born in subjection to their parents, and the King's authority is founded on the paternal. Adam was an absolute monarch, and so are all princes ever since; they are above the laws (p. 99).

Locke meets him with principles drawn from Aristotle, Sydney, and Hooker, and, so far as he is guided by any, it is by Hooker; but he professes himself "little acquainted with books, especially on those subjects relating to politics."[20]

By nature, he says, men are free and equal (ii. 135, § 67); children are born *for* this, and mature manhood *has* it (ii. 188). Government exists by compact for the good not of the governor but of the governed. The "law of nature" wills the peace and preservation of all mankind, and a liberty which is consistent with the liberty of others. If it be said that men were never in a state of nature, the answer is that States are so now towards each other, and individual men are so till they see the advantages of society. But the state of nature is by no means always as Hobbes fancied—a state of war; Society exists to make the war impossible, and, even before Society, though possible, the war was not necessary or universal. The freedom of nature is subjection to nothing but laws of nature, civil freedom being subjection to a *common* rule.[21]

By the "original law of nature," all things were common, and by the same law there was property, and it was a property founded on labour. To be used is to be appropriated. Every one has property in his own labour and his own person; and as regards things, it is my labour on them that makes them my property. Even now fish of the sea belong to him who catches them, and in principle labour is the foundation of all property. God gave the world "to the use of the industrious and the rational, and labour was to be his title to it, not to the fancy or covetousness of the quarrelsome and contentious."[22] God by commanding man to subdue the earth gave him authority to appropriate that part of it that he could subdue; and "the condition of human life which requires labour and materials to work upon necessarily introduces private possessions." A man should have as much as he can use and no more: the earth is still large enough for all.[23] The chief end of civil society is the preservation of the property so constituted;[24] its citizens have given up the power to be judges and executioners for themselves, and have accepted the empireship of the State; they have passed out of the "state of nature"[25] into that of a Commonwealth by a mutual consent and compact, giving authority to the majority. The law of nature indeed is "plain to all rational creatures," but men are biassed in the application of it to their own case. Political Society provides them with a common impartial tribunal, and with power to execute its decrees, with taxation only for common ends and by common consent. The purpose of its foundation is the common good, for no rational creature changes his state in order to be worse but to be better off. The result is the Commonwealth, which is a wider word than city and less wide than community. A community or society is not identical with a government, but where the government is dissolved the society becomes a confused multitude. This dissolution, the subversion of the commonwealth, is the only real rebellion; it is truly rebellion, it is the return of *bellum*; and resistance to it is certainly lawful.[26]

We have thus in Locke as in Hobbes the individual men as the starting-point, and a deliberate compact as the beginning of Civil Society. We have further a distinction between the State and the Society; Locke sees that the very nature of men and women leads to a social life that is quite distinct from the political and might exist in separation from it. Moreover the law of nature is simply the pursuit of happiness in obedience to a natural impulse; it is not a moral law written on the heart. So, in civil society, "law in its true notion is not so much the limitation as the direction of a free and intelligent agent to his proper interest, and prescribes no further than is for the general good of those under that law;—could they be happier without it, the law as a useless thing would of itself vanish." But the end of law is not to secure the freedom of doing as I please, but the freedom of "disposing and ordering" as I judge best, in accordance with the laws.[27] Viewed in connection with the passages previously quoted, this means that the law, and the State which makes the law, exist in order (in later phraseology) to secure to every man the fruits of his labour.

This purely economical view of the origin of Property and therewith of the State may be paralleled on the one hand by Plato's account of the growth of the State out of division of labour in the 2nd book of the Republic, and on the other hand by Adam Smith's description of the "original state of things" when the wages of labour were identical with the product of labour. But Adam Smith does not represent labour as historically giving rise to property; it is appropriation that *destroys* the original state of things; and Locke does not, like Plato, see that the individual previous to society is imperfect, and only in society and the State realizes all that is in him.

Apart from parallels, however, we must ask how Locke meets the difficulties that present themselves as soon as we compare property as it exists in States as they are now with property as described in his theory of its nature and origin.[28] The actual possessors do not always (or even very often) hold their possessions by their labour, and those that labour do not always have property. His solution is that the invention of money made accumulation possible, and by agreeing to the use of money men have tacitly "agreed to a disproportionate and unequal possession of the earth" (*Civil Govt.*, ch. v. vol. ii. p. 187). This would be practically a condemnation of things as they are if we were not expressly told by Locke so often that the political compact is indissoluble, and the political compact ratifies the general order of things as it now is. "The power that every individual gave the society when he entered into it can never revert to the individual again so long as the society lasts, but will always remain in the community" (vol. ii. p. 245). Property therefore, if at first due to labour, is now due to law. Locke does not sufficiently consider, too, that historically possessions were due to the "right of occupation," even if the first comer was one who wished to labour. Where there were several individuals, all willing and anxious to labour, say on a given piece of ground, nothing else but the right of the first comer could be claimed, unless indeed it were the right of the strongest; the right to apply labour would be asserted before there could be any right to the produce of labour. But, taking the theory as expressing not the historical origin so much as the *rationale* or justification of property, we find it much harder to apply in a civilized European community than in a new and wide unpeopled territory. The labour in a civilized State can only go on when the right of property in tools and materials or the *use* of them has been first conceded; and, apart from that concession, the labour, when it does go on, owes its efficiency to the social surroundings of the work-man, and to the division of labour and inventions, without which he as an individual would realize a very inferior product indeed. What he produces therefore is what society has helped him to produce; and in apportionment of property according to labour, even if the latter could be taken as the only standard of desert, the society would have a claim as well as the indi-vidual. The individualism of Locke prevented him from keeping this truth in view; and yet economically and philosophically it is a truth of first-rate importance.

It may, finally, be noted that Locke distinguishes the "*sponte acta*" and the prescriptions of custom in human society from political action.

Political action itself is of two kinds. The act by which political society is established is not the same as the act by which Government is established, and the dissolution of the Government does not involve the dissolution of the political society. Of the spontaneously formed societies (ranked as if co-ordinate with the civil society) religious bodies are the best instance.[29] Economic institutions are another instance. The invention of money is not (according to Locke) even a consequence of the union of men in a State, but is independent of a State. "Since gold and silver, being little useful to the life of man, in proportion to food, raiment, and carriage, has its value only from the consent of men (whereof labour yet makes in great part the measure) it is plain that men[30] have agreed to a disproportionate and unequal posses-sion of the earth,—*they having by a tacit and voluntary consent found out a way* how a man may fairly possess more land than he himself can use the product of by receiving, in exchange for the overplus, gold and silver, which may be hoarded up without injury to any one, these metals not spoiling or decaying in the hands of the possessor. This partage of things in an inequal-ity[31] of private possessions men have made practicable, out of the bounds of society and without compact, only by putting a value on gold and silver, and tacitly agreeing in the use of money."[32] He sees, too, how this spontaneous action apart from the State goes on in trade even under the State, and no laws to forbid (for example) the exportation of coin will ever succeed in their purpose. When he draws attention, too, to the power of custom in retarding even beneficial political changes[33] he is again allowing the existence of a joint action of men that is not political, and not even deliberate or conscious. The truth that lay in the doctrine of "*laissez faire*" as expounded by later writ-ers, was simply the necessity of leaving room in a political society for the spontaneous action, joint and several, of its individual members.

Notes

1 *Essay on the Human Understanding* (1690), II. xx., § 3
2 Journal quoted in King's *Life of Locke*, p. 86.
3 *Essay*, II. xxi., § 46.
4 *Essay*, II. xxi., § 45.
5 *Essay*, II. xxi., § 45.
6 *Civil Govt., Wks.* (1740), II. 183.
7 Journal in *Life*, page 87.
8 Only in parts reproduced in *Essay*, IV. xii.
9 *Considerations on the Lowering of Interest, Wks.*, vol. ii. 7.
10 *Further Considerations, Wks.*, ii. 78.
11 *Considerations*, II. 37, cf. ii.
12 Cf. *Wealth of Nations*, I., end of ch. i. There is the same idea in Mandeville, *Fable of the Bees* (ed. 1723), i. 181 *seq.* (Remark P). It is worked out in Locke's Journal, Feb., 1677 (*Life*, by Lord King, p. 85).
13 *Civil Govt.*, 187. Cf. Goethe, *Wilhelm Meister*, "America is here or nowhere." But Locke's utterance is not meant to be a compliment.
14 Cf. *Consid. on Int., Wks.*, II. p. 65.
15 To whom the *Considerations* were a reply (1691).
16 "As to money, and such riches, and treasure taken away, these are none of nature's goods; they have but a fantastical imaginary value." *Civil Govt., Wks.*, II. 228. See John Law, *Money and Trade* (1705), ch. i.
17 A discussion of the whole "Quantity" theory of Currency, as well as a criticism of Locke, may be found in Zuckerkandl, *Theorie d. Preises*, 13, 139, 141, etc.
18 *Further Consid., Wks.*, II. 69. Even the word "eternal" is used (II. 134, § 64) of the "natural right" of parents over children.
19 *Patriarcha, or the Natural Power of Kings* (1680).
20 Letter to Rev. Rich. King in *Wks.*, vol. i. 109, iii, cf. 74.
21 Vol. ii. 179. Locke can hardly be said to have pushed his criticism of Innate Ideas very far in Political Philosophy.
22 ii. 182.
23 ii. 183.
24 Cf. *Letter concerning Toleration, Wks.*, ii. 268.
25 ii. 198, top.
26 ii. 239. This passage shows that Stahl is wrong in representing Rousseau as the first writer to maintain that the uprising against a monarch is no rebellion (*Philos. des Rechts*, i. 297). Cf. the passagè in the *First Letter on Toleration*, where it is said that the one cause of Sedition is Oppression (*Wks.*, II. 272).
27 ii. 189.
28 For another discussion of this aspect of Locke's theory, see Mr. D. G. Ritchie's article on "Locke's Theory of Property," in the *Economic Review*, January, 1891.
29 See the *Letters on Toleration*, and cf. *Life*, by King, p. 297. For other societies see *Third Letter on Toleration, Wks.*, II. 356, etc.
30 2nd ed. reads "that the *consent of men* have agreed" (p. 202).
31 4th ed. has "equality." 2nd ed. reads (after "unequal possession of the earth"): "I mean out of the bounds of society and compact, for in governments the laws regulate it, they having by consent found out and agreed in a way how a man may rightfully and without injury possess more than he himself can make use of by receiving gold and silver (which may continue long in a man's possession) for the overplus," etc., etc. (p. 202).
32 *Civil Govt.*, bk. II. ch. v. (vol ii. p. 187).
33 *Ib.*, vol. ii. pp. 217, 238.

6   David Hume (1711–1776)

The interval between Locke and HUME is better filled up by the philosophers than by the economists. Bishop Berkeley, the most important philosopher, was one of the most important economists. Yet this last is little to say. Berkeley always took up the subject of econommics rather from a desire to carry out a particular reform than to gain truth for its own sake in this region; and his economical writings are suggestive rather than systematic. The effects on English society of the South Sea Scheme and kindred speculations impressed him deeply, and led to his *Essay towards Preventing the Ruin of Great Britain* (1721). He took too gloomy a view of the decadence of England; and his own suggestions are not far in advance of current economics. He proposes, for example, a bounty on children, and the confiscation of half the estates of those who die unmarried. His *Alciphron*[1] (1732) contains, besides an attack on freethinkers generally, a reply to "the wickedest book that ever was," namely, Mandeville's *Gambling Hive: or, Knaves Turned Honest* (1714), expanded (1723) into the *Fable of the Bees: or, Private Vices, Public Benefits.*[2] In the course of this reply he points out some obvious economical sophisms of Mandeville; and he gives at some length his own ethics and political philosophy. He had already given a sketch of these in his sermon *Passive Obedience on the Principles of the Law of Nature* (1712), which is largely a criticism of Locke's *Civil Government*. The ethics are a "theological Utilitarianism," such as we meet again in Abraham Tucker, Paley, and Malthus. The political philosophy adds nothing new to the points of controversy; and his remarks on subjects connected with economics are always most valuable when they are elicited, not by authors and theories, but by pressing social questions of the day. In his *Journal of a Visit to Italy* (1717) he is careful to notice the economical features of country and people; and in the *Querist* (1735–37), he deals with the condition of Ireland, as he has seen it and known it, and with the improvements in it which he and his friend Prior hoped to make by the promotion of arts and sciences and a National Bank. The *Querist* is the happiest of his economical writings, and adds to the admiration which all philosophical students have felt towards "one whom the wicked are not worthy even to praise." But Berkeley rendered no such service to the political philosophy of Locke as he rendered to the metaphysics of that author. In this region the "dry light" of the less enthusiastic Hume will help us further.

Hume was no missionary or social reformer. He was not even an iconoclast; but he was a studious seeker for philosophical truth, and a keen lover of argument. In one particular he believed himself a reformer. He believes himself the founder of the science of human nature as an experimental science (*Hum. Nat.*, 1st ed., vol. i., p. 474, bk. I. pt. iv.). He believes in the possibility of a science of ethics and a science of politics. He believes, lastly, in the possibility of a science of Economics. He does not indeed use the term, but he describes the study itself. Its scope is, he says, an inquiry into the nature of commerce and riches, and their effect on the greatness of the State and the happiness of individuals.[3] Till England and Holland (he says) had shown what commerce could do to make a State prosperous, no one had thought the subject worthy of special study.[4] It is a vulgar weakness, he continues, to think that general principles are out of place in such a region—"general principles, if sound, must always prevail in the general course of things, though they may fail in particular cases; and it is the chief business of philosophers to regard the general course of things."[5] His own way of distinguishing causal from accidental may be gathered from what he says in the Essay on the "Rise and Progress of the Arts and Sciences":[6] "What depends upon a few persons is in a great measure to be ascribed to chance or secret and unknown causes.[7] What arises from a great number may often be accounted for by determinate and known causes." If the die has a bias, it may not appear in one throw, but it certainly will in a great number. Moreover, causes that act on the multitude as compared with those that act on the select few are "gross as a mountain, open, palpable"; they are strong and stubborn, and can be made a basis of calculation, With these principles in mind, and without separating economics by name as a study distinct from other branches of political philosophy, he proceeds to take up current generalizations, and examine their truth.[8] For example, it is usually said that the power of the State and the wealth of its private citizens mutually depend on one another; but there are certainly cases where "the commerce, riches, and luxury of individuals" are such as to weaken the State instead of strengthening it.[9] The labour devoted to supplying the superfluous as distinguished from the necessary wants of rich subjects might have been employed in the fleets and armies of the State, to better advantage from the public point of view. Sparta had no luxury nor commerce, and therefore could be powerful in war. But Sparta was a kind of political miracle; "were the testimony of history less positive and circumstantial, such a government would appear a mere philosophical whim or fiction, and impossible ever to be reduced to practice."[10] "Ancient policy was violent and contrary to the more natural and usual course of things." "According to the most natural course of things, industry and arts and trade increase the power of the sovereign as well as the happiness of the subjects, and that policy is violent which aggrandises the public by the poverty of individuals." Luxury, with its attendant arts and manufactures, leads to the increase of industry, which is a reserve fund on which the State may draw in case of need, without imperilling the means of subsistence; "the more labour therefore is employed beyond mere necessaries, the more powerful is any State."[11] Public spirit is not now a sufficient motive;[12] "it is requisite to govern men by other passions, and animate them with a spirit of avarice and industry, art and luxury." Thus the public and individuals alike are the gainers.[13] "Avarice or the desire of gain," unlike the desire of knowledge, is universal among men.[14] In society man's wants are not a fixed quantity, but "multiply every moment upon him."[15]

This is an example of Hume's manner of dealing with economical subjects. They are always, to him, mixed with politics. And the above passages incidentally show us his conception of wealth. Wealth must not include merely a few fixed and simple elements; it must embrace "luxuries" as well as "necessaries." The distinction of the two was brought into prominence by Mandeville. The Bees in his Fable had prosperity for their little commonwealth so long as they had luxuries and vices, and they lost all their good fortune and "flew into a hollow tree" as soon as the vice and luxury gave place to virtue and plain living. Frugality (says Mandeville) enriches the individual household, but impoverishes the State. Everything is a luxury which is not "immediately necessary to make man subsist as he is a living creature."[16] Nobody, as a matter of fact, even in savage countries, confines himself to necessaries in this strict sense; and yet this is the only line that can be drawn. If the above definition is not right, then nothing is a luxury, for the necessary comforts of life, beyond the strict necessaries in the above sense, vary with the persons concerned. Mandeville thinks that all luxury (in the sense defined) is exceedingly wrong, but, for the general weal, exceedingly expedient. It is (in modern language) ethically wrong, but economically right.

Hume deals with Mandeville's position in more than one part of his writings. He expresses himself most tersely on the subject when he says that luxury once condemned as a vice, is now (namely, by Mandeville) recommended as *useful, and, therefore, not a vice.*[17]

The Utilitarian ethics of Hume enable him to solve the contradiction that Mandeville flaunted in the faces of philosophers, between economics and politics on the one hand and morality on the other. The merit of the social virtues, he thinks, is due to "that regard which the natural sentiment of benevolence engages us to pay to the interests of mankind and society."[18] In the case of justice, utility is the sole source; and in the case of other virtues, it is the chief source of merit.[19] Virtue demands "just calculation and a steady preference of the greater happiness"; yet reason and calculation alone are not enough to move to action; there must be "feeling for the happiness of mankind, and a resentment of their misery." Reason, in fact, tells us the tendencies of our actions; humanity (or sympathy) tells us which to approve; and the ones approved are those which "give to a spectator the pleasing sentiment of approbation." I approve those acts of my own, in which if they were done by another, I should find pleasure.[20] The test is thus the pleasure of the agent;

but it is his projected or reflected pleasure; the agent puts himself in the place of a spectator of his own conduct, and asks himself how it would impress him if he were not agent, but spectator.

This is not the place to enter into a full statement or criticism of the ethical doctrine of Hume. It involves a rejection of the view of Shaftesbury and Hutcheson, that man distinguishes moral good from moral evil through a "moral sense," by showing the elements into which the alleged "sense" may be analysed. But, looking simply at its relation to economics, we have to consider whether the above conception of virtue justifies us in concluding from the tendency of all virtue to public good, that whatever tends to public good implies a virtue; does a public benefit necessarily involve a private virtue?

Hutcheson[21] had seen that in cases where the intention of the agent was far from the public good, we could not count the action meritorious, though, as a matter of fact, it may have turned out advantageous to the public. Hume himself has to make similar concessions; but, though necessary, they seem fatal to his reply to Mandeville. Private vices might be public benefits, and yet remain vices. A deeper objection is that no reason is given why the pleasure of the projected sort should have greater claims to be preferred by me than any other pleasure; and, if it be answered (as it is by Hume) that my interest is involved, for private utility in the end does coincide with public, there still remains the question of fallibility. With the best intentions a man may go wrong in judging of the tendency of actions to the *public* advantage—witness the conflicting views of statesmen. He will frequently disagree with the general opinion of men on this point, public opinion itself being fallible. He may even go wrong about his *own* advantage; and Hume expressly admits there are occasions in which "men knowingly act against their interest, and the view of the greatest possible good" does not influence them.[22]

Hume is not so abstract and rigorous in his Utilitarianism as Bentham; he knows the world too well. He would allow that the individual is not always the best judge of his own, still less of the public interest; and that even when he judges rightly he does not always follow up the judgment by action. Hume, again, does not make it plain whether the pleasure of reflected approbation, which is the standard of virtue, is the pleasure of approving that which the public (including myself) believe to be tending towards the public advantage, or the pleasure of approving that which I (perhaps against the opinion of all others) believe to be so tending, or that which retrospectively is seen, as a matter of fact, to have so tended, The great difficulty is to explain, on the principles of Hume's philosophy, any objective and permanent standard at all; and this applies to the ethical and to the economical theory quite as much as to the theory of knowledge. In the latter, we are at a loss to account for an irrepressible belief in permanent objects and uniform causes; in the former, to account for a belief in a common standard of what is good or bad, and what is economical or wasteful.

The beginning of Hume's psychological analysis is simplicity itself, at first sight. He reminds us of his distinction of ideas and impressions, which are, according to him, the two ultimate constituents of human knowledge.[23] Where action, as distinguished from knowledge, is concerned, men are affected less by impressions than by ideas.[24] There are no doubt (as Bishop Butler had taught) certain appetites which move to action, not by any idea, such as a remembrance of pleasure, but directly (before we have had any pleasure from satisfaction of them) by an unexplained stimulus driving us to their object. We have the hunger, and desire the food, not the pleasure of eating it. But these are exceptions. The ordinary action of men in managing the affairs of life, and in pushing their way in the world, involves the holding up before the mind's eye of an idea of a pleasure; and this idea of a pleasure constitutes a desire and excites to action. Now this suggests to a modern reader the comment that the remembrance of a pleasure, the "idea" as opposed to the "impression," is very far from being the pleasure itself; it is, or (it might be more true to say) it *brings with it*, more pain than pleasure. It is something which, if we desire to have, we thereby confess that we do not now have. How far the desires are from being simple and direct like the appetites, we may see when we take the desire which is most important for the present subject, the desire of wealth.

Among the psychological aspects of the Desire of Wealth are the following:—(1) The relation of the individual to *other* individuals, in the way of *interest* secured by connection with them, or in the way of *sympathy* with them; (2) the effort of the individual for the satisfaction of his own wants, the relation of Pleasure to Desire, and the relation of Will to both of them, which involves, *inter alia*, the contrast of permanent and transitory, present and future. The light thrown by Hume's incidental consideration of these points is, perhaps, as important as his services to what are, by comparison, the more mechanical and external parts of the subject, treated consecutively in the essays on Commerce.

To be quite thorough, the philosopher who was examining the assumptions made by the political economist would need to go back to the whole theory of knowledge and human experience in general. We should need, for example, in this case to examine Hume's doctrine of the genesis of our experience from impressions and ideas by association. But this would involve discussion of subjects that are beyond our scope here. It will be enough to remark that "economy," even in its widest sense, is an adaptation of means to ends; it implies that the subject is in conscious relation to a world of objects from which he distinguishes himself, but on which he believes himself to act under the guidance of permanent principles of causation. If, indeed, no causes were permanent, but every fresh event were a miracle, economy of any kind would be impossible and useless. Or, if there were no permanent subject, or none that is conscious of its own permanence, there could be no economy, for each want would be a feeling by itself, to be stilled by itself without co-ordination or comparison with others. There could be no desire of wealth, as of a "permanent possibility" of the satisfaction of wants, any more than there could be any plan of living of any kind. In the battle of Philosophies the possibility of Economics is as much at stake as the possibility of Physical Science.[25]

Without, however, discussing whether Hume's philosophy explains either possibility, let us look more particularly at his Economical doctrines. According to Hume there are three kinds of goods:—(1) goods of the mind; (2) goods of the body; and (3) external goods.[26]

Human happiness consists in three ingredients—"action, pleasure, and indolence";[27] all indispensable, but occurring in various proportions in various men, and in various nations according to their civilization. These ingredients are most harmoniously combined where industry and the arts have prospered most. "Men are kept in perpetual occupation, and enjoy as their reward the occupation itself, as well as those pleasures which are the fruits of their labour. The mind acquires new vigour, enlarges its powers and faculties, and by an assiduity in honest industry both satisfies its natural appetites and prevents the growth of unnatural ones, which commonly spring up when nourished with ease and idleness."[28] In another place he says that men's happiness "consists not so much in an abundance of the commodities and enjoyments of life as in the peace and security with which they possess them."[29] "Inward peace of mind," too, is very requisite to happiness.[30] Happiness (says his Epicurean) is not to be produced artificially; it is an affair of the desires rather than of the reason. A propensity to hope and joy is (says his Sceptic) real riches; one to fear and sorrow, real poverty.[31] The life of business does not pall so soon as the life of pleasure; but no one situation in life is absolutely better than another.[32]

There is here the distinction between wealth and happiness, and the sentiment of the last sentence could be strained to imply that there was no necessary difference in happiness between poor and rich. Francis Hutcheson, whose *Inquiry into Beauty and Virtue* (1720) had great influence on Hume, was of opinion that all the best pleasures in life were nearly as open to the poor as to the rich (*Inquiry*, 4th ed., 1738, p. 94). Adam Smith in his *Moral Sentiments*, and Hume in the above quoted passage, follow suit.[33]

They seem all three of them to have meant no more than Aristotle. Wealth does not make a man happy, but neither as a rule can men be happy without it. Without a certain equipment of external goods ordinary men cannot realize the internal goods at all. In adopting this view we assume (and nearly every economical argument involves the assumption) that other men are so far like ourselves that external objects are, with them (as they are with ourselves), a necessary means of satisfying wants. The precise nature and degree of these wants and therefore the precise relation of the external objects to them may vary in others, as they do in ourselves. We reason from what men *do* to what they *are*, presuming that action, agent and object are in the case of others what they are in ourselves.[34]

This is the assumption made by Hume when he speaks of our power to put ourselves by "sympathy" in the place of others, and even when he pronounces happiness to depend less on our control over worldly goods (or on the purely economical element) than on the state of the mind itself apart from such external relations.[35]

Looking further at economical facts, we find more implied in "economy" than a simple relation of outward and inward. We find a relation of past, present, and future. A large part of economy is provision from the past in the present, and for the anticipated wants of the future. Wealth itself includes the idea of such a provision, or it would be identical with the satiety of the moment. It is rather a permanent power to be satisfied than a state of being or having been so. But it is provision for a near future, not a distant. "Men are principally concerned about those objects which are not much removed either in space or time, enjoying the present and leaving what is afar off to the care of chance and fortune. Talk to a man of his condition thirty years hence and he will not regard you. Speak of what is to happen to-morrow, and he will lend you attention. The breaking of a mirror gives us more concern when at home than the burning of a house when abroad and some hundred leagues distant."[36] Distance in space, however, "weakens the ideas and diminishes the passions" less than distance in time. West Indian merchants are anxious about what is passing in Jamaica, though few of us, merchants or not, are affected by the possibility of accidents less distant in time than Jamaica is in space.[37] Hume explains the difference by the fact that parts of space are co-existent and may be viewed as one in the imagination, whereas moments of time are always separate. (Aristotle would have said that whereas space is divisible time *is* divided.) To the imagination therefore it is harder to pass from the present to the future than from the near to the distant in space. It is hardest of all to pass from the present to the distant *past*, for this inverts the natural order of thought which follows succession of time. On the other hand the very difficulty of so using the imagination becomes a reason for a greater admiration of things past and for an attachment of greater value to things associated with past events.[38] "Distance lends enchantment to the view." Hume does not in these passages take special note of the economical bearings of his observations. They are important economically, because a great number of the phenomena of trade are due to the divergence between one man and another in the view taken of present as compared with future advantages. It has even been argued in our own day[39] that the phenomenon of interest on capital (as distinguished from profits) is due simply to the higher value attached by ordinary men to things present as opposed to things future. Hume himself does not entirely overlook the social and political effects of this underestimate of the future. One advantage of the institution of government is (he says[40]) that it enables men to defeat their own liability to be carried away by influences that are near them in time and space, and their temptation to seek present advantage to the detriment of their own interest, namely, the maintenance of order in society and (thereunto) the administration of justice. Knowing our weakness, we provide against it, deliberately (by "reason") making it impossible for ourselves to yield to it.

Observe that Hume's language implies that circumstances may in a sense be moulded by the will. The will is vaguely described as "the internal impression we feel and are conscious of, when we knowingly give rise to any new motion of our body or new perception of our mind."[41] The will itself is governed by uniform causes like everything else; otherwise, general reasonings about human affairs would be impossible, whether in history, or in "politics, war, commerce, economy."[42] But Hume does not (like Robert Owen) reason as if the outward and economical circumstances were the sole determining influence, and as if the inward should count for nothing.[43] "Prosperity is naturally, though not necessarily, attached to virtue and merit, as Adversity is to vice and folly."[44] The desire for worldly prosperity, too, at least in the shape of the love of wealth, is not regarded as the ruling passion of mankind, though Hume lays stress on this passion when he wishes to show the need for rules of justice to defeat it. "The avidity of acquiring goods and possessions for ourselves and our nearest friends is insatiable, perpetual, universal, and directly destructive of society"—unless turned against itself by justice.[45] Unlike Adam Smith, Hume by no means regarded the desire of wealth as a force which shaped society, in any good sense. It is rather a disintegrating influence which needs to be counteracted. In this respect at least he is no individualist.

The same regard to the spiritual as distinguished from the external conditions of human action appears even in his view of Production. His "Stoic"[46] declares that "everything is sold to skill and labour"; man must direct his industry not only on nature but on himself; he must improve his talents, mind and body, if he would be victorious over the obstacles that encompass him. "Labour" is always understood by Hume to include intellectual as well as physical toil.

His account of the growth of the wealth of nations is in substance as follows:—"Our passions are the only causes of labour," and labour is the means of purchasing from nature all the wealth in the world.[47] The passions are first of all directed to procuring the necessaries of life; and these are obtained by agriculture. Now agriculture will not be studied as a science unless manufactures and arts are also prospering; but, if so, the result will be that the land will produce not only food for the tillers but food for the manufacturers and artisans, with whom the tillers will exchange it for luxuries.

Luxury thereby becomes a political safeguard. For the men thus supported as manufacturers by the additional produce of the land could on emergency be supported, in the same way, as soldiers. In a civilized State therefore Hume represents agriculture and manufacture as mutually necessary to each other, while (he says) trade and commerce grow up with them, and commerce, especially foreign commerce, is a fruitful cause of improvement in the arts.[48] He recognises too the difficulty of separating town occupations from country occupations as if their spheres were quite distinct. In the country, he points out, perhaps as many as a third of the inhabitants are not husbandmen but artisans.[49] He has no leaning to the exaggerations of the "Agricultural System."[50] Labour, as Locke and Berkeley had seen, is the great source of wealth. Hume adopts the principle which Locke, with reservations, had applied to Property:—"Every person, if possible, ought to enjoy the fruits of his labour in a full possession of all the necessaries and many of the conveniencies of life. No one can doubt but such an equality is most suitable to human nature, and diminishes much less from the happiness of the rich than it adds to that of the poor," besides augmenting the power of the State and making taxation bearable.[51]

There is hint here of no little sympathy with the idea that the necessaries of a civilized life should be accessible to all persons in society. The principles of Locke's *Civil Government* were beginning to receive their full application in the popular philosophy of France and England at this time. The fashionable political doctrine is (Hume says in his *Human Nature*, III. II. VIII. 145), that all men are born free and equal. His own verdict on all schemes for equality in the distribution of wealth or of any other distribution than the existing, is that they are very fine but very impracticable.[52] He rejoices in the high wages of workmen in England as compared with the Continent, and he cannot be represented as (like Mandeville[53]) even in appearance the favourer of low wages and ignorance among the poorer classes; but neither is he a convert to the New Learning that tried to look at social problems from the poor man's point of view. The place of labour, however, in his economical theories is hardly less important than in Adam Smith's after him; and Hutcheson's influence may perhaps be traced here as we have seen it elsewhere.[54]

As Hume does not exaggerate the importance of agriculture as compared with other kinds of labour, neither does he connect wealth too closely with money and commerce. "Men and commodities," he says,[55] "are the real strength of any community. Money is nothing but the representation of labour and commodities and serves only as a method of rating and estimating them."[56] It is not a wheel of circulation; it is only a lubricating oil.[57] It has merely "a fictitious value" arising from convention.[58] But he admits that an increase in its quantity and consequent rise in prices will give a temporary stimulus to trade, which may last if the production is so much increased that there are as many goods (in proportion) to be exchanged by the new money as there were by the old.[59]

The domestic happiness of a people, or, in other words, the happinesss of a people within its own boundaries, is not affected by the great or small quantity of money it employs; and though its foreign trade is so affected, foreign trade is not essential to national prosperity. Like Berkeley, Hume thinks that commercial isolation might be no calamity for a nation.[60] This is, however, hardly consistent with his express admission that every improvement Britain had made in the previous two centuries had been due to imitation of foreigners and importations from them;[61] or that a single country can hardly be rich and industrious when its neighbours are idle, any more than a single man.[62] The two positions are not to be reconciled by the assumption that Hume is in the former case looking at the matter from a purely economical point of view, while in the latter he is reasoning as the political philosopher who has regard to the whole civilization of a nation, and to its wealth only as one element out of many therein. It does not occur to him to reason in the "abstract" method at all; and the explanation is rather to be sought in his love of posing as a sceptic on all occasions.

At the end of a long argument, when the whole has been converging to a seemingly unavoidable result, he likes to point out a loophole, by which to escape the appearance of a dogmatic conclusion. His decided opinion that public debts would eventually ruin the indebted nation is one of the few exceptions to his rule.[63] The same spirit of philosophical criticism, which in economics as in metaphysics drives him beyond common assumptions down to the foundations of the truth, keeps him almost painfully aware of the difficulties of his own theories.[64] He is acting perhaps in this spirit when he first demonstrates that the interest of loans does not depend on the variations in the amount of the metal currency and that the usual explanations of depreciation are wrong, and then adds a suggestion that the value of the currency may be altered, after all, by banks and paper money.[65] To take another instance, he first demonstrates that restrictions on foreign trade are worse than useless if they are meant to keep gold in a country, and then adds that they may be useful enough if they are meant to encourage manufactures.[66] In both cases he goes straight to the concrete conditions of the case, whether psychological or social. But, though we cannot say that Hume reasons down from abstract principles to their modification by concrete conditions, he certainly distinguishes generalizations that maybe called universal because they apply without distinction of social conditions, from generalizations that are directly drawn from the latter and are therefore in a sense narrower. This is what may be termed, in the words of a later economist, the distinction between economical and historical categories. The principles that regulate the value of money are of the first class, those that regulate the rate of interest on loans are of the second. Hume does not deal exhaustively with economical theory. His view of value (so far as he distinguishes it from price at all) is even less fully stated by him than by Hutcheson.[67] Scattered suggestions are happy. He speaks of property as being only in things limited in amount, and therefore being sometimes in water only (the wells of the Desert) and sometimes in land only, where water is unlimited. There is something more than an analogy (we shall find) between this view and that of later economists who restrict Political Economy to things "limited in supply" and "capable of appropriation."[68] The connection of Property with Value would have been a fruitful theme; but Hume passes it by, and selects only a very few (and those of the most current) economical principles, on which to deliver his mind fully. One of these is the subject of Interest. The rate of interest, he says, depends on the demand for loans, on the ability to supply that demand, and on the contemporary profits of trade.[69] There must be a body of proprietors of land and their manners and customs must be such as to lead some to be spendthrift. There must also be a body of frugal people in whose hands loanable wealth has accumulated, and this means that merchants and manufacturers have come into being, in whom the *amor habendi* has taken fast root.[70] In the third place the profits that can be made by merchants in their trade will determine the minimum rate at which they will lend sums away from their trade, even to debtors known to be secure. Competition of traders will keep down profits, and competition of lenders will keep down interest. But abundance of metal currency will not of itself affect either; the cases are quite distinct.[71]

We see, therefore, that Hume recognises how much the historical conditions of a case affect the working of economical principles. He never indeed deliberately detaches the two. Still, even in regard to such a "historical" category as the rate of Interest on loans his language would imply that, given the combination of circumstances described, human nature would always show itself in much the same way. Even the "historical" categories have thus a general economical element. Taking men not as individuals but as communities, caprice may be disregarded, for it will not disturb general reasonings and prevent general conclusions.[72] In other words, the action of men in communities will have a uniformity on which investigators may count, and a logic in it which they may decipher.

In his general theories of Society and the State Hume presses this doctrine rigorously. In outward nature we expect uniformity of causation; much more with men; we not only know that "men always seek society, but can also explain the principles on which this universal propensity is founded."[73] If every man could propagate his kind and preserve his being without need of the other sex or other men, there would be no society; but it is not so. The union of the sexes is as certain as any mechanical attraction—say of "two flat pieces of marble." The care of parents for their children is no less certain; and the provision for members of various families made by their union in a society is as certain as any of the others. Men cannot live without society, and (as the next step) they cannot be joined together without government. Government makes a distinction of property, and with it of ranks of men. "This produces industry, traffic, manufactures, law-suits, war, leagues, alliances, voyages, travels, cities, fleets, ports, and all those other actions and objects which cause such a diversity, and at the same time maintain such a uniformity in human life."[74] This reasoning "from the actions of men, derived from the consideration of their motives, temper, and situation," is so mixed with our life that we cannot act or subsist a moment without having recourse to it.[75]

A Society without Government is not indeed impossible, where the pleasures and the possessions are few and simple. Government probably arises when two societies quarrel; and this would be after considerable wealth had been formed. "Camps are the true mothers of cities."[76]

This view of Hume's reminds us of Plato's idea of the City of Pigs. It was only when the simplicity of the City of Pigs was exchanged for luxury that the development of the State could fairly begin. Mandeville had gone farther and said that not only was vice the beginning, but it was an inseparable condition of political development throughout. Hume, taking another view of the nature of vice, thinks that civilization as it progresses tends to free us from vice, or at least to counteract its effects. The Golden Age and the State of Nature are to him fictions—the one of the poets and the other of the philosophers—and contradictory fictions, the one of a state of Peace, the other of a state of War. The idea of a Golden Age, Elysian fields and Arcadia, is a poetic representation of the fact that if goods were abundant and all men were benevolent no civil society would be needed, and there would be no need of justice.[77] On the other hand he allows that in a universal scarcity Justice would be impossible, for it would be as useless as in universal abundance (*Essays*, II. 262). The idea that after a State of Nature men entered into a Contract to make Society and Government is not, he considers, supported by what we know of the origin of States. Theoretically it is true that the consent of the people should be made the foundation of government; but, if we had as a matter of history to "choose a period of time when the people's consent was least regarded in public transactions, it would be precisely on the establishment of a new government," when military force or political craft usually decides the controversy.[78]

The use of Nature and Natural, as if these words contained in themselves an unanswerable argument, was sure to receive no mercy from Hume. If, he says, "nature" is opposed to miraculous, it is too wide a word to be useful; if it is opposed to rare and unusual, it may always be doubted what these are; if it is opposed to artifice, then we must ask whether human artifice is not itself natural; finally, if it is opposed to civil or moral, then such a virtue as justice is unnatural, for there is no justice without moral and civil relations, and no love of mankind in the abstract, without relation to particular persons. The passions of men incline them (especially in the distribution of external goods) to give preference to themselves, their families, and their friends, and the passions are therefore by no means the origin of justice. The origin is in this sense moral and not natural.[79] Justice and the civic relations are, however, "natural" in the sense that they are inseparable from human nature.[80] Human nature must necessarily come to them. In this sense Society and the State are both natural.

The distinction of Society from the State in historical growth, and also contemporaneously, within any given community is practically admitted by Hume. To say nothing of religious and moral institutions, manners and customs in regard to everyday life, dress and behaviour, we must note (he says) the tacit conventions by which men have agreed to employ gold and silver as money, and certain sounds and signs as a language. These are of Society, not of the State. Bentham would have called these "*sponte acta.*" Hume describes these things as not traceable to the State, but nevertheless done by a number of men together and losing advantage unless done together.[81] The whole system, by which trades are separated while their produce is exchanged and used by mutual consent, is of this nature. There is no contract or promise, but "a common sense of interest."[82] This spontaneous union is not only distinct from any political arrangement, but it may be, and often is, distinct from any clear consciousness of union at all; it is the sense of an objective common interest and purpose, to be served by common action; but the solidarity is not always clearly understood, still less does it always imply a bond of conscious sympathy. Hume does not enter into this matter; but he dwells on the relation of Justice to other virtues, pointing out that there is not always the same vivid Sympathy present in Justice as in the rest. The other virtues, including the "natural abilities" (or intellectual virtues) of Prudence, Good Sense, etc.,[83] are in ultimate logic regarded as virtues from their utility, but they do not at first show themselves in a deliberate or conscious regard for utility. They are rather revealed by a "natural sense or feeling," a kind of sympathy which implies that "men consider the sentiment of others in their judgment of themselves."[84] But, in the case of justice, public utility is consciously and deliberately intended, and regard for it is the sole foundation of merit."[85] Placed as we are between two extremes, universal abundance and universal scarcity (either of which would be fatal to justice), and related as we are to other beings recognised by us as equally human, we find justice necessary to the regulation of these relations. Without equality, in the sense of recognition of our common humanity, there is no justice. We may be kind or merciful to the lower animals, but cannot strictly speaking be just or unjust to them.[86] On the other hand, neither an equal distribution of property, nor an assignment of the lion's share of property to the greatest virtue is demanded by justice. Not the first, because men are unequal in skill and industry. Not the second, because men are fallible in their judgment of merit in each other. "It must indeed be confessed that Nature is so liberal to mankind that, were all her presents equally divided among the species and improved by art and industry, every individual would enjoy all the necessaries and even most of the comforts of life, nor would ever be liable to any ills but such as might accidentally arise from the sickly frame and constitution of his body. It must also be confessed that, wherever we depart from this equality we rob the poor of more satisfaction than we add to the rich, and that the slight gratification of a frivolous vanity in one individual frequently costs more than bread to many families and even provinces.[87] Moreover, the Spartan government and the Roman agrarian legislation gave an impression that such an equal division might be practicable. This is a strong statement of the case, and there are other passages that show it to reveal more of Hume's own feeling than is usually noticed. For example, he says in the Essay on the Original Contract,[88] that in our modern society the artisan or peasant is not free in the sense of being able to leave his country if he is ill off in it; his poverty ties him to his country, as effectually as the passenger is tied to his ship in mid-ocean. But Hume, whether from the influence of Hutcheson[89] or from his own love to pose as a sceptic, is careful to show that equality of possessions is impracticable, or at least it is destructive to society. The motives to industry would be gone and the resources of society would immediately decline. "Instead of preventing want and beggary in a few, you render it unavoidable in the whole community."[90] Politically, too, it means either tyranny or anarchy.[91]

If then we are not to attempt to introduce equality, what rules for the regulation of external goods are we to adopt in order to secure justice? The answer seems to be that each nation discovers them for itself in accordance with its peculiar character and situation. Hume, himself a historian, agrees with Montesquieu (*Spirit of the Laws*, bk. XIV.) that the laws of a nation are relative to its particular kind of government, manners, religion, climate, and other idiosyncrasies,[92] though he elaborately refutes that author's exaggerated estimate of the influence of climate on national character.[93] There is therefore (to Hume) no such thing as an abstract justice, discoverable everywhere and valid everywhere, whether in regard to property or any other relation of life. But neither is justice purely local and particular in the sense that every separate nation has a separate notion of justice, and that laws grow up as irrationally as superstitions. The human nature common to all nations reveals itself in common ways; or else there could be no science of politics or of human nature at all. The marriage union of men takes different forms, whereas the union of the sexes in animals takes in the same species the same form; so there are many types of human houses, but only one type of robins' nests.[94] But the variation is not inconsistent with uniformity. We can trace, for example, certain rules of marriage that can be pronounced good, not only for one special case, but in a broad sense. In the same way the benefits of the institution of property are not peculiar to one place and nation. Its justification is very different from its history, It did not begin from the idea of rulers that it was wise to encourage industry by allowing their subjects to acquire property; such an idea could only occur among a people already civilized. Historically, even as government was often founded by violence, so property was often founded by mere "occupation," and not by industry; the sympathy of men for actual possessors and regard for the common interest, supposed to be secured by stability of property, have led to prescription, accession, and the other usual titles to property.[95] In this way the great end was gained of giving to external goods the same security that nature has given to the goods of the mind.[96] Hume feels the force of Locke's view, that property arises "where we join our labour to anything." He is careful, as usual, to note the objections; but he seems not unfavourable to it when taken as prophecy instead of history.[97] It is possible that he regarded any departure from the rule that property should go with labour as one of those cases where (he says) "a single act of justice is frequently contrary to public interest." When a miser or a seditious bigot has a large fortune restored to him, the act is just, though the public suffer.[98] But the public gains by the invariability and inviolability of justice over the whole field; and it is to the broad general effect that we must look.

We see that in essence Hume's view is not much more than an expansion of Plato's hint in the first book of the *Republic*. Even a band of robbers could not hold together without justice, still less can a political society. But we fail to get any positive conceptions, such as are presented in the later books of the *Republic*. Hume, while maintaining that a general doctrine is possible, is careful to avoid even the appearance of construction, and his empirical generalizations are few and vague, We get no dogmatic philosophy of society; and our author's ideal State can only be inferred from casual expressions.[99] In politics too, he says, prophecy is as rash as it is in medicine.[100] Yet he gives a forecast of political development, especially in his own country, and in connection therewith his views of the relation of politics to trade and commerce and the distribution of property. Harrington's theory that the balance of power depends on the balance of landed property seems to him unsupported, Government is always founded on the "opinion" of the governed,—their opinion that it is for their interest, and their opinion that it is supporting ancient rights and justice.[101]

Therefore, though the balance of power be not that of property, the government may be unchanged for years. When the depression of the nobility and the rise of the commons, and the statutes of alienation, and the growth of trade, had really altered the old balance of property and power in England, the readjustment was only made slowly and gradually by the House of Commons. Besides, "property" may mean either accumulated or dispersed property engrossed by a few or extended to many; and, if it be the former, a much less amount of it would involve greater power than a much greater amount dispersed in many hands. Combination of small owners is difficult, and engrossment in a single hand gives much greater influence over dependants.[102] Peace and security, too, are valued by men even more than wealth; and, as they can get them only from government, they are not often willing to risk the loss of them by a change which may weaken government.[103] The interests of classes are often at one when they seem divergent; trade and agriculture have the same political interests.[104] The character of a government is not indeed indifferent, especially to foreign trade. Unlike the Fine Arts, commerce can only flourish under a free government, not because property is less secure under despotism (for "avarice, the spur of industry," would not be scared by fancied dangers of confiscation) but because commerce has less honour under an absolute government than under a popular.[105] Yet the decline in the prosperity of France, which was observable in Hume's days, was due (he says) not to the amount of taxation but to the arbitrariness and inequality of it. France was the standing instance of an absolute monarchy which had prospered; and he himself saw no reason why all the advantages of a free government should not be obtained under a limited monarchy in England. If the government of England was to change, he would rather see it become absolute than become republican.[106]

But, as usual, after pointing the contrast as keenly as possible, Hume ends by representing the rival governments as differing much less than might be thought. The most important feature (for our present purpose) of his political reasoning is his subordination of the economical element to the rest. It was left to Adam Smith to take up Harrington's assertion of its predominance and state it in his own way, with clearer consciousness of the bearings of the position and greater mastery over the proofs.

Note

The ethics of Hume are treated by Hasbach, *Untersuchungen über Adam Smith* (1891). Readers may compare with Professor Hasbach's the account of Hume's views given by Professor T. H. Green in his introduction to the 2nd vol. of Longman's reprint of Hume's *Philosophical Works*, pp. 42 *seq.*, esp. 57, 58. The economics are estimated perhaps too highly by Hill Burton, in vol. I., 355, and vol. II. p. 520 of his *Life and Correspondence of David Hume* (1846)—the most charming of the many books written on the subject. Economists are indebted to Hill Burton also for *Letters of Eminent Persons addressed to David Hume* (1849), where letters of Turgot, Tucker, Morellet, etc., are given, and hints on economical subjects abound.

Notes

1 *Alciphron, or The Minute Philosopher, i.e.* the Freethinker. The book was composed at Rhode Island on Berkeley's farm of Whitehall.
2 See esp. *Alciphron*, 1st, 2nd, and 3rd dialogues. For Mandeville's relation to Rousseau see below (Ad. Smith).
3 See the *Essays on Commerce*, first publ. in 1752. They form the second part of the first vol. of the collected *Essays* publ. in 4to by Cadell in 1768. An excellent account of the editions is given by Mr. Grose, *Essays of Hume*, Longmans, 1874.
4 *Essays*, I. 95.
5 *Essays*, p. 286.
6 *Ibid.*, p. 120.
7 This is not the place to discuss whether such language is logical in a writer who takes Hume's view of Causation in general.
8 Joseph Harris, in his *Essay on Coins*, 1757, reached the generalization that the rate of profits tends to be the same in all trades in the same neighbourhood, and he is sometimes reckoned the first to declare an economic law; but, to say nothing of Gresham, Hume was before him and before Cantillon, whose *Essai sur le Commerce* (though written about 1732) was first published posthumously in 1752, and who did not become an English classic till 1881. Marx declared that Hume borrowed his theory of interest from J. Massey, *Natural Rate of Interest* (1750). See *Kapital*, I. 537, n. So Coleridge accused Hume of borrowing his ethics from Thomas Aquinas (*Life of Hume*, by Burton, I. 286).
9 *Essays*, I. 287. He is not using State in the narrow sense.
10 *Ibid.*, 291.
11 *Ibid.*, 294.
12 He forgets that it was not so even in Greece and Rome, for the slaves worked from necessity, not from choice.
13 *Ibid.*, 296.
14 *Ibid.*, I. 82, cf. 122.
15 *Hum. Nat.*, bk. III., § 2, p. 51.
16 *Fable of the Bees*, vol. i., Remark L, cf. Q.
17 *Essays*, II. 257 (Of Benevolence), cf. I. 315 (Of Refinement in the Arts).
18 *Ibid.*, II. 311.
19 *Ibid.*, 313.
20 *Ibid.*, I. 368–378, cf. II. 239.
21 *Inquiry into the Original of our Ideas of Beauty and Virtue* (1st ed. 1720); 4th ed. 1738, pp. 117, 118.

22 *Hum. Nat.*, II. 253; cf. *Essays*, I. 520: "Were all men possessed of so just an understanding as always to know their own interest."

23 *Human Nature* (1739), I., beginning.

24 *Ibid.*, vol. ii., II. 288. Reason in the same way is distinguished from Passion only as the calm from the violent.

25 See the acute papers in the *Giornale degli Economisti* (last half of 1891), on the relation of Political Economy to Evolution, written by T. Martello under the pseudonym of "Hiatus."

26 *Hum. Nat.*, vol. iii. 55 (ed. 1739).

27 *Essays*, vol. i. 303, 304 (Of Refinement in the Arts). By pleasure he means amusements and actual consumption of wealth as distinguished from production. "Indolence" may have been suggested by Locke (*First Letter on Toleration*, p. 252).

28 *Ibid.*, 304.

29 *Ibid.*, I. 50 (Of Parties).

30 *Ibid.*, II. 372 (Principles of Morals, Conclusion).

31 *Essays*, I. 154 (Epicurean), 187 (Sceptic).

32 *Ibid.*, 188, 189.

33 "How small of all that human hearts endure,
   That part which laws or kings can cause or cure!
   Still to ourselves in every place consigned,
   Our own felicity we make or find."—(*Traveller*, 1764.)

34 Cf. Hume, *Essays*, II. 268.

35 See *Human Nature*, bk. II. part ii. sect. v. (Of our Esteem for the Rich and Powerful).

36 *Hum. Nat.*, II. 272. The compensation is that far-off ills are not allowed to poison present happiness. *Essays*, I. 196.

37 It might be doubted if time and space are commensurable at all.

38 *Hum. Nat.*, 273–278, 279–289, bk. II. pt. iii. sect. vii. and viii.

39 By Prof. Böhm Bawerk, *Positive Theorie des Capitals*, Innsbr., 1889. See *Harvard Quarterly Journal of Economics*, April, 1889.

40 *Human Nat.*, III. 132 *seq.* (part II., sect. vii.).

41 *Ibid.*, II. iii. sect. i. (Of Liberty and Necessity), 1st ed., p. 220.

42 *Ibid.*, II. iii. sect. i. p. 229.

43 *Essays*, vol. i. "The Sceptic," pp. 191, 192. Character can be changed, *e.g.*, by the constant pursuit of a good model.

44 *Essay on Impudence and Modesty*, 1741. Not reprinted in collected essays.

45 *Hum. Nat.*, III. ii. ii. 62, 63. On the other hand, cf. *Essays*, I. 339.

46 *Essays*, I. 162 *seq.*

47 *Ibid.*, I. (Of Commerce), 294.

48 *Essays*, I. 297, etc. (Of Commerce).

49 *Essays*, I. 288.

50 See below, ch. vii.

51 *Essays*, I. 298.

52 *Essays*, II. 270, 271. See below, p. 124.

53 Mandeville, *Essay on Charity Schools. Fable of the Bees*, 2nd ed., pp. 326 *seq.*

54 Hutcheson, *Inquiry*, p. 284.

55 Essays, I. 331 (Of Money). How far the Mercantile System involves too close a connection will be considered later.

56 *Ibid.*, 321.

57 *Ibid.*, 317.

58 *Ibid.*, 334.

59 *Ibid.*, 322, 329, etc.

60 *Ibid.*, 324, cf. 298, 343. Berkeley, *Querist*, 134: "Whether, if there was a wall of brass a thousand cubits high round this kingdom, our natives might not nevertheless live cleanly and comfortably, till the land, and reap the fruits of it?"
61 *Essays*, I. 370 (Of the Jealousy of Trade).
62 *Ibid.*, 370, 371.
63 *Essays on Commerce.*
64 Cf. the remarkable passage in *Hum. Nat.*, I. iv., sect. vii., 457 *seq*: "But, before I launch out into those immense depths of philosophy which lie before me, I find myself inclined to stop a moment in my present station," etc.
65 *Essays*, I. 333 *seq.* (Of Interest).
66 *Ibid.*, 348 *seq.* (Of the Balance of Trade).
67 Hutcheson, *Moral Philosophy* (Foulis, 1747), pp. 209 *seq.*
68 *E.g.*, to take one instance out of many, Rich. Jones in his Introductory Lecture, 1832.
69 *Essays*, I. 335 (Of Interest).
70 *Ibid.*, 339.
71 He does not think of the phenomenon mentioned by Cliffe Leslie (*Fortn. Rev., Nov.*, 1881, page 7 ft.). The silver discoveries, by enlarging the stocks of silver, enlarged the loanable capital, and thereby lowered interest.
72 *Essays*, I. 120, 121, above quoted; cf. *Hum. Nat.*, I. iii. xi. 227.
73 *Hum. Nat.*, bk. II., pt. iii., sect. 1., p. 224.
74 *Hum. Nat.*, 225.
75 *Ibid.*, 229, 230.
76 *Ibid.*, III., pt. II., sect. VIII., 141–144; cf. *Essays*, II. 268, 269 (Of Justice).
77 *Essays*, II. 260, 263, 266, 267. *Hum. Nat.*, III. 64–66.
78 *Essays*, I. 520 (Of the Original Contract).
79 *Hum. Nat.*, III. II. II. 61. Hume wrote to Hutcheson, Sept., 1739: "Your definition of natural depends on your solving the question, What is the end of man?" (a question Hume gives up). "I have never called justice unnatural, but only artificial." *Life* by Burton, I. 113.
80 *Ibid.*, III. I. II. *seq.*; III. 32–49.
81 *Essays*, II. 390 (Further Considerations with regard to Justice).
82 Cf. *Hum. Nat.*, III., pt. II., sect. II., p. 59.
83 *Hum. Nat.*, III., pt. III., sect. IV., pp. 256 *seq.* See below [ch. viii., Ad. Sm.]. For criticism of the classification of Virtues, see Bentham's *Deontology*, vol. i. ch. xviii.
84 *Essays*, II. 214, 236, etc. cf. *Hum. Nat.*, III. III. VI. 276: Hasbach (*Unters, über Ad. Sm.*, p. 94) considers that Hume gives to Sympathy in the *Essays* an altruistic character which it does not possess, in the *Human Nature*.
85 *Essays*, II. 259.
86 *Essays*, II. 268 (Of Justice). He adds that Women have been wrongly treated as lower animals, and so have Indians by American colonists.
87 *Ibid.*, II. 271. Montesquieu (*Esprit des Lois*, VII., ch. i., beginning, cf. ch. vi.) had similarly asserted that one man's luxuries meant another man's labour.
88 *Essays*, I. 522.
89 Hutcheson, *Beauty and Virtue*, p. 286 (4th ed.).
90 *Essays*, II. 272 (Of Justice).
91 *Ibid.*
92 *Ibid.*, II., 274. *L'Esprit des Lois*, which had appeared in 1748, is expressly cited in this passage.
93 *Essays*, I. 226 *seq.* (Of National Characters).
94 *Ibid.*, II. 281.
95 *Essays*, II. 393 n.; *Hum. Nat.*, III. II. III. 85 *seq.*

96 *Hum. Nat.*, III. ɪɪ. ɪɪ. 58.
97 *Ibid.*, III. ɪɪ. III. 85 n.
98 *Ibid.*, III. ɪɪ. ɪɪ. 71; cf. *Essays*, I. 298, etc.
99 See above, p. 116.
100 *Essays*, I. 43 (The British Government).
101 *Essays*, I. 31 (Principles of Government).
102 *Ibid.*, I. 34 (Principles of Government).
103 *Ibid.*, I. 50 (Of Parties).
104 *Ibid.*, 55 (Of Parties).
105 *Ibid.*, I. 100 (Of Civil Liberty).
106 *Essays*, I. 102, cf. 49 (The British Government).

7 The Mercantile System and The Physiocrats

It is impossible to understand the position of Adam Smith in the history of Economics without forming some idea of the two economical systems which influenced him most (the one by attraction, the other by repulsion), and which were identified neither with Hume nor with any other of the writers already considered. These were the Mercantile System and the Agricultural System. The latter was the body of doctrine taught by the French Economists or Physiocrats, who formed the first school of Economists in the strict sense of the term and first gave the whole study its place among the sciences.

I. The principles of the MERCANTILE SYSTEM were not taught by any School; there was no master, there were no disciples. From one of its aspects it was a popular economics and not in the best sense of the term. Though Adam Smith turned to Mun[1] when he looked for a discriminating statement of the Mercantile views, it is clear from his various criticisms on them in the 4th book of the *Wealth of Nations* that he does not regard them as a body of arguments and conclusions carefully worked out by thoughtful men from desire of truth, but rather as a scheme of commercial policy[2] which different governments had adopted on the advice of interested merchants and manufacturers. Its principles, so far as they were ever elaborated into a system, seem to him to be the maxims of practical men of business, who know how trade benefits themselves and have no concern how it benefits the nation at large. On the other hand, the motive of governments in adopting the Mercantile policy. could hardly have been disinterestedly to benefit the merchants and manufacturers. The time of its first appearance and the time of its decline will help us to understand the matter. It is usually said to have begun with the Reformation and ended with the French Revolution; and this means that it began when foreign commerce was becoming a power in Europe and ended when governments were beginning to be constitutional and popular. The common notion of Mercantilism represents it as confusing wealth with money, or at least with the precious metals. The charge thus blankly stated is not strictly true; but it is true that views were adopted and made the ground of political action for more than two centuries which might fairly be represented as logically involving the fallacy in question. The intelligible motive for adopting a policy which promised to multiply the precious metals in a country was clearly the desire of the rulers to have a full treasury for warlike and other purposes.[3] There was also a belief that for general reasons (the reasons of the "merchants and manufacturers") it was good for the country that as much of the precious metals as possible should be attracted into it. The measures adopted to secure this end were the prohibition to export gold and silver "forth of the kingdom," the careful watching of the balance of trade, to see that our exports should in value exceed the imports, in order that there might be a balance in money to come into the country, restraints (by duties or prohibitions) on importation from foreign countries, and encouragement (by bounties and drawbacks) of exportation, special encouragements of home manufacture and of the growth of a home population to labour on it, treaties of commerce to secure privileges for our exporters, and finally the foundation of Colonies and the retention there of our monopoly of trading.

It has been stated[4] that Mercantilists agreed in displaying an exaggerated care for the mere numbers of the people. The fallacy of considering a large population to be of itself a source of strength to a nation may indeed be connected with the military view in which the Mercantile System seems to have originated; but it is not necessarily of a piece with the rest of the policy. Not only the adherents of the Mercantile policy but nearly all economical writers before the Physiocrats were more or less tainted with this fallacy; and it is no more safe to identify this view with Mercantilism than it is to identify Mercantile theorists with the supports of an absolute monarchy. No doubt the policy arose at a time when Monarchies in Europe were becoming strong, and the regulation of trade may have seemed as natural in an absolute monarchy as the regulation of religion, morals and literature. But the Mercantile System prevailed even under the Commonwealth; and it survived the expulsion of the Stuarts. Its absence in Holland was due rather to its impracticability there than to the popular form of the Dutch government. It is true that Colbert, the great bugbear of the Physiocrats, was the minister of an absolute monarch; but the Physiocrats who successfully contended against the continuation of his policy were themselves suspected of inclining to an absolute form of government. The Mercantile system was no immediate consequence of the decay of feudalism and the rise of powerful monarchies. The first efforts of these monarchs were rather in the direction of sumptuary measures; their interference with foreign importation was meant not to bring money into the country but to prevent their own people from being corrupted by foreign luxuries. It is not till a century after the discovery of America and the fall of feudalism that we find Mercantile views coming forward with authority. All we can safely say seems to be that, when the separate States became more conscious of their own national life than of the ties that bound them to their neighbours, they were easily led to confound commercial dependence with political,[5] and it was not hard for jealousy and suspicion to convince them that their neighbours' gain could not at the same time be their own. We can understand too that in the days when governments did not understand the limits of their omnipotence they would feel bound to regulate the spirit of trading which seemed to be becoming a passion with their citizens to the detriment of their patriotism. This would seem to them the more imperative because trade is not the creation of any government, but is one of the *"sponte acta"* that have a life of their own. There was therefore an interference at every point. Isolated writers, especially in England, expressed doubts about the wisdom of this interference; but it was not till the middle of the 18th century, when a great School of Economists arose in France, that both rulers and people were forced to pay some regard to the demand for freedom of trade. The demand was simply that what was spontaneous in its origin should be allowed to be spontaneous in its development.

II. This demand was first made (in connection with a system of doctrine) by the remarkable group of French writers, known in their own day as the "Economists," and perhaps best known in ours as THE PHYSIOCRATS. They were not metaphysicians, but their system was a political philosophy conjoined with a political economy. Though they themselves kept up the conjunction, they were the means of establishing the position of political economy as a distinct branch of study.

With the Peace of Aix la Chapelle (1748), at the close of the war of the Austrian Succession, France entered on the period of political ferment which led up to the Revolution. In 1748 Montesquieu published his *Spirit of the Laws*. In 1753 Rousseau printed his *Discourse on Inequality among Men*, and in 1762 his *Emile* and his *Social Contract*. Throughout the century the increasing financial difficulties of the French monarchy had made a brisk market for writings on taxation and finance.

Vauban's *Dîme Royale* and Boisguillebert's *Détail de la France* had appeared in the reign of the Grand Monarque (1707); and the projects of John Law, which led to an active discussion on currency, banking and finance, were early in the reign of Louis XV. But even in Montesquieu's financial chapters there was no systematic or logical economical doctrine. Cantillon (*Essai*, 1755) may have furnished to the Physiocrats one, if not more, of their leading ideas; but Cantillon shared the fate of other anticipators.[6] It was reserved to the Physiocrats to carry on both the financial and the philosophical lines of discussion in the light of principles, from which they professed to deduce at once an economical and a political system.

The pioneer of the new doctrines was Quesnay, the physician of Madame de Pompadour. His articles in the *Encyclopédie* of D'Alembert and Diderot on "Fermier" and "Grains," contain a sketch of the physiocratic principles. "Political Economy" remained, in the pages of the *Encyclopédie*, a theory of political philosophy. Rousseau, who is the writer of the article so headed (*Economie politique*, 1755), discusses the relation of the State to its members, in the manner of his maturer work on the "Social Contract" (1762), and with little or no reference to what we should now call economical matters proper.[7] But in the articles of Quesnay, as well as in the later writings of himself, Gournay, Mercier de la Rivière, Dupont, and the elder Mirabeau,[8] the economical element bulks at as largely as the political. Turgot, a greater personality than any of them, is not to be reckoned among the physiocrats; but he in turn influences them and is influenced by them. Their power over public opinion seems to last with his life, and to cease at his death (1781). When their doctrines were criticised by Adam Smith in 1776, Quesnay had been dead two years, and the influence of the School was already beginning to wane. It was Turgot who defended them (with some reservations) against the charge of being systematic (as if that were a fault), by saying, "Every thinking man has a system."[9] They presented a "body of doctrine defined and complete, which clearly lays down the natural rights of man, the natural order of Society, and the natural laws most advantageous to men united in a society" (Dupont; see Schelle, *Dupont* (1888), p. 44). We have now to see what that system was, and what permanent service it has rendered to economics and philosophy.

The consumption (says Quesnay[10]) which is most profitable for the sovereign, and brings greatest happiness to the people, is "that general consumption which satisfies the wants of life." And this does not mean such provision as will barely keep soul and body together. No one, if he can help it, will drink only water, and wear only rags, and eat the worst bread. "All men try by their labour to procure *good* food and *good* clothes."[11] It is not good policy to keep people poor in order that their poverty may spur them to industry; wealth is a much better incitement, for it has hope in it.[12]

This might be a general maxim of all economists; but in the hands of Quesnay and his followers it had a special application. Clear revenues are the produce of land and of men. Without the labour of men land has no value. The original wealth (*les biens primitifs*) of a great State consists in men, land, and cattle.[13]

Land furnishes the raw materials of all industry; those raw materials are the original wealth, always renewed, which sustains all classes in the kingdom. Without means of doing justice to the resources of the land, the farmer not only keeps himself poor, but injures the prosperity of the whole nation. It is therefore of the first importance that the farmer should not be poor. When Quesnay says Farmer he does not mean the agricultural labourer, though as nearest to the actual work on the land the labourer might be conceived to be the more important person. To Quesnay the farmer is the *"entre-preneur,"* employer, and director, and organiser of labour on the land. He must be in a position to spend what is necessary on the soil itself, and on the wages of the labourers. He was so in France in the days of Sully; he has not been so since, for Colbert, unlike Sully, has neglected agriculture, and forced France into manufactures that have prejudiced the farmers, and with the farmers Agriculture, and with Agriculture the solid prosperity of the whole nation.[14] For it is not true (says Quesnay)[15] that commerce and agriculture are two coordinate sources of wealth. Commerce is only a branch of the tree of agriculture, and a less important branch than manual labour. It is only in agriculture (or, more generally, in the procuring of raw materials) that the return to expenditure more than balances expenditure, and leaves a surplus, clear gain,[16]—a gain which is no other man's loss. Hence, agriculture should be a subject of interest not only to farmer and labourer and landlord, but to the entire nation. It is every one's interest that the produce of the soil should be as great as possible, and hence every obstruction to agriculture should be removed. There should be free exportation of corn and other raw produce. The result would be better prices to the cultivator, better capacity on his part to do justice to his lands, and consequent increase of cultivation, followed by an increased population, which again would extend consumption, and keep up the market for the produce. Most of the trade of the kingdom, as it now is, does not really increase the wealth of the nation; (as Locke says) it means no more than money changing hands in a game or a lottery; it does not add to the stakes.[17]

The economical principles given in Quesnay's two articles,[18] became the basis of Physiocracy. His strong expressions of patriotism, and (perhaps even more) his special pleading for one particular industry, give his readers the impression that the general principles are in some degree an afterthought. However, it is a matter of history that both in Quesnay's own writings and in the voluminous writings of his school, the principles were expanded and applied economically and philosophically far beyond these simple positions. The theory of taxation and the theory of Free Trade were worked out more elaborately; and the notion of a "natural order," natural rights, and a corresponding theory of Government, were developed. The term Political Economy became once for all identified with the study of the subjects now embraced under it.[19] It is true that the Physiocratic system embraced much more than economical matters; but its economical positions are its most characteristic feature, and the Physiocratic writers have perhaps done more for economics than (much as they strove after it) for political philosophy.

It has been said that Philosophy touches Economics most closely at the starting point and at the close. The doctrines of wealth and value rest on psychology, and the economical relations of men to each other in society cannot be fully understood without a political philosophy. Now, the first of these points of connection was not fully considered by the Physiocrats; but indirectly they have rendered help to its consideration by their clear statement of first principles, and especially by their analysis of value and rent. It is Quesnay who says (*Dialogue sur les travaux des artisans*, Daire, 192):— "To obtain the greatest possible increase of enjoyments by the greatest possible diminution of expenses is the perfection of economy." The distinction of Value in Use from Value in Exchange comes in its modern form from the same writer. "We should distinguish in a State the goods (*biens*) which have a value in use (*valeur usuelle*), and no market value (*valeur vénale*) from the wealth (*richesses*) which has both a value in use and a market value. For example, the savages of Louisiana enjoyed many goods, such as water, wood, game, fruits of the earth, which were not wealth because they had no market value. But, after the establishment of trade between these savages and the

French, English, and Spaniards, part of their goods acquired a market value and became wealth. So the government of a kingdom should try to procure for the nation at once the greatest possible abundance of productions, and the greatest possible market value, because by means of great wealth the nation can procure in trade all the other things which she may need, in precise proportion to the state of her wealth."[20] Money is a form of wealth which acts as an intermediary between the sellers and the buyers, but its function is to be the means of exchanging other forms of wealth. It adds nothing to the "real wealth" of the country, in the sense of leaving the total greater than it found it; and it is a mistake to suppose that an accumulation of money is the way to make a nation really rich.[21] This was a view directly opposed to the Mercantile Theory, to which theory the Physiocrats may be considered as dealing the death blow.

But it was not only money which was sterile, in the view of those Economists. Quesnay represents society as divided (economically) into three great classes—the cultivators, who are alone productive, the proprietors (including the State) who draw from the first class what they spend on the 3rd or Industrial class, and the last, who are called emphatically the Sterile or unproductive class.[22] Their materials all come from the first class, and their outlay of labour and capital does not bring to the nation in material goods more than and equivalent.[23] If we depended on them and had no agricultural surplus, but just enough to feed our own people, the wealth of the country could not grow. Growing national wealth must mean growing produce of agriculture. Agriculture alone yields a net produce or clear gain after reimbursement of expenses; and the agriculturist is not the labourer, but his employer. Physiocracy, therefore, as an economical theory is a glorification not of the labourer, but of the capitalist, though only in one field of action. The theory of capital is, as a matter of fact, more fully elaborated by Quesnay and his followers than the theory of Rent, though the later theory of Rent had no doubt its first beginnings in their doctrine of net produce. They speak of "advances laid out on the soil" (see Dupont, *Abrégé des principes de I écon. pol.*, 1772, Daire, I. p. 375) and "original advances" (which are roughly identical with sunk capital, and permanent instruments for agricultural work), and "annual advances" (which correspond to circulating capital). The notions of fixed and circulating capital seem little more than an extension to all industries of the broad distinctions made by the Physiocrats for agricultural capital in particular. We should not, however, find in Quesnay or the rest any very satisfactory explanation of the first origin of the "original advances" and "annual advances" themselves. We are told that even in order to rear children "advances" are necessary, and the hunter's bow and arrows have needed "advances" and are his capital. But the phenomenon of interest and profits, except in agriculture, are left practically unexplained,[24] and the relation of the idea of capital to that of property is only touched in so far as it is necessarily covered by the philosophical doctrines of natural right, natural laws, and natural order.

Quesnay's thoughts on these matters follow the lines of Grotius and Locke. He is giving his contribution to the development of the notion of a Law of Nature; and his "new science" is the study of "Physiocratic" or that constitution of government which is best for man, because most in accordance with Nature.

The natural right of man (says Dupont in his Preface to Quesnay's[25] *Physiocratie*) is the right which he has to do that which is advantageous to him, the right which he has to the things proper to his enjoyment; and this right is founded on the imperious necessity by which we are charged with our own preservation under penalty of suffering and death. To give effect to that right we must of course know what is advantageous to us; and so it is an essential corollary of that right that we should seek to be enlightened by reflection, judgment, and the calculations of self-interest. Else we might use our faculties to do what is hurtful to us, and that could not be in pursuance of natural right. The exercise of our natural right is prescribed for us by the absolute causes which our intelligence ascertains for us. As the natural right existed for the first man, and exists for men in isolation now, it is in one sense antecedent to the social order. But it is not the less limited by the physical laws of the natural order, the laws of the general order of the universe; and hence is in need of an enlightened understanding. If men violate physical laws, they will suffer death; and, if they violate the laws of social order, which are equally natural, they will ruin and destroy each other. There are no rights without duties, or duties without rights.[26] Natural order, then, in this large sense, is antecedent to natural right, whether exercised in isolation or in society. Natural laws, as distinguished from the natural order, are simply the conditions under which the members of the natural order play their part in conformity therewith. The natural laws of the social order are accordingly the conditions under which men must act in order to secure to themselves the advantages of society. They prescribe the rules of union; and the rules are no arbitrary contrivances, but flow from the essential justice that secures to men their subsistence and their enjoyment of their possessions without detriment to others; without them there is no security of life or possessions. "Nature" does not mean the savage state. The noble savage of whom we at present hear so much [from Rousseau] is often in his tribal life much more regardful of the laws of the social order than civilized men are in a badly constituted State, with positive laws that conflict with the laws of nature.[27] But his condition is far from being the best possible for humanity. Civilization is better; and it began with agriculture. "The first wheat sown in the earth was the germ of empires." With agriculture came settled life, property, and political government. There followed too a great increase of people, for "men only multiply in proportion to the wealth necessary to their subsistence; and so it is that agriculture, which is the only source of the wealth of empires, occasions a rapid increase of population."[28]

To facilitate this production of wealth by agriculture, government must grant the utmost freedom of trade, in order that the cultivator may have the best market possible. Free trade is thus one of the natural laws of the social order. From the economics of the school it follows that the expense of government must be met by a taxation laid on the only shoulders that can bear it, namely, the proprietors of land.[29] The Physiocrats had a partiality for a sort of patriarchal monarchy, like the Chinese, on the ground that a patriarchal monarch would feel his interests identical with that of the agricultural classes. They were not careful to avoid language which seemed to justify despotism,[30] and the famous pamphlet of Voltaire (1768), *L'homme aux quarante écus*, which was directed against them, makes much of this feature. Logically (as their candid friend Turgot pointed out to them[31]) there was no such connection between their ideas and those of absolutism that they needed to incur the odium of this reproach.

For our present purpose it is more important to inquire what was the exact sense in which they understood rights of property. There were, according to the Physiocrats, three kinds of property, equally founded on the "natural order." These were property in one's own person, property in moveables, and property in land. The right of self-preservation demands the first of these, and the consequence of its admission is not only the abolition of Slavery (the Physiocrats were many of them active abolitionists), but the removal of all restrictions on employment. The economists joined with Turgot in demanding the abolition of corvée, guilds, and other mediaeval obstructions to freedom of labour; they certainly helped towards the final removal of them in 1789. The second kind of property is the extension of the first; by joining my labour to objects I make them mine.[32] But then comes the hard question:—In a world already tenanted by others have I a right to everything, as Hobbes had declared? Quesnay answers that this is a physical impossibility; the right of nature is therefore only to such means as I can obtain by my own efforts for the satisfaction of my wants. In a state of "pure nature" this would mean that my labour was my only title; and the right of all to all would be reduced to the right of every one to that portion which his labour procured for him.[33] But we find in men a great inequality of powers, an inequality neither just nor unjust, for it simply results from natural laws. As men benefit by laws of the physical world as much as they suffer from them, so (it is suggested) they benefit from the social order more than they are restricted by it. It secures to them what otherwise could not be secure, the fruits of their labour; and their labour in society is much more economical and effective than it could have been in isolation. They suffer no injury by the fact that their rights are limited by those of others.

This justification of personal Property is exposed to the same criticisms as the doctrine of Locke; and a like remark applies to the Physiocratic justification of property in land. "In employing his person and his moveable wealth on the labour and outlay necessary to cultivation, man acquires property in the soil on which he has laboured. To deprive him of that soil would be to rob him of his labour and the wealth he has laid out on the cultivation; it would be to violate his property in his own person and moveables. In acquiring property in the land, he acquires property in the fruits produced by it, and this was the object of all his expenditure, and the object for which he seeks to gain that property in land. Unless he had this property in the fruits of the soil, no one would spend wealth or labour on the land; there would be no landlords; and the soil would remain waste, to great detriment of population, present and future."[34] Become landowner, he may associate with him another who voluntarily and by free contract may continue the cultivation for him, on terms freely arranged between them. Thus we have farmers as well as landlords.[35]

We have here a more explicit declaration than in Locke or Hume of the political reason for allowing the appropriation of land; the land should be allowed to become property not only because men have worked on it, but in order that they may have the motive to go on working upon it.

This tacitly implies that, if they do not work upon it, their title is *pro tanto* insecure, and the State would not be bound to treat them as absolute masters of their land. But the existence of proprietorship without work is certainly tolerated by the Physiocrats.[36] The absentee landlord and his neglect of his duties are indeed criticised by them, as by all enlightened Frenchmen of the time; and we must not forget that it was Dupont de Nemours himself who in 1789 proposed the confiscation of the estates of the Church. But in the previous generation the time had not come for economical discussions to touch the deepest foundations of property. The communism of men like Morelly[37] was an isolated opinion. There was more need in the beginning of the second half of that century for the assertion of liberty in the sense of the removal of obstacles. It was better that the outward instruments and material aids to the progress of the poorer classes should be made ready *before* than *after* the change of the old social order. Free trade in the sense of freedom of contract and movement was a necessary step. If the material wealth had been placed in the hands of the poor at that time, they could not have used it so effectively as the capitalists (especially in England after the Peace of Paris) were able to do.

The practical services of the Physiocrats were not small. They gave an impulse to scientific agriculture both in and out of France; they helped Turgot to abolish the *corvée*; they helped the removal of restrictions on the corn trade within the kingdom of France; they prepared their nation for the commercial treaty with England in 1786.[38] They exerted an influence on American finance.[39] Their theories drew the attention of the Empress Catherine; and the Margrave of Baden tried to carry them out in his dominions.

Their services to economic science can hardly be overestimated; and their political philosophy had a greater influence than has always been recognised. Their doctrine of natural rights, though interpreted by themselves in a way that rendered it safe to existing institutions, was (like Locke's theory of property and view of the social contract) easily convertible into a revolutionary doctrine.[40] The "right of man to the things proper to his enjoyment" was (as Schelle remarks) not easily distinguished from the "right to live" to which the

Abbé Raynal appealed, or the "right to labour" invoked by other popular leaders at a later date. The Physiocrats so far granted the correctness of this interpretation that they claimed the intervention of the State in education and in relief of the poor. Their system was not one of laissez-faire in the sense in which the phrase is sometimes employed, or they could never have been accused of tending to make government too paternal and despotic. But they believed that the course of trade was best left to organize itself, and, too optimistically, considered that self-interest and justice were in most cases identical. It must be allowed too that the political government which they described was one too exclusively dominated by reference to material wealth; their study of the relations of economics to politics had led them to make the economical element in a nation the governing element; and on the other hand their political philosophy had introduced into economical discussion a body of philosophical principles, from which they reasoned deductively without sufficiently clear distinction between economical and philosophical elements. But systematic study of economical subjects begins with them. We shall find their principles entering as a factor into all later developments of economical doctrine.

Note

Quesnay's view, that the moral law of nature coincides with the physical, was probably a tradition from Stoicism. It seems hardly necessary to trace it (with Hasbach) to Richard Cumberland, or (with Dr. Stephan Bauer) to Malebranche, though both theories are plausibly supported. The best English account of Malebranche is given by Dr. Martineau (*Types of Ethical Theory* (1885), I. 151–233).

Notes

1 *England's Treasure by Foreign Trade*, published 1664, though written perhaps thirty years earlier.
2 See *W. of N.*, IV., Introd., p. 187 (MacCulloch's edition):—"Political Economy *considered as a branch of the science of a statesman or legislator.*"
3 See, *e.g.*, Cunningham, *Growth of Engl., Industry, and Commerce*, p. 150 (1st ed.). Miaskowsky, *Die Anfänge der National-Oekonomie* (1891).
4 *E.g.* by Roscher, *Gesch. der. Deutschen Nat. Oekonomik* (1874). Roscher treats the Mercantilists as if they were really a "School." He is closely followed by Ingram, *Hist. of Pol. Econ.* (1888), p. 229.
5 Cf. List's idea of a "*National Political Economy,*" and Fichte's of a "closed commercial State."
6 Espinas, *Histoire des doctrines écon.*, 1892, pp. 179–197, gives a good account of Cantillon. See also Mr. H. Higgs, *Quart. Journ. of Ec.*, July, 1892.
7 According to a quotation given by Oncken, *Der ältere Mirabeau* (Berne, 1886), p. 41, Mirabeau at a later time tried hard to convert him but wrung from him only a cry for mercy: "I am an old man. Send me no more books !"
8 We should need to add Le Trosne, St. Péravy, Vauvillers, Roubaud, Baudeau, to make the list of leading writers more nearly complete.

9   *Éloge de Gournay*, reprinted in the volume *"Turgot"* of *Petite Biblioth. Ec.*, p. 39.
10 *Encycl. of Did. and D'Alemb.*, vol. vii., 1757, art. "Grains," pp. 812 *seq.*
11 *Ibid.*
12 Cf. *Maximes génér. du gouvern. écon.* Daire's *Physiocrates* (1846), I. p. 99 n. *Encycl.*, art. "Fermiers" (vol. vii., 1756, p. 528 *seq.*).
13 "Grains," 821, 2.
14 "Grains," 819, cf. 821, 2.
15 *Ibid.*, 820 n.
16 Quesnay's word is *"revenus."* *"Produit net"* became his favourite phrase some years later. Benj. Franklin was Physiocratic when he spoke of manufactures as "subsistence metamorphosed." *Works* (Sparks), II. 374 (quoted by Dugald Stewart, *Pol. Econ.*, I. 262).
17 "Fermier," 539, 1.
18 Much of the space is taken up by a discussion of the merits of horses versus oxen, and similar details.
19 It is fair to remember that Verri in Italy (in 1763), and Steuart in Scotland (1767), were perhaps the first to use "Political Economy" in the titles of distinctly economical treatises.
20 Quesnay, *Maximes génerales du gouvernement économique d'un royaume agricole*, 1758. Note on Max. XVIII. (Daire, I. p. 98). Elsewhere he speaks of *"biens gratuits"* and *"biens commercables."* See Schelle, page 81.
21 *Maximes générales*, XIII. note (Daire, p. 93).
22 Condillac, the philosopher, departed from them on this point in his *Commerce et gouvernement* (Amsterd.), 1776 (*e.g.* ch. vii. p. 67), though otherwise Physiocratic.
23 See above and cf. the *Tableau économique* of Quesnay given in Dupont's *Physiocratie ou constitution naturelle du gouvernement le plus avantageux au genre humain*, Paris and Leyden, 1768. See Daire, Introd. to vol. i. pp. xliv., etc.
24 See, *e.g.*, Dupont's Correspond. with Say, in Daire, I. p. 401.
25 *Physiocratie (Droit Naturel*, etc.) (1768). He is giving the main points in Quesnay's *Droit Naturel*, which comes directly after his preface. See Daire, vol. i.
26 See Dupont, *Origine et progrès d'une science nouvelle*. Daire, I. 342.
27 We find in Adam Smith something like a deliberate avoidance of "laws" in matters economical. Malthus seems to have been the first English economist to use the term in this connection, and he may have borrowed it from the Economists, though his use of it is slightly different from theirs. But see below [*Natural Rights and Law of Nature*].
28 *Loc. cit.*, XLIX.
29 *E.g.* Dupont, *Origine et progrès d'une science nouvelle*. Daire, I. 364.
30 They spoke of *"autorité tutelaire"* and even *"despotisme légal."*
31 See his letter to Dupont, quoted by Schelle, *Dupont de Nemours*, 1888, p. 178.
32 See, *e.g.*, Dupont, *Origine et progrès*. Daire, I. 362 ft.
33 Quesnay, *Physioc. Droit Naturel, e.g.* Daire, I. 44.
34 Dupont, *Origine et Progrès*. Daire, 344.
35 One opponent of the Physiocrats, De Graslin, gained a prize given by the Political Economy Society of St. Petersburg, 1767, for an essay, in which he advocated nationalization of the land.
36 So Condillac, *Commerce et gouvernement*, 1776, ch. xii. p. 94.
37 *Code de la Nature*, 1755. So Mably, *Doutes proposés aux économistes* (The Hague), 1768.
38 Vergennes entrusted Dupont with the negotiations, and the treaty was on the French side his work. See Schelle's *Dupont*, p. 231 *seq.*
39 See Prof. Dunbar, *Quarterly Journ. of Economics*, July, 1889 (p. 437).

40 See Playfair's Preface and Notes to his edition of Ad. Sm. *W. of N.* (1805), esp. vol. i. Pref. v., vii., xvi., and vol. iii. 495, 505, 513, 517, 518. We get from him the entirely false impression that the Physiocrats were directly responsible for the Assignats, and for almost every bad feature of the Revolution. "When they were committing and instigating others to commit the most atrocious actions, it was all done under the pretence of advancing the happiness of mankind!"

8   Adam Smith (1723–1790)

The fame of ADAM SMITH in his own lifetime rested as much on his *Theory of Moral Sentiments* (1759) as on his *Inquiry into the Nature and Causes of the Wealth of Nations* (1776), but the influence of the latter book in after times has been beyond comparison the greater. The author cannot indeed claim to have created economical study in England. His friend Hume, following up Locke and Petty and many pamphleteers, had done good preparatory work; and Hutcheson's lectures at Glasgow, to say nothing of his *Moral Philosophy* (1747)[1] had probably an influence on Adam Smith's ways of thinking. There had been considerable public interest in economical subjects, towards the middle of the century, whether through Hutcheson and Hume, or through French influences. Foulis and other Scotch publishers had reprinted the tracts and treatises of Gee (1750), Law (1750), Mun (1755), and others, as well as Mores *Utopia* (1743). Montesquieu's *Spirit of the Laws* had been translated for them (1750). Original treatises were fewer; but Sir James Steuart, Jacobite and Mercantilist, had written in 1767 an *Inquiry into the Principles of Political Œconomy, being an Essay on the Science of Domestic Policy in Free Nations*, in which he had covered the ground of political economy in the modern sense. Complaint has sometimes been made that Adam Smith borrowed from Steuart without acknowledgment.[2] It was, however, to the philosophers of his native country rather than the economists that Adam Smith was indebted; and Steuart, though he wrote a little on philosophy, was hardly a philosopher. Adam Ferguson, himself an eminent writer on political philosophy, says that the author of the *Moral Sentiments* was the man from whom was expected "a theory of national economy equal to what has ever appeared on any subject of science whatever."[3]

Adam Smith was professor of Logic in Glasgow, 1751, and from 1752 to 1763 professor of Moral Philosophy there. The biography (by Dugald Stewart) prefixed to the posthumous edition of his *Essays on Philosophical Subjects* (1790), along with some passages in the *Moral Sentiments*, shows us his programme of work, and also his view of the relation of Philosophy to Political Economy. From the concluding words of the *Moral Sentiments*[4] it appears that he considered Ethics and Jurisprudence to be the only two "useful" parts of Moral Philosophy, excluding casuistry as a useless relic of the middle ages. He had no special liking for "Logic, or the science of the general principles of good and bad reasoning" (*Wealth of Nations*, V. I. 345, 2); and is said during his professorship (1751) to have devoted himself chiefly to Rhetoric, then as now included in the proper work of the Logic chair in Glasgow.[5] He had previously lectured on literary criticism at Edinburgh in 1748–50; and readers of the *Moral Sentiments* will believe him to have done full justice to his subject.[6] There is no doubt, however, about his contributions to "Moral Philosophy," which he understood, with the Greeks, as an inquiry into the "happiness and perfection of a man, considered not only as an individual but as the member of a family, of a State, and of the great Society of mankind" (*Wealth of Nations*, V. 1. 346).

His lectures on Moral Philosophy[7] embraced four parts, (1) Natural Theology, dealing with the Being and Attributes of God, and "those principles of the human mind on which religion is founded." Except for scattered hints in the *Moral Sentiments*, we have no materials for judging of his views on these matters. We only know (from more than one passage in his works) that anything like a metaphysical treatment of them would be rigorously excluded, for our author hated metaphysics, scholastic or otherwise.[8] (2) They embraced Ethics in the narrower sense, the doctrines chiefly discussed in the *Moral Sentiments*. (3) They embraced justice in particular, as a virtue susceptible of precise and accurate rules, and therefore admitting a full and particular explanation. He followed the plan of Montesquieu, and traced the progress of jurisprudence, public and private, from the rudest to the most refined ages, pointing out the effects of the industrial arts and of the growth of wealth on laws and government.[9] He had it also on his programme[10] in this connection to sketch out a system of natural jurisprudence (or law of nature), of which he regarded every system of positive law as a more or less imperfect embodiment. This would give "the natural rules of justice independent of all positive institution." Grotius, he says, was the first who attempted this, and he left much to be done, which our author, writing in 1759, hoped to live long enough to do himself.[11] He partly fulfilled this hope in 1776 (*Wealth of Nations*), but like Grotius he left much undone; and with something of sadness in his last edition of the *Moral Sentiments* he repeats his promises (6th ed. 1790) with only a faint hope of fulfilling them:—"In the last paragraph of the first edition of the present work, I said that I should in another discourse endeavour to give an account of the general principles of law and government, and of the different revolutions which they had undergone in the different ages and periods of society, not only in what concerns justice, but in what concerns police, revenue, and arms, and whatever else is the object of law. In the *Inquiry concerning the Nature and Causes of the Wealth of Nations*, I have partly executed this promise, at least so far as concerns police, revenue, and arms. What remains, the theory of jurisprudence, which I have long projected, I have hitherto been hindered from executing, by the same occupations which had till now prevented me from revising the present work. Though my advanced age leaves me, I acknowledge, very little expectation of ever being able to execute this great work to my own satisfaction,[12] yet, as I have not altogether abandoned the design, and as I wish still to continue under the obligation of doing what I can, I have allowed the paragraph to remain as it was published more than thirty years ago, when I entertained no doubt of being able to execute everything which it announced."

He had at least dealt with the fourth and last subject of Moral Philosophy as he conceived it,—the regulations made by States to increase their power and prosperity, for this subject will cover the main topics of the *Wealth of Nations*, commerce, finance, ecclesiastical and military establishments.

Adam Smith undoubtedly started with the purpose of giving to the world a complete social philosophy. He accomplished the greater part of his design, and yet he is seldom remembered except for his economical work and only for part of that. He is reckoned not among the architects but among the iconoclasts of the eighteenth century. But it is to the former class he would have wished to belong. Philosophy, to him, is "the science of the connecting principles of nature"; "philosophy, by representing the invisible chains which bind together all these disjointed objects, endeavours to introduce order into this chaos of jarring and discordant appearances."[13] It removes the appearance of fits and starts, and "renders the theatre of nature a more coherent and therefore more magnificent spectacle" to the imagination. But to do this its connecting principles must be such as are "familiar to all mankind." This general notion of Philosophy is first applied by him to the Physical Sciences; but it applies equally well to his Ethics and Economics, where the connecting principles are sympathy and commercial ambition, principles familiar to all mankind.

After so describing Philosophy, he goes on to tell us that it can only arise in a well ordered society, a society where there is security for life and possessions. In place of philosophy the savage has his polytheism and fetishism, and whatever he finds irregular he ascribes to the "invisible hand"[14] of some god, who "stops or alters the course which natural events would take if left to themselves."[15] When Adam Smith himself recognises the presence of an "invisible hand," it is as a cause of order and law in human actions, as opposed to irregularity,[16] a calm philosophical view, which can, as he admits, only arise where there is civic calm and tranquillity, permitting wonder to take the place of terror. The first motive of philosophy, he says, is not utility but curiosity, and the study is pursued as a good in itself without regard to any supposed usefulness,[17] Adam Smith himself was in this sense a philosopher to the end of his days. His motive for studying economics as well as for studying ethics was neither as with Malthus philanthropy, nor as with the Physiocrats patriotism, in the first instance.[18] It was essentially the discovery of truth for its own sake, the love of finding order where there had seemed to be chaos. This appears even from the similes with which he illustrates his general descriptions of Philosophy. Systems, he says, resemble machines. A machine is a little system, to perform and connect together all the movements which its artist designs for it. A philosophical system is an imaginary machine that endeavours in fancy to connect movements already existing in reality. Now, as the first machines are the most complex, so are the first systems. Such were the Ptolemaic and Copernican, as compared with the Newtonian system.[19] They are inventions of the imagination, though they fit the facts so well that they easily seem to us the real chains by which nature binds together her several operations.[20] The business of philosophers is not to work but to think, "not to do anything but to observe everything," and they are "upon that account often capable of combining together the powers (*sic*) of the most distant and dissimilar objects."[21] They try too to fill up the gaps between one process and another in sequences so near and familiar that mere custom hinders the ordinary man from even perceiving that there are any gaps to be filled.[22]

We have now to consider Adam Smith's own application of these principles to economics as a branch of Moral Philosophy in its larger sense, and we have to see how far the "connecting principles" of ethics and of economics, have themselves any principle of connection.

From the programme above quoted[23] compared with the *Inquiry into the Nature and Causes of the Wealth of Nations*, as we now have it, it is plain that the *Inquiry* was, like the writings of the Physiocrats, intended to embrace political philosophy as well as economics.[24] In his 4th book indeed the author deliberately applies the term Political Economy in a narrow sense. "Considered as a branch of the science of a statesman or legislator" (he says) it has two objects, to enrich the people, and to provide a public revenue; and it is from this narrower point of view that he criticises the mercantile and the physiocratic systems.[25] But in dealing with the Physiocrats he says, that their works "treat not only of *what is properly called Political Economy, or of the nature and causes of the wealth of nations*, but of every other branch of the system of civil government."[26] This passage seems to make it clear that Adam Smith understood the title of his own book to be a good general description of Political Economy; and we must remember how comparatively small a part he allots to politics and governments in the the creation of the wealth of nations. Quesnay, he says,[27] seemed to believe that the desire of men to better their own condition in the world would not act effectively unless complete liberty were granted,—whereas in point of fact (according to Adam Smith) it has been acting throughout the centuries already, and has been triumphing in spite of governments; economical forces not only ought to be but are and have been more powerful than political. The "causes of the wealth of nations," therefore, are found to act within society indeed but apart from the action of the State and often in defiance of it; and an *Inquiry into the Nature and Causes of the Wealth of Nations* begins earlier and ends later than mere politics. Though Dugald Stewart struggled hard to preserve the wider notion of Political Economy, as dealing with "the happiness and improvement of political society" and not merely its wealth,[28] he was only followed by a few of the minor economists; and the desirableness of narrowing the range of inquiry has been generally recognised.

Turning now to the inquiry itself, we find it very unlike a text book for students, or a treatise addressed to a group of professional economists. It is addressed, like Hume's Essays, to all the world of educated people;[29] and, without troubling himself about definitions, the author launches *in medias* res in his first sentence:—"The annual labour of every nation is the fund which originally supplies it with all the necessaries and conveniencies of life which it annually consumes, and which consist always either in the immediate produce of that labour or in what is purchased with that produce from other nations."[30] Plain reason tells us that "the real wealth" of a society is "the annual produce of the land and labour" of it. The mercantile writers have therefore been wrong in regarding a nation as wealthy in proportion to its supply of the precious metals; and the Physiocrats came nearer the truth when they "represented the wealth of nations as consisting not in the unconsumable riches of money, but in the consumable goods annually reproduced by the labour of the society."[31] The really important "balance" of trade is the balance of the annual produce over consumption.[32] In other words, Adam Smith sides with the Physiocrats, but he refuses with them to limit "real wealth" to raw produce; to him, every product of labour is part of the national wealth. Wealth means consumable goods of every sort. "Every man is rich or poor according to the degree in which he can afford to enjoy," etc., page 13. Unfortunately in the *Wealth of Nations* there is no complete theory of consumption; and the treatise is far more on the causes than on the nature of wealth.[33] We have indeed near the end of the book[34] a distinction between the consumable goods that are necessaries and those that are luxuries. The former are such as nature renders necessary for the support of life and also such as custom, which is a second nature, has rendered necessary for decent living. We are told too[35] that it is not necessarily a losing trade that a man drives with the ale-house. Consumption is not the same as loss or waste. But, for the author's view of this subject, and Mandeville's paradox in regard to it, we have to go to his *Moral Sentiments*.[36] There he tells us that virtue does not mean insensibility or absence of passion, but a restraint of it so that it hurts neither the subject of it nor society at large. Mandeville's assertions are only plausible if morality means asceticism; and it must be allowed that on that assumption civilization could only develope at the expense of virtue. But this is far from being the case. Our author, indeed, allows that there may be happiness without wealth. God made the "machine of the universe so as at all times to produce the greatest possible quantity of happiness."[37] "When providence divided the earth among a few lordly masters, it neither forgot nor abandoned those who seemed to have been left out in the partition. These last too enjoy their share of all that it produces. In what constitutes the real happiness of human life they are in no real respect inferior to those who would seem so much above them. In ease of body and peace of mind, all the different ranks of life are nearly upon a level, and the beggar who suns himself by the side of the highway possesses that security which kings are fighting for."[38] On the other hand, it is one of his theses in the *Wealth of Nations*, that in civilized society there is not only greater wealth than in the savage state but it extends even to the humblest classes in society. The English peasant is better accommodated than the African king.[39] The wealth of the nation means in greater or less degree the wealth of every member of it. With an obvious reference to the opposite contention in Turgot[40] and the Physiocrats, he points out that the wages of labourers are not merely a bare subsistence but considerably above that (*Wealth of Nations*, I. viii. 33 *seq*.). What are the causes of the greater wealth of civilized societies?—This becomes the important question at starting. The first cause (and it is the pivot of all the rest) is the division of labour in manufacture, which increases dexterity, saves time, and leads to inventions. The result is a much greater quantity of produce than before. But, besides that, division of labour implies social or joint efforts at starting; and it requires a wide social area for the distribution of its products, unless it is to be waste instead of gain. The result is opulence to the community, and yet the design was (says Adam Smith) mere individual gain. So completely is our author imbued with the growing individualism of his time[41] that he thinks of each human unit as at birth almost exactly the same in character and capacities as every other unit; it is division of labour that alters character, not character that determines a man's selection of his particular task in the division.[42] We have seen how differently Plato regarded the subject.[43] If we ask how it comes that men ever thought of dividing labour, we are told it was through a propensity they had to truck or barter. Man is by nature a trader, from the very fact that he possesses reason and language.[44] Being more dependent on his kind than other animals are, he is soon compelled by stress of circumstances to appeal to his kind for help. As it is more easy to gain it by giving them an equivalent than by securing their friendship out of benevolence (for a whole life is scarce sufficient to gain the friendship of a few persons),[45] he sets himself to making what circumstances have accustomed him to make best, and then he offers his wares to his neighbours in exchange for theirs. It seems clear (though Adam Smith barely touches the point) that division of labour assumes a society or at least a common understanding ready formed, and does not itself create such. Given the common understanding, however, it may be granted that the division of labour will constitute a new means of binding men into a society, or of binding society more firmly together. The idea that division of labour in society is analogous to the division of function among the organs of a living individual body did not occur to Adam Smith,[46] and he does not even trace out the division of labour, like Aristotle,[47] in the Family. But like Aristotle he deduces from it a doctrine of Exchange, Value, and Money. The first form of exchange is the direct form, exchange in kind or barter; and the difficulties and awkwardness of barter lead to the use of a common medium of exchange and common measure of value called money. When one thing is exchanged for another, they are said to have a value, by which is simply meant that the one purchases the other. This is one sense (according to our author) in which we may use the word value; it is the power which a given commodity possesses of purchasing other goods. There is however another sense; there is a value which simply means the "utility of some particular object." This is Value in Use, as the other was Value in Exchange—a distinction very nearly identical with the Physiocratic distinction of *valeur usuelle* and *valeur vénale*. Adam Smith adds that the two are so far from depending on each other that "the things which have the greatest value in use have frequently (like water or air) little or no value in exchange" and *vice versa*. Like the Physiocrats, he makes no attempt to analyse value in use, but devotes his attention to value in exchange.[48] The ordinary common measure of it, he allows, is money, and he adds little or nothing to Aristotle's account of the nature and functions of money. But the real measure of the purchasing power of anything is (he says) not its price in money but the quantity of labour which it will enable the purchaser to command. From the seller's point of view, the article he sells is of great or of little value according to the power which the equivalent that he gets for it has of purchasing labour; from the buyer's point of view, the article he buys is of great or little value, according as it saves him his own labour or purchases the labour of others, in a great or a small degree. So far as Adam Smith is consistent (and he is not so always), he understands the measure of value to be the labour that the exchanged articles will purchase. This seems to him the only factor which remains unchanged through the centuries. The wear and tear of tissue in human beings is (he considers) always the same. When we read of corn as having a certain price in shillings or pounds 300 years ago and a very different price now, we cannot tell which of the two, the corn or the money, has altered; but, when we are told that corn would purchase so many days' labour 300 years ago and so many fewer or so many more now, we can tell at once how much the corn has altered in value, for we know that labour is the same to human beings to-day, yesterday, and at all times. The postulates here are simply that the human race is identical in the whole length of its history, and that the physiological cost of labour to the labourer is always the same, on the very ground of the identity of race. It is the same idea as was noticed in the case of division of labour; human beings are at all times alike, and we can reason from their similarity. It is the same idea as in the striking passage of Hume:[49] "There is a great uniformity among the actions of men in all nations and ages; and human nature still remains the same in its principles and operations. ... Would you know the sentiments, inclinations and course of life of the Greeks and Romans? Study well the temper and actions of the French and English. ... Mankind are so much the same in all times and places that history informs us of nothing new or strange in this particular. ... So readily and universally do we acknowledge a uniformity in human motives and actions as well as in the operations of body." To Adam Smith's particular application of this doctrine there are many objections, ill and well founded. The objection that skilled labour is paid more than unskilled, is not of the latter sort. We have to consider not only the workman's present labour but the labour he has spent in gaining his skill, and we have to allow for inconstant employment and any risks the employment has to face; we might, after all allowances,[50] discover that the average was not higher for the whole working life than it is for unskilled labour. Nor is it a fatal objection that the author seems to consider only manual labour; the principle may equally apply to intellectual; the strain of it is the same now as it was 300 years ago; the alteration in the human body and brain has, at least in comparison with the alteration in the materials and processes of industry, been inappreciable.

But a more serious objection is that "value" is not really used by Adam Smith in the same sense throughout his reasoning on this subject. When he says that "Equal quantities of labour at all times and places may be said to be of equal value to the labourer; in his ordinary state of health, strength, and spirits, in the ordinary degree of his skill and dexterity, he must always lay down the same portion of his ease, his liberty, and his happiness,"[51]—it is clearly not value in exchange that is meant, but value in use; and, according to Adam Smith's own account, the two kinds of value have no fixed relation to each other; and the one can be no measure of the other. There was therefore every need for his own admission that most people will employ as their measure of value some "other commodity" than labour, such a measure as money or corn being a "palpable object," while labour is really in this connection "an abstract notion, which, though it can be made sufficiently intelligible, is not altogether so natural and obvious."[52]

Adam Smith, in fact, had put himself in the position of working men, and had pronounced that wealth changed and on the whole man did not, and that in toil, as in pleasure,[53] human beings were more nearly equal than was usually supposed. He then descended into the market and found that labour was a "commodity" like others.[54] Once upon a time "in the original state of things," the "natural wages" of labour were simply the produce of labour; but the appropriation of land and the accumulation of capital have made the labourer dependent on landlords and capitalists; and, though it is "the annual labour" of the society that supplies it with its consumable wealth, many share in the latter who have not laboured for it. Working men have as a rule no considerable property, and are "under the necessity of submitting for the sake of present subsistence" to the terms offered them by the employers. These terms are favourable or not, according as their numbers are small or great in comparison with the "funds destined for the payment of wages."[55] "The demand for men, *like that for any other commodity*, necessarily regulates the production of men."[56] He does not however say that it does so in the same degree or same way; and the chapter from which these extracts are taken is largely devoted to a proof that wages are *above* bare necessaries, and have been rising with national prosperity. It is clear, therefore, that he does not consider the production of men to be in all points similar to the production of material goods. There is an analogy on certain points, as there must always be where we are dealing with quantities in relation to each other. For the purpose in hand the labourers are similar units in relation to similar material goods. But our author does not forget that they are human beings, members of a society of men, and therefore an end in themselves as well as means to one another. "Servants, labourers, and workmen of different kinds make up the far greater part of every great political society. But what improves the circumstances of the greater part can never be regarded as an inconveniency to the whole. No society can surely be flourishing and happy, of which the far greater part of the members are poor and miserable. It is but equity, besides, that they who feed, clothe, and lodge the whole body of the people should have such a share of the produce of their own labour as to be themselves tolerably well fed, clothed and lodged." He here contradicts his own statement (about the general diffusion of happiness[57]) in order to make it plain that he does not, like Mandeville, conceive general poverty to be the condition of commercial prosperity.

For the most part, however, he gives us a colourless statement of things as they are, without suggestion of any radical reforms. He describes industrial society, after the manner of Turgot and the Physiocrats, as divided into three classes—Labourers, Landlords, Capitalists. He considers the revenue of each, and then how far the interest of each is or is not in harmony with the interest of Society as a whole. The interest of the landlords, when they know their own interest, is, he says, always identical with that of the public; their rents can be kept up only by the prosperity of the country. The interest of the labourers is so too, but they are incapable, from their circumstances, of understanding the public interest and its connection with their own. But the interest of employers, such as dealers and manufacturers, is often different from that of the other two classes, as well as from that of the public.[58]

We need not examine the truth of these statements from an economical point of view. But it will be noted that "the Public" are treated as distinct from the three classes, although the three classes are treated as an exhaustive division of the public itself. In the same way, the Consumer figures not only in Adam Smith, but in later economists as a distinct entity. The meaning in both cases is that the "great body of the people" are regarded from one particular point of view, abstraction being made from the fact that they necessarily belong to one or other of the three classes. As consumers, the Public may be regarded as one; as producers or drawers of income, they are many. The abstraction is not wholly justifiable, for all consumption is dependent on an antecedent revenue; it may be allowed however that the consumers of any one particular article must always outnumber the producers of it, and in the case of necessaries they will be actually co-extensive with the "great body of the people." To press the claims of the Consumers, therefore, is to press the claims of the majority; and Adam Smith in doing this is as democratic as Rousseau.

It is remarkable then that our author, who gives no complete theory of consumption, makes the Consumer (see esp. IV. VIII. 298) almost the central figure of his book. In this he is at one with the Physiocrats; but without their reservations in favour of agricultural producers. To him all labour is productive if it realizes itself in a "fixed and vendible commodity." The category of productive labour is thus widened. His successors have challenged even this limitation. Why not include all services useful to society, if division of labour is to have its perfect work,[59] and if it allows some to devote themselves to the "production" of services merely, and some to that of the crasser "vendible commodities"? No doubt Adam Smith has brought this question on himself by including capacities and skill under the wealth of a nation. But to "produce" evidently struck him as, in ordinary language, inapplicable to services. He does not doubt the usefulness of the labour, *e.g.*, of public servants or doctors, but simply indicates that it does not produce a commodity in the ordinary sense of the terms. "To produce" is to present society with more or less permanent wealth as distinguished from a momentary or intangible satisfaction; in Mill's language, it is to furnish a "permanent possibility of satisfaction." The distinction of productive and unproductive labour leads into a troublesome dialectic, if it is supposed to mean anything other than this. To separate useful from useless labour is as hard as to separate the tares from the wheat or good from evil. But it is an intelligible practical distinction to say that expenditure is more or less certainly a benefit, according as it is expenditure on what will last long or what will perish at once. A "fixed and vendible commodity" like the *houses* and even the *furniture* of the rich, may pass into the hands of the poor;[60] the luxurious *food* of the rich will not be so widely shared. If we describe all as wealth which satisfies desire, we may still with clearness distinguish that which does so often and for many, from that which does so once and for one. The productive labour of which Adam Smith spoke was in this sense more of a public benefit than the unproductive. Its benefits extended to a greater number; and it is the benefit of the greater number, "the whole body of the people," which he is always considering. The long discussions of the 4th book of the *Wealth of Nations* are a vindication of freedom of trade on behalf of "the great body of the people." As against the Mercantile system, and even as against the Physiocratic,[61] all preferences and restraint are to be taken away, and then the "*simple system of natural liberty*" will establish itself of its own accord.[62]

Private interest (he considers) is most likely to coincide with the public interest when private action is left most free. This is the baldest statement of the doctrine of natural liberty; but, as the doctrine has been of great influence, and is sometimes regarded as the very essence of Adam Smith's teachings, we must inquire more closely into its meaning.

In the *Moral Sentiments* (ed. 1759, p. 181) we are told that "every man is by nature first and principally recommended to his own care," being much fitter to take care of himself than of any other person. "Every man, therefore, is much more deeply interested in whatever immediately concerns himself than in what concerns any other man." In the same way *Nature* (unlike the Stoic philosophy) has made it not man's chief business but only his occasional consolation, to consider the affairs of the Universe. His chief business is to govern the affairs of his own daily life;[63] and in them, fortunately, while intending simply his own gain, he is "led by an invisible hand to promote an end which was no part of his intention,"[64] and which he could not have promoted so well if he had deliberately aimed at the public good. There is no reason (on Adam Smith's general philosophical principles) why human Society should have been deliberately contrived by its members any more than the planetary system consciously framed by its own parts; and the pursuit of separate interests is conceived to have had a social result without any intention on the part of the separate individuals, and without any help from governments. The majority of men have common sense, and do not either miscalculate or mis-spend; the principle of frugality, the "desire of bettering our condition," "though generally calm and dispassionate," is born with us and lasts with our whole life, while the "passion for present enjoyment," the principle that prompts to expense, is on the whole momentary and occasional.[65] This desire to better one's condition has shaped Society, even when Society was putting obstacles in its way. It has never had its *perfect* work, and the simple system of natural liberty has never been fully realized. But it has been the ruling principle of the majority of men, and its influence has been on the whole a civilizing and beneficent one.

The teaching of Adam Smith is quite plain thus far. But in his *Moral Sentiments* he recognises the limitations of these principles more clearly than he is called upon to do in the *Wealth of Nations*. In the first place, he recognises that the desire of advancement has more forms than one, and the desire of wealth is only one out of many alternative objects of ambition (6th ed., vol. i., 148; cf. 1st ed., 304). The great admiration felt for the rich and powerful may become a source of corruption in a State (6th ed., i. 146). Moreover, selfishness of some kind is not the only motive of men. Epicureanism, in so conceiving men, was taking nature for something more simple than she really is, and trying to explain her complexity by a few inadequate simple principles. By Adam Smith's leaning to Aristotle's doctrine of the mean (1st ed., 452) he is led to remark that, like other desires, the desire for personal advancement may become excessive and therefore vicious. He objects to piece-work because "reason and humanity" are against excessive labour, and should overbear "emulation and gain" (*W. of N.*, 37). But even in moderation the desire of gain, though commendable enough, is not a positive duty, and may be absent without shocking (even if not without surprising) us.[66]

Moreover, though its effects are social, it is not itself the root from which society springs. There is a regard for others which is (in Adam Smith's opinion) a reflected regard for ourselves, but which leads to conduct that is essentially different from desire for mere personal advantage. It is due to Sympathy in the wide sense of the word, that power we have of placing ourselves by imagination in the place of other persons and looking at matters as we suppose they would look at them. We do this most readily in the case of those brought most closely into contact with us, and especially those dependent on us; and hence the regard for others is strongest towards children, then towards friends, and then in a less degree towards fellow-citizens and towards men as such.[67] Nature formed men for society, for "mutual kindness" which is necessary to their happiness,[68] but "that wisdom which contrived the system of human affections, as well as that of every other part of nature, seems to have judged that the interest of the great society of mankind would be best promoted by directing the principal attention of each individual to that particular portion of it which was most within the sphere both of his abilities and of his understanding."[69] And the standard by which we judge of others is our own imagined similarity to them: "I judge of your sight by my sight, of your ear by my ear, of your reason by my reason, of your resentment by my resentment, of your love by my love; I neither have nor can have any other way of judging about them."[70] That is to say that in ethics as well as economics Adam Smith postulates the generic identity of human beings as the foundation of his reasoning. But, just as we know men as individuals before we know them as a genus, so we form moral ideas about individuals before we do so in regard to groups of men. Strictly speaking, sympathy exists only between indidividuals. Nature made the individuals; the groups are artificial and secondary. There is such a thing as a general fellow feeling, a regard for a man simply because he is a fellow creature (*M. S.*, 1st ed., 199). The concern we take in the fortune of individuals is never due to the fact that they are members of a society of men, any more than our distress at the loss of a guinea is due to the fact that it was a certain aliquot part of a total in the purse. Our regard for the multitude is "compounded and made up of the particular regards which we feel for the different individuals of which it is composed."[71] In the same way, a regard for the advantage of society and for our own advantage simply as bound up therewith, comes later than a regard for the advantage of individuals. The immediate sympathy is indeed antecedent to any consideration of utility, personal or social.

By sympathy Adam Smith understands not pity or compassion but "fellow feeling with any passion whatever."[72] It arises when we put ourselves in the place of another and have the feelings that his situation would have excited had it been ours. Our author does not try to deduce it from anything else, but goes on to say that the pleasure of mutual sympathy, when I find my neighbour entering into my situation as I into his, cannot at least be resolved into self-interest. He adds that to obtain the pleasure of mutual sympathy a man must moderate his passions. I cannot give sympathy (and therewith approval) to a man whose passion, for example, is greater than the particular cause of it would be conceived by me to produce in my own case, in short, where "the affection" is disproportionate to the cause that excites it. From this point of view I am judging of the "Propriety or Impropriety" of men's actions. I expect men, as it were, to tone down their outbursts of feeling till they reach my pitch; and in like manner I tone down my own to reach theirs.

But I also sit in judgment on the "Merit or Demerit" of actions, and then I am considering not the cause but the end, the beneficial or hurtful nature of the effects which the affection aims at or tends to produce."[73] In either case our "rule or canon" is "the correspondent affection in ourselves." The "man within the breast," "the impartial spectator" there, is our guide.

The "impartial spectator" in judgments of propriety is clearly a reminiscence of Aristotle's prudent man who knows where to place the mean;[74] and
a critic would point out that the decisions of such a "prudent one" or "spectator" would be very different according to his race, his place, and his time.[75]
The individual's judgment would be one formed unconsciously to himself by
the Society in which he was born. "Others" have influenced him before he
knew that he had a "self."

This criticism seems sound in relation to "Propriety" where the question is
one of degree. It seems relevant also in regard to questions of "Merit." There
is "Merit," Adam Smith says, in actions which, if another did them to us,
would excite our gratitude and prompt us to reward it, and Demerit where
resentment would follow, and, prompted by resentment, punishment.[76] Merit
means deserving of reward, demerit deserving of punishment. We attribute
merit where in addition to propriety (as above described) we find a beneficent
motive and beneficent tendency in the action, the whole thus earning our
sympathetic gratitude, and, "if I may say so, calling aloud for a proportion-
able recompense."[77]

Here the difficulty seems to be that it will depend on the particular society
whether an act would produce resentment or gratitude. The sympathy of the
individual has been trained by his society, and, if Adam Smith is trying to
show us[78] how the "moral sentiments" grow up when individuals are for the
first time brought into contact with each other, he is assuming as his starting
point an impossible isolation of individuals.

Apart from this assumption the theory of *Moral Sentiments* is essentially
social. The majority of men regulate their conduct by "general rules" formed
in accordance with the principles described. The regard for these general rules
and maxims of conduct is "what is properly called a sense of duty, a principle
of the greatest consequence in human life, and the only principle by which the
bulk of mankind are capable of directing their actions."[79] "Upon the tolerable observance of these duties depends the very existence of human society," and they "are to be regarded as the commands and laws of the Deity,
promulgated by those vicegerents which he has thus set up within us."[80] Most
men content themselves with a mechanical and general conformity; even the
offenders are not able to shake off all allegiance; but only a minority exhibit
that high degree of morality which we call virtue and which aims at perfection. Exact conformity is easily practicable in the case of justice, the rules of
which are as exact as the rules of grammar; but not so with the other virtues,
where the rules are as indeterminate as the rules of style.[81]

It would be beyond the scope of the present inquiry to discuss in detail
Adam Smith's derivation of moral ideas, whether of Propriety or of Merit,
from the notion of sympathy. It must be observed however that sympathy is
perpetually spoken of as that of the "impartial spectator," the "man within
the breast," whose judgment is not in the ordinary sense that of a particular
man, but that of one who looks beyond his particular feelings, guides himself
by general maxims (cf. 1st ed., 276), and takes up an attitude which places

him in touch with his fellows.[82] The essentially social character of this notion is recognised in such statements as the following: "Was it possible that a human creature could grow up to manhood in some solitary place without any communication with his own species, he could no more think of his own character, of the propriety or demerit of his own sentiments and conduct, of the beauty or deformity of his own mind, than of the beauty or deformity of his own face. Bring him into society, and he is immediately provided with the mirror which he wanted before."[83] "Every man may be the whole world to himself, but to the rest of mankind he is a most insignificant part of it."[84] This last saying is applied specially to a man's desire of "wealth and honours and preferments." There are rules of the game which he must observe, there are unfair advantages which must not be taken, though within certain limits he is not only allowed but expected to be more assiduous on his own behalf than for others.[85]

What these limits are, will appear specially from our author's view of Justice. The members of a society may or may not be kind and generous and affectionate to each other, but they *must* be just, or else their society, like the robber bands mentioned by Plato in the *Republic*, will dissolve. As Adam Smith curiously puts it: "Society may subsist among different men, as among different merchants, from a sense of its utility, without any mutual love or affection,"[86] if only they refrain from doing injury to each other. "Justice is the main pillar" of the whole political edifice: "if it is removed, the great, the immense fabric of human society, that fabric which to raise and support seems in this world (if I may say so) to have been the peculiar and darling care of nature, must in a moment crumble into atoms."[87] Accordingly Nature has implanted in man a consciousness of good and ill desert, and a fear of merited punishment as "the great safeguards of the association of mankind." But for them "a man would enter an assembly of men as he enters a den of lions."[88] Yet, advantageous as justice is, it is not its advantageousness that gave rise to it in the first instance, but the fellow feeling which we have with our fellowmen simply as such. Even justice begins with sympathy, though (as Adam Smith tells us), it is a weak sympathy compared to others.[89] Adam Smith is less Utilitarian than Hume; regard for consequences is always secondary to immediate regard to virtue for its own sake.[90] The state of the agent's mind must be the great consideration in ethics; the action must be done for duty's sake, ἕνεκα τοῦ καλοῦ, or it is not ethical.[91] Even rules of conduct are secondary; they are generalised from individual acts. Yet moral rules are binding, and they are as truly "laws" as any other general rules, being especially analogous to the laws which a sovereign prescribes to his subjects.[92] They were intended by the Author of Nature to be governing principles of human action. In framing them He could have had no other purpose in view than "the happiness of mankind as well as of all other rational creatures";[93] and, if we examine the works of nature, we find them all "intended to promote happiness and guard against misery." By obeying His moral laws, therefore, we are furthering the plan of Providence, and are fellow-workers with God

(1st ed., p. 284). Even in human fortunes the disorder is less real than apparent.[94] Success in business is the reward most adopted to encourage industry,
prudence, and circumspection, and it is the reward they usually obtain. The
goodwill of others is the reward most adapted to encourage truth, justice,
and humanity; and except in rare cases this reward is secured by them. We
are prone to wish that, besides their own proper reward, truth, justice, and
humanity should be crowned with wealth and power, with which they have
in fact no necessary connection. So we grieve to see the "industrious knave"
prospering and the "indolent good man" reaping no harvest; but it is the
"natural course of things" that decides in favour of the knave; he used the
proper means to the proper ends.[95] "What a man soweth that shall he also
reap,"—not something else.[96] Man is disposed to correct nature in such cases;
he tries to "alter that distribution of things which natural events would make
if left to themselves"; "like the gods of the poets, he is perpetually interposing
by extraordinary means in favour of virtue, and in opposition to vice, and,
like them, endeavours to turn away the arrow that is aimed at the head of the
righteous, but accelerates the sword of destruction that is lifted up against the
wicked; yet he is by no means able to render the fortune of either quite suitable to his own sentiments and wishes." The industry and attention of men
are best aroused by the very rigour of Nature's laws, and the impossibility of
securing any end except by the means that she prescribes.[97]

The optimism[98] of the above view of Fortune has a counterpart (as we
already saw) in our author's view of Happiness. He thinks that men differ in
happiness far less than in wealth and fortune. He points to the "never-failing
certainty with which all men sooner or later accommodate themselves to whatever becomes their permanent situation," and thinks there is something to be
said for the opinion of the Stoics, that in real happiness there is "no essential
difference" between one situation and another.[99] But he agrees with this view
only under reservation of a minimum; as there are necessaries of life, so there
are necessaries of a happy life. "Happiness consists in tranquillity and enjoyment," and "in all the ordinary situations of human life a welldisposed mind
may be equally calm, equally cheerful, and equally contented."[100] "In ease
of body and peace of mind, all the different ranks of life are nearly upon a
level."[101] "What can be added to the happiness of the man who is in health,
who is out of debt, and has a clear conscience? To one in this situation all
accessions of fortune may properly be said to be superfluous." Yet (he adds)
this is the ordinary state of mankind everywhere.[102] Irregularity and uncertainty of employment would seem from this point of view to be real evils,[103]
destroying "tranquility"; and yet on the other hand, either excessive labour
or deficient food by destroying good health will destroy the power of "enjoyment." Below a certain point poverty is associated with misery;[104] and savage
life, though sometimes noble, is rarely happy.[105] The happiest time for the
bulk of any society is when that society is advancing towards its maximum of
wealth, but has not yet reached it. "The progressive state is in reality the cheerful and hearty state to all the different orders of the society. The stationary is

dull, the declining melancholy."[106] When there is evidently much to be done, and every one can feel assured that, if he works, "bread shall be given to him, and water shall be sure," the necessary conditions of happiness are present. Unfortunately it would seem from our author's own statement that every nation reaches its full complement of wealth some day, and therewith passes from the progressive into the stationary state. It thus becomes a question how far the stationary state can be deferred indefinitely, or else be made as happy as the progressive. Both these alternatives are discussed by later economists; they are not even suggested with any distinctness by Adam Smith, who leaves us to draw (if we like) a somewhat pessimistic conclusion from his silence. Mandeville's proposition that private vices are public benefits, would imply that the progress of the progressive state was made at the expense of morality. Adam Smith sees the fallacy here. Mandeville, he says, wrongly represents every passion as wholly vicious which is so in any degree and in any direction.[107] The result would be that all beyond the necessaries of an ascetic would be culpable luxury. Custom, however, as well as physical requirements, may rightly convert into necessaries "those things which the established rules of decency have rendered necessary to the lowest rank of people";[108] and even indulgence in luxuries, when kept within bounds, has no vice in it. Progress in wealth, therefore, may carry us quite lawfully beyond physical necessaries to superfluities.[109] At the same time we must never forget that wealth and happiness are not cause and effect, still less identical.

The satisfaction shown (in the *Inquiry into the Nature and Causes of the Wealth of Nations*) at the growing improvement in the production and distribution of wealth, that seemed to be discernible in the author's own century, as compared with previous epochs, is not due so much to the philanthropic thought of the increased happiness which would result, as to the philosopher's recognition of natural laws, working themselves out, in spite of would-be lawbreakers, and even by means of their hallucinations. Men struggle for wealth in a great measure because they take an illusory view of the pleasures obtainable by it, and they are thus decoyed into a course of action which has beneficent consequences due to no human designing. The power of imagination, as a factor of industrial progress, is finely described in the *Moral Sentiments*: "It is well that nature imposes on us in this manner. It is this deception which rouses and keeps in continual motion the industry of mankind. It is this which first prompted them to cultivate the ground, to build houses, to found cities and commonwealths, and to invent and improve all the sciences and arts which ennoble and embellish human life, which have entirely changed the whole face of the globe, have turned the rude forests of nature into agreeable and fertile plains, and made the trackless and barren ocean a new fund of subsistence and the great high road of communication to the different nations of the earth. The earth by these labours of mankind has been obliged to redouble her natural fertility and to maintain a greater number of inhabitants. It is to no purpose that the proud and unfeeling landlord views his fields, and, without a thought for the wants of his brethren, in imagination consumes, himself, the whole harvest that grows upon them. The homely and vulgar proverb that the eye is larger than the belly,[110] never was more fully verified than with regard to him. The capacity of his stomach bears no proportion to the immensity of his desires, and will receive no more than that of the meanest peasant. The rest he is obliged to distribute among those who prepare, in the nicest manner, that little which he himself makes use of, among those who fit up the palace in which this little is to be consumed, among those who provide and keep in order all the different baubles and trinkets which are employed in the œconomy of greatness,—all of whom thus derive, from his luxuries and caprice, that share of the necessaries of life which they would in vain have expected from his humanity or his justice. The produce of the soil maintains at all times nearly that number of inhabitants which it is capable of maintaining. The rich only select from the heap what is most precious and agreeable. ... They are led by an invisible hand to make nearly the same distribution of the necessaries of life which would have been made had the earth been divided into equal portions among all its inhabitants, and thus, without intending it, without knowing it, advance the interest of the society, and afford means to the multiplication of the species. ... In what constitutes the real happiness of human life, they [the poor] are in no respect inferior to those who would seem so much above them."[111]

Adam Smith, therefore, is not found guilty of the fault he blames in Epicurus,—attempting to explain all phenomena by a few simple principles.[112] Commercial ambition is not by any means the only or the chief subject of his admiration. If he had really taken the exaggerated view of its importance which is sometimes attributed to him, he would have been tempted to rank it in the category of intellectual virtues, a category which otherwise (unlike Hume[113]) he does not acknowledge. The claims of morality are never lowered by him. What he really does is to treat commercial ambition as (in later language) a principle of development. On the principles of evolution by natural selection, the individuals and the species, whose development results in a higher order of species and individuals than themselves, could have no credit for the result, and yet the result might be pronounced good. To Adam Smith the same seemed true of industrial progress. It was "Nature's" doing, not man's. It was according to law, but not a law of man's making; indeed, man could not try deliberately to make it without spoiling the work of Nature. Throughout, Nature is used in contrast to human art and artifice, especially the art and artifice of societies of men, small and great. Thus it is that Trade combinations, whether of masters or men, commercial companies, with or without the aid of the State, are equally disliked by him.[114]

If the objection be made that society in the larger sense is allowed by him to be "natural" and its collective acts cannot logically be refused the name, and that the interference of collective humanity has seemed in history (in regard to industry for example) to grow up as "naturally" as society itself, he would possibly have answered that by a "natural order" he does not mean one which is first in time. Historically the development of the towns has led to that of the country, but by nature the development of the country should come first.[115] America, following the natural order, has grown faster than Europe, where the order is disturbed.[116] The order is called "natural" simply because it is the better means to a given end.[117] In all such cases (he seems to think) we discover the best means (and therein the natural order) by leaving the commercial ambition of men free to act in the way each individual prefers. Thus left free, if the individuals are really pursuing wealth and not one of the other objects of human aspiration, they will light upon the fittest means, and the fittest means involve *e.g.* that the progress of agriculture should come before and not after progress of manufactures. To say that the disturbance of this order is not natural is therefore only to say that it prevents the use of the best means to the given end. This is the meaning of the apparent selfishness of the *Wealth of Nations*; there are many ends of life besides wealth, but, *given this end*, Adam Smith points out what he considers to be the best means of securing it. He believes that he can discover, even in things as they are, clear proofs that, on the whole, men have had an inkling of these proper means and have laid hold on them in spite of all deterrents. Intense individual interest and assiduity are indispensable for the making of wealth. It is not and it cannot be a fit work for societies and States.[118] The presumption is thus always against the interference of the State and in favour of "natural liberty" and the spontaneous unrestricted action of individuals.

Though (to Adam Smith) the progress of wealth is thus not due to collective action, it is in a very real sense not possible without it, for it is not possible without security and justice, which it is one of the main objects of the State to guarantee. The "natural liberty" of men would be a mockery without the limitations of it which are enforced on all for the benefit of all. "*Laissez-faire*" beyond these limits is not the doctrine of our author, but of William Godwin and modern Anarchists, who think that public spirit may be one day the universal substitute for the fear of the magistrate and the constable. Adam Smith could not have entertained such a view. What we call public spirit, he says, is frequently found in men without any humanity or humaneness of feeling; it is frequently a desire to improve a political system because of the mere love of order and method for their own sakes, as men remedy faults in a machine from a purely intellectual pleasure in beholding a perfect mechanism. On the other hand, men may be full of good nature (like James I. of England) without any public spirit.[119] That all men should be always alike imbued with all the virtues seems the only contingency that would make an enforced justice unnecessary.[120] But ideal virtue is very distantly approached, even by the chosen few; and ordinary virtue is far below such requirements.[121] Gradual progress, whether in politics,[122] ethics, or economics, seems to Adam Smith the natural and safe progress. He never speaks as if it could ever go so far as to make the State superfluous.

Human affections seemed to him to extend from narrower circles to wider by a natural order of precedence and succession.[123] One of the larger circles was a man's own country; and the love of country involves two different and

not always harmonious principles, regard for the good of society and regard
for the stability of political institutions. When there is conflict between them,
as in times of Revolution, the former should prevail.[124] Reconstruction of
political institutions may be indispensable; the "greatest and noblest of all
characters" is that of the reformer and legislator of a great State,[125] though, in
general, stability and order should be sedulously maintained. For himself, our
author is more cosmopolitan than patriotic. He speaks severely of the idea
that nations can be natural enemies.[126] Both nations gain by a trade between
them, just as both parties to every fair bargain between individuals gain by it;
and, if trade were only free, the different countries of the earth would (in matters of trade) resemble the different provinces of a single empire.[127] The progress of cultivation, invention, art and science of every kind, and everywhere,
means a "real improvement of the world we live in. Mankind are benefited;
human nature is ennobled by them" (Moral Sent., II. 98).

To our author, therefore, economical truths are like the matters of science
generally: they have no nationality; the facts are true for all the world, not
for one nation only, but for all societies of men everywhere. But the State is
treated as something mechanical. We hear of "the political machine,"[128] and
of "that insidious and crafty animal vulgarly called the statesman or politician."[129] There is a natural jurisprudence, certain principles on which every
legislator should proceed; but they are the "natural rules of justice, independent of all positive institutions."[130] The State is profitable for defence, justice,
and for public works; in other words, for such works as are every one's
business and no one's business.[131] Beyond these limits our author has little
regard for the State; he respects society so long as it is not acting collectively.
He regards the personal head of the State as ordinary flesh and blood: "All
the innocent blood shed in the civil wars provoked less indignation than the
death of Charles I.," and yet the agony of dissolution is the same to those of
low degree as to those of high rank.[132]

"Nature" here at least is (he admits) not identical with Reason. Reason
teaches us that kings are the servants of the people; nature teaches us rather
that they are superior beings who may exact abject obedience.[133]

This last admission points us to a weakness in Adam Smith's whole argument. He cannot in the case of man avoid sliding from the notion of Nature,
as the divine reason working in him without his will, into the notion of
Nature as mere instinct and custom, rational or irrational.

"Natural liberty," like Christian liberty, might easily become a cloak of
maliciousness without ceasing to be "natural" in the *latter* sense. Our author
was influenced by Hume, whose *Treatise of Human Nature* he had read as
early as his college days.[134] There are "a natural price," "natural wages," a
"natural order," which human nature, as distinguished from human institutions, will discover for itself; and men's "natural liberty" will be simply the
absence of any hindrance to this spontaneous action of human nature. Adam
Smith's *Wealth of Nations* is in fact, so far as it has one single purpose, a
vindication of the unconscious law present in the separate actions of men

when these actions are directed by a certain strong personal motive. It is an attempt (in later language) to show the purely economical categories bursting through all historical hindrances. There is an objective standard of good and bad economy, and it is possible to say that the mass of men have been tending towards good economy so far as their hindrances have allowed them. Our author's system of natural liberty would not lead to perfect economy unless men are, for the sake of the argument, supposed to be infallible in judging their interests and singleminded in pursuing them. Our standard would thus be the acts and results that follow from these suppositions, in other words from the method criticised very generally now as abstract and deductive. The method consists in considering one particular end and motive of human life in detachment from the rest, and afterwards replacing it in its context. It would be beyond criticism if only it could be applied to each and every one of the separate ends and motives, and not to one (desire of Wealth) alone. But the others, *e.g.* desire of Honour, relate to less tangible objects and less imperious needs, and are (largely on this account) less definable and less separable even in thought from one another. Malthus may be said to have treated one of them in this way, but he quickly saw how short a distance this method could carry him. Adam Smith tries to show the strength of one desire in midst of modifications as well as in abstraction from them,—whereas Malthus, in the case of a different desire, spends nearly all his strength on the concrete modifications. Even in regard to the pursuit of wealth the abstraction from all other motives is difficult, for (except to a few misers) wealth is not an end in itself, and yet when we abstract from all other motives we seem to be treating it as such. Adam Smith runs the risk of this misconception in almost every chapter of his *Wealth of Nations*. It is clear, from such passages as the eloquent description of the ideally Prudent Man, in the *Moral Sentiments*,[135] that there is no narrowness in his own mind; but he certainly would have saved himself obloquy if he had in all cases made it clear when he was reasoning abstractly from the supposition above mentioned and when he was giving the historical facts. There is room for suspicion that he overpasses the limits between theoretical economy and history when he speaks in one place of "the property which every man has in his own labour" as the "original foundation of all other property" and also the "most sacred and inviolable,"[136] and in another place of the "sacred regard" to life and property, in the conventional sense, as the foundation of justice and humanity.[137] There would not be even the appearance of contradiction if the notion of liberty were more positively defined, so as to include opportunities of development[138] and not simply relief from interference, and if the notion of law had not been opposed to that of custom. The respect accorded to superior rank and fortune seems to him healthy on the whole because it is custom; and yet, we all know, in great measure the distinctions of rank and fortune are preserved if not created by laws in which the customs are embodied and defined. It is possible that Adam Smith's projected treatise on Natural Jurisprudence would have dealt with such points. As his work stands, they are not adequately treated.

Neither is the distinction of Society and State consistently maintained. After accustoming us to view the State as a body almost hostile to progress and mainly of use in protecting us against injustice and violence,[139] a committee of the nation with less than the virtues and more than the faults of the average citizen, he commits to the State the maintenance of popular education, in the Schools and even (with reservations) in the Churches. He does not see that, once we admit that the State can act as parent and guardian of the people, if only in matters sanitary[140] and educational, we have passed beyond the mediæval notion to a modern notion of the State which has more affinity with Greece than with mediæval Europe, involving an action that is more than purely regulative. This modern notion would colour even the economical conception of Taxation; the taxes could not be treated (as for the most part they are in the *Wealth of Nations*) as a *quid pro quo*, an equivalent for a service rendered by State to individual, a service as exactly measurable as the recompense for service rendered by a tradesman to his customer, or by an agent to his principal. Adam Smith probably means no more than that the advantages of government should be at least equal to the cost of it; and his inclusion of Church and University, to say nothing of schools, among benefits to which the State makes contribution, would itself show that he thought better of the State than his own language sometimes suggests. It is only in the earliest statement of his views [141] that we find protection and light taxes brought forward as substantially the only desiderata in a good State.[142] Both philosophy and economics were conconcerned in the solution of these difficulties; but the solution was not then ready.

Note (I.) Books on Adam Smith

Professor Wilhelm Hasbach, of Königsberg, has lately published two books in which the economical doctrines of Adam Smith are brought into relation with his philosophical. The earlier of these (*Die allgemeinen philosophish-cen Grundlagen der von F. Quesnay und Adam Smith begriindeten politis-chen Oekonomie*, 1890) is largely a comparison of the Physiocratic doctrine of natural rights and laws with the views of Adam Smith. The second (*Untersuchungen über Adam Smith*, 1891) includes an elaborate comparison of the ethical views of our author with those of his predecessors, especially Hutcheson and Hume. The above chapters cannot compete with such monographs in exhaustiveness. Professor Hasbach argues that in spite of Adam Smith's own declarations, his doctrine of Sympathy is essentially that of Hume's. (See especially *Untersuchungen*, pp. 90 *seq.*)

Besides the work of Oncken already cited (pp. 169, 170), there may be noted here, out of the multitude of other writings on Adam Smith, the essays of Cliffe Leslie (*Essays in Moral and Political Philosophy*, 1879), and Bagehot (*Biographical Studies*, 1881), the bibliography appended to Mr. R. B. Haldane's *Adam Smith* (1887), J. A. Farrer's analysis of the *Moral Sentiments* ("Adam Smith," 1881). In French there are the books of Du Puynode (1868) and Delatour (1886). No one has as yet "dragged the ponds" so thoroughly for biographical details as the German Professor E. Leser, *Lebensgeschichte Adam Smith's* (1881). Dr. R. Zeyss, in his *Adam Smith und der Eigennutz* (1889), takes the pains to give grave refutation to the notion of Skarzynski (*Adam Smith als Moral-Philosoph*, 1878), that our author changed in 1776 the doctrines he had taught in 1759, because in the interval he had travelled in France and become a Materialist. Zeyss disposes also of Buckle's idea (*History of Civilization in Europe*) that in the one book men were regarded as moved purely by selfishness, and in the other as moved purely by benevolence. As regards Adam Smith's relation to French writers, it has hardly been noticed how he himself describes the opinions of Rousseau and the Encyclopedists in his *Letter to the Authors of the Edinburgh Review* (1755). He says of Rousseau's treatise on *Inequality among Men:* "Whosoever reads this last work with attention will observe that the second volume of the *Fable of the Bees* has given occasion to the system of Mr. Rousseau, in whom however the principles of the English author are softened, improved, and embellished, and stripped of all that tendency to corruption and licentiousness which has disgraced them in their original author. Dr. Mandeville represents the primitive state of mankind as the most wretched and miserable that can be imagined. Mr. Rousseau on the contrary paints it as the happiest and most suitable to his nature. Both of them, however, suppose that there is in man no powerful instinct which necessarily determines him to seek society for its own sake; but, according to the one, the misery of his original state compelled him to have recourse to this otherwise disagreeable remedy; according to the other, some unfortunate accidents, having given birth to the unnatural passions of ambition and the vain desire of superiority, to which he had before been a stranger, produced the same fatal effect. Both of them suppose the same slow progress, and gradual development of all the talents, habits, and arts which fit men to live together in society, and they both describe this progress pretty much in the same manner. According to both, those laws of justice which maintain the present inequality amongst mankind were originally the inventions of the cunning and the powerful in order to maintain or to acquire an unnatural and unjust superiority over the rest of their fellow creatures. Mr. Rousseau however criticises Dr. Mandeville; he observes that pity, the only amiable principle which the English author allows to be natural to man, is capable of producing all those virtues whose reality Dr. Mandeville denies. Mr. Rousseau at the same time seems to think that this principle is in itself no virtue, but that it is possessed by savages and by the most profligate of the vulgar in a greater degree of perfection than by those of the most polished and cultivated manners—in which he perfectly agrees with the English author.

"The life of a savage, when we take a distant view of it, seems to be a life either of profound indolence or of great and astonishing adventures; and both these qualities serve to render the description of it agreeable to the imagination. The passion of all young people for pastoral poetry which describes the amusements of the indolent life of a shepherd, and for books of poetry, chivalry, and romance, which describe the most dangerous and extravagant adventures, is the effect of this natural taste for these two seemingly inconsistent objects. In the descriptions of the manners of savages we expect to meet with both these, and no author ever proposed to treat of this subject who did not excite the public curiosity. Mr. Rousseau, intending to paint the savage life as the happiest of any, presents only the indolent side of it to view, which he exhibits indeed with the most beautiful and agreeable colours in a style which, though coloured and studiously elegant, is everywhere sufficiently nervous, and sometimes even sublime and pathetic. It is by the help of this style, together with a little philosophical chemistry, that the principles and ideas of the profligate Mandeville seem in him to have all the purity and sublimity of the morals of Plato, and to be only the true spirit of a republican carried a little too far " (*Edinburgh Review*, 1755, part ii. pp. 73–75).

Note (II.) Duties as Divine Commandments

In view of Oncken's comparison of Adam Smith and Kant, a passage of the first edition of the *Moral Sentiments* (p. 203) may be quoted here, as it was omitted in later editions, and is probably new to many readers. It shows how Adam Smith, unlike Hume, kept in view not only the Greek idea of vice, but the Hebrew sense of sin. It may also explain the popularity of the book in clerical circles, attested by Hume.[143]

"That the Deity loves virtue and hates vice, as a voluptuous man loves riches and hates poverty, not for their own sakes but for the effects which they tend to produce, that he loves the one only because it promotes the happiness of society which his benevolence prompts him to desire, and that he hates the other only because it occasions the misery of mankind, which the same Divine quality renders the object of his aversion, is not the doctrine of nature, but of an artificial though ingenious refinement of philosophy. All our natural sentiments prompt us to believe that, as perfect virtue is supposed necessarily to appear to the Deity as it does to us, for its own sake and without any further view, the natural and proper object of love and reward, so must vice, of hatred and punishment. That the gods neither resent nor hurt was the general maxim of all the different sects of the ancient philosophy; and, if by resenting be understood that violent and disorderly perturbation which often distracts and confounds the human breast, or if by hurting be understood the doing mischief wantonly and without regard to propriety and justice, such weakness is undoubtedly unworthy of the Divine perfection. But, if it be meant that vice does not appear to the Deity to be for its own sake the object of abhorrence and aversion, and what for its own sake it is fit and right should be punished, the truth of this maxim can by no means be so easily admitted. If we consult our natural sentiments, we are apt to fear lest before the holiness of God, vice should appear to be more worthy of punishment than the weakness and imperfection of human virtue can ever seem to be of reward. Man when about to appear before a being of infinite perfection can feel but little confidence in his own merit or in the imperfect propriety of his own conduct. In the presence of his fellow creatures, he may often justly elevate himself, and may often have reason to think highly of his own character and conduct, compared to the still greater imperfection of theirs. But the case is quite different when about to appear before his infinite Creator. To such a being he can scarce imagine that his littleness and weakness should ever seem to be the proper object either of esteem or of reward. But he can easily conceive how the numberless violations of duty, of which he has been guilty, should render him the proper object of aversion and punishment; neither can he see any reason why the Divine indignation should not be let loose without any restraint upon so vile an insect as he is sensible that he himself must appear to be. If he would still hope for happiness, he is conscious that he cannot demand it from the justice, but that he must entreat it from the mercy of God. Repentance, sorrow, humiliation, contrition at the thought of his past conduct, are, upon this account, the sentiments which become him, and seem to be the only means which he has left for appeasing that wrath which, he knows, he has justly provoked. He even distrusts the efficacy of all these, and naturally fears lest the wisdom of God should not, like the weakness of men, be prevailed upon to spare the crime, by the most importunate lamentations of the criminal. Some other intercession, some other sacrifice, some other atonement, he imagines, must be made for him beyond what he himself is capable of making, before the purity of the Divine justice can be reconciled to his manifold offences. The doctrines of revelation coincide in every respect with those original anticipations of nature; and, as they teach us how little we can depend upon the imperfection of our own virtue, so they show us at the same time that the most powerful intercession has been made, and that the most dreadful atonement has been paid for our manifold transgressions and iniquities."

Note (III.) Machines

With the references on page 151, etc., compare *Moral Sentiments*, 6th ed., I. 455 (on the accuracy of watches), and the essay on the *Formation of Languages* (*ibid.*, II. 455), where the gradual simplification of languages is likened to the simplification of a mechanical invention. It should be remembered that Adam Smith took an active part in befriending James Watt, when, in 1757, "he was molested by some of the corporations who considered him as an intruder on their privileges," and was allowed to open his shop within the precincts of the University (see Arago, *Life of Watt*).

But see Hasbach, *Allgemeine philosophische Grundlage*, pp. 140–147.

Notes

1 See especially bk. II. ch. xii.: "Of the Values of Goods and of Coins," pp. 209 *seq.*
2 General Steuart, who gives a biography of his father in the sixth vol. of the collected works of the latter (Cadell, 1805, pp. 388 *seq.*) compares the two authors

very impartially, and makes no such complaint. The question is fully discussed in Prof. Hasbach's *Untersuchungen über Adam Smith* (1891).

3 *History of Civil Society*, 4th ed. 1773, p. 242 (not in 1st ed. 1767). Ferguson's *Moral Philosophy* (1769), written for his Edinburgh students, includes a chapter on "public œconomy," partly borrowed from Harris.

4 1st ed. p. 546. Cf. *Wealth of Nations*, V. 1. 346 (MacCulloch's edition).

5 His lectures on Logic were destroyed before his death. *Essays*, page xvi.

6 See his *Essays* (1790), on the Imitative Arts and Italian Verses, for a taste of his quality as a critic; also on the State of Literature in Europe, in the old *Edin. Review*, 1755, No. ii.

7 *Life*, by Dug. Stewart, in *Essays*, p. xvii. *seq.*

8 See *W. of N.*, V. 1. 346.

9 Dug. Stew., *loc. cit.*

10 *Mor. Sent.*, 1759, last paragraphs.

11 Compare 1st ed. 1759, p. 549, 6th ed. 1790, vol. ii. p. 397.

12 George Wilson's letter to Bentham, 14th July, 1787 (Bentham, *Wks.*, vol. x. 173, 174) gives us an idea how Adam Smith was hampered by ill health in the later years of his life: "Dr. Smith has been very ill here of an inflammation ... The physicians say he may do some time longer. He is much with the ministry, and the clerks at the public offices have orders to furnish him with all papers, and to employ additional hands, if necessary, to copy for him. I am vexed that Pitt should have 'done so right' a thing as to consult Smith; but, if any of his schemes are effectuated, I shall be comforted."

13 *Essays* (publ. 1790)—"The History of Astronomy," pp. 20 *seq.*

14 *Ib.*, 25; cf. *W. of N.*, IV. ii. 199, 2.

15 *Essays*, p. 25.

16 *W. of N.*, IV. ii. 199, 2.

17 *Essays*, p. 26.

18 From this point of view the passage in *Moral Sent.* (1st ed.), p. 351 *seq.* and esp. 355, may seem an "apologia pro vitâ suâ."

19 *Essays*, p. 44.

20 *Ibid.*, p. 93. He himself so applies them when he says in *Moral Sent.*, II. 118, that God made the "machine of the universe" so as to produce "the greatest possible quantity of happiness."

21 *W. of N.*, I. 1. 5, 2.

22 *Essays*, p. 18.

23 Above, pp. 147–149.

24 He seems to have begun the book as early as 1764. See Burton's *Life of Hume*, II. 228.

25 *W of N.*, IV., Introd.

26 *Ib.*, IV. ix. 307, 1.

27 See *W. of N.*, 304, 2.

28 Dug. Stewart, *Pol. Ec.* (ed. Hamilton, 1855), vol. i. p. 9 (written *circa* 1810). Cf. Pryme, Introd. Lecture (Cambridge), 1823.

29 Cf. Courcelle-Seneuil, *Ad. Smith* (*Petite Biblioth. Écon.*), p. xix.

30 *W. of N.*, I. Introd., pp. 1, 2. Cf. II. iii., 149, 1, 150, 151, etc.

31 IV. ix. 307, 1.

32 *Wealth of Nations*, IV. iii. 220, 2.

33 Professor Leser makes a praiseworthy attempt to draw a complete theory of wealth from Adam Smith. See his *Begriff des Reichthums bei Adam Smith* (1874).

34 Bk. V., ch. ii., p. 393. "Taxes upon consumable commodities,"1874.

35 IV. III. pt. ii. 217, 2.

36 1st ed., p. 483 *seq.*

37 *Moral Sent.* (6th ed.), II. 118, cf. 414, 1. Cf. the attack on Asceticism in *W. of N.*, V. 1. 346.
38 *Moral Sent.* (1st ed.), pp. 350, 351.
39 *W. of N.*, I. 1. p. 6. Locke had said the same before him. See above, page 93.
40 E.g. *Formation et Distribution des Richesses* (1766), § 16, cf. § 6.
41 It may be said to appear even in the early essay on the Formation of Languages (*Moral Sent.*, 6th ed., vol. ii., appendix). All words are represented as at first absolutely concrete and particular; their generalization comes gradually afterwards. Cf. Romanes, *Mental Evolution in Man* (1888).
42 *W. of N.*, I. II. 7, 8. Cf. Hume, *Essays*, I. 531.
43 See above.
44 *W. of N.*, I. II. 6, 2.
45 *Ib.*, p. 7, 1.
46 Though he uses similes from Physiology, *e.g.* IV. ix. 304, 2.
47 One of the latest and most complete monographs on the hackneyed subject of Division of Labour is that of Schmoller in *Jahrb. für Gesetzgebung*, 13th series, 3rd part, 1889, pp. 57 *seq.*
48 *W. of N.*, I. iv. 13; cf. I. xi. 79.
49 *Human Understanding*, § viii. Of Liberty and Necessity. *Essays*, vol. ii., p. 98.
50 See *W. of N.*, I. x.; cf. VI. 22.
51 *W. of N.*, I. v. 15, 1.
52 *Ibid.*, 14.
53 See above, p. 153.
54 Amongst his followers, Edmund Burke expressed this view with startling frankness. See *Thoughts and Details on Scarcity* (1795).
55 I. VIII. 31.
56 I. VIII. 36, 1.
57 For the passage implies that below a certain point the want of wealth produces a want of happiness.
58 *W. of N.*, I. XI. 115, 156.
59 From this point of view it is not fair to argue that, if *all* labour were like that of domestic servants or doctors, there would be no wealth for anybody (Cf. *W. of N.*, IV. v. 224.)
60 *W. of N.*, II. III. 154.
61 IV. IX. 311, 1.
62 IV. IX. 311, 1.
63 *Moral Sent.*, 6th ed., ii. 263.
64 *W. of N.*, IV. II. 199, 2.
65 *This locus classicus* is *W. of N.*, II. III. 151; cf. 128.
66 *Moral Sent.*, 1st, 465; 6th, II. 62, 295–6.
67 *Ibid.*, 6th ed., II. 69 *seq.*, 93–99, cf. 88.
68 1st, p. 188: "he can subsist only in society," etc.
69 *Moral Sent.*, 6th ed. II. 99.
70 1st ed., p. 29. Compare the passage of Hume quoted above, p. 156.
71 1st ed., 198.
72 *Moral Sent.*, 1st ed., p. 6. 6th ed., I. p. 7.
73 1st ed., p. 27 *seq.*; 6th, I. 29.
74 Cf. 1st ed., p. 49; 6th ed., I. p. 53.
75 Adam Smith says so himself in his chapters on the Influence of Custom, but he thinks the effect is of degree only, 1st ed., p. 371 *seq.*, and esp. 412, 6th ed., II. 1 *seq.* and 48.
76 1st ed., p. 141 *seq.*; 6th ed., I. 161 *seq.*
77 1st ed., p. 158; 6th ed., I. p. 179.

78 See *e.g.* 1st ed., p. 254. The chapter is altered in later editions.
79 1st ed., p. 273; 6th ed., p. 402.
80 1st ed., p. 283. Altered in later editions.
81 1st ed, pp. 45, 308, 310; 6th ed., pp. 48, 439, 442.
82 See the title page of 6th edition: "*The Theory of Moral Sentiments*, or an Essay towards an analysis of the principles by which men naturally judge concerning the conduct and character first of their neighbours and afterwards of themselves." The title of the first edition is simply: *The Theory of Moral Sentiments*.
83 1st ed., p. 254. Contrast Rousseau. See note to this chapter.
84 *Ib.*, 181.
85 *Ib.*, 183.
86 *Ib.*, p. 189.
87 *Ib.*, 190, cf. 6th, I. 407.
88 1st ed., 191.
89 1st ed., p. 199.
90 *e.g.*, 203.
91 *e.g.* 1st ed., 208. This is one of the positions in which Oncken finds Adam Smith akin to Kant; but it is really Greek.
92 1st ed., 283; cf. 6th, I. 395.
93 1st ed., 284.
94 Cf. Dante, *Inf.*, VII. 68.
95 1st. ed., 289; cf. 6th, II. 50, etc.
96 See the well-known sermon of Robertson of Brighton on this text.
97 *Moral Sent.*, 1st. ed., 290–292; 6th, II. 65. Such passages lead Oncken to say that Adam Smith re-introduced Teleology into Philosophy. *Adam Smith und Im. Kant* (1877), p. 61.
98 Optimism, he considers, is natural to men; most men have an overweening confidence in their own luck (*Wealth of Nations*, I. x. 48, 2).
99 *Moral Sent.*, 6th ed., I. 366.
100 *Ib.*, 368. Happiness depends more on the mind than on the body. Cf. *Wealth of Nations*, V. I. 353, I.
101 *M.S.*, 1st ed., 351.
102 1st ed., 97, 98.
103 *Wealth of Nations*, I. VIII. 37, 2.
104 *Ib.*, I. VIII. 36.
105 *Moral Sent.*, 1st ed., 398.
106 *Wealth of Nations*, I. VIII. 37, 1.
107 *Moral Sent.*, 1st ed., p. 485; cf. whole passage, 474 to 486.
108 *Wealth of Nations*, V. II., art. IV. 393.
109 Necessity is a great spur to exertion. See *Wealth of Nations*, V. 1. II. 341, etc. But ambition is treated as a greater, throughout.
110 See Swift, *Gulliver* (Brobdingnag, ch. viii.).
111 *Moral Sent.*, 1st ed., pp. 348–351 ("The Effect of Utility"). Compare Dr. Johnson (*Life of Drake*, in Dodsley's *Fugitive Pieces*, I. 211): "Happiness and misery are equally diffused through all states of human life."
112 *Moral Sent.*, 1st ed., pp. 452, 453.
113 See above [Hume, p. 124].
114 *e.g. Wealth of Nations*, I. x. 57, 59.
115 *Ib.*, I. x. 59.
116 *Ib.*, III. I. 169, IV. 185.
117 Cf. *Moral Sent.*, 1st ed., pp. 290–292.
118 *Inter alia, W. of N.*, II. III. 154; cf. 199, 1, etc., etc.
119 *Moral Sent.*, 1st ed., 350–353.

120 *Moral Sent.*, ıst ed. 357.
121 6th ed., "Of the Character of Virtue," II. 146 *seq.*
122 See the passage apparently aimed at the Revolutionary parties of France, 6th ed., 106–108.
123 See above, p. 162.
124 *Moral Sent.*, 6th, II. 104.
125 *Ib.*, 106; cf. II. 94 *seq.*
126 *Ib.*, II. 100.
127 *W. of N.*, IV. v. 240.
128 *Moral Sent.*, ıst ed., 352.
129 *W. of N.*, IV. ıı. 201.
130 *Moral Sent.*, 6th ed., II., 397–398.
131 *W. of N.*, Bk. V.
132 *Moral Sent.*, ıst ed, 114.
133 *Ibid.*, ıst ed., 115.
134 It was probably a copy sent by the author. See Burton's *Life of Hume* (1846), I. 116.
135 6ᵗʰ ed., II. 50–65
136 *W. of N.*, I. x. 55.
137 6th ed., *Moral Sent.*, I. 378–379.
138 This gap is partly filled by *W. of N.*, V. ı., where *inter alia* he insists on Popular Education to remedy the bad effects of division of labour, already pointed out by Ferguson, *Civil Society* (1767), Part IV.
139 Violence against *property* in particular. See the striking passage in *W. of N.*, V. ı., pt. ii., 319.
140 *W. of N.*, V. 1. 353. (To prevent the spread of diseases.)
141 *I.e.* the paper quoted by Dugald Stewart as having been drawn up by Adam Smith in 1755. See *Life of Adam Smith* prefixed to his *Philos. Essays*, p. lxxxi.
142 For a different vindication see Prof. E. Sax, *Theoret. Staatswirthschaft*, pp. 48, 49 (1887).
143 In a letter quoted by Dug. Stewart, *Life of Adam Smith* (prefixed to *Essays*), pp. xlvii.–xlix.

9   Natural Rights and Law of Nature

The expression natural rights played so conspicuous a part in the politics and political philosophy of last century, especially at the time of the Encyclopedists and Physiocrats and Adam Smith, that a few words must be added here on the connection between natural rights, law of nature, and state of nature. It is important not only to know the ambiguities and errors[1] associated with these terms, but the sense (if there be such) in which they may still safely be used. The commonest use of "natural" is probably in the sense of "instinctive." Macduff "wants the *natural* touch," the *instinct* of an animal to fight for its young. Hamlet's father considered his own murder to be "most foul, strange, and *unnatural*," because against the instincts of kindred. This sense throws no light on "natural rights," for instinct might be pleaded to justify a frank selfishness that defied all claims but its own.[2] But it frequently passes into a sense which has a decided bearing on "rights." In such passages as "unnatural deeds do breed unnatural troubles,"[3] the second "unnatural" implies that there is a certain order or harmony, the preservation of which would be "natural." It leans on the idea of a law of nature, analogous to the order that makes the sun rise. It is implied in such sayings as "nature abhors a vacuum," "leave nature to work her own cure," "leave him to time and the medicating effects of nature." This is an intelligible conception. It is that of deliberate human action on the one side, and all the materials and forces with and on which it works on the other side; and it implies that sometimes it is best to abstain from all deliberate action, and simply drift with wind and tide, acting spontaneously or not at all.

It might, however, be shown that not *all* but only some classes of spontaneous action result in any *order* at all as far as human life is concerned. "Nature" sometimes kills as well as cures. There is no consistency possible here; the same people who contrast "nature" with human deliberate action would not deny that human deliberation is itself perfectly "natural." This popular contrast of nature with deliberate human action was at one time a theory of the philosophers (*idolon theatri*), as well as a vague theory of common folk (*idolon fori*). Theories founding human society on a law of nature have often defined nature negatively by contrast with deliberate human contrivance. Institutions like the Post Office or the Board of Trade which result from the deliberations of a legislative assembly are contrasted with those which, like the family and the commercial relations of men, seem to have grown up spontaneously, and to have been the collective result of separate human actions in which nothing more than a separate result had been intended by the several agents. This is to a large extent the notion of nature to be found in the Physiocrats. It is the foundation of their demand for "*laissez-faire*," and it lurks in Adam Smith's notion of the "simple system of natural liberty."[4] To do the doctrine justice, we must however look to its philosophical origin and growth in the pages of Grotius, Hobbes, and Locke. In the last of these we find the conception of the law of nature not as a moral law written on the heart, but as the pursuit of happiness in obedience to a "natural" impulse; and civil laws secure this happiness by securing to every man the fruits of his labour.

Locke was the source of the doctrine of *natural rights* as it afterwards appeared (1) in America, and (2) in France. By nature (he says, as we saw above) men are free and equal; children are born *for* this and mature manhood *has* it; the law of nature wills a liberty that is consistent with the liberty of others. But the doctrine came to the American Colonies and to the French people, not directly from Locke, but filtered through the medium of French writers. Hume's criticism (that the Golden Age is the fiction of the poets, and the State of Nature the fiction of the philosophers) made no impression; Hume's criticisms were only accepted, like Voltaire's, where they were palateable, which meant chiefly where they touched theology. The law of nature was still preached by French philosophers and economists; and by the people it was welcomed, as vaguely felt to be the opposite of things as they then were, in a highly artificial society full of political and other inequalities. In the popular mind, however, the idea of a State of Nature bulked more largely than any Law of Nature; and it was Rousseau[5] who brought the former notion into favour. In the state of nature men were uncorrupted; their manners were rude, and their life had its discomforts; but they were nearer what the law of nature made them than in society and under civil government. "Men are born free, and they are everywhere in chains." Men are good by nature and made bad by society. Civil society begins with the first claim to private property. "He, who first enclosed a strip of land, and said, 'it is mine,' and found folk simple enough to believe him, was the real founder of civil society" (*Inégalité*, part ii.). The social contract which creates the State is perhaps necessary, for men are stronger when so combined, but the ideal political government (as well as the ideal private Education) is that in which there is the minimum of interference, and "Nature" is allowed to do her own work.

But, as men are stronger to carry out the law of nature in society and the State, these latter come into being; only (be it noted) the "sovereignty of the people" remains as absolute after the foundation as before it. The government is only justified in existing when it represents the "general will." And there is emphasis on *will*; it is not a mere superior force—not might asserting itself as right. The difficulty is that this sovereignty of the people is represented as one and indivisible, qualities hard to reconcile with the domination of *majorities*, where there is simply a "general will," not the "will of *all.*' This will of all may be expressed best by assemblies of the whole people, though often they may err and not seek really the good of all, through defective information and bias of private interests in their advisers (see *Contr. Soc.*, II., chap. iii., etc.). But, however the difficulties are surmounted, Rousseau's contention at least is quite plain. The same natural rights that belonged to men *before* government must belong to them after its foundation. No State is legitimate in which this is not so, and, as this is so (according to him) only by the constant reference to the *whole* people, we may infer[6] that the Swiss federation of small States—small enough to admit such a reference—was in his thoughts. The dominance of the idea of a Federation of Communes in the minds of many Frenchmen if not due only to Rousseau's influence,[7] has been evidently assisted by it.

There are two public documents in particular in which the Rights of Man are described and asserted with special emphasis. The first is the American Declaration of Independence, 4th July, 1776,[8] a document prepared by Thomas Jefferson, who was well read in English philosophy. The influence of Locke is unmistakeable. "Men are created equal, they are endowed by their Creator with certain inalienable rights—among these, life, liberty, and the pursuit of happiness. To secure these rights, governments are instituted, deriving their just powers from the consent of the governed, and whenever any form of government becomes destructive of these ends, it is the right of the people to alter or abolish it and to institute a new government."

The second document is the Declaration of the Rights of Man and of Citizens adopted by the National Assembly of France, in 1789. "Considering that ignorance, neglect, and contempt of human rights are the sole causes of public misfortunes and corruptions of government," they "set forth in a solemn declaration these natural, imprescriptible and inalienable rights, in order that, this declaration being constantly present to their minds, the members of the social body may be ever kept attentive to their rights and to their duties," etc. The following are some of the rights of man and of citizens:—

1   Men are born and always continue free and equal in respect of their rights. Civil distinctions therefore can only be founded on public utility.
2   The end of all political associations is the preservation of the *natural rights of man*, and these are liberty, property, security, and resistance to oppression.
3   The nation is the source of all sovereignty.
4   Political liberty consists in the power of doing whatever does not injure others.
5   The law ought to prohibit only actions hurtful to society.[9]

There is something here not only of Locke and Rousseau but of the Physiocrats. It is curious that Burke[10] found fault with the Declaration as inconsistent with any hereditary right, while Bentham saw in it an attempt to bind posterity by a premature definition of eternal truths.[11] Paine, who defended it against Burke, tends to the same conclusion as Bentham; and their conclusion may be described in the words, "*laissez-faire*," a Physiocratic maxim. "Government," says Paine, "is nothing more than a national association for the good of all, individually and collectively. Every man wishes to pursue his occupation and to enjoy the fruits of his labours, and the produce of his property in peace and safety, and with the least possible expense. *When these things are accomplished, all the objects for which governments ought to be established are answered.*"[12] Bentham, for his part, was the father of the Philosophical Radicals, who were identified with *laissez-faire* for two generations after the French Revolution. Yet of "natural rights" he is a keen critic.

One of the chief objections to "natural rights" imprescriptible, inalienable, anterior to civil society, was the connection of them with a supposed State of Nature anterior to Civil Society. As a historical fact, no such state is known to have existed, and no such "social compact" is known to us. A contract of the kind would only be possible to people already "civilized," or disciplined by civil society. Primitive men seem to have been nearer than we are to Hobbes' State of War, not farther away from it; and they seem to have escaped by nothing so deliberate and definite as a contract. Historically men seem to be born not only not free or equal, but not even conscious that they ought to be so.

But apart altogether from history the question may be asked if there are not certain rights which are essential to the life of men as reasonable beings in whatever society they are and which may therefore be called in a special sense natural or at least fundamental. It is possible that in all the necessary relativity of governments there is a certain absolute element, the presence or absence of which determines whether or not a given society and government are to be considered really civilized.

In dealing with this question we may first of all give up the attempt to detach rights *from* society. Rights are *claims* on others, our fellows. Community of life is essential to the notion of a right. If there are any rights of animals,[13] for example, these could only be founded on the notion of a community of living beings of which they and we were members. Rights are not anterior to society in the sense of possibly existing where there was no society, or for one individual in abstraction. But neither are they purely the creation of the State. In the sense in which we have spoken of them as implying a common life—they are simply the other side of duties. No doubt "legal" rights have a narrow sense and imply discretion of the individual.[14] The right to send letters by the post, or to obtain gold from the Bank of England for one of its notes is the creation of law. But even many of such legal rights (defined by statutes) were once (undefined) customs, and are thence derived. This means that society and not the State is the ground on which they grow. Commercial law in particular is even yet in England the customs of the mercantile community, which the State ratifies but did not create.

It follows that a right might be anterior to the State, though not anterior to society. Does this countenance the use of the adjective "natural" in the sense of spontaneous?

Historically, it is doubtful if we are justified in going even so far. The recognition of the "rights" above quoted from the American and French Declarations has historically come very late, for the conviction that the end of good government is the good of the entire body of the governed was of slow growth. It is a logical result of the Christian principle of the equality of men and the value of each individual soul. But it is a result that has needed philosophy and politics, that is to say, deliberate analysis, to unfold it. The spontaneous development of the Church was not enough to bring it out.

When unfolded, the claim of right based on the Christian idea of human equality comes to be as follows:—

The moral life of man requires certain outward conditions for its development. This is the postulate to which we have in our own time arrived as the necessary postulate of all States and Governments;—they must be so ordered as to allow and secure for each individual as a member of society the conditions necessary for the development of the faculties of the said member.[15] On this general postulate may be founded the several claims distinguishable as "rights of man." The moral ideal being recognized, it follows that the external conditions necessary to realize it should he secured. Now, as the development of the individual is bound up with the development of the society in which he is (his action being powerless and purposeless apart from the others with whom he lives),—the securing of the required external conditions depends largely (though not wholly) on the society and on its organ of conscious deliberate collective action—the State. The postulate may be called natural in the sense of spontaneous, in so far as the right secured is the right to develop spontaneously. But (1) the right itself is not spontaneously present to every man, and (2) the action by which this right is asserted is by no means without deliberate consciousness, still less (3) is the action by which it is secured. It is therefore not strictly natural in the sense of spontaneous. It is rational, and it is that claim which reasonable beings come (after centuries) to make; and, if to be rational is to be natural, it is "natural," and the resulting rule of conduct may be called a "natural law." But there is no clear advantage in using words that could never dispense with a note of explanation.

Though it is anticipating a little of what will be said in the next book,[16] we may take three cases very familiar to us in our own times and more or less eagerly discussed for the last century or more,—the "right to live," the "right to work," and the "right to have leisure." These are frequently described as natural rights.

The first of these is only natural in the sense that a civilized society, being bound to secure the outward conditions of a moral life, is bound to secure the first of them—that the means of support be within reach of its members. But it does not follow that it must force each member to turn the possibility into actuality. There is no claim on society for more than a start in life, unless the claimant is beyond the power of starting of himself any more. Even the claim to secure the start goes beyond what Bentham and Paine had conceived to be the function of the State. It implies that the State is not simply "Anarchy plus the Constable," but has the positive function of trying to fit the runners for the race. This is a requirement of the public interest as a whole. In education and similar acts, it is not for the sake of the parents, but for the sake of the future citizens and the future commonwealth themselves, that we see that all have a fair start, so far as human arrangements can so order it.

The difficulty which is felt in regard to the "right to live" turns largely on the relation of the numbers of the people to their welfare as a whole. Children are brought into the world, whose parents have no means of feeding them. Are we to recognise indefinitely a right to be supported at the expense of others? The answer is that in childhood we are all so supported, and the question is on *whom* we are to depend. The question, instead of that of a child's claim to support, becomes that of a claim of grown-up people to bring children into the world improvidently. There is no right on any one's part to do this; there is no duty of which this right is the converse, or claim warranted by any ideal of society known to us now. The fact that more citizens may be ushered into the State than the State desires, is a proof that the State has been too indulgent to those that have become parents. That the children, once there, have a claim, seems beyond question.

The second claim of right which we have taken as an instance of alleged "natural rights" is the claim to be provided with such employment as will provide a living. It is the first claim (or claim to live) in a more advanced stage; and the difficulty here lies in making sure that the individual is really seizing the opportunities presented to him already. It needs to be remembered that a right is the converse of a duty. It must also be remembered that the claim is now advanced in a special form of society, in which the relation of wages-earner and employer is the dominant feature of industrial organization and livelihood is precarious. The utmost that seems lawful to grant is, that the accidents of life may make it necessary for the State to save the lives of its citizens by directing these citizens to a particular opportunity for labour, in the way of wages-earning or otherwise. But, as the main end is that the individual develope his own special faculties in his own way, the end is not served but foiled, when the work is chosen for him and prescribed to him by the State or by any other agency. Spontaneity is better than government, whenever there is a choice.

The third claim also (the claim for leisure) so far as it is justifiable is involved in the first. There is to be secured by the State to each citizen opportunity for the development of his faculties; and this development may be impossible if the inequalities of wealth are so great that the rich hold the poor at their mercy and compel them to work for bare living so long or so hard that no powers but the muscular are exerted, and these overexerted. But before we allow this to be a claim on the State we must be sure that it is possible for the State to fulfil it. "What cannot be accomplished ought not to be accomplished." Without the action of the persons concerned the State's action will not be successful; and the claim need go no farther than such a regulation on the State's part as will give the individual action the possibility of success. It is every man's duty to seek leisure enough to develop his whole man and his special gifts. It is therefore his right to do so. But his claim upon the State is simply that he shall find no hindrance not over-comeable by his own efforts, whether by vigorous personal action or action in combination with his fellows at his own discretion.

It will have appeared that the "natural rights" of man are not capable of being applied like a code of commandments to be learned by memory and carried out in a uniform way everywhere. They are founded on the necessity that certain external conditions be fulfilled before a rational or moral life can be lived, and these conditions may mean more or less according to the men and the circumstances. The term "natural rights," or even "rights" pure and simple, has often been used with a covert understanding of the *legal* meanings of rights, claims enforceable in a court of law and defined by statute. It is impossible to give them any such definiteness, and almost impossible to avoid risk of this confusion. When our forefathers talked of natural rights there was a truth in the conception conveyed by their words, but it is a truth perhaps more safely and clearly expressed now-a-days in some other way.

It may seem otherwise with the word "law," which in Economics at least has become too familiar to be easily dropped, and in Social Philosophy seems to be rather gaining than losing ground. But there are reasons for seriously restricting if not abandoning the use of this term also, whether accompanied or not by the adjective "natural."

There are two senses in which "law" is constantly used outside of economics and social philosophy. The first and oldest is that of a prescribed rule of conduct, issuing from the command of a legislator. The second (which was possibly derived from the first, Deity being taken as the legislator)[17] is that of a sequence of physical events from physical causes. Under certain conditions a certain phenomenon is expected to occur; and the uniformity of its occurrence is stated as a "law."

There is now a general agreement among modern economists than an "economic law" cannot mean a precept; but among ordinary men now (as among economists of past generations) the associations of "law" in the sense of precept have had an influence when "economic laws" have been mentioned; there has been a vague idea that Political Economy had prescribed courses of action which men were expected to follow. The "law of *laissez-faire*" is an expression which itself reveals the dangers of the ambiguity.

Apart from this objection there is another, that when mention is made of "economic laws" the hearer most readily thinks of something like the physical laws, with which science has tried to make him familiar. It may no doubt be contended that the laws of economics are on the same footing as physical laws; they are statements that, when certain conditions are given, certain phenomena will tend to present themselves. But there is this difference, that the economic conditions are more subject to change than the conditions contemplated in physical laws. Even physical science is not in haste to apply the term to all cases where under certain conditions certain phenomena occur, but confines it very largely to the primary uniformities from which large groups of others are derived. The law of gravitation is the most hackneyed instance, but none the less valid. It would be possible to confine the term law in political economy to such wide generalities as are likely to be exemplified in every community, civilized or uncivilized. It might be an economic law that under the conditions of human life on this planet human wants tend to multiply indefinitely: it might be an economic law that men tend to prefer the greater to the less gain, or to prefer the greater to the less quantity of the means of satisfying their wants. When we descend from such primary laws to laws of production and distribution, such as are described by J. S. Mill, in his *Political Economy*, we come to principles, no doubt as rigorously true under the conditions assumed for them, but far less frequently exemplified, because far less often finding their conditions fulfilled.

It seems by no means necessary to use the term at all. Adam Smith speaks of "principles" (which may be taken to mean simply general truths), not of laws.[18] The Physiocrats used the term freely, but there was in their reasonings a covert personification of the "order of nature," and law in their writings suggests legislative precept rather than the law of physical science. Still they are not far from the modern use; and Turgot, who was very closely in contact with them, seems to use the term in the later sense. "To recognise the primary and unique *laws* founded on nature itself, by which all values in commerce are balanced with each other, and fixed at a definite value, ... to perceive the reciprocal dependence of trade and agriculture, their close connection with laws and morals and all the operations of the government, etc. ... this is to look at the matter with the eye of a philosopher and a statesman" (*Éloge de Gournay*, 1759, near beginning). Malthus, when he speaks, of the "law" of population, might be considered to use the word in the physical sense; and the rhetoric of Burke, who speaks of the "laws of commerce" as "the laws of nature and therefore the laws of God" (*Thoughts and Details on Scarcity*, 1795) is hardly to be regarded as the language of an economist. Perhaps the earliest use of the term by an economist in the sense of what is now called "economic law" occurs in Ricardo's tract (1810) on the *High Price of Bullion*. Gold and Silver, he says, obey "the same laws as every other commodity." After this date the use became common;—we hear of laws of rent, profits, interest, etc.[19]

Since Jones, Cliffe Leslie, and the later Historical Economists, the term has perhaps been used more sparingly. It has been felt to be awkward to speak of general principles as "laws" when they are only exemplified in one or two countries, and inoperative in the greater number. This awkwardness has lent an apparent justification to the assertion that every land has its own economic laws as well as its own laws of government.

Whether or not there are permanently true principles, sequences of which the conditions are always realized, is a position which must not at this stage be discussed.[20]

Note

Mr. Herbert Spencer defends the use of the terms "natural rights" against Bentham, and later writers (including Jevons and Matthew Arnold) in *The Man versus the State*, pp. 87 *seq.* In substance his conclusion is that of T. H. Green. "To recognise and enforce the rights of individuals is at the same time to recognise and enforce the conditions to a normal social life. There is one vital requirement for both" (102). This is not the place to discuss Individualism *versus* Socialism: and it may only be remarked that Mr. Spencer furnishes another instance of the affinity of a doctrine of "natural rights" with *laissez-faire*. The affinity appears less strongly in Lorimer (*Institutes of Law*, Blackwood, 1880), who makes a powerful defence, on the principles of Krause, Trendelenburg, and Ahrens, which are closely akin to the view of T. H. Green (as will be shown in a later chapter) and Mr. H. Spencer.

Notes

1 Detailed, *e.g.*, in Bentham's *Anarchical Fallacies* (*Wks.*, vol. ii.), Lewis' *Use and Abuse of some Political Terms* (1832).
2   "Thou, nature, art my goddess; to thy law
      My services are bound."—*Lear*, I. ii.
3 *Macbeth*, V. i. 79.
4 See above, p. 162. As Cowper wrote: "God made the country and man made the town," so Adam Smith says, nature made early education domestic, and the education of a public school is man's invention (*Moral Sent.*, 6th ed., II. 79). "Those parts of education, it is to be observed, for the teaching of which there are no public institutions, are generally the best taught." *W. of N.*, V., ch. i., art. ii., p. 344, 1.
5 *Inégalité*, 1753; *Contrat Social*, 1762; *Émile*, 1762.
6 With Prof. Caird, *Essays on Literature and Philosophy* (1892), vol. i. p. 110.
7 See Prof. T. H. Green, *Works*, vol. ii. (Political Obligation), p. 398.
8 The text is given, *e.g.*, in the *Annual Register* [261], 1776.
9 The document is quoted in full in Paine's *Rights of Man* (1791–2).
10 *Reflections on the French Revolution* (1790).
11 *Anarch. Fallacies, Wks.*, vol. ii.
12 *Rights of Man*, II. 378.
13 A tract on the *Rights of the Brute Creation* is quoted in the *Annual Register*, 1776, *Miscell. Essays*, p. 176. A book on the subject was published a few years ago by Mr. E. B. Nicholson.
14 See Godwin, *Political Justice* (1st ed.), Book II. v., vol. i. p. iii.
15 See T. H. Green, *Polit. Obligation. Works*, II. 341, etc.
16 See below [Malthus], [Fichte], [Hegel].
17 Compare Eucken (Prof. R.) *Grundbegriffe der Gegenwart*, 2nd ed., 1892, pp. 173 *seq.* There is a full discussion of "Economic Laws" in Prof. Menger's *Methode der Socialwissenschaften* (1883).

18 Though in *Moral Sent.*, 1st ed., page 283, 6th ed., vol. i., 412, he says, "All general rules are commonly denominated laws," yet the examples he gives are the laws of motion and the laws of morality.
19 *E.g.* Malthus, on Rent (1815), p. 22, *Pol. Ec.* (1820), p. 13. Ricardo, *Princ. of Pol. Ec. and Tax.* (1817). Pref.
20 See below [J. S. Mill, and Marx].

Book III

Modern Philosophy (II)
Utilitarian Economics

1   Malthus (1766–1834)

In Pitt and Burke, Adam Smith at once obtained followers of his economic policy. In economic theory, Bentham early showed himself at once disciple and critic (*Letters on Usury*, 1787); but it was not Bentham's political philosophy but William Godwin's that led to the next step. Godwin's two books, *Political Justice* (January, 1793), and the *Enquirer* (1797) gave occasion to the Essay of Malthus on Population (1798).

Godwin's *Political Justice* has little or nothing to do with economics. It is a treatise on Society and Government and their relations to individual men. The ethics are not those of the *Moral Sentiments*. Godwin follows more closely the lines of Locke, and he has studied Swift, Rousseau, and Helvetius. Though he levies contributions on Hume and to a less extent on Adam Smith, he is no disciple of the latter.

Nevertheless, even in its ethics and political philosophy, his books have points of contact with Adam Smith's. The ruling individualism of the age appeared in both, though in different ways and in different degrees.

Burke in his *Vindication of Natural Society, or a View of the Miseries and Evils arising to Mankind from every Species of Artificial Society* (1756) had professed to apply to political philosophy the same destructive reasoning which he conceived Bolingbroke to have applied to religion and morals; but the deduction was meant as a *reductio ad absurdum*. Godwin in all earnestness adopts the thesis of the pseudo-Bolingbroke. Godwin may be said to have extended to political philosophy the doctrines which Adam Smith confined largely to trade. The institutions of society are represented by Adam Smith as hindering the commercial progress of nations; so in the *Political Justice* they are conceived as hindering moral and intellectual progress.[1] Like Adam Smith, Godwin takes deep thought for the independence and originality of men, and distrusts all associations.[2] He would abolish government so far as coercive, and would have no collective organization larger than the parish.[3] Society is to him only an "aggregation of individuals. Its claims and duties must be the aggregate of their claims and duties, the one no more precarious and arbitrary than the other."[4] Rousseau is wrong; civilization has been a benefit and not an evil,[5] but it is not identical with positive institutions, which have been on the contrary an obstacle to all movement and progress. "Government, even in its best state, is an evil."[6]

Individuality is of the very essence of human perfection.[7] If as a body we would reach truth, each man of us must be taught to inquire and think for himself, while at the same time communicating his thoughts to others, and getting the benefit of joint as well as independent effort. In any other sense there is no such thing, as collective wisdom; it is "among the most palpable of all impostures."[8] Patriotism, and even universal philanthropy, are too abstract. It is individual men that we are to make happy; happiness, to be real, must be individual; and, wherever there are individuals that understand the nature of political justice, *there* is my country.[9] Political justice itself is simply morality viewed in relation to other men (ἀρετή ἡ πρὸς ἕτερον); it is "that impartial treatment of every man in matters that relate to his happiness, which is measured solely by a consideration of the properties of the receiver and the capacity of him that bestows." Its impartiality does not make it a special virtue, but is simply the feature common to all moral acts. "The true standard of the conduct of one man towards another is justice. Justice is a principle which proposes to itself the production of the greatest sum of pleasure or happiness. Justice requires that I should put myself in the place of an impartial spectator of human concerns," without regard to my own predilections. "Justice is a rule of the utmost universality, and prescribes a specific mode of proceeding in all affairs by which the happiness of a human being may be affected."[10] Political philosophy, therefore, is a branch of ethics. We must not think we can justify political arrangements by referring to their historical origin; our only standard must be public welfare.[11]

Observe that Justice is now conceived positively instead of (as in Smith and Hume) negatively. Whatever conduct secures the maximum of happiness to the world of men, generally—that is justice. It is not avoidance of injury; it is positive beneficence. Morality, too, is the object for which external freedom from restraints of all kinds is desirable; if a man have moral qualities, there is little left for him to aspire after. Yet he cannot obtain them without a certain degree of intellectual enlightenment. Eminent virtue implies a large understanding and is inconsistent with stupidity and ignorance[12] (IV. iv. 259). It is a calculation of consequences, and therefore dependent on perception of truth.[13] Vice is unquestionably no more in the first instance than an error of judgment. But men differ less by nature than by circumstances; and enlightenment may become universal, for there is a "tendency to improvement" in the human race.[14] When men are enlightened, plain living and high thinking will be the order of the day, and the inequalities of riches and poverty that disgrace our present society will disappear of themselves. We shall attain "that simplicity which best corresponds with the real nature and wants of a human being" (VI. vii. 662). The glamour of distinction that leads men to strive after riches would vanish; and, though we should need more than the necessaries to which Mandeville would limit us, we should need much less than the superfluities of modern wealth. All property would be recognised to be a trust held for the public good, not as now, "a patent entitling one man to dispose of another man's labour" (3rd ed., vol. ii. 309, 311; cf. 1st, VIII. 1. 788 *seq.*, VIII. ii. 804). The ideal life would be one including work for each of us along with time for relaxation (V. xiii. 485); and, if all men worked now, the division of labour and the inventions of machinery would lose their present drawbacks and become pure gain to mankind (*Pol. J.*, VIII. vi. 844 *seq.*). They would in fact make it possible for all of us to live comfortably at the cost of only half-an-hour's labour a day.[15] Every one will have enough; no one will wish to commit the injustice of accumulating property. The only distinctions will be moral and intellectual.[16] Costly gratifications of sense will lose their charm; sensual desires will be weakened. As the earth becomes filled, men will probably cease to propagate and will live indefinitely long on the earth, instead.[17] Franklin's idea, that mind will one day become omnipotent over matter, will be perhaps so truly realized that we shall conquer the matter of our own bodies, so that the bodily machine shall never wear out. The objection[18] brought against systems of equality from "the excessive population" they would cause is thus groundless. Even on lower ground it could be met by the consideration that "things find their level," population is somehow proportioned to the food, and it will be a long time before the supplies of food will be exhausted. The earth itself may not last so long (VIII. vii. 861). Such is Godwin's theory.

The last conjecture is, no doubt, separable from the main argument. The main argument itself depends on an abstraction. Error, as Malebranche[19] said, is the universal cause of the misery of mankind; but men are reasonable beings; therefore truth will prevail over error; and of their own accord men will adopt the one perfect form of society, without laws or central government. In modern language, they will be not Socialists but Anarchists. In Platonic language, they will have no need of kings because they will be themselves philosophers. The idea is (as after 2,000 years it might easily be) larger than that of Plato, who thought that the redemption of society depended on the appearance of philosophic kings. But if the idea is greater, it is only the more impracticable. If it is a mistake to suppose men governed by a ruling passion, it is equally wrong to suppose them influenced by reason without any passion at all. Godwin allows that the victory of reason may be slow in coming; but he seems wrong in imagining that it could ever be complete, even in a single man, at any time, however far in the future. He was abstract, too, in his conception of rational society; it could only (he thinks) have one form, as opposed to the diversity that now prevails (III. vii. 181 *seq.*), the diversity allowed to individuals being denied to societies, for societies are mere aggregates of individuals, and have nothing that the units have not. Godwin's theory is the apotheosis of individualism and (in a sense) of Protestantism; a purified and enlightened individualism is not to him (as to Rousseau) the beginning, but the end of all human progress. He is the father not so truly of philosophical radicalism as of Anarchism.

The great objection to the theory is its violation of the axiom above quoted from Hume—of the uniformity of human nature. The axiom does not mean that men can never change for better or for worse, but that they cannot entirely lose an old attribute or gain an entirely new one,—men as such having specific qualities, the absence of which makes them cease to be men. While the race remaineth, reason and fancy, feeling and desire will not cease. We cannot suppose primitive man to be without intellect, and we cannot suppose millennial man to be without passion. But Godwin was not alone in those ideas.

Not long after the first appearance of Godwin's *Political Justice*, Condorcet, in hiding from the Committee of Public Safety (1794), was writing his *Outlines of a Historical Picture of the Progress of the Human Intellect*.[20] Though "the rights of man are written in the book of nature," by studying the laws of the development of the human faculties, as they present themselves in history, we learn (he thinks) how errors and prejudices arise, and therewith how they may be removed. He divides history into ten great epochs; 1st, that of hunters and fishermen; 2nd, that of shepherds; 3rd, that of tillers of the soil; 4th, that of commerce, science, and philosophy in Greece; 5th, that of science and philosophy from the conquests of Alexander to the decline of the Roman Empire; 6th, that of the decadence of science till the Crusades; 7th, from the latter date till the invention of Printing; 8th, from the invention of Printing to the attacks on the principle of Authority, by Luther, Descartes, and Bacon; and 9th, from Descartes to the French Republic, when reason, tolerance, and humanity were becoming the watchwords of all. In conclusion, he looks forward to the future, and sees not only enlightenment extending, but science more and more completely mastering nature. The progress of the race, in every respect, is without limit; and it will result in equality of material, comfort and security of livelihood, as well as moral and intellectual perfection, universal peace, and political liberty.[21] Industry, by aid of the sciences, will make the soil capable of yielding support without limit.[22] He pauses to ask, Will not the increase of men be without limit, too? and answers, In any case, at a very distant time, and before that time arrives we shall no longer be prevented by "superstition" from limiting our numbers in ways obvious enough, but not now followed.[23]

The equality of the sexes, which progress will certainly bring with it, will make this consummation more easy of fulfilment.[24] Progress in the art of medicine will so prolong life, that death will be the exception rather than the rule.[25] Persecuted philosophers may console themselves by looking away from the present to this glorious future.[26]

It was this picture of the future, drawn in similar outlines by Godwin and Condorcet, that impressed the French and English public at the end of last century. Malthus called on them to distrust the picture utterly. He drew attention to one appetite in particular, which was permanently hostile to systems of equality. This was the appetite of sex. Its economical effects had been noticed by Hume, Adam Smith, and lesser writers,[27] but had been first directly brought to bear on systems of equality by Dr. Robert Wallace (*Prospects of Mankind*, 1761), who had failed to do it justice. Physical impulses (says Malthus) must have their satisfaction; and the passion of sex has not been abolished, or even weakened by civilization; there is no "tendency" to remove it. And for the human beings that are thereby brought into the world food is always necessary. These two facts, taken together, make it impossible that a reign of equality should either come about, or if it did appear, should ever last.

As things are now, there is a perpetual pressure by population, on the supplies of food. Vice and misery cut down the numbers of men when they grow beyond the food. The increase of men is rapid and easy; the increase of food is, in comparison, slow and toilsome. They are to each other as a geometrical increase to an arithmetical. In the United States of North America, the people double their numbers in twenty-five years; and yet they have not perfectly healthy conditions of life, nor perfect immunity from vice. Godwin's regenerated race would, by supposition, be free from vice, and they would increase faster than the Americans. The result would be a struggle for existence, and the reappearance of inequality. The causes are acting now; and, as they act now, they would act then. Godwin believes that, if the allurements of fancy and ornament were removed, and the appetites were presented to us in bare simplicity, their attractiveness would vanish,—that we should see what a mean thing they are. But (says his critic) so long as men are men, the fancy and ornament will be part and parcel of the attraction of appetite; asceticism can never be universal, or even general. There will be families wherever there is food for them, and even (sadly enough) where there is not. This is a source of suffering with which human institutions have little or nothing to do. But it is one of the great causes of human activity. Adam Smith had dwelt on the powerful influence of commercial ambition in modifying society and securing progress in spite of bad political institutions. Godwin had considered the love of praise as a great motive to exertion, which would not disappear, but only take a higher form in his ideal society (VIII. iv. 825). Neither of them sufficiently noticed the sharpness of the spur applied by the pressure of population on the food. It is this ever-recurring necessity that keeps human wits constantly on the stretch. The Maker of the World takes this way of drawing out the faculties of man, which would otherwise languish. Leisure for all would be apt to mean indolence for all.[28]

When Malthus re-wrote his *Essay*, in 1803, he amended his argument considerably. He felt that, as a controversialist, he had been tempted to meet one abstraction by another. His second statement of his position is more guarded. The tendency of population to increase beyond subsistence may be checked (he now allows) not only by vice and misery, but by an effort of will, which he calls "moral restraint," though it need not be more moral than the temperance which Plato describes as due to a kind of intemperance, the essence of it being simply that the appetite is not gratified. The power of reason over passion is thus conceded, and the critic's point of view is made less remote from that of the author originally criticised. Moreover, the teleological argument is weakened, for it is now admitted that below a certain grade of misery the fear of starvation leaves men helpless and hopeless and does not lead to progress. But the question is now discussed more fairly on its own merits, apart from the particular application to Godwin's political philosophy. As Adam Smith traced the effects of one particular kind of ambition on human industry and human progress, so Malthus traces the effects of one particular appetite. He takes the whole series of nations known characteristically as savage, barbarian, and civilized, and considers how far this particular appetite has been checked in its effect upon them by moral restraint, and how far simply by the "positive checks" of vice and misery. Like Adam Smith, he has an idea of how one cause would operate if taken by itself; and, like that author, he observes how, as a matter of fact, it is modified by other causes. The modifications are by far the larger part of his completed *Essay*. The desirable state of things (in Malthus' opinion) is that in which the various aims of civilized men, including commercial ambition, enter in and prevent or delay the gratification of this appetite, giving the tortoise a long start before the swift hare. Instead of plain living and high thinking, he desires high living (in the sense of a high standard of living) and high thinking together. We need not (he thinks) wait till all men are perfectly disinterested, and absolutely raised above the temptations of appetite, before hoping for them a comfortable life. On the other hand, he agrees with Godwin that, if anything is to be done, it must be by individual conviction, responsibility, and initiative, and not by laws and institutions; he condemns all attempts to regulate population by laws, almost as heartily as Godwin condemns such attempts to regulate human thought and conduct in general. Like Godwin, he was a Utilitarian, and like Godwin, an individualist,—two features which were to be associated with English economists for a long time to come. On the other hand, he stands almost alone among English economists in his strong regard for the principle of Nationality, which led him, amongst other things, to countenance the Corn Laws.

The amended argument of Malthus against Godwin undoubtedly brings him nearer to the latter. It is admitted to be possible for men to remain in a state of equality on the supposition that all are perfectly prudent and self-restrained in the matter of marriage. The main argument, however, of the *Essay on Population*, as a criticism of the *Political Justice*, had been that political institutions were not the only, or even the main Cause of suffering and poverty, but that individuals, whether left to themselves or oppressed by governments, were a cause of their own sufferings and poverty by yielding to their passions. "The very admission of the necessity of prudence to prevent the misery from an overcharged population removes the blame from public institutions to the conduct of individuals. And certain it is, that almost under the worst form of government, where there was any tolerable freedom of competition, the race of labourers, by not marrying and consequently decreasing their numbers, might immediately better their condition, and under the very best form of government, by marrying and greatly increasing their numbers, they would immediately make their condition worse."[29] We may add that Malthus saw, in this prudence, the possibility of an immediate and certain benefit to the human race, as opposed to the remote and comparatively uncertain benefit of a complete conversion of the race to the principles of Political Justice.

This main doctrine of Malthus has influenced modern thought in two different ways. It has (first of all) had an influence on men more interested in Political Philosophy or in broad philosophical and scientific theories, than in Political Economy as a special branch of study; and (in the second place), either (*a*) as a substantive economic doctrine, or (*b*) as a foundation for such, it has affected Political Economy itself.

In regard to political philosophy Malthus is not original. The details of his views on the State and government are those of an advanced Whig of the school of Fox and Grey. His adherence to Adam Smith did not prevent him from departing from "*laissez-faire*" even more than his master. Though a Utilitarian, he was not wholly an individualist; and he was not pronouncedly cosmopolitan. He applied the doctrine of Population to politics; it was the interest of tyrants (he thought) that population should grow without any preventive checks, for this meant distress and restlessness, and the constant need of a strong military power. It was not the interest of any constitutional government to hold out direct encouragements to the growth of population, whether by a bounty on large families, or by a lax system of poor relief. There was never any fear but that numbers would increase where trade and wealth were increasing; there was no need of a bait; a bait would simply increase numbers beyond resources. We must therefore convince governments, imperial and local, that they must not interfere in these matters. We must also convince every man in the country that he has no right to bring children into the world if he cannot reasonably expect to maintain them.

This is the real meaning of the statement, which Malthus advances against the Abbé Raynal and others, that there is no "right to live," and that a man may find that at "Nature's mighty feast" there is no cover laid for him. Not this man sinned, but his parents; and yet this man bears the consequences. Malthus is contending not that the poor should not be relieved, but that they should not be able to claim relief as a right, for, if dependence is not made more irksome than industrious independence, there will be no limit to the number of dependent families. "*Si quantum pauperum est petere pecunias caperint, singuli nunquam exsatiabuntur; respublica deficiet.*" The right to relief is illusory, because if all made the claim, it could not be granted. The English Poor Laws had practically conceded the right, and Malthus thought they had relieved suffering at the cost of creating more of it. If there had been no Poor Laws, "the aggregate mass of happiness" would have been greater than it was in his days, though there might have been more instances of severe distress. By the rule of the "Greatest Happiness,"

Malthus has a strong position here; and he has succeeded in impressing on all thoughtful political reformers the necessity of considering how far any project, otherwise desirable, would tend to encourage the tendency of men to do nothing for themselves if they can get others to do it for them. If a man's family will be supported by his neighbours, there will be a great temptation to him to marry without having himself made provision for the future.

This is the one aspect of the Malthusian argument against systems of Equality; and it is undoubtedly one that must be faced with frankness. It is not the aspect that most concerned Godwin's scheme, for the realizing of the latter implied that all men were intellectually and morally enlightened and weaned from indolence. But it applied to such a scheme as Robert Owen's, which was prominently before the public a quarter of a century after the *Political Justice*, and was, unlike Godwin's, socialistic, or largely dependent on Government for its execution.

It was a mistake of Malthus to regard all systems of equality as expressions of a few identical fallacies that persisted in recurring from age to age, only to be as regularly refuted. The very necessity he himself experienced of adopting an almost entirely new plan of attack should have shown him that the positions he was criticising were not identical with the old. The Utopias of his day were an attempted solution of social problems that were substantially new. The main argument of Malthus was not so, though there were circumstances of the time that no doubt gave it peculiar force. It was his pointed application and statistical justification of it, and his careful statement of its qualifications, that made his work effective for its purpose in the first instance, and permanently valuable afterwards. The idea that the struggle for existence was a wide principle of progress, through the survival of the fittest, was suggested to Darwin long afterwards by a study of the Essay on Population.[30] But this positive application did not occur to Malthus himself. He saw that the struggle for existence was the law of all living beings; and, if he had thought of the matter in the light of the reasoning of the *Wealth of Nations*, he might have seen that in nature's free competition the survivors are those that make best use of their advantages. But, when he takes a positive view of his subject at all, he looks rather to the effects of the pressure of population as stimulating men to action,[31] than to the effects of the consequent struggle for existence in sifting out the strongest, and *pro tanto* improving the breed of men. Whether or not the special form of the Evolution theory, known as the theory of Natural Selection, helps us to an adequate explanation of the forms of social development, will be considered afterwards. The biological question is of course beyond our scope in any case.

It has sometimes been doubted whether the theory of Population belongs strictly to Political Economy at all, and we cannot pass to the consideration of the influence of that theory on economical speculations without saying a word on this objection. The doubt seems to arise because of the very closeness of the connection between political economy and political philosophy. Malthus himself seemed to regard the effects of the tendency of population to outstrip food as bearing even more vitally on the happiness than on the wealth of nations, which he thought Adam Smith had too exclusively considered. This means in substance that Adam Smith had paid more attention to production than to distribution of wealth; the latter may be of such a character as to nullify the good of the former for a great part of the people concerned. In this matter Malthus agrees with Godwin; and his book is a study of the nature and causes rather of the poverty than of the wealth of nations. If people take his advice, the distribution, he thinks, will be less faulty than it is now.

But the pressure of population affects production as well as distribution, for it is a strong spur to the former. We may go further and notice that the desire of marriage is usually one element in commercial ambition; individualism does not exclude family life; the strongest opposition is between the family and the society, not between the latter and single individuals, as if they could usually be severed from the family. The motive of commercial ambition is the aggrandisement of the family, as often as personal gain, though in certain cases marriage and the desire of marriage may hinder commercial ambition instead of forwarding it.

Coming to questions of theory, we find Malthus directly deriving a theory of Rent from the tendency of population to press upon subsistence, and his contemporary, Ricardo, building on the theory of population a theory of Wages, Profits; and Value, which kept its ground in England with obstinacy till near our own time. It is true that Malthus distinguished between economical theory and its application, being perhaps the first to recognise the character and limitations of the abstract method of economical inquiry; but he certainly included among the first principles of theory the principle which was expounded and illustrated in his own essay.

Malthus is sometimes said to have introduced into political economy the notion of Law. It is true that his emphasis on a principle which (in Mill's language) partook largely of the nature of physical fact may have encouraged economists to look for general principles that should be as binding and far-reaching as physical laws. This would have been a doubtful service. But a law in the sense of a uniformity of sequence from permanent causes was in practice the quest of Adam Smith (to go no farther back), though instead of using the word law, Adam Smith spoke of what "naturally" happened, or of a "principle" merely. In regard to the uniformities of economic theory (as supply and demand, rent, wages, etc.), the phrase "principle" was preferred even by Malthus himself, and it seems to have been Ricardo that first taught English economists to speak freely of "economic laws."[32]

In the last place, the doctrines of Malthus have several points of contact with Psychology and Ethics. Though he gives no satisfactory psychological basis for his theory of Value (attributing value, as he does, somewhat vaguely to a Supply and Demand which are not fully defined or analysed), he brings us directly face to face with ethics and psychology, in his doctrine of moral restraint, and in his view of the standard of living. His view is Utilitarian. The civilized man restrains himself—"reason interrupts his career"—because he sees that the immediate pleasure will bring him ultimately a large balance of pains; the calculation of consequences (to Malthus as to Godwin) is the decisive element. Again, the civilized man finds that his wants keep pace with his civilization, and the modicum of comforts that satisfied him once is not enough for him, as his civilization has gone further; he has wants which compete with the desire of marriage, and his powder of restraint (which is only "moral" in the sense that it is due to deliberate will) is confirmed by regard to a number of pleasures which now permanently form part of his calculations. Barely to keep soul and body together is not now his object, and in fact when a man is so placed that he can have no other object he is too depressed to be self-restraining.

There is a point of depression where necessity leads to no vigorous or healthy efforts after progress. It is a standard of living and a desire for comforts considerably above physical necessaries that act as the healthy stimulus, and compete successfully with physical cravings. It has been said[33] that Malthus was Utilitarian, but not Utilitarian enough; he should have kept more constantly before him the Greatest Happiness of the Greatest Number. But Malthus was a Utilitarian of the old school; the greatest happiness of the great body of the people seemed to him to be best secured by the devotion of the individual members of it each to his own permanent and real happiness. The difficulty of consistently explaining economic facts by a Utilitarian ethics of any kind will appear when we see the Utilitarian theory in the hands of Bentham, the Utilitarian *par excellence*, who had Godwin's supreme confidence in his abstractions, and much more than Godwin's acuteness.

Note. Malthus and Darwin

"It [Darwin's own doctrine] is the doctrine of Malthus applied with manifold force to the whole animal and vegetable kingdoms, for in this case there can be no artificial increase of food and no prudential restraint from marriage." *Origin of Species* (pop. ed.) ch. iii., p. 50, cf. 143, 297. Compare *Descent of Man*, pt. I., ch. iv., pp. 131, 132 (ed. 1871). *Domestication of Plants*, vol. i., p. 10 (ed. 1868). *Life*, (1887), vol. i., p. 83, ii. II *seq.*, cf. 316, 317. A passage in the *Voyage of the Beagle* dated 1834 (p. 175 of ed. 1870), shows how the language and idea of Malthus were even then working in his mind: "Some check is constantly preventing the too rapid increase of every organized being left in a state of nature. The supply of food on an average remains constant; yet the tendency in every animal to increase by propagation is geometrical." This is seen for example in European animals left to run wild in America during the last few centuries. The check can, as a rule, be seldom pointed out precisely, though (on p. 191) he observes that the horses on the Falkland Islands are a case where this can be done.

Mr. A. R. Wallace, in his book on *Darwinism* (Macmillan, 1889) has, like Darwin himself, retained even the phrase "geometrical ratio." In his statement (which is given in substance below [end of Book IV.], he makes the Malthusian law an integral part of Darwinism. In regard to the descent of Man, Mr. Wallace (*Darwinism*, p. 458) employs a deductive argument which is of interest in this connection. From the theory of natural selection it follows (he says) that there must have been "a large population spread over an extensive area," to supply "an adequate number of brain-variations for man's progressive improvement." The theory of progress by variations is thus made in some measure to support *a priori* the theory of Malthus.

Notes

1 *Pol. J.* (1793), Bk. VI. 1. 589.
2 *Ib.*, Bk. IV. ii. 215, 216.
3 *Ib.*, V. xxii. 564, 565.
4 *Ib.*, II. ii. 90.
5 *Ib.*, VIII. iii. 815. In 3rd ed., vol ii. 491, he expressly refers to Rousseau. Cf. 1st ed. V. xv. 503.
6 III. vii. 185, 186; cf. 3rd ed., IV. ii. 264: "That civilization is a benefit may perhaps be conceded"—a sentence not in the 1st ed.
7 *Pol. J.*, VIII. vii. 841 *seq.*; cf. 3rd ed., vol. ii. 500.
8 *Ib.*, V. xxiii. 572, 573; cf. IV. ii. 212, etc. Godwin's political philosophy is expressed by Shelley in *Queen Mab*, and (more finely) in the sonnet on *Political Greatness*.
9 *Pol. J.*, II. iv. 106, 107, V. xvi. 515.
10 "Summary of Principies." *Pol. J.*, 3rd ed., vol. i. p. xxv.
11 Vol. i. (3rd ed.) 122, 123. Godwin is in this at one with Bentham.
12 A step beyond Hume, who ranked intellectual excellence with moral virtue. We may compare with this the view of Prof. Perry, that commercial ambition is not "materialistic," because it involves great mental energy (*Pol. Econ.* 1891, p. 22).
13 3rd ed., vol. i. 342. The 1st ed. is less clear on this point.
14 1st ed., I. vi. 43 *seq.* and *passim*.
15 *Pol. J.*, VIII. iv. 823.
16 *Ib.*, VIII. II. 807, VIII. iv. 825.
17 *Ib.*, VIII. ii. 802.
18 The objection was stated and answered in his own way by Condorcet. It was not suggested by English circumstances in particular.
19 *Recherche de la vérité*, beginning.
20 *Esquisse d'un tableau historique des progrès de l'esprit humain*. 3rd ed., 1797.
21 *Esquisse*, p. 334; cf. 345, 375 *seq.*
22 p. 361 *seq.*
23 p. 364.
24 p. 373.
25 *Esquisse*, pp. 385–387.
26 p. 390.
27 *Essay*, 1st ed., p.8.
28 For the theology of Malthus, see *Malthus and His Work*. Bk. I., ch. i., 35, and Bk. III.

29 Letter of Malthus to Godwin, quoted in *Life of Godwin* (K. Paul), I. 324. See *Malthus and His Work*, Bk. IV. "The Critics."
30 See the note to this chapter, and compare end of Book IV.
31 *E.g. Essay*, 7th ed., I. iv. 38.
32 See above, p. 193 *seq.*
33 By an American economist, Prof. S. N. Patten.

2 Bentham and James Mill

Bentham (1748–1832) was the contemporary of Malthus, and shared with him the credit of defeating the famous Poor Law Bill of Pitt (1797–1798). In his *Letters on Usury* (1787) he extended Adam Smith's "simple system of natural liberty" to bargains about loans of money. In his *Manual of Political Economy* (published piecemeal in 1798 and afterwards) he presented Adam Smith's economical doctrines in more abstract language than their author's and with an arrangement of his own. He divided actions bearing on political economy into three groups, "*sponte acta*," or the acts of individuals and their results, "*agenda*" or "things to be done" by the State, which should be reduced to the lowest possible dimensions, and "*non-agenda*" "things not to be done" by the State, or cases of unwise interference. The last he denounces not as merely unwise but as unjust, for the individual is in economical matters all in all. Consideration of the community, however, cannot fail to come in, for Bentham differs from Adam Smith almost as much in his bent for legislation as in his indifference to history, and the legislator (in Bentham's own language) must regard "the greatest happiness of the greatest number." Even his economical definitions show the prominence in his mind of this point of view. National *wealth*, or the total of the means of enjoyment in a nation, is distinguished from national *opulence*, or the proportion of the said total to the numbers of the nation. The chief end of wealth is "well-being," and a material object is wealth if it possesses "value, namely subservience to well-being." We even hear (though at random in a conversation) that "the value of money is its quantity multiplied by the felicity it produces,"—a saying which illustrates the fondness with which Utilitarians dwell on what later writers have called the subjective element in value.

It is to Bentham that we owe the close association of English political economy with Utilitarianism in Philosophy. Not only in matters of trade, but in all cases, men act (according to Bentham) with a view to their personal interests. In other words individualism means the same thing in ethics as it does in political economy. "To obtain the greatest portion of happiness for himself is the object of every rational being. Every man is nearer to himself than he can be to any other man, and no other man can weigh for him his pains and pleasures. Himself must necessarily be his own first concern."[1] This is nearly the language of Adam Smith;[2] but without his qualifications. Bentham has no reserve. "To interest duty must and will be made subservient."[3] "There is no true interest but individual interest." "Nature" (he says in the famous introductory chapter of the *Principles of Morals and Legislation*) "has placed mankind under the governance of two sovereign masters, pleasure and pain. It is for them alone to point out what we ought to do, as well as to determine what we shall do" (Clar. Press ed., p. i). A man's actions result from his calculation of the balance of consequences in favour of greater pleasure or less pain to himself individually. Utility (he says) is not a new principle, but it has been vaguely defined. The sense it must bear is the tendency to produce happiness, and the sense happiness must bear is the greatest possible sum of pleasures.

In the same way (he goes on in the introduction to *Principles of Morals and Legislation*) that which tends to increase the total happiness of the individuals composing a community is the Utility of the said community. Every individual is to count as one and no one as more than one.[4] The aim and intention of all legislation should be to secure the Greatest Happiness of the Greatest Number.[5] We must put aside all theories of a supposed Natural Law, or of Ascetic, or even of Sympathetic moralists. We start with Greatest Happiness as our first principle. Like other first principles, it cannot be proved directly, but it cannot be rejected without absurdities.

Both morals and legislation therefore deal with the tendency of actions to produce pleasure and pain. And these feelings are viewed as being identical in all men; they are palpable and familiar facts, with no mystery or mysticism about them. Pleasures (and pains) differ in intensity, duration, certainty, nearness in time, fecundity (or likeliness to give rise to other pleasures or pains), purity (or freedom from admixture of their opposite), and finally extent (or the great or small number of persons in whom they occur).[6] These are differences on which all are agreed and about which all can appeal to their own experience.[7] But we cannot say that pleasures and pains differ in kind or quality one from another. No one can pronounce on their quality except the subject of them. The moralist and legislator have to deal with the palpable, comparable and measurable differences of quantity above mentioned; these are the criteria by which alone the tendency of an action is to be judged, and the action itself pronounced good or evil. The good of the individual is the greatest sum of pleasures possible to him; the good of society is the greatest sum of pleasures possible to the greatest number of its members.

With the influence of Bentham on Legislation, we have of course nothing directly to do, and the application of his ideas to Jurisprudence will be best viewed in connection with James Mill. But the general effect on the thinking public of England was precisely what Godwin had tried to produce in the case of political philosophy as a whole;—the appeal to custom and tradition was discredited, and writers were forced to give a reason for the steps they took and a first principle for the doctrines they advanced, as well as to define the terms they used.

The influence of Utilitarianism, and especially of Bentham's Utilitarianism, on Political Economy has been profound and enduring. It is certainly not by accident that nearly all leading English economists, and a large proportion of Continental economists since his time have been Utilitarians when they have had any philosophy at all. This applies to Ricardo, James and John Mill, Say, Sadler, Destutt de Tracy, Jevons, Cairnes, and Sidgwick. Going back to economists before Bentham we find the conjunction in Malthus, and earlier still in Beccaria and Verri.[8] It will be best to consider the affinity (thus indicated) in special relation to the form of Utilitarianism which is, from one point of view, the purest, and, from another, the crudest,—the theory of Bentham himself, as distinguished from the later modifications of J. S. Mill, Spencer, and others.

A man like Ricardo, whose first and chief intellectual training in mature life had been derived from political economy, seemed to fall at once into line with the principles of Bentham as soon as he tried to express for himself a political philosophy at all. The two bodies of doctrine seemed to agree (1) in being directly related to palpable and tangible, or (to put it more bluntly) mundane and materialistic aims. Carlyle speaks of the monster Utilitarianism and the dismal science (of political economy) in the same breath, as symptoms of one and the same disease.[9] John Stuart Mill speaks of Bentham's whole system as dealing almost entirely with the "business" relations[10] of human life, the relations in which men are competing or contracting parties, not members conscious of their membership in the same body. To both (2) the body politic is a "*fictitious body*, composed of individual persons who are considered as constituting *as it were* its members."[11] The alliance of political economy with Utilitarianism may be said to have given a new lease of life to the individualism of the 18th century. Comte saw how close the connection was when he spoke of "Benthamism" as "the main origin of what is called political economy."[12] Besides individualism there was (3) a point of contact in the emphasis laid by both on the deliberate calculation of means to ends, as opposed to action from habit or instinct. Then (4) the notion of an indefinite sum of satisfactions is common to both. "Consumption is a quantity almost indefinite, for there is no end to the desire of enjoyment."[13] To Aristotle there was a definite limit of wealth, but Aristotle was not a Utilitarian.[14] In the same connection (5) we may note that the calculus of pleasures and pains which is so striking a feature of Bentham's Utilitarianism has been turned to account in the exposition of the economical notion of final utility in relation to Value. In the pages of a recent Italian writer, for example, "homo economicus" and hedonist are convertible terms.[15] Finally (6) (especially by recent writers of the School of Final Utility), the absolutely individual character of economical judgments is asserted in the same way as the absolutely individual character of the hedonistic by the older Utilitarians. The individual is not only the best but the only judge of his own interests, as of his own pleasures.[16] All desires are equally legitimate; all objects satisfying a desire (of whatever character the desire may be) are equally wealth. This is nearly the point of view described by Hegel in his *Philosophy of Right* as that of Civil Society as distinguished from the Family and the State; and in Civil Society, abstractly considered, the chief end is simply Greatest Happiness.[17]

To take the points of affinity in their order—we must note that, though it is true that Political Economy deals with palpable and tangible goods and makes provisional abstraction of goods that are not such, and motives that do not relate to such, it by no means follows that Political Economy is consistent only with a Utilitarian ethics. It is a sufficient warrant for the existence of Political Economy as a separate study that the tangible goods *are*; there is no need or wish to claim that the others are not. Nor is there need or wish to claim that self-interest, whether directed to tangible or intangible goods, is the only motive of men. It is enough that self-interest directed to tangible goods is certainly one motive of men, and a motive, comparatively speaking, more uniform than the rest, so that abstraction from the rest will yield results (again comparatively speaking) more fruitful than abstraction from this particular motive itself would be.

In the second place Political Economy needs no necessary assumption of individualism in politics. Its abstraction would apply to the acts of the State as well as to those of individuals, and to those of families and societies as well as those of the State. It would consider them in their relation to "tangible goods" in the first instance. This implies no historical judgment as to what has been, and no postulate of this relation as the one and only relation, still less a pronouncement that the State and other groups of men are more "artificial" than their component individuals. It may even be doubted whether the merely economical aspects of society themselves could ever be exhaustively understood by individualism. Men who have confined their studies mainly to abstract economics have sometimes been led to forget that they were dealing with abstractions which gave no complete guidance in the handling of concrete social problems. But in this they were exceeding the scope of their own method.

In the third place, though political economy must assume that men calculate means to ends, there is no need to assume that the calculation is deliberate, and that men are in every case clearly conscious both of their ends and of their means. What Bentham called the "*sponte acta*" were "*sponte*" in a wider sense than he intended. Not even the acts done from self-interest and concerning only "tangible goods" can be truly described as always deliberate in any or every individual case. The end is often forgotten in the means, and the means are often borrowed, without reflection, from habit and tradition. If no more is meant than that the actions are voluntary, this does not mean that they involve deliberate calculation. It is one of the paradoxes of Bentham's Utilitarianism (as of Godwin's *Political Justice*) that though founded on a Sensational Psychology it tended to the undervaluing of feeling.

The older Utilitarianism (of Bentham) may be described as the most conscious of ethical teleologies. Some chief end (τέλος τí) is no doubt an indispensable conception in all Ethics, from the Socratic downwards; but in no Ethics is it so distinctly conceived to be consciously followed in every part of the regulation of life. Utility in the sense of personal self-interest was the general description of the end and the motive both in economics and in the older Utilitarianism. *"Sponte acta"* to Bentham are not, as we might have supposed from their name, the unconscious results of a groping after ends only dimly known if known at all, but the results of conscious individual effort as compared with those of collective or governmental action.

Teleology was read into political economy by Adam Smith, and seen in it after him with great delight by Hegel. The end reached was public utility, the motive was private utility. This might or might not point to a conception quite alien to the older Utilitarian. It at least introduces an end gained without being deliberately sought. It has an affinity rather with the later Utilitarianism of John Mill than with the older of Bentham. John Mill thinks of the ethical end as one to be sought not directly but indirectly. But in his Economics he is less inclined than Adam Smith to allow private self-interest to work out its results without interference, in faith that they will result in public benefit. In short, he does not see economic teleology from Adam Smith's point of view, nor ethical from Bentham's. Economists need not assume in their "economic man" any more deliberate or precise teleological action than is common to all ordinary men.[18] They assume that man as such acts with a view to ends, and they investigate that special kind of action of which outward wealth is the end. But they need not assume, for example, that, even when men are clearly conscious of their proximate ends, they are with equal clearness conscious of their remoter ends, any more than that they are all alike in preferring the present to the future. Indeed, to make this last assumption would go far to make the phenomenon of interest on capital almost unintelligible.[19]

In the fourth place there is no need to assume that, because the desires of human beings are unlimited, their desires for tangible goods must be so. The expansion in men's conception of "necessaries" often falls behind the growth of their resources, though there is undoubtedly a *tendency* for the former to overtake the latter. The idea of insatiable desire for tangible goods seems inconsistent with the existence of a class of capitalists. Capitalists prefer a limited satisfaction secured for a long time to an indefinitely greater satisfaction in the present.

It might be answered that when they are rich enough to secure both they will not fail to do so. But we see as a rule that men who have made money in business are not great spenders of it in the present, and have often no other notion of spending it than to make new businesses to bring them in future returns.

Upon the whole (*a*) it may be true of the human race generally that there is no end to the variety of goods that will be desired by them as a whole. But of any one particular class, or of any individual man, it is not true. There are many who could say for themselves that as regards the tangible and palpable good things of this life (which are now in question), there is a definite limit to the amount wanted. Their pleasures go in a "round," not in an infinitely extended line. Else it would follow that plain living and high thinking were never honestly preferred by any one; and this is against evidence. Desires may be for objects that are not tangible in the sense of material; they may be for what can be enjoyed by many together, as well as for what cannot be enjoyed by one except at the expense of another.

It is true (*b*) not only of the race, but of all individuals and classes in it, that there is an infinity of wants, though not of material wants. Therefore we may grant the postulate in this sense; but in this sense it furnishes no principle that is economically of much advantage.

In his *Essay on Education* James Mill admits that the desire of wealth and power does not include the mere love of eating and drinking, "or all the physical objects together which wealth can purchase or power command. With these every man is in the long run speedily satisfied." The difficulty is (*c*) that "it is impossible to define what is corporal pleasure" (*Westm. Rev.*), and the pleasures of sense have much that is not of the senses in them. How far do the intellectual and spiritual pleasures depend on material provision? Do they do so to such an extent that the proposition in discussion becomes true, and demand becomes constant, in one direction or in another?

On the assumption of insatiableness of desire for tangible goods, it would follow (*d*) that the sum total of desires would remain constant, at least in proportion to the numbers of the people. Demand then would depend entirely on resources. It would never be wanting on the side of desire. Ricardo speaks as if demand might always be taken for granted; if desire does not go out in one direction, it goes out in another, and so long as men have some superfluity to offer, so that the desire can become effective demand, they will always be willing to offer it to satisfy new wants.[20] This idea is present in Hume,[21] Hobbes,[22] Pufendorf,[23] and is taken for granted by later authors; but there is no need to assume it, and it seems (for the above reasons) ill-founded. The new wants might be of intellectual goods, and not of tangible and material. The fewer half-accurate assumptions we make in Political Economy, the less trouble we shall have in modifying our abstract conclusions to adapt them to things as they are.

To recur to the main questions—in the fifth place the calculus of pleasures and pains is not a necessary foundation, even for abstract economics. The notion of means and ends, and personal advantage in the gaining of the latter, will enable us to work out the theory of value without placing ourselves, even provisionally, at Bentham's point of view. All that mathematical economics needs to assume is that a material quantity of goods will be in a certain proportion to a greater or less strength of motive; whether the motive be taken as "pleasure," or not, is not essential. The most intelligible statement of the Utilitarian doctrine certainly is that each action is to secure the greatest pleasure possible at the time, the maximum *then* possible, not a sum in the remote future. But for economical reasoning, at least, it seems better to paraphrase this—the attainment of the ends before the agent at a given time by the most economical means before him at that time. Finally, it is not necessary to assume with the older Utilitarians and many economists who follow them, that the individual is the only judge of his own interests, and therefore infallible in pursuit of these.[24] All economical theory proceeds on the tacit assumption that he *does* know it and follow it; but this means that there is a discoverable right (or economical) course, and a discoverable wrong (or anti-economical) course which the individual may follow, and that abstraction is made from the fact that he very often (either from high or from low motives) takes (what is from this point of view) the wrong course. But here, as before, it would seem that, from gazing constantly at the abstraction, theorists fell into the delusion that it was a concrete reality.

Again, it is not necessary to assume that all desires are equally legitimate, and all that satisfies desire is equally good, simply because there is always a more and a less economical way of reaching an end of that kind, whatever be the judgment to be passed on the end itself, and therefore on the means, from other points of view.

But the older Utilitarians were bound by their principles to assume that the individual was infallible in following his interest. Bentham may have been led to it by his Political Economy. From the abstraction which the economist adopts when he assumes that men are following the quickest road to their own advantage, it is conceivable that Bentham passed to a similar (but unperceived) abstraction applying to all human life. In fact, if our own pleasures and pains are taken as our only motives to action, and there is no other standard but our own feelings, it is clear, by the terms of the supposition, that no one else can judge for us; and, as, according to Bentham, we always do (as well as should) act with a view to our maximum pleasure,[25] we must always be said to attain this maximum in any given circumstances. To suppose anything else is to put ourselves outside of our own feelings, and outside of the given circumstances themselves. This indeed is one of the difficulties of the older Utilitarianism. It may be said to do precisely what John Mill thought in his early life it prevented us from doing—to set up the sentiment (the feeling of pleasure) as its own reason (*Autob.*, p. 65). To say nothing of such desires as are (as we say) instinctive, and lead us to an end which we have not deliberately calculated and could not have anticipated, the greater part of human calculation is (even when it is *of* or *for* a pleasure) not itself a pleasure, and even when it is so, it is not the same pleasure as that which it is designed to bring. Calculation implies means to an end; and in any calculation the end as such is not present but future. If connected with pleasure at all (and if pleasure be not, as Aristotle says, a mere appendage to some action or concomitant of it), it implies not the presence but the *idea* of a pleasure, which idea has something of pain in it, the pain of an unsatisfied want. But psychologically this is not Pleasure but Desire; and desire is not, for pleasure so much as for the object that brings it. If we would apprehend some joy, we comprehend some bringer of that joy. "Good-pleasure," again, is not emotionally pleasure at all; it is our "good-pleasure" to do even the most unpleasant act; but this means simply that, when we act, it is we that act.

Nor does it make matters clearer to suppose that the motive is always the greatest ultimate, and not the greatest immediate amount of pleasure. The ultimate sum, so long as still in the future, is not a pleasure but only the idea or anticipation of one; moreover, if the wants of man are really infinite, it is an idea that can never be realized. Man never *is*, but only *to be* blest. Even for the individual, then, the notion that pains and pleasures are the only motives to action seems (however valued for its supposed concreteness) to be perfectly abstract. Condillac did not explain the phenomena of the mind by calling them all sensations,[26] nor did the older Utilitarians explain motives by calling them all pleasures and pains. The designation remains abstract till it is defined for us in the various concrete activities of daily life.

It is true that Political Economy is concerned not only with certain actions but with certain impulses to action. But it is concerned with the latter only in their relation to the former, and as taking character from that relation. The actions which are the special subject of its consideration are those in which there is adaptation of means to a particular end, the end of procuring tangible goods. Its main work is to pronounce on the more or less successful adaptation—a purely intellectual process which has only indirectly to do with the pleasures that are supposed to be secured by the gaining of the end and with the pains of unsatisfied desire that urge to the adoption of the means. It may be added that, if the end be a future sum of pleasures, there is in that a general notion of the "permanent possibility" of satisfaction, for a being that is thereby supposed capable of something beyond mere pleasures and pains, for in a mere feeling there is nothing permanent and nothing general. It approaches, from the side of sentiency, the idea of idealistic ethics that the chief end of man is the harmonious development of all the powers that are in him. This development may involve a concomitant pleasure; but the end will be the exercise of the faculties rather than the pleasure of exercising them, and the "tangible goods" will be means to that exercise. This ethical view seems more consistent than the Utilitarian with economical study; and it at least makes it possible for us, without contradiction, to judge the individual to be following a course that is objectively right or wrong, instead of one that simply seems so to him.

We have still to touch on the Utilitarian idea of the Greatest Happiness of the Greatest Number,[27] as distinguished from that of the individual by himself. This idea certainly introduces an objective element, but it is at the expense of consistency. As it has been happily put by Dr. Martineau: from "each for himself" to "each for all" there is no road (*Types of Eth. Theory,* II. 308). The only course open to the older Utilitarians would have been to have shown that the individual best secures his own happiness by securing that of his fellows; but that is not shown by Bentham, who in fact rather takes his maxim for granted than proves it in any way.[28] Even if they had taken this course, there would have been a difficulty. If each man is his own best judge, how can another (Bentham or any other legislator) judge for him.[29] The simple statement of any individual, that he for his part did not find his happiness in the general good, would be unanswerable. It could only be answered on principles that go beyond the older Utilitarianism, with its principle of individual infallibility. It can only be answered when we recognise that the individual's pleasures or pains are no criterion even of his own good, and that there is an ideal of human life which is none of the individual's fixing.

Bentham was less troubled with such difficulties than he might have been; he was always more of the legislator than of the moralist. He argued that, as the interest of the individual was his own greatest happiness, the interest of a Society was its own greatest happiness as a whole;[30] and further that, if its rulers are to secure this, their interest must coincide with that of society, so that they shall lose more by injuring society than by benefiting it. Now the Majority are the only body of whom this is true, and government should therefore be in the hands of the majority. Again, since "the legislator can know nothing of individuals" as such, he must only interfere with their action "with respect to those broad lines of conduct in which all persons or very large and permanent descriptions of persons may be in a way to engage."[31]

Government and Society (for Bentham seems to make the distinction[32]) are not identical; and governments should do rather too little than too much. Their plainest functions are to give protection and security. All government is, in a sense, an evil, for it is an infraction of liberty,[33] but it is the less of two evils if it is wisely carried on. There are cases such as Property where legislation may be said to create private ethics, for, till property is settled by legislation, the general rules of ethics would guide no one in regard to it.[34] But Bentham explains his views on the positive functions of government much less fully than his friend James Mill.

James Mill (1773–1836) "the last of the eighteenth century,"[35] resembled William Godwin in his firm belief in the final victory of Reason in the world through the power of education and discussion,[36] and was also at one with Godwin in regard to the determination of character by circumstances.[37]

He speaks too of "that grand and distinguishing attribute of our nature, its progressiveness," in a broad unqualified sense in which his son could accept no such doctrine.[38] But in calm, not to say cold reasoning, where feeling is really and not simply in theory excluded, he stands almost by himself, with his master Bentham as his nearest rival.

James Mill, in his article on Government in the Supplement to the *Encyclopedia Britannica*, 1820, takes us a step further back than Bentham in regard to this subject. "The business of government," he says, "is to increase to the utmost the pleasures, and diminish to the utmost the pains which men derive from one another. The necessity of labour for obtaining the means of subsistence as well as the means of the greatest part of our pleasures is the primary cause of government, for, if nature had produced spontaneously all the objects which we desire, and in sufficient abundance for the desires of all, there would have been no source of dispute or injury among men, nor would any man have possessed the means of ever acquiring authority over another. The results are exceedingly different when nature produces the objects of desire not in sufficient abundance for all. The source of dispute is then exhaustless, and every man has the means of acquiring authority over others in proportion to the quantity of those objects which he is able to possess. In this case the end to be obtained through government as the means is to make that distribution of the scanty materials of happiness, which would insure the greatest sum of it in the members of the community taken together, preventing every individual or combination of individuals from interfering with that distribution or making any man to have less than his share."[39]

Mill goes on to say that, since most objects of desire are products of labour, "the means of insuring labour must be provided for as the foundation of all." His view on this point is more fully explained by a reference to a passage of his *Analysis of the Phenomena of the Human Mind* (chap. xxi., pp. 208–209, ed. J. S. M.), where he says that those three "remote causes of pleasure,"—"Wealth, Power, and Dignity, which appear to most people to sum up the means of human happiness," are the means of procuring for ourselves pleasurable sensations "only by procuring for us the services of our fellow creatures." So far as wealth is used to subserve Power and Dignity it is included under these. So far as it subserves our direct consumption, it stands by itself. But in either case it is "the great means of procuring obedience through the medium of good" (*i.e.*, of procuring service through an equivalent offered). Power on the other hand procures services through the medium of evil (pain or fear), and its range in human affairs is much wider than that of wealth. Where the wealth of an individual commands at most a few thousands of men, his power (*e.g.*, in the case of an Emperor) may command millions. Dignity is the respect procured for us "without the immediate application" either of reward or fear, though it is really due mainly to both of them, and arises from "association" with them of our actual gain from the Wealth and actual suffering from the Power. The Essay on Government proceeds to say that enslavement is plainly contrary to the very end of government, the happiness of the greatest number; we must leave labour to be secured then "by allurement or the advantage which it brings." "To obtain all the objects of desire in the greatest possible quantity, we must obtain labour in the greatest possible quantity; and to obtain labour in the greatest possible quantity we must raise to the greatest possible height the advantage attached to labour." In other words (he explains) we must secure to every man not more indeed than the whole product of his own labour, but so far as possible no less; "the greatest possible happiness of society is attained by insuring to every man the greatest possible quantity of the produce of his labour." But will not the stronger take the product of the weaker? Yes, unless men unite to protect one another, and delegate to a small number the power necessary for protecting them all. This is government. It may be in few hands or in many, but, if it is in few, the interest of the governors may be opposed to the general interest; and this cannot be if the majority are the governors. We must assume that men will always follow their interest. "Government is founded upon this, as a law of human nature that a man, if able, will take from others anything which they have and he desires."[40] Men's desire of power is as unlimited as their wants are. Otherwise government is unnecessary, for *ex hypothesi* human beings will of their own accord abstain from injuring one another.

Here we have a theory like that of Hobbes or of Glaucon in the 2nd book of Plato's *Republic*[41]—government is formed for the protection of the weak against the strong—together with an economical element which reminds us of Plato's own account of the genesis of Society. Plato says that men combine in a society because otherwise they would not get the benefits of division of labour. James Mill says that men form governments because they would not otherwise have the fruits of their labour secured to them, and therefore would not give all the labour needed (in a world where nature is niggardly) to secure a maximum production of goods, and there-with a maximum sum of happiness. Government comes into existence to secure property in order to secure labour. If this theory had been only incidentally advanced in the course of an economical discussion, it might have been thought that the writer was stating not a completely adequate theory of government, but simply a justification of government from the special point of view of Political Economy. But the article in which the theory is given is not professedly economical at all; and we must suppose that it was advanced in all good faith as an adequate general theory of the genesis of government. It was not difficult for Macaulay[42] and Mackintosh[43] to point out the weaknesses of it. Mackintosh observes that the word "interest" in the sentence "every man pursues his own interest" is ambiguous. If it means a man's own general welfare, it is not true that men always pursue that; they may pursue the welfare of another. If it means gratification of desire (or better if the sentence means simply that what we will we will) it is a tautology; "interest is a mere general title for all subjective motives of will[44];" and it does not at all imply that men always pursue their own general welfare. Not only individuals but Nations often prefer passion to interest in the latter sense of the word interest. What can a philosopher make of such complex notions as "interest," and "general interest" without breaking them down into the elements of which they are composed?[45]

It is remarkable that the companion articles to that on Government, especially the articles on Law of Nations and on Jurisprudence contain some of the very features which we most miss in the first. International law,[46] for example, is said to be a law without a command and without a sanction, without combination for a common interest in the sense in which the terms would apply to the laws of a single nation. Its binding force is due to the fact that men are powerfully influenced by the praise and blame of other men; indeed in private morality this is the chief motive to good conduct. Mill considers that this regard to the opinion of others can only tell upon a democratic government, for a monarch or an aristocracy does not need to care what others think about it.[47] But "what others think" really enters far more into the motives of rulers than is here admitted. John Stuart Mill saw his father's mistake, and recognised that the character and actions of all rulers, without exception, are influenced "by the habitual sentiments and feelings, the general mode of thinking and acting, which prevail through the community of which they are members," as well as by those of their own particular class. "And no one will understand or be able to decipher their system of conduct who does not take all these things into account."[48] Besides private interest, *sensus communis* must be taken into account; and it may be in certain circumstances as powerful in producing the desired effect as any "responsibility to the governed." But Bentham and his disciples[49] were backward in allowing for peculiarities of national character; their scheme of government was in an unfavourable sense "abstract." It must be added that any theory must be inadequate which derives the origin of government from purely economical causes. History and the facts of present society are alike inconsistent with such a theory; and it is no necessary postulate of political economy that the State should have come into being from purely economical causes. The same applies to the theory of Property.[50] James Mill's utterances on the subject could bear an interpretation which would justify for example the dispossession of all capitalists and landlords. In another connection he speaks of the rich being almost of necessity prone to vices from which the poor are kept free by their poverty.[51] But in his *Elements of Political Economy* he is nearer *laissez-faire* than socialism. He thinks the existence of a comfortable middle class is for the public advantage (p. 49). He does not try to press home his own suggestion that the rent of land is a good fund for the exigencies of the State (198, 199, cf. 50). Such hints, however, brought forth fruit in John Mill.

In one particular, James Mill and Bentham seem nearer to Socialism than to *laissez-faire*, Government by the majority is their great concern; the minority and single individuals are to be subject to the majority so absolutely that originality and innovation run the risk of being crushed under a "despotism of public opinion."[52] But in this Bentham's political philosophy was again showing its affinity to the political economy of the older economists. Under the "system of natural liberty" the "great body of the public" benefit; but the minority and single individuals suffer keenly.[53] As in Benthamism, there is the temptation to argue that a greater pleasure in the many counterbalances a greater pain in the few. The main apology offered for this suffering is that "in the long run" the minority will share the benefit; and yet this final settlement has no sooner come for one class than the causes of suffering are set at work for another.

It was nevertheless perhaps the chief service of Bentham's school to have laid emphasis on the claims of the Greatest Number as against the aggrandisement of the few. Their principle (however we may criticise it in details) had a broad general tendency to secure the recognition of equality of rights. Every one is to count as one, no one for more than one.[54] The question bequeathed by the eighteenth century was, how far can human institutions be said to do justice to human nature? How far are they an evil, how far a good? Bentham was dealing rather with this question than with the problems of ethics; and his test, of the Greatest Happiness of the Greatest Number, was applied ruthlessly to English institutions, especially English laws. The democratic opinions learned from Bentham and from James Mill (in his Essay on Government) helped to make the moderate reform of 1832 possible. Negatively Bentham did much to discredit the notion of natural rights as used by the philosophical precursors of the French Revolution;[55] and if he substituted an abstraction of his own it was at least one that could be turned to practical service by his own countrymen. Indeed, it might be contended that Bentham was only opposed to the letter and not to the spirit of the doctrine of Natural Rights. "Every one to count as one, no one as more than one," does not get from him more than a dogmatic justification; and the notion that every one has a "natural right" to life, liberty, and the pursuit of happiness, is fully in keeping with the dogma of Greatest Happiness, whether as expounded by him or by James Mill. The idea of natural and non-natural is rather redefined than discarded; and we read in John Mill[56] of what is "naturally pleasurable" and "naturally painful," as we might have read it in Adam Smith himself, and simply as opposed to fictitious, artificial, or derivative.

Note on Carlyle

"That is one definite objection of Carlyle's; political economists in his day confine their attention to the production and exchange of wealth, and say too little about the distribution of it. This was largely true. But he goes on:— 'Political Philosophy? Political Philosophy should be a scientific revelation of the whole secret mechanism whereby men cohere together in society: should tell us what is meant by "country" (*patria*), by what causes men are happy, moral, religious, or the contrary. Instead of all which it tells us how "flannel jackets" are exchanged for "pork hams," and speaks much about "the land last taken into cultivation." They are the hodmen of the intellectual edifice, who have got upon the wall and will insist on building as if they were masons.' This is in reality a second objection: political economy in his opinion claimed to be a political philosophy, and had no right to do anything of the kind. This was really because there was no political philosophy except the Utilitarian before the English public at that time, and the economists were usually Utilitarians. How far such charges could be maintained even against the Utilitarians I will not say; but, when Carlyle foresaw that the Utilitarians were soon to 'pass away with a great noise'? (*Life*, vol. ii., p. 79), he might have allowed that after that event political economy would have something to say for itself, when it had ceased to be associated with Utilitarianism. It would not *miss* its associate. To many of us it seems a positive hindrance to the fair fame of political economy now, that its professors still talk of a 'calculus of pleasures and pains', as if that were the foundation on which all economical theory must rest. If the economist is no longer supposed to assume that all men act only from self-interest in the narrowest sense, why should he be supposed to measure only 'pleasures' and 'pains'? Human interests (as Carlyle quite rightly protested) are not rightly or fully described in terms of pleasure and pain (unless these words are so twisted as to mean what does not belong to them in ordinary speech at all). The economist measures the effects of certain motives and certain conduct in relation to a particular subject—namely, the material good things of this life, and without any necessary concern with the motives and conduct themselves as a subject of psychology.

"Men have wants and satisfy them by material means; the outward acts and the intentions and aims they indicate are of economical concern. The relation of the motives to the acts, and the relation of human reason to human action, are, no doubt, of the highest concern, to the moral philosopher, but not to the economist as an economist. He may have opinions about them because he may be philosophically minded and study them; or, without any detriment to his economics, he may not be inclined to go beyond them as they stand, in which case he should not adopt the language and conclusions of a particular philosophical theory. Yet this was what Malthus, Ricardo, James Mill, and Jevons did in their time; I fear the like has been done in our own time. The result is to prejudice people who are not Utilitarians against a study which they naturally think must be bound up with the particular psychology and ethics of Utilitarianism. Something like this may have happened in the case of Carlyle."—From a paper on the *Relations of Carlyle to Political Economy*, 10th December, 1890 (Glasgow Philosophical Society).

Notes

1 *Deontology*, vol. i., p. 18 (ed. Bowring, 1834).
2 *Moral Sent.*, 6th ed., II. 99. See above, p. 37.
3 This quotation also is from the *Deontology*, which it is fair to remember is more paradoxical than any of the works published in Bentham's own life-time.
4 As to this phrase, see below, p. 234 n.
5 For the history of this motto see Palgrave's *Economical Dictionary*, art. "Bentham."
6 See *Table of the Springs of Action* (1817), p. 3. The last seems as compared with the rest to be an external difference. It goes beyond the mere sensation.
7. Except surely "extent."
8 Beccaria, *Dei delitti e delle pene*, 1764. Verri, *Sull' indole del Piacer*, etc., 1773.
9 *E.g.* Carlyle, *Signs of the Times* (1830). Macaulay deplores the association of Benthamism with Political Economy as tending to discredit the latter. *Edin. Rev.*, June, 1829, pp. 298, 299. See too Palgrave's *Econom. Diction.*, article "Carlyle," and note to this chapter.
10 J. S. Mill, Essay on Bentham (*Dissert. and Discuss.*). Cf. *Ricardo's Letter's to Malthus*, Clarend. Press, Preface.
11 *Princ. of Morals and Legisl.*, I. iv.
12 *Letter to Mill*, 20th Nov., 1841, p. 4.
13 Jas. Mill, *Pol. Ec.*, p. 1.
14 Unless the 7th book of the *Nicom. Ethics* is really his.
15 Pantaleoni, *Economia Pura* (1889).
16 Even Böhm Bawerk and Sax use language that implies this.

17 § 189; cf. § 258, p. 306, etc.
18 Compare Prof. Marshall, *Principles* (1st ed.), I. vi.
19 See Böhm Bawerk, *Positive Theory of Interest on Capital*, 1889.
20 *Letters*, p. 34; *Works* (ed. MacC.), 176, 178.
21 *Essays*, vol. i. (ed. 1768), p. 122 ("Progress of Arts and Sciences"); *Human Nature*, vol. iii. 62, 63 (1st ed.).
22 See above, pages, 78, 81.
23 See *De Jure Nat. et Gent.* (Engl. Trans.), 1703, p. 77; but contrast 129.
24 Ricardo consistently enough writes to Malthus (*Letters*, p. 138): "Happiness is the object to be desired, and we cannot be quite sure that, provided he is equally well fed, a man may not be happier in the enjoyment of the luxury of idleness" than in a neat cottage, etc.
25 As stated by Mr. Alexander, *Moral Order and Progress*, II. v. 199, the idea of a maximum of happiness seems quite an intelligible one, whatever else we may think of it. It is "not a happiness than which no greater is possible, but the happiness which is greatest under the given conditions."
26 The criticism of John Mill, *Diss. and Disc*, I. 410; "Coleridge," written 1840.
27 Bentham is said to have amended the formula, and adopted "Greatest Happiness" *sans phrase*. See the *Deontology*, published after Bentham's death by his friend and executor, Dr. Bowring (2 vols., Longmans, 1834). See esp. vol. ii. 328 *seq.* The *Deontology* is not entirely at one with the previous writings of Bentham, and the book has lain under suspicion. Perronet Thomson claims to have converted Bentham to the change in the formula. *Exercises*, vol. iii., 125. *Westm. Review*, 1st July, 1834. Dr. Southwood Smith quotes the MS. of the *Deontology* in his *Lecture on the Remains of Bentham* (1832), p. 32.
28 This was pointed out by Macaulay. It was admitted by James Mill.
29 In Bentham's own words (*M. and L.*, ch. xvii. 319): "It is a standing topic of complaint that a man knows too little of himself. But is it so certain that the legislator must know more?"
30 *E.g., Morals and Legislation*, chap. xii., p. 313. For a keen criticism of Bentham's views on legislation as well as ethics, see Prof. F. C. Montague's Introduction to the Clarendon Press edition of the *Fragment on Government* (1891)
31 *M. und L.*, 319.
32 *E.g., Fragment on Government*, I. ix. x., *seq.*
33 *Mor. and Legisl.*, chap. x.
34 *Mor. and Legisl.*, xvii. 322.
35 J. S. Mill, *Autob.*, p. 204.
36 *Ib.*, p. 106.
37 *Ib.*, p. 108.
38 James Mill, *Political Economy*, 1st ed. (1821), p. 48. Compare J. S. Mill on Guizot in *Dissert. and Discuss.*, II. 237–238 (written 1845).
39 It was no doubt such passages that gave colour to the caricature of Utilitarianism ("Pig Philosophy") in the Latter Day Pamphlets. See Note to this chapter.
40 Mill quotes Montesquieu to a like effect. *Esp. d. L.*, II. 4.
41 Mill was familiar with both authors. He was indeed the reawakener of interest in Hobbes.
42 *Edinburgh Review*, 1829. Perronet Thompson replied in *Westminster Review* of same year.
43 *Dissertation on Eth. Phil.*, vol. i., p. 210, ed. Longman, 1854.
44 Prof. Caird, *Kant* (1889), II. 180.
45 Cf. John Mill, *Dissertation*, I. 450 (" Coleridge"), written 1840.
46 Bentham (or rather Dumont) introduced this adjective into the English language. See *Principles of Morals and Legislation* (written 1780), chap. xvii. Clar. Press ed.,

p. 326, n. For other coinages of Bentham see works (ed. Bowring), vol. x., pp. 570, 571.

47 Cf. the passage to the same effect, quoted by Macaulay, from the article on Jurisprudence. *Edinburgh Review*, March, 1829, p. 167.

48 *Logic*, vol. ii., p. 484.

49 James Mill rejects this designation (see *Fragment on Mackintosh*, 1835, pp. 123, 124). He admits a close general agreement in opinion.

50 Macaulay rightly reminds us that protection of person is as truly a *raison d'être* of Government as protection of property. *Edinburgh Review*, March, 1829, p. 163.

51 Article on Government, p. 31 (of reprint), etc. Cf. J. S. Mill, *Autob.*, p. 71.

52 J. S. Mill, *Diss. and Disc.*, I. 378 ("Bentham"), written 1838.

53 *E.g.* on the introduction of machinery or a change of fashion, or under the application of a rigid poor law.

54 A phrase attributed to Bentham. I can trace it no further than to J. S. Mill, *Utilitarianism*, p. 93. He calls it "Bentham's Dictum," but gives no reference. The doctrine at least is undoubtedly Bentham's.

55 *Princ. of Legisl.*, ch. xiii., *Anarch. Fallacies* (*passim*).

56 *Diss. and Disc.*, I. 137 ("Sedgwick"), written 1835.

3   John Stuart Mill (1806–1873)

"With those who (like all the best and wisest of mankind) are dissatisfied with human life as it is, and whose feelings are wholly identified with its radical amendment, there are two main regions of thought. One is the region of ultimate aims, the constituent elements of the highest realizable ideal of human life. The other is that of the immediately useful and practically attainable. ... It is in these two extremes principally that real certainty lies. My own strength lay wholly in the uncertain and slippery intermediate region—that of theory, or moral and political science—whether as political economy, analytic psychology, logic, philosophy of history" (*Autobiography*, p. 189).

This is John Mill's judgment on himself; it is frank and accurate. Born in 1806, he had been trained by his father from earliest boyhood to weigh arguments and evidence. "The education which my father gave me was in itself much more fitted for training me to *know* than to *do*" (*Autob.*, p. 37). But we cannot wish this fault undone, the issue of it being so proper. The boy grew up in the habit of thinking for himself, and by following his father's rules arrived in manhood at conclusions very different from his father's (*Autob.*, p. 179). At first it was not so. From about 1821 to 1826 he was devoted heart and soul to Bentham's principles; his aim in life was to be a reformer (*Autob.*, p. 132); his philosophy was Bentham's Utilitarianism in conjunction with Ricardo's Political Economy, Malthus's doctrine of Population, and James Mill's Psychology (*ib.*, 64 *seq.*, pp. 105, 108, etc.) "No youth of the age I then was can be expected (he himself says) to be more than one thing," and the thing he then most desired to be was an eighteenth century *philosophe* (*ib.*, p. 109). After his great mental "awakening" in 1826, he ceased to be "only one thing," and became really a philosopher. He discovered the value of feeling and of a "due balance among the faculties." He gained the habit of avoiding half-truths, and of looking at questions from his opponent's point of view, with a constant sense of his own fallibility (*Autob.*, pp. 132–162). The beginning of the change seems to have been a reflection on the results of "victorious analysis" in his own person; he feared it had worn away his power of feeling. One result of the change was a correction of his old Utilitarianism. He now thought that the way to attain happiness is not to pursue it directly, but "to treat some end external to it as the purpose of life" (*ib.*, p. 142).

Accordingly in the Essay on Liberty, the chief end of man is described, in the language of Humboldt, "as the highest and most harmonious development of his powers to a complete and consistent whole" (p. 103), or, in his own words, "the permanent interests of man as a progressive being" (p. 24). This was one of the first of his many modifications of the Utilitarianism of his father and Bentham. He was also led to abandon their political philosophy. French influences were becoming a large factor in his life. His early visit to France (in 1820) had impressed him with the superior openness of the French character and absence of false shame in contrast with English reserve and the English custom of taking low motives for granted (*Autob.*, pp. 58, 59). "Both in a good and in a bad sense," he says long afterwards, "the English are farther from a state of nature than any other modern people." They not only *act* but *feel* according to rule.[1] His later visit (at the Revolution of 1830) was of more direct influence on his Political Philosophy. It introduced him to the new ideas of History and Social Science that played so large a part in his thinking in after times. He had been only half convinced by Macaulay's criticisms of the *Essay on Government*. He saw that one great defect of the school of Bentham was its neglect of history. But he also recognised the defect of the merely historical and experimental political writers, who appeal to "specific experience" (*Autob.*, 157–160). He now came to learn the meaning of a Philosophy of History, which was to have neither defect. "To find on what principles derived from the nature of man and the laws of the outward world each state of society and of the human mind produced that which came after it, and whether there can be traced any order of production sufficiently definite to show what future states of society may be expected to emanate from the circumstances which exist at present," that is the problem of a philosophy of history (*Dissert.*, II. 129, *Edin. Rev.*, Jan., 1844, "Michelet"). He had read such ideas in Coleridge and the Germans (see *Autob.*, p. 161, *Diss.*, I. 425, "Coleridge"), but it was French statements of them in Guizot, Michelet, Comte and the St. Simonians, that carried them fairly home to his mind[2] (*ib.*, pp. 162, 163; cf. *Dissert.*, II., "Michelet" and "Guizot"). He had new reasons now for agreeing neither with Bentham in his neglect of history nor with the English historians (like Macaulay) in their neglect of all attempts at a philosophy of history.

His views of Political Economy were undergoing a corresponding change. The *Essays on Some Unsettled Questions in Political Economy* were written between 1829 and 1831,[3] and are the fruit of the deliberations of a small economical club in which the writer took a leading part between 1825 and 1830. The *Essays* are essentially Ricardian, the last (which was re-cast in 1833, and published in *London and Westminster Review*, October, 1836) being perhaps the most adventurous ("On the Definition and Method of Political Economy"). Another stray economical paper, on the Currency Juggle (1833, *Dissert.*, I. 42) showed no tendency on Mill's part to leave the old lines. Nevertheless, the St. Simonians in 1830 had helped to convince him of "the very limited and temporary value of the old political economy, which assumes private property and inheritance as indefeasible facts, and freedom of production and exchange as the *dernier mot* of social improvement" (*Autob.*, pp. 166, 167). He became (through the St. Simonians) a modified Socialist and (through De Tocqueville) a modified democrat, full of care for the rights of minorities (*ib.*, p. 191). He learned, also through the St. Simonians, to press the claims of women to the legal rights that are claimed for men.[4] By the time he wrote his *Principles of Political Economy*, in 1848, all the main ideas of his writings had become a part of him.

This slight sketch of Mill's mental history will be of service when we try to trace the effect of his philosophy on his political economy and of the latter on the former. His aim in writing the *Political Economy* was (as he tells us in his Preface) to produce a work after the model of the *Wealth of Nations*. The distinctive feature of Adam Smith's work was (he thinks) that it invariably considered principles in close conjunction with their applications.[5] Now for practical purposes political economy is "inseparably intertwined with many other branches of social philosophy," and there are perhaps no economical questions which can be decided on purely economical premises. Adam Smith himself never forgot this, but since his time no attempt (Mill says) has been made to write on economical matters as he wrote on them, and to apply the wider knowledge of social philosophy that has been gained since his time. There has been no attempt, in short, "to exhibit the economical phenomena of society in the relation in which they stand to the best social ideas of the present time, as he did, with such admirable success, in reference to the philosophy of his century" (Preface to 1st edition of *Political Economy*, 1848). Hence the title of Mill's book is, *Principles of Political Economy with Some of their Applications to Social Philosophy*.[6] It was to combine the abstract theories of economics, as worked out by Ricardo and others, with the modifications of economic theories shown in the practice of men and nations, and required by a general philosophy of society.

On the threshold we are met by questions which touch philosophy in its larger sense, the questions of Definition and Method. How are we to define Political Economy, and what is its scope and method? These questions are much better treated in the last of the *Essays on some Unsettled Questions in Political Economy*, and in the 6th book of the *System of Logic* (1844) than anywhere in the *Political Economy*, where in fact we need constantly to read between the lines. When we are told in the introduction (*Pol. Econ.*, Preliminary Remarks) that it is no part of the author's design to aim at "metaphysical nicety of definition," that every one has a notion sufficiently correct for common purposes of what is meant by wealth, etc., we do well to remember Mill's own idea of an intelligible style, "to say a little more than the truth in one sentence and correct it in the next"[7]; and, further, his belief that the definition of a science usually comes later than the creation of the science itself.[8] "The facts classed themselves" before there was any intentional classification of them; and it requires the highest powers of analysis and abstraction to determine the logical definition of any science. The first principles of all sciences belong not to the particular sciences themselves but "to the philosophy of the human mind," and are rather *last* than first in order of time.[9]

Political Economy, like the rest, has fared very ill in the matter of its own definition. Even Adam Smith's definition "an enquiry into the nature and causes of the wealth of nations" might convey the notion that it teaches nations how to become rich; but it is a science, not an art. For a like reason it is not well defined by analogy to domestic economy,[10] which is nothing if not an art, or as "the science of the laws which regulate the production and consumption of wealth," for that might include all the physical sciences in any way concerned in production. It is one of the moral or psychological sciences (*Uns. Questions*, 129), and it is "the science which treats of the production and distribution of wealth so far as they depend upon the laws of human nature" (*ib.*, p. 133), or (more strictly still) as "the science which traces the laws of such of the phenomena of Society as arise from the combined operations of mankind for the production of wealth,[11] in so far as those phenomena are not modified by the pursuit of any other object" (*ib.*, p. 140).

We see that the final definition involves the conception of a particular Method of studying the science; and of this Mill is aware. Definition (he says, p. 141) must always be closely connected with Method. "Political Economy considers mankind as occupied solely in acquiring and consuming wealth," not that economists suppose that mankind are really thus constituted, "but because this is the mode in which science must necessarily proceed" (*Uns. Quest.*, pp. 138, 139). There are certain departments of human life in which the gaining of wealth is the main and acknowledged pursuit of men, and Political Economy investigates this pursuit by itself, in abstraction from all other pursuits, proceeding *à priori* and getting results that are true in the abstract, and therefore "true in the concrete with proper allowances." The amount of these allowances (the modifications due to competing motives and disturbing causes) constitutes "the only uncertainty of Political Economy" (*Uns. Quest.*, 138–150). In other words the concrete part of Mill's book on *Political Economy* is the only uncertain part of it.

When he wrote the *Unsettled Questions* Mill was of opinion that this *à priori* method was the only right method of inquiry in Social Science generally as well as the Economical branch of it. Comte convinced him of his mistake, and in the *Logic* (which was completed at a time when he was in active correspondence with Comte[12]) he describes the method of Social Science in its other branches as the Concrete Deductive Method. It is not the Experimental or Chemical, which relies on specific experience;[13] we cannot reason, for example, from the facts that are true of a nation at one period of its history to the facts true of it now, and we have no power to make experiments. No two events in history are ever the same. Nor can we, except in Political Economy, use the Geometrical method of reasoning from one assumption (or at most a very few assumptions), as Bentham did when he assumed that the majority of men will be governed by their personal interests. "It is unphilosophical to construct a science out of a few of the agencies by which the phenomena are determined and leave the rest to the routine of practice or the sagacity of conjecture." We must treat Social Science as dealing with a complicated case of the Composition of Causes, and consider not a few but *all* of the causes at work, as is done in Astronomy and Physiology. The difficulties, however, of this complicated phenomenon, Society, are so great that, when we have first deduced our conclusions from our knowledge of human nature, we need to verify them by specific experience. It may even happen conversely that the specific experience first suggests a generalization and then we verify it by our knowledge of human nature, following an Inverse Deductive Method. Comte thought that this inverse method was the only one admissible in social science; social science was to generalize from history and then verify the generalizations by the laws of human nature. But there is scope also, Mill thinks, for direct deduction.[14] "Different species of social facts are in the main dependent immediately and in the first resort on different kinds of causes, and therefore not only may with advantage, but *must* be studied apart,"—just as there is a physiological and a pathological study of the separate organs, although every organ is affected by every other. So Political Economy, by reasoning from "the familiar psychological law that a greater gain is preferred to a smaller one," and from the outward circumstances of societies in relation to that law, can explain the one particular class of social phenomena.[15] From this position Mill did not afterwards depart. He hints that he would have recognised the same deductive method in other cases could he have seen the possibility of a similarly fruitful abstraction. The theory of population we have seen to be an instance of the kind, but Mill (not quite logically) incorporates it with political economy itself "for the sake of practical utility" (*Uns. Quest.*, p. 140). The antagonistic principles to the desire of wealth, namely, aversion to labour and desire of present indulgences are incorporated also, on the ground that they are "inseparably mixed up with" the desire of wealth (*ib.*, p. 138). In reality, therefore, Mill's *Political Economy* is an inquiry into the operation not of one desire, but of four distinct desires, and it might be doubted whether its method would not be more truly described as concrete deductive than geometrical. The four would be included if we abridged and amended the final definition and made it read as follows: "The science which traces the laws of such of the phenomena of society as arise from the combined operations of mankind in the production, consumption and distribution of wealth." Mill himself (though he is not perfectly consistent, see, *e.g.*, *Uns. Quest.*, p. 138) excludes Consumption as having no laws distinct from those of human enjoyment, generally (*ib.*, p. 132) and in his final definition he does not mention Distribution, perhaps for the reason given in the *Political Economy*, that its laws are not determined by fixed conditions of nature and human nature, but are wholly of human institution (*Pol. Econ.*, Prelim. Remarks, and bk. II., ch. i.). His account of Production includes Malthus' doctrine of Population, under the title of the "law of the increase of labour"; and, as he does not profess to confine himself to abstract political economy, he has no difficulty in treating of all the four motives under one head or

184 Modern Philosophy: Utilitarian Economics

another, the desire of wealth being the main abstraction, and the others the first of the modifying concurrent causes. We might suppose the order to be as follows: After considering by themselves the effects of the desire of wealth, we combine with them the effects of the desire of marriage, when the latter have first been considered by themselves in their abstractness. We then combine with these two the effects of the desire to avoid labour and the desire of present indulgences. Last of all we combine our results with the results of the other ordinary motives of everyday life, thus coming gradually down from abstractness to concrete facts.

The desire of wealth, though the reasoning from it is *à priori*, is not itself of course regarded as so purely *à priori* that it is not itself derived by induction from experience. To Mill nothing is purely *à priori*. Even the Uniformity of Nature, the ground of all induction, is considered (*Logic*, bk. III., ch. iii.) as itself an induction. The axioms of geometry are inductions; and deductions are made from them on the hypothesis (which, like the economical, is never quite true) that the points, lines and angles are in nature what they are said to be in the definitions (*Logic*, bk. II., chaps, v., vi.). The only ultimate unexplainable facts are certain psychological phenomena, such as belief in the truthfulness of Memory and the recognition that Pleasure is a good.[16] The relation of the derivative desire of wealth to its simpler elements was touched on by James Mill among the "remote causes of our pleasures and pains" (*Analysis*, ch. xxi., p. 207 *seq.*; vol. ii. of ed. 1869). John Mill touches it even more slightly. We gather (from *Uns. Quest.*, p. 132) that he regarded it "simply as a form of human enjoyment," and its meaning as too obvious to need explanation. In the *Political Economy*, after saying that "every one has a notion sufficiently correct for common purposes of what is meant by wealth" (*Pol. Econ.*, 1st ed., p. 2), he offers the usual caution against the notion of wealth favoured by Mercantile theorists, and then gives a description which is wider than theirs, but not wide enough: Wealth is "everything which serves any human purpose and which nature does not afford gratuitously. Things for which nothing could be obtained in exchange, however useful or necessary they may be, are not wealth in the sense in which the term is used in *Political Economy*" (*ib.*, p. 8). This limitation is in the spirit of Ricardo and MacCulloch; but it is open to the objection that it really reduces wealth to value and makes it hard to understand why common language, and even the language of Ricardian economists, distinguished the two at all. According to Mill's own account of the matter (*Pol. Econ.*, III. i) exchange is no "fundamental law of the distribution of produce" but only "part of the machinery for effecting it." Why then should Mill, who recognises no value except value in exchange, adopt a definition of wealth which makes it a sum of things valuable?

The truth seems to be that he was (or thought himself to be) precluded from devoting special attention to things valuable in use by the terms of his definition of economical science, for that definition represents Political Economy as relating not directly to individuals but only to societies of men.

But no one knew better than Mill that in order to know a society we must know individual men; and he could not have shown reason for refusing to trace the workings of "familiar psychological laws" in the case of the economical unit. To the philosophy of history, he considers psychology an indispensable preliminary, understanding by psychology not introspection but the study of sequences in the world of mental phenomena; and he allows that political economy assumes all the laws of other sciences that are the necessary conditions of its matter. He grants too that value in use, or the value which people put upon a thing, is the condition and also the "extreme limit" of value in exchange.[17] But he omits to notice that it is not every means of gratifying inclinations which the individual counts valuable in use, that in one sense even value in use (as distinguished from mere usefulness) is a scarcity-value, and that the psychological causes which lead the individual to value or not to value particular possessions quite apart from the power of exchanging them, are important links in the whole chain of an economical system. When this was observed by Jevons and others twenty years or so after the publication of Mill's *Principles of Political Economy*, a fresh impulse was given to the study of deductive economics.[18] A doctrine of Consumption became an essential part of the whole; and it was no longer possible to suppose that all exact political economy depended on the assumption of free competition in exchanges.

To Mill wealth consists in "utilities fixed and embodied in material objects"[19]—just as in his philosophy material objects themselves are "permanent possibilities of sensation."[20] He gives us no special account of utility as an economical phenomenon, or of value in relation to it. Outside of political economy, he has given us his view of the gradations of human wants. Although economically he treats all pleasures as alike, this is far from being his view in ethics. His Utilitarianism, as distinguished from that of Bentham and James Mill, recognises a difference in *quality* between pleasures. The pleasures arising in connection with the higher or distinctively human faculties are "more desirable" than the merely animal pleasures; and we know that they are so because those that have tried both tell us so (cf. *Diss. and Disc.*, I. 158; *Utilitarianism*, p. 12, cf. 15). This is the proof used by Plato (*Republic*, IX., §§ 582 *seq.*[21]) when he decides that the philosopher's pleasure is the pleasantest of all. Mill goes on to say that the higher pleasures give greater happiness but not so easy contentment. The desires of an ignorant or uncivilized man are satisfied sooner and with greater ease; but in the higher grades of existence wants are more numerous and more difficult to satisfy; "a highly endowed being will always feel that any happiness which he can look for, as the world is constituted, is imperfect," but he has a sense of the dignity of man which makes him always prefer rather to be a human being dissatisfied than a pig satisfied,[22] and to be a Socrates dissatisfied than a fool satisfied. If the fool thinks otherwise, it is because he only knows his own side of the question. Tannhäuser in Wagner's drama did not take this view of the matter when he taunted his fellow bards with having no practical knowledge of the pleasure of love; but the concession itself, whether logically maintainable or not, deprives Utilitarianism of a great part of its difficulties in relation to Economics, and we need not pause to criticise the theory. Mill's own answer to Tannhäuser would be (see *Utilitarianism*, p. 14) that when a man returned to the baser pleasures he had lost capacity for the higher and therewith real knowledge of them. He recognises frankly that men are not always the best judges of their own wants (*Diss. and Disc.*, 1.28).

Desires, it appears, thus only tend towards infinity and insatiableness when the subjects of them are civilized and instructed men. In modern civilization Mill elsewhere (*Diss.* I., "Civilization," pp. 177, 178) remarks another feature. The individual, owing to the comparative security of political institutions, relies very little on himself for protection of his person and property, and devotes all his energies to personal aggrandisement, virtue, philanthropy, or the gaining of wealth. These motives vary greatly in different cases, but the desire of wealth may be considered almost universal; and wealth being as a rule "the most accessible means of gratifying all their other desires," "nearly the whole of the energy of character which exists in highly civilized societies concentrates itself on the pursuit of that object." The highest classes in society have too much wealth already to make them incur the toil of procuring more, and as a rule they have no dominant pursuit, while that of the middle classes is almost wholly the pursuit of wealth.

Abstract economics, therefore, would seem to be an analysis of the effects of the dominant desire of the middle classes. This desire is to be considered as not only the most powerful but the sole ruler; all parties are to be supposed in the first instance "to take care of their own interest" (*Pol. Econ.*, III. i., § 5; 1st ed. 519; 5th, 531 to 533), and it is implied that they make no mistakes about it. We are to suppose free competition and enlightened competitors.

Such are the premises of Mill's abstract political economy. The economical doctrines which he proceeds to draw from them are in the main Ricardian. Perhaps the most original feature of his first book (on Production) is his ingenious introduction into it of the "law of the increase of labour" as affecting the numbers of the producers and being therefore co-ordinate with the "law of the increase of capital" and the "law of the increase of production from land" (chaps, x., xi., xii.). As before noticed, this is really a composition of causes, and logically a departure from the severity of the first abstraction. In dealing with the "Requisites of Production" (I. i.) he discusses the relation of human labour to nature, and decides that the part which "nature" plays in any work of man is incommensurable with man's part. Man "puts things into fit places for being acted upon by their own internal forces and by those residing in other natural objects." He can do nothing but *move* them from one position to another.[23] In the first of the Essays on *Nature, the Utility of Religion, and Theism* he goes more fully into this point, and shows how widely the 19th century is removed from the opinions of the 18th. "Nature" (he tells us) "means the sum of all phenomena together with the causes which produce them, including not only all that happens but all that is capable of happening" (p. 5). In this sense, it includes Art, for "Art has no independent powers of its own.

Art is but the employment of the powers of Nature for an end. Phenomena produced by human agency, no less than those which, as far as we are concerned, are spontaneous, depend on the properties of the elementary forces or of the elementary substances and their compounds. ... We move objects. ... Even the volition which designs, the intelligence which contrives, and the muscular force which executes these movements are themselves powers of Nature" (pp. 7, 8). But the usual antithesis has been between the doings of man and the doings of the *rest* of nature. In this sense the Law of Nature was made a standard of ethics and of jurisprudence.[24] The modern use of the terms natural, and unnatural points to a third distinction, namely, between what is and what ought to be, though there is always in the minds of those who use the terms an idea that observation of what *is* will guide us to a knowledge of what ought to be (pp. 8–13). We can only make sense of such a notion by translating the precept "follow nature" into the precept "study nature." We cannot escape from nature as a whole; but by study of the laws of nature we can use one law to counteract another (pp. 16, 17). But, if it is intended that we should imitate in our action the spontaneous course which the rest of nature follows when left to itself, human wisdom would be folly; to dig, to plough, to build, and to wear clothes would be direct infringements of the injunction to follow nature (pp. 19, 20). The arts of life and civilization generally are so many admissions that nature is from man's point of view imperfect. They are intended to supply what is lacking on nature's part, τὸ τῆς φύσεως ελλεῖπον αναπληρεῖν. Because we cannot imitate the vastness of natural forces, it does not follow that we ought to imitate external nature in its other attributes from mere awe of its vastness.[25] Nature goes straight to her ends with a reckless indifference to all moral considerations. "Nearly all the things which men are hanged or imprisoned for doing to one another are nature's everyday performances" (pp. 27, 28). This applies to the causes at work on and in human society. It is "part of Nature's habitual injustice that to him that hath shall be given, but from him that hath not shall be taken away even that which he hath." It is the good who become more good; it is the person who already knows much that can learn most easily; "those who find it easy to gain money are not the poor but the rich, while health, strength, knowledge, talents, are all means of acquiring riches; and riches are often an indispensable means of acquiring these,"—and the tendency of evil is towards further evil, of ill health to worse health and poverty, of poverty to a thousand mental and moral evils, of vice to multiplied vice (pp. 34–36).

We have nothing here to do with Mill's theological conclusion, which is that the Creator is not omnipotent. But we see how closely this reasoning (in an essay written between 1850 and 1858) bears on Mill's economical views. The laws of production are of physical necessity, and therefore (we infer) they partake of the general imperfection of nature, and are to be turned one against another, in order to be of service to man. Similarly the distribution and the exchange of wealth (however Ricardian is the treatment of the latter by our author) are by no means to be left to take their spontaneous course as if that were necessarily the best. The works of nature, including the spontaneous action of economical laws, are no more to be passively taken on trust, and taken as patterns for imitation, than the actions of our fellow men.

But our first duty as intelligent men is to ascertain what they are. The facts of production are (he considers) a body of facts partaking of the nature of physical truths. No modification of external nature, or of human nature, can go so far as to modify them. While the earth endureth, the production of wealth by material agents and by labour, and of human beings by procreation from human beings, will not be otherwise than it is now. To believe otherwise would be to give up belief in fixed laws of nature altogether. Some evolutionists would perhaps dispute the assumption that physiologically men will always remain essentially as they are;[26] and even in later life Mill devotes no discussion to this point, thinking it settled perhaps by Malthus in his controversy with Condorcet and Godwin. There is probably no one who would dispute the assumption that the constitution of the material world is unalterable.

Mill had, however, been so strongly impressed with the power of human beings, and especially human societies, to grow from strength to strength both in intellect and in character, that he seized perhaps too eagerly the opportunity of marking out an apparently clear line of distinction between the province of unalterable laws and the province of human institutions in matters, economical. He recognised the first in Production, and the second in Distribution. But even his chapters on production are full of illustrations from contemporary life and from history, which show how large is the effect of social arrangements, and of ideas, in that region also; the laws of production are no doubt not of man's invention, but they are turned to much or little use according to the wisdom or unwisdom of human arrangements. In other ways Mill himself fails to preserve his distinction between distribution and production. It appears that distribution itself has at certain stages certain laws that are not of man's creation. It depends no doubt on man whether they have the conditions of their operation supplied to them or not; but, these once supplied, the further steps (or their actual operation itself) are "determined by laws as rigid as those of production itself."[27] They are not the result of deliberate human invention, but are "*sponte acta.*" Mill was referring to the laws of Exchange and Value, and he could not himself have denied their hypothetical exactness without ceasing to be a deductive economist. But the principles of currency, for example, are less truly described as hypothetical than the principles of commercial value, and we feel the want of some distinction like that of Rodbertus between historical and theoretical categories, which embraces distribution and production alike. Mill's admission even of a hypothetical exactness in the field of distribution would forbid us to say that distribution is arbitrary, and production is not so. The laws of Exchange are not of "human institution," or at least not "*solely.*" On the other hand, the law of Population, which is ranked under Production, is not a physical law unmodifiable by man, though it appears under Production. Mill has himself said of Malthus again and again that in expounding it he had not shut the gate of progress, but really for the first time opened it.[28] Mill's recognition of fixed economical laws and his recognition at the same time of man's power to turn them, as he turns any other laws, to his own uses are among the most distinctive features of his treatise; and the two features are found together in the book on Production as well as in the book on Distribution.

But the modification of economical tendencies is made to occupy a far larger place under Distribution than under Production. The modifications actual, possible, and contemplated, are described at length. We are told of the influence of Custom in preventing rents from being rack-rents, wages from being the lowest possible, or highest possible, prices from being in the retail trade what competition makes them in wholesale dealings. We are confronted with the experience of countries where competition hardly exists. We are led to examine the various schemes, prominently before the public at the end of the first half of the 19th century, for toning down or altogether abolishing the severities of competition in modern societies.

The whole book (II., on Distribution) may be regarded as an introduction to the next one (III., on Exchange), for the author is really discussing how far the social and legal conditions, which the Ricardian principles of exchange assume to be existing, really do exist in the world generally, and how far, where they do exist, they can possibly be modified or entirely supplanted by deliberate contrivance. First and foremost stands the institution of private Property. Mill clearly recognises (as against the theories of Locke and others) that historically, the legal recognition of private property was not based on any philosophical theory of its public utility, economical or otherwise. But "social philosophy" (he says, II. I., § 2) may consider what would be the view taken by a society of men, say a body of colonists now, if they were to consider whether they should conduct their production on the principle of common ownership or of individual property. Common ownership of the land and the instruments of production is the feature of all Socialism; Communism is a species of it which insists on absolute equality in the distribution of the comforts of life. Such schemes are, he says, not *à priori* impracticable. To say that under Communism the individual would have no interest in doing good work is to forget that the greater part of the work of our present society is done by wage-earners for a master, and therefore without any "interest" on the part of the worker. Besides, "mankind are capable of a far greater amount of public spirit than the present age is accustomed to suppose possible," and a communist society would excite an *esprit de corps* that might be as efficacious as competition. Emulation in the public service would not be discouraged. Reckless increase of families would be condemned by public opinion. A real difficulty, however, is the apportionment of work, and the appraisement of different kinds of it, apart from the standards of competitive trading. But "human intelligence, guided by a sense of justice," might be equal to the task.

If, therefore, we had to choose between private property as it is now, and Communism, we might elect for the latter in spite of its difficulties. But it is a rule of good criticism to compare the best form of one theory with the best form of its rival; and we should take private property not as it is, but as it might be. "The principle of private property has never yet had a fair trial in any country. The laws regarding it have never anywhere conformed to the principles that justify its existence; they have converted into private property what could not justifiably become so (in sanctioning slavery); and they have recognised absolute property where there could only be a very modified right (in the matter of the land). They have been so framed as to increase inequality rather than to diminish it. But these abuses have no necessary connection with the principle of private property itself. The guarantee to every individual of the fruits of his labour and abstinence is the essential feature with which (if individual property is to be fairly tested) nothing inconsistent should be established. In addition we must assume two conditions which are the conditions of all reforms, Socialistic or otherwise,—universal education and restraint on population. "With these, there could be no poverty even under the present social institutions." Socialism is therefore not our sole refuge, but simply one of two alternatives, the comparative merits of which are hard to determine. "We are too ignorant either of what individual agency in its best form, or Socialism in its best form, can accomplish, to be qualified to decide which of the two will be the ultimate form of human society." It will probably be that one which is most consistent with the greatest amount of liberty and spontaneity. For, next to food and clothing, liberty is the great necessary of human life. Socialism might give more of it than the great body of the people have now; but Mill clearly fears that, under it, the will and the opinion of the majority might leave even less room for "eccentricity" than they do now. After touching on the St. Simonians, and the experiment of the Jesuits in Paraguay,[29] he goes with more detail into Fourierism, which takes into account capital and talent as well as labour in distribution. In reference to the claim made by Fourier to make labour "attractive," he notes that "scarcely any labour, however severe, undergone by human beings for the sake of subsistence exceeds in intensity that which other human beings, whose subsistence is already provided for, are found ready and even eager to undergo for pleasure." We must not therefore (he says) dismiss such schemes as impracticable, and the experiment should be tried. However till we have more experience to guide us we may expect that for some time to come the conditions of social existence and progress will include private property and individual competition, and our aim must be to make these institutions work for the full advantage of the community.[30] In other words we must in the first place make the best of things as they are.

Mill tries to be faithful to the inductive and *à posteriori* method in social reform as distinguished from political economy. On the other hand, in dealing with the law of Inheritance, he reasons directly from first principles, without waiting for experiment. Land, so far as it is not improved by its possessor, should not be counted his private property as a chattel should be. Later in life he proposed that all the "increment" in the value of land that was "unearned" should be taken by the State in taxes.[31] The basis of property is labour, and that is absent in the possessor of the unearned increment. Again, he argues (in the *Political Economy*) that bequest might be limited to an amount that would give sufficiency, not luxury, to the heir, and that (as Bentham urged) in intestacy, failing direct heirs, the crown should inherit. Elsewhere he had pleaded strongly for the desirability of turning old endowments to public uses when the times had so changed that to carry out the intentions of the founder was no longer to confer the public benefit intended by the founder.[32] His arguments against Turgot, in favour of liberty to found Endowments, are largely drawn from the observation that progress often begins in the "eccentricities" of individuals (cf. *Liberty*, I. 33), ideas that are not at first popular, but must create a demand for themselves slowly and gradually. There is in fact hardly any case in which Mill would say that *a priori* an alteration of present arrangements is absolutely forbidden. He is consistent with his general Utilitarian position, and rejects certain schemes (*e.g.* nationalization of land and capital) on grounds of expediency and experience.[33] Though he believes firmly in the relativity of all institutions, economical as well as political, and in some few passages traces the growth of an idea (like that of property) from ancient forms to modern, he can hardly be said to look for guidance to any idea of development. He recognises the fact of it, and thinks that it will lead us to some form of associated industry; but he makes no attempt to forecast in detail the steps by which the change will be produced, and he regards competition in some form or other as indispensable to progress (*Pol. Econ.*, IV. vii., § 7).

Mill is an optimist so far as he allows that society has on the whole been becoming better. The reign of brute force is over, and the reign of reason begun.[34] Even in the matter of the distribution of wealth there is progress. The working classes, as things are, have gained and are gaining ground. The pressure of population has not increased but diminished. "The permanent causes all operate in the direction of improvement."[35] The Socialists who have done service by pointing out the evils of competition, have not themselves realized the advantages of competition. "There are many things which free trade does passably; there are none which it does absolutely well, for competition is as rife in the career of fraud as in that of real excellence."[36] But the evils of privilege are greater still, and to be protected against competition is to be protected in idleness and mental dulness.[37]

We may therefore regard Mill as taking up the abstract discussion of the problems of exchange without any strong bias either for or against the realizing of the abstractions and the universal adoption of the ruling motive of the middle classes. The "stationary state" of material wealth and population is to him personally more attractive than the "progressive," which was eulogised by Adam Smith; but it is an aspiration of which he does not confidently foresee the fulfilment.[38] He hopes that the future of the working classes will be co-operative industry, in place of work for an employer.

The mere intellectual enlightenment and increased worldly wisdom of the great body of the people, the present industrial relations of employer and employed, remaining as they are, would have realized the ideal of the Manchester School of politicians; but this was not the ideal of Mill, or of any English economist, whose works have claim to be in the first rank. It was really a political theory with the stamp of the 18th century on it; it was an enlightened "anarchy *plus* the constable." Free competition was to Mill only the necessary assumption of abstract economical science; he went so far as to say that Political Economy would not be a science without it.[39] But he usually[40] recognised that the science so constituted was hypothetical, and it is with full recognition of this hypothetical character of it that he drew out in detail the doctrine of Value and Prices, Profit, Wages, Rent, International Exchange, and even Credit and Currency. For the present purpose, it is not needful to discuss the body of doctrine thus presented by Mill. It is enough to say that even in deductive economics his attitude of mind was so far from dogmatic, that as late as the year 1869 (see *Fortnightly Review*, May of that year), he abandoned what had since the days of MacCulloch and Senior been reckoned as a demonstrated economic doctrine, the theory of a Wages Fund, while otherwise his economical teaching is in principle that of the Ricardians.

There is one topic, however, on which we might expect to find his new views of political philosophy transforming the old economical theories, and that is the relation of society to government and of both to the individual citizens.

The distinction between Society and Government is practically recognized by Mill. There is (he says) a powerful natural sentiment, a desire to be at one with our fellow creatures, which is not innate in the sense of being present perceptibly always with all of us, but natural, in the sense in which speech and reason are natural. The social state is at once so natural, so necessary, and so habitual to man, that except in some unusual circumstances or by an effort of voluntary abstraction, he never conceives himself otherwise than as a member of a body. This association (without "express inculcation" and simply from "the influences of advancing civilization") is riveted more and more as mankind are further removed from the state of savage independence. Any condition therefore which is essential to a state of society becomes more and more an inseparable part of every person's conception of the state of things into which he is born and which is the destiny of a human being. It becomes impossible, for men, living together, working together and having common interests, to be without a strong feeling for the welfare of others as well for their own. To attend to the good of others becomes as much a matter of course with them as any of the physical conditions of their existence.[41]

Yet the body, of which the individuals feel themselves to be members, is conceived by Mill (in the spirit of Bentham) as artificial. "We of this generation are not addicted to falling down before a Baal of brass and stone; the idols we worship are abstract terms; the divinities to whom we render up our substance are personifications. Besides our duties to our fellow country-men, we owe duties to the *constitution*; privileges which landlords or mer-chants have no claim to must be granted to *agriculture* or *trade*; and, when every clergyman has received the last halfpenny of his dues and expectations, there remain rights of the *Church*, which it would be sacrilege to violate. To all such rights we[42] confess our indifference. The only moral duties which we are conscious of are towards living beings, either present or to come, who can be in some way better for what we do or forbear. When we have done our duty to all these, we feel easy in our minds, and sleep with an untroubled conscience the sleep of the just—a sleep which the groans of no plundered abstraction are loud enough to disturb."[43] As Mill was prouder of the article in which these words are written than of almost any other he ever wrote (see *Autob.*, p. 182), we may conclude that he did not give up this individualistic point of view. It is indeed the only one consistent with the nominalism of his *Logic*.[44] A class, he says there (vol. i. 104) is nothing but individuals denoted by a general name. Inseparable association (we may infer) can make "soci-ety" *appear* to be more than this, but the only *reality* will be the feeling of the individuals that others are as they are.

Artificial or not, societies exist and societies develope (Mill thinks) in morality and in speculative knowledge, hindered and helped by governments and rulers, but at the same time, in a sense, independent of them. They are so far independent that they have a distinct character of their own which rulers cannot make for them, but must more or less consult even when they would pervert it to their own purposes.[45] Industrial organization amongst other things is determined by this national character; and nothing is more strictly relative to national character and peculiarities than government. Mill differs from his father in refusing to believe that rulers can govern simply with a view to their own selfish interests; they must adapt themselves to the character and customs of the nation they rule, and they are always themselves more or less under the influence of the *sensus communis*. It follows that there is no absolutely best form of government, but that each nation, according to its historical circumstances, will have a government peculiar to itself. He differs from Ricardian economists in refusing to believe that competitive industry is the final and best type; national character will to a large extent determine the type of industrial organization as well as the government. Yet he does not allow this view to become a fatalism; nations, like men, are never above criticism. Political Philosophy may show flaws in a constitution; and Political Economy may "emphatically teach" that a certain industrial arrangement is necessarily bad. Nations, like men, are not free to begin the world as if they were the creators of it; but they are free to direct their circumstances so as to modify their own character by their acts.[46]

Now one of their ways of doing so is by the action of government. Governments are not, as the writers of the school of Godwin and Paine supposed, purely a human invention and purely a mischief: Neither are they, as writers like Burke and Macaulay have argued, purely a natural growth, where man's deliberate invention plays no part at all. "In every stage of their existence they are made what they are by human voluntary agency." They are neither machines nor plants. A people will not be made to substitute a good government for a bad without preparation, but it may be prepared for one or other by having the desire of it implanted by political propaganda or otherwise. Its government is in this sense a matter of choice; and its choice is not a fixed quantity that outside influences cannot affect.[47] But what is our criterion of a good or bad government?[48] Simply the Utilitarian; the good is that which is best fitted to promote the interests of the society concerned. These interests are, it is true, not easy to define; the constituents of social well-being cannot be exhausted in a formula like that of Coleridge, "permanence and progressiveness," or that of Comte, "order and progress," for all depends on what is included under order and progress, on the qualities which are to be cherished and developed in a people. Even in matters economical there is no real contrast between the two principles; a good system of taxation and finance which is essential to order, is conducive to progress also. It is best indeed to say simply that a good government is that which is most conducive to progress, for progress involves order, while order may not involve progress. Progress[49] in wealth, for example, is impossible unless there is some sort of order in the sense of preservation of gains already made, but there might be the latter without any steps being taken to go beyond them. Progress, then, is the chief concern of government. It must be taken as including not only conservation of the past gains, but prevention of positive relapse. Mill, unlike Godwin, realizes that human beings and human affairs may drift strongly towards evil as well as good. He even hints that the service of philanthropists and reformers is much greater in preventing relapse than in assisting progress.

Good government, in fact, (Mill argues) depends most of all on the personal "qualities of the human beings composing the society over which the government is exercised."[50] The best institutions will fail if corruptly directed and not supported by a popular sympathy with their spirit. No form of government, it is true, would be rational that depended on the absolute disinterestedness of the average citizen.[51] But there must be a sense of common interest, such as has been already described as belonging to all members of a civilized society;[52] and, besides this, there must be adequate machinery. Mill would have the representative machinery so constructed as to provide for the representation of minorities. We need not dwell on the political problem, but look rather at the general question—in what institutions the good sense of a society is to express itself, and what can and cannot be expected from the institutions so formed. Government (Mill answers) has certain public business to carry on for the people, and it has a certain guiding influence to exert upon the people. The first class of functions (called in the *Political Economy*[53] the "necessary" as distinguished from the "optional" functions of

government) include the maintenance of the laws of property and the administration of justice and police, taxation, finance, and such public works as
coinage and sanitary regulations. They might conceivably be the same for all
societies. The second class (or optional functions) include all those actions of
government which are usually said to go beyond the principle of *laissez-faire*
or non-interference. "Whatever theory we adopt respecting the foundation
of the social union and under whatever political institutions we live, there is
a circle around every individual human being which no government ought to
be permitted to overstep."[54] But how large should this circle be? Mill decides
that it ought to include all that concerns mainly the life of the individual
himself, and only affects the interests of others by way of example,—and the
burden of proof should always be laid on the advocates of interference. "In
the most advanced communities the great majority of things are worse done
by the intervention of government than the individuals most interested in the
matter would do them or cause them to be done, if left to themselves."[55] This
applies, for example, directly to industrial operations. Government may regulate them (as it regulates railways by a Railway Commission), but it cannot
so successfully conduct them. Even if it had at its disposal all the talents of the
community instead of a small fraction thereof, it would not be desirable that
the training which the conduct of business gives to a people should be taken
away from them and confined to a small number of officials. "Letting alone,
then, should be the general practice."

On the other hand, where the consumer is not the best judge either of his
own wants or of the article to be provided (as in education and scientific
enterprises and research, and in the case of children, the insane, the lower animals, the Poor Laws, colonization, and even perhaps the hours of labour)[56]
Mill will allow no abstract principle to forbid the interference of the State.
Where expediency is distinctly shown, that is to him the highest principle and
must prevail. He makes full recognition of the fact that much of our law is
simply custom made definite and written, this being more especially true of
Commercial law which consists in great part of the usages of merchants and
has thus been created by those who have most interest in keeping it good.[57]
But he sees clearly that besides this almost spontaneous growth of law out of
custom there must be a legislation that is ahead of custom while not contrary
to national character.

In political philosophy and in political economy Mill's work, if not that of
a mere formulator,[58] is not that of a great constructor. In the former he has
emphasized, perhaps even exaggerated, some neglected views; he was so anxious to avoid the narrowness of his own early days, that he too often leaves
us with the impression that of two opposing theories both are true, though
the principle that reconciles them is not clearly discoverable. In political
economy, too, in his anxiety to avoid representing the postulates of abstract
economics as the literal truths of concrete life, he leaves the impression that
the qualifications are too great to make the abstract theory very useful. It was
the less useful in his case because he never dealt quite freely with the work

of Ricardo, whom from his early training he regarded as the creator of the science. He prepared the mind of English economists for new ideas, but he did little to introduce these himself. The latest developments of economical doctrine were to come from an entirely different direction and to follow a path to which he had not pointed.

Note

In the pamphlet *Gneist und Stuart Mill. Ait-Englische und Neu-Englische Staatsanschauung* [Anon.], 1869, the principles of Mill on Representative Government are compared with those of the German historian Gneist. The main question is, how far is it possible for a people to adopt the institutions of another and more highly developed people, without passing through all the stages in which the latter had developed. The anonymous writer sets Gneist against Mill on this point, Mill's view being to him the unhistorical one. We must remember however that the stress laid by the school of Bentham on political mechanism may be a needful corrective of the extreme "historical" view from which it would almost appear that all teaching of one nation by another is impossible, and all institutions are spirit without machinery. It is no doubt true that division of labour must not be allowed to justify bureaucracy (*Gneist*, p. 31). The State is not a workshop. But, even in industry, division of labour does not mean absence of all knowledge and control of the work of others outside of one's own subdivision.

The best general estimate of Mill as an economist, is given by F. A. Lange, *J. S. Mill's Ansichten über die sociale Frage* (1866). Professor Bain's *J. S. Mill, a Criticism* (1882) is a disparaging account which is well corrected by Mr. W. L. Courtney's *Life of John Stuart Mill* (1889). M. Taine's *Study of John Stuart Mill* (transl. 1870) relates chiefly to the philosophy; it received the commendation of Mill himself.

The *Lettres inédites de Stuart Mill* printed by Laveleye (Brussels, 1885) are of very inferior interest to the correspondence with Comte. The letters are few and short, the commentaries long. There is an interesting description of Mill's house and person; but Mill's character appears far more clearly in the letters printed as Appendix to the *Journals and Letters of Caroline Fox* (1881), and addressed to her brother Robert Barclay Fox (1840–43).

Notes

1 *Subjection of Women* (first written in 1861. See Bain's *J. S. Mill*, p. 130), 2nd ed., p. 124. In *Diss. and Disc.*, II. 355 (*Fr. Rev.*, written 1849), on contrary made it a reproach against the English people that "a theory which purports to be the very thing intended to be acted upon fills them with alarm."

2 Even in his later days Mill could see nothing valuable in Kant except his refutation of his predecessors (*Exam. of Hamilton*, p. 636, n.).

3 See Preface to edition 1844; but cf. *Autob.*, pp. 120, 121, 180.
4 Mill allows that he might have learned the same lesson from Owen's followers, *e.g.* from W. Thompson (*Distribution of Wealth*, 1824). See Mill, *Pol. Econ.*, II. 1., § 4. He might in fact have learned it from Bentham. See *Reform Catechism* (1818), p. 36, and note. "A peremptory exclusion, by which one-half of the species is excluded from that security for a regard to their interests, which in the case of the other half is pronounced indisputable." Cf. *ibid.*, p. 128 ft., and Mill, *Autobiogr.*, p. 105.
5 It is fair to Malthus to remember that his *Political Economy* avowedly attempted the same conjunction. J. Hill Burton made the same attempt in the year after Mill.
6 Prof. Ingram's criticism on the full title of the *Political Economy* is perfectly fair. It ought to have read, "with some of their applications to *other branches* of Social Philosophy."
7 *Diss.*, I., "Bentham" (1838), p. 391.
8 Cf. Burke, *Sublime and Beaut.*, Introduction (1756).
9 *Uns. Questions*, p. 120; cf. above (Ad. Sm. on Philosophy), p. 149.
10 *E.g.*, Mrs. Marcet, *Conversations on Pol. Econ.*, 1817, pp. 17, 18.
    The definition up to this point was anticipated by the German economist, L. H. Jacob, the contemporary of James Mill. See Roscher, *Nat. Oekon. in Deutschland*, p. 688. For a good discussion of present views of Definition and Method, see J. N. Keynes, *Scope and Method of Pol. Econ.* (1891).
11 See *Lettres d'Aug. Comte à J. S. Mill*, 1841–46 (Leroux, 1877).
12 He was thinking amongst other things of Macaulay's criticism of the Essay on Government.
13 "All true political Science is in one sense of the phrase *à priori*,"—*Inaug. Address, St. Andrews*, 1867, p. 51.
14 Comte rejected both Psychology and Political Economy; but in this he was not followed by all his disciples.
15 Memory: see *Exam. of Hamilton* (1865) p. 209 n. of ed. 1872. Pleasure: *Utilitarianism*, p. 6, "admitted to be good without proof." Social Feeling: *Utilitarianism*, pp. 43, 45.
16 *Pol. Econ.*, III. i., § 2; cf. II., § i.
17 See *Harvard Quarterly Journal of Economics*, Oct., 1888, April, 1889.
18 *Pol. Econ.*, I. iii., "Of Unproductive Labour." Compare *Uns. Quest.*, p. 82: "The wealth of a country consists of the sum total of the permanent sources of enjoyment, whether material or immaterial, contained in it."
19 *Exam. of Hamilton*, p. 225, etc.
20 τίς ἐμπειρότατος πασῶν ὧν εἴπομεν ἡδονῶν, etc.
21 Perhaps a rejoinder to Carlyle's epithet, "the Pig Philosophy."
22 Jas. Mill is said by his son to have been the first to apply this observation to economics. It occurs as a general maxim in Bacon's *Novum Organum*, IV.: "Ad opera nil aliud potest homo quam ut corpora naturalia admoveat et amoveat; reliqua natura intus agit."
23 The doctrine of Natural Law (he says) has now exhausted what good influence it ever had (*Diss, and Disc.*, III. 243. "Austin.").
24 A philosopher should not be frightened by mere bigness (*Unseen Univ.*).
25 The human race might say with Omar:—

> "Think that to-day you are what yesterday
> You were; to-morrow you shall not be less."

The assumption is implied in Mill's expression, "the inherent properties of their own bodily and mental structure" (*Pol. Econ.*, II. 1., §1). We may compare Hume's remark, above quoted, p. 156.

26 So *Pol. Econ.*, 1st ed., Preliminary Remarks, last sentence but one. In later editions the sentence stood thus: "As much a subject for scientific inquiry as any of the physical laws of nature."
27 *Diss.*, II. ("Claims of Labour," 1845), 183, etc., etc. So Thomas Chalmers in his *Pol. Econ.* (1832), I. 44.
28 He says this was "of short duration." But it lasted 150 years. There are reasons to believe that it was built on primitive native communism. See Letourneau, *Property, its Origin and Development* (1892), pp. 42 *seq.*
29 *Pol. Econ.*, II. i., § 4.
30 See *Diss. and Disc.* IV. 239 *seq.*: Papers on Land Tenure.
31 *Diss. and Disc.* I. 1 *seq.*: Corporation and Church Property. IV. i. *seq.*: Endowments.
32 See posthumous papers on Socialism, *Fortnightly Review*, April, 1879, p. 525.
33 *Subj. of Women*, p. 10.
34 Papers on Socialism, *Fortnightly Review*, March, 1879, pp. 373 *seq.* It should be noted that the often quoted passage in *Pol. Econ.*, IV. vi., § 2, about the failure of machinery to benefit the working classes is really a protest against over-population.
35 *Diss.*, IV. (Endowments, 1869), p. 13.
36 *Pol. Econ.*, IV. vii., § 7.
37 *Pol. Econ.*, IV. vi. (Of the Stationary State.)
38 *Pol. Econ.*, II. iv., § 1.
39 Not always. In *Diss.* IV. 149, for example ("Maine," 1871) he says that political economy "teaches emphatically" that the status of a tenant at will is essentially vicious.
40 *Utilitarianism*, pp. 44–47.
41 Editorial.
42 *Diss.* I. 20, 21 (Corpor. and Church Prop.), 1833.
43 The doctrine of kinds maintained in that book would have made another view possible.
44 See *Aug. Comte and Positivism*, pp. 113, 114, etc., etc.
45 See, *inter alia*, *Representative Govern.* (1861), ch. i. "To what extent forms of Government are a matter of choice."
46 *Repres. Gov.*, loc. cit.
47 *Ib.*, ch. ii.
48 Mill's curious idea of the limits of the progress of Art, shown in his fear lest musical combinations of notes should be exhausted (*Autobiogr.*, p. 145), may be compared with Condorcet (*Esquisse*, p. 376).
49 *Repres. Gov.*, ch. ii.
50 *Ib.*, ch. vi.
51 *Utilitarianism*, 44–47.
52 See above [p. 259].
53 Bk. V., ch. i.
54 *Pol. Econ.*, V. xi., § 2.
55 *Ibid.*, § 5.
56 *Pol. Econ.*, V. xi., § 12. Mill is as cautious here as in his admission of the possible desirability of Protection in "young communities."
57 *Pol. Econ.*, V. viii., § 3.
58 Bagehot, *Econ. Studies*, p. 19.

Book IV

Modern Philosophy (III)
Idealistic Economics

1   Kant (1724–1804)

In speculative philosophy Kant was roused from his dogmatic slumbers by Hume. He saw that in carrying out the principles of Locke and Berkeley to their logical consequences Hume had proved too much; he had proved human experience itself to be untrustworthy and scientific law to be based on fictions. Since this *reductio ad absurdum* follows from supposing that knowledge comes entirely from sense, we ought now (said Kant) to ask how matters stand if we suppose all knowledge of the data of sense to depend on conceptions of the subject knowing. Hence arose his doctrine of the *a priori* conditions which make all experience possible; experience has no meaning, unless forms of intuition and categories of the understanding are conjoined with sensations.

The question of chief interest to us here is how far Kant has also parted company with Hume in regard to Moral Philosophy and the Philosophy of Law. In regard to the former, at least, the breach is complete. Moral experience is only possible[1] on the condition of a connecting principle (expressed in the word "ought") which has nothing like itself in our sensible world, and could not be derived from any data of sense; it is the principle that reason is an end and a law to itself, and is not under the conditions of space, time, and causality.

Even the ordinary moral notions of men, imply that there is "nothing absolutely good but a good will," a will which is simply reason, ignoring all consequences and desires, and fixing itself on good for the sake of good. Duty is "the necessity of an act, the only motive of which is reverence for the law," and an act is in keeping with duty only when its maxim (or principle) could be willed to be universal law (or, as he says sometimes, a universal law of Nature[2]) without contradiction. The precept "so act that you could universalize the maxim of your action," is a categorical imperative, as distinguished from the hypothetical imperatives which prescribe certain actions as necessary to ends that we may or may not adopt according to circumstances. The morality of an act thus concerns its form, not its matter. Pleasures are purely relative and accidental; happiness is merely a general name for satisfactions of desire. Whereas morality deals with reason itself, as sufficient for itself and as opposed to all desires and pleasures which depend on an outside world. In other words, morality deals not with happiness, but with worthiness to be happy.[3] Kant will not hear of any distinction (such as is made by J. S. Mill) between pleasures that are high, and pleasures that are low; pleasures, as Epicurus rightly held, differ only in degree and not in kind. Moreover, so far as man is guided by feelings and desires, he is under the same law of necessity as the physical world,—whereas, when reason is its own end and law, man is (in respect of this autonomy) free. In the first case we have a phenomenal man, and in the second a noumenal (just as for the Speculative Reason we have a phenomenal world and a noumenal[4]),—and the two are separated, and contrary the one to the other. In spite of the separation, Kant thinks of man the noumenon, man the moral and rational being, as transforming man, the phenomenon, and making the latter his servant. He has even the idea of a "realm of ends" or one great society of moral beings, members one of another and working to secure the realization of the moral and rational life. He goes farther than Butler, and thinks that the moral law must have might as well as right and will govern the world. But, as on his own first principles the world and the moral law were defined as excluding one another, they are never fairly reconciled in one system. Oncken has laboured to show that Kant and Adam Smith were at one in their conception of the absoluteness of the law of duty. Smith no doubt expressed a stronger sense of reverence for the law, than many moralists of his time. But his ethics are widely removed from the ascetic or Stoical position of Kant, and the coincidence between their descriptions of religion (duties considered as divine commandments), on which much stress is laid by the author in question, relates after all to a matter not purely ethical.[5] The points of contrast are at least as important as the points of resemblance between two philosophers, one of whom has hardly an economics and the other of whom has no metaphysics.

When Kant goes on to consider how the law of reason is to be realized in the world as it is, he says that reason takes the phenomenal world and tries to make out of it a "type" of the purely rational world. Now, among the objects of the phenomenal world are other rational beings like ourselves. What is to be their relation to one another? Each of them, as rational, is end and law to himself; and, when brought into relation with each other, they must "so act that humanity in the person of others as well as in their own person shall be an end and never a means." Still each must work out his own salvation, and they must all be guided by the rule that the freedom of one (or his power to realize the law of duty in the world) shall not prevent another from having the same freedom. This is the first principle of Law (or Right) as distinguished from Morality: so act that your freedom shall not be inconsistent with the freedom of another man.

Law relates in this way not to the matter but to the form of what is willed. It concerns the outward action, not the motives of it; and it is negative where morality is positive.[6] When a man buys goods from me, for example, the question of law is not whether the transaction profited both or either of us, but whether each was free in the making of it.[7] Every action is legally right (as distinguished from morally good) if "the maxim allows the freedom of each man's will to exist in harmony with the freedom of every other man's according to a universal law." This (it will be noticed) is simply an application of the supreme canon of morality. Kant deduces from it the rightfulness of *compelling* one man to abstain from hindering the freedom of another, and the rightfulness of organizing Civil Society to carry out that compulsion. Civil society exists to secure the freedom, not the happiness of its members.[8] Each is to secure his own happiness for himself, and it depends on his own particular desires and his knowledge of nature what shape it takes. No man can judge for another in this matter. But liberty, equality, and independence are only secured by civil society, by a political government (VII. 132). Before its establishment, men are under the law of Nature; they may be socially brought together as one people; but that people is not a nation till it has a civil constitution; and the act by which it gets this is the "original contract." By this contract the several individuals (*omnes et singuli*) give up their wild freedom in order to receive all together (*universi*) the civil liberty secured by the State. Till this is done men are in a state of war with each other; Hobbes (VI. 194) was only wrong in saying they are warring instead of in a state of war;[9] till then, all rights (of property or otherwise) are merely provisional; and till rights are secured there is no *wealth* (IV. 326). Kant does not mean that there was such a social contract as a matter of history; it is simply his way of stating the fact that the rational basis of civil government is the "*volonté de tous.*" The supreme legislative authority is the collective will of all, "all" being soon explained to mean only mature persons and those whose personality is not bound up with that of others.[10] The supreme executive and judicial powers once established, no resistance to them is tolerable. The execution of Louis XVI. seemed horrible, because it overturned the whole foundation of law and order. Hobbes himself is thus hardly more autocratic than Kant, though Kant regards the Republican form of government as the best when men are ripe for it. As there is an original contract so there is an original common ownership of land (*communio fundi originaria*) as distinguished from a primitive common ownership (*commiunio fundi prirmava*). As a matter of history, all was disorder and violence in early times; but civil government implies as a matter of logic a common ownership, before private ownership can begin. Right in anything is right to make private use of it, and this is a right which implies concurrence of others, who agree with me in respecting *mine* while I respect *theirs*; otherwise no one does me a wrong in dispossessing me. We have agreed to grant each other the same rights and that which we have thus allotted we must first collectively have had in our disposal.[11] From this follows the State's right of taxing landowners and of preventing corporations and castes from perpetuating any use of land which may prove prejudicial to the public interest.[12] The right of the State to impress soldiers is deduced from its *creation* of them. Since without the civil government there would be less production and fewer men, the State has (indirectly) *made* men; and so, since "every one has undisputed property in what he has made himself," the State can rightfully impress the men who owe to it their existence.[13]

The sentences last quoted may be thought to convey the idea that Kant, like Locke, deduced property from labour. But this is not the case. In regard to land, for example, he says that actual cultivation is not necessary to appropriation, but rather implies an appropriation already made.[14] Something like a demand that every person should have property is involved in the statement[15] that the power to give temporal benefits in the way of charity, depending as it does on gifts of fortune, is really due to the "injustice of Government," which has created inequality of wealth. But he does not follow up this idea, and his State is undoubtedly regulative rather than socialistic. Law and order are to be preserved, and then men are to pursue their happiness in their own way. Economical questions are treated under "Contracts" more fully than anywhere else. Rights of property are divided into three classes—*jus reale* (*jus in re*), *jus personale* (right to require the doing of particular acts by another person, in regard to things), and *jus realiter-personale* (over persons who are things, as in the relation of husband and wife, father and children). In this last case what the one person loses by being the other's property, he gains by having property in the other. The case is not that of pure contracts (*jus personale*) Contracts of the ordinary sort Kant divides into three classes, all concerned with the conversion of *meum* into *tuum* and *vice versa*. We have *first* those aiming at the gain of only *one* out of the two parties. These are benevolent contracts and *pacta gratuita*. Next come those aiming at gain on *both* sides,—onerous contracts. Last of all are those aiming not at a greater gain of possessions, but a greater security for possessions already held—*cautio*, including pledge, suretyship, and personal guarantee.

Under the second class (or the reciprocal and onerous contracts) come (*a*) alienation or exchange of goods for goods, purchase and sale, goods for money, loans (whether of goods for goods, or goods for money, or money for money), and (*b*) hiring (*locatio*), whether of goods for interest, or of labour (*locatio operce*) for wages, "the use of my powers for a stipulated price," or finally, in the form of a business undertaking (*mandatum*).[16]

Of money he says that its nominal definition is—something of which the only use is, to be exchanged for something else, which implies that a mutual gain is intended. It is a "medium of trade (*Mittel des Handels*) which in itself has no value, in contrast to a thing, as a commodity [or ware], which has value and is related to the *wants* of another man;—it *represents* all commodities" (VII. 86 *seq.*). The value of commodities (like corn) is direct; they satisfy wants. The value of money is only indirect; yet it is a useful *medium*. "It is the general means of exchanging [? the product of] one man's labour with another's."[17] National wealth, so far as obtained by means of money, is the sum of the labour [? products of the labour] with which men mutually reward one another, and which is represented by the money circulating among the people. Now the thing which is to be Money must itself have cost labour to produce it, in order that it may be equivalent to the labour by which the commodities (natural or manufactured) have been acquired. Otherwise, if it were easier to get money than goods, there would be more money than goods in the market to be sold. The sellers would give more labour than the buyers. Industry and wealth would decay. Bank notes and assignats are not money, for they cost no labour, and only circulate so long as their supposed basis of hard cash is not found to be wanting. The labour in gold and silver mines, which yields us our bullion, is probably even greater than in home industries, owing to the number of unhappy speculations in the former. The individual possessor of gold is no doubt indifferent to what it has cost, and asks only what it will fetch (V. 24); but the cost enters into the consideration of the general place and action of money. If the question is asked, How is the selection made of a material for money? one answer is, that the rulers may originate a custom by taking one particular material in tribute and encouraging merchants to use it in their traffic. Kant thinks that the case of Money is analogous to that of Books,—as the universal means for exchange of *ideas*; there is in both cases a rational meaning underlying the empirical or current view of the matter. Money is a commodity in which the price of all others (and even of sciences so far as taught for fees) is defined. Its abundance makes the opulence (*opulentia*) of a State. "For price (*pretium*) is the public judgment about the value (*valor*) of a thing in relation to the proportional quantity of that which is the general representative means of the mutual exchange of industry." Hence, on a large scale, not gold or copper, but silver is the real money for reckoning prices. Money, as Adam Smith says,[18] is at once the means of exchanging and the means of measuring the labour concerned in trade. To harmonize the empirical notion of it with the rational we must look only to the common *form* of mutual services in (onerous) contracts, the merely legal aspect of this conversion of *meum* into *tuum*.

This is the only case where Kant has given us anything like a full analysis of any economical notion. The abstraction and universality involved in the notion of money, wherever found, are the features that strike Kant because in harmony with his own notion of the philosophy of Law. His emphasis on the element of Labour may have been due to his study of the first part of Adam Smith's book; and it is possible that the prominence thus given to labour in the only attempt at a full economical analysis presented by the founder of modern German Philosophy may have had some influence on his followers when they turned their minds to economical questions.

Kant had no very strong prejudice against moneyed men. Though he speaks of the commercial spirit as being, like the aristocratic, unsocial,[19] he thinks that the moneyed classes are, on the whole, the most trustworthy servants of the State.[20] His remark that the English have given the world the language of trade (as the French that of polite conversation), and the English say a man "is worth a million," where the French say he "possesses a million,"[21] is not made in any unfriendly way. In fact, trade is (to him) one of the chief means of securing a Permanent Peace among the nations of the earth. The spirit of trade is inconsistent with war, and the spirit of trade sooner or later lays hold of every nation. Thus Nature, by the mechanism of motives that are non-moral, secures a result (permanent peace) which is demanded by morality.[22] The realizing of this permanent peace is rather the chief end of Law than simply one form of it amongst many (VII. 173), for this is the only state of things in which "mine" and "thine" are secured under rational principles. When people say "the best constitution is that in which the laws and not men have supreme power," they are admitting that the true objective reality is an *idea*; and it is an idea which logically involves in it permanent peace. Peoples, like individuals, should come out of the State of Nature[23] and form an International Commonwealth or State. Such a union would be too great in extent for a single government such as is known to us now, and for the present it is merely an ideal, the ideal of a cosmopolitan community, where each member respects the rights of every other. Nature has shut men up on a finite globe with limited lands to inhabit; nations have the right of offering mutual commerce and intercourse with each other, which implies a possible union under general laws, *jus cosmopoliticum*. Practical Reason (or morality) postulates this union, and we must work towards the best constitution to carry it out—"perhaps the Republicanism of all States collectively and severally,"—or else we are declaring our practical reason treacherous, and may as well fall back among the brutes.[24]

We naturally ask how far Kant considers that humanity has advanced and is advancing on the road indicated. His writings on Universal History, the "Probable Beginning of history," etc., will give the answer. Kant tells us[25] that, though the human will is free, its *phenomena* are under natural law. Even the births, deaths and marriages of human beings have a regularity of their own; and law governs the results of human actions quite apart from the intentions of the agents. Since men are guided neither by instinct nor by mere reason, history is not perfectly systematic; but, still, we may gather certain intentions of nature in regard to man, and they may be stated in the following propositions:—

1. All human capacities are destined to be developed.

2. The *rational* or intellectual capacities are to be fully developed in the *race* not in the individual. A step may be good for the race that is bad for the individuals who take it (*e.g.* from Paradise into Freedom).[26]

3. Nature wills that the individual shall choose and make his own happiness, and no one else can do so for him. Nature, in short, provides for the race, and the individual provides for himself. We must not forget that Kant considers the individual bound as a *moral* being to consider and to promote the happiness of others.[27]

4. Antagonism is Nature's chief means of developing human capacities. Man has *social* tendencies because in society he feels that his powers are developed; but he has also tendencies to *solitary* life and isolation from others and rest and quietness. "Man wills harmony; and Nature for the sake of the race wills discord." Nevertheless Nature herself wills an ultimate harmony (cf. IV. 321), and so—

5. The greatest problem of the race is to found such a civil society as will realize law everywhere.

6. This problem will be the last to be solved, "so crooked is the wood out of which we are carved."

7. Its solution depends on the possibility of an orderly relation of States to one another, a *fœdus Amphictyonum*. All wars may be regarded as experiments in that direction.

8. That is the end to which Nature is working in human history;—it is the state of things in which all human powers will be developed. "A mans chief concern should be to fill his place in creation fitly, and learn to be really a man."[28]

Thus the ways of providence are vindicated. At present, no doubt, though civilized, we are not yet made moral. The Enlightenment spoken of by the French philosophers is simply our coming of age, when we claim to think and act for ourselves.[29] This is a rational claim; but it is only a condition not the chief end of progress.

Kant, like Herder, regards development or evolution[30] as "organic." Between organized bodies and the State there is an analogy; every member of the body politic is to be at once means and end, at once helping to hold up the State, and itself dependent on the whole for its own support.[31] But (he says) this idea of organic evolution goes beyond physical science; it is a metaphysical notion implying the unity of all organic forces in the world. This is a wide conception which science would rightly regard as inadmissible from its point of view.[32] Teleology is excluded by science from its interpretations of facts; it is not "constitutive," though it is always present as an impulse and guide to the provisional inquiries; in other words, it is "regulative."[33] Physical science is bound to explain by mechanical principles and experience. Experience tells us how things are and have been, but does not tell us that they cannot be otherwise in the future.[34]

Rousseau had no such optimistic view of history. Kant, for whom Rousseau's writing had a magical attraction,[35] differs from that author in his very starting-point; "Rousseau proceeds synthetically and begins with the natural man; I proceed analytically, and begin with the civilized man." Kant considers that in civilization what is too often lost in simplicity is gained in opportunities of progress. The idea of the organic development of human powers was the form which the eighteenth century's conception of progress, such as we have seen it in Godwin, took in the case of Kant. He worked out no more than the bare outlines of a philosophy of history; but he and Herder had done enough to plant the idea in German philosophy. This service of theirs which seems remote from economics was in reality to be of great importance to that study.

Notes

1 But see Prof. Caird's *Kant*, II. 173, n.
2 *e.g. Metaphys. of Ethics* (Hartenstein's ed., IV. 269).
3 Hart., VI. 309, cf. VII. 293 ("Fragment of a Moral Catechism").

4 The noumenon, there, is the "thing in itself," which can never be an object of knowledge.

5 Austin whose ethics are hardly Kantian has a similar view of religion. See *Province of Jurisprudence* (1832).

6 A distinction substituted for that of Pufendorf between duties of imperfect and duties of perfect obligation.

7 *Rechtslehre* (Hart., VII. 27, § B.).

8 Hart., VI. 322, etc.

9 Hart., VII. 635 (Anthrop.), VII. 133–134, VI. 194, 321.

10 Hart., VII. 132. Kant mentions amongst his instances women apprentices, and workmen who work for a master.

11 Hart., VII. 60. The passage is quoted by Proudhon, *Contrad. Econ.*, II. 188.

12 VII. 142.

13 Hart., VII. 163.

14 VII. 64, 68.

15 VII. 262, cf. 62 ("On Acquisition by *Occupatio.*")

16 Hart., VII. 84, 85.

17 This is its real as opposed to its nominal definition.

18 Kant professes to quote Smith's words, but in reality gives only the general sense. Hart., VII. 88.

19 *Anthropologie*, VII. 639, n.

20 *Permanent Peace*, VI. 435.

21 *Ib*. VII. 636, n.

22 VI. 435, cf. VII. 172, 173.

23 Nature is sometimes used by Kant in sense of Reason, but not in this connection. Cf. VIII. 619: "Nature never makes a man a citizen." How deeply the contrast between the state of Nature and Civil Society impressed Kant appears *inter alia* from his applying it analogically to morality with and without a Church. VII. 194.

24 *Rechtslehre*, VII. 168–173.

25 IV. 143 *seq.*

26 *Probable Beginning of Human History*, IV. 321. So Hegel looked on the Fall as the "eternal mythus of man"; man passes from innocence to sin and then to conscious morality.—*E.g. Works*, VI. 54, XII. 265.

27 *e.g. Tugendlehre*, VII. 205, 256 *seq.*

28 VIII. 623.

29 IV. (*Aufklärung*), 161.

30 The word "evolution" occurs *e.g.* IV. 188. Cf. *Kr. d. Urtheilskraft*, § 81, V. 436. In its modern sense it was as old as Leibnitz. See Prof. R. Eucken's *Grimdbegriffe der Gegenwart*. Second Edition, 1892, p. 104.

31 *Urtheilskraft*, V. 387, note.

32 IV. 161.

33 *Urtheilskraft*, V. 391.

34 IV. 182.

35 VIII. 618. The relation of Kant to Rousseau is considered in Dietrich's *Kant und Rousseau* (1878) and Fester's *Rousseau und die deutsche Geschichtsphilosophie* (1890), ch. iii.

2   J. G. Fichte (1762–1814)

Economists of the school of Adam Smith have been often blamed for putting wealth instead of man in the forefront of their inquiries. Fichte goes farther than most of these critics. In his essay on the *Dignity of Man* (1794) he puts the Ego in the centre of all philosophy, and explains that by the Ego he means the Man.[1] It is the conception of a self-conscious spirit, or Man, that first shows to us that the world is a cosmos, and (he considers) the remark is true not only speculatively but practically and physically. "Man makes raw materials organize themselves after his ideal; he tames the wild animals and domesticates the wild plants." Science, first awakened by hard necessity, gradually knows and subdues Nature (*Destiny of Man*, 1800).[2] Men in company with men become more truly human, and human society reveals and developes the true nature of humanity. Though all outward embodiments of his ideal decay, the ideal itself remains, ever tending to transform the material world to its own likeness, and it remains an elevating feature in the lowest forms of humanity; the down-trodden slave on an American plantation is a temple of the Holy Ghost.[3]

Nothing could be more spiritual and less egoistic (in the vulgar sense of the term) than the teaching of Fichte with whom the modern socialism of Germany may be said to begin. "All progress," he says, "is due to unselfish devotion to ideas" (VII. 41). The State is no mere economic association (VII. 144, 157). Yet no modern socialist is more deeply dissatisfied with the condition of the labouring classes. "The majority of mankind are all their life long bowed down by hard toil to provide food for themselves and for the minority who do their thinking for them; immortal spirits are forced to tie down all their thoughts and schemes and efforts to the earth that feeds them" (*Destiny of Man*, *Wks.*, II. 266, 267). But the destiny of our race is "to be united into one body completely in accord with itself and uniformly developed" (*ib.*, 271). History shows a progress in this direction. Greek culture was good; but modern extends over far larger numbers of men, and the extension must go on till not merely as now a few nations but all nations of the earth share the benefits of it. This end reached, there is a further end: "When all useful things over the world have been discovered and distributed, then without stay or relapse, with united forces marching well in step, men will steadily rise to a culture of which we can at present form no conception" (*ib.*, 272, 273). In 1800, when these words were written, the idea of the Perfectibility of Man had not lost its fascination, and it is one of Fichte's points of contact with the Revolutionary writers. Another is his view of contemporary political institutions. Existing States are no true States but "strange combinations formed by senseless accident." He does not, like Godwin, consider the State to be in itself a mere necessary evil, and his idea of the course of its development is not like that of Godwin. Godwin foresaw a gradual and peaceful evolution of Society; Fichte thinks that the change will come through an attempt of the upper classes to tighten their grasp on the lower, resulting in a desperate effort of the latter to secure freedom, abolish privilege, and introduce equality (*Dest. of M.*, 273). Then will arise a true State in which every man will be secured against violence, and there will be a reign of true peace. Foreign wars will cease, for there will be no motive for wrong-doing. Men are not wicked for the sake of wickedness (cf. 314), but because as things are they get gain by it. When they have all their wants supplied, not at the expense of others, but with mutual advantage to their neighbours and themselves, vice itself will cease and emulation will take no hurtful forms (276, 277). But this happy state of affairs is only a finite and earthly perfection (279). It is only a mechanism or means to an end (281), the human race cannot be redeemed by a mere mechanism; and the goal itself towards which the union of spirits, of free human wills is striving, is a moral perfection, not a heaven beyond the grave, but a heaven here in this world. The kingdom of heaven is within us (283, cf. 289). Perfect external conditions are only desirable as a means to this higher spiritual perfection (285) which is no doubt never reachable by any individual, but is postulated by the moral law, and involves therefore an infinite progress to it—an endless life for the human spirit (287).[4] Without the law of duty there would not even be a present world: with it, there is also another world (288). In other words, the consciousness of a spiritual bond, of union with other men, is what constitutes our world; it is as real a fact as any in our experience, but it is not attested by the senses;[5] it is spiritual, and its possibilities are all the greater (cf. 301, etc.).

We need not follow Fichte into his further metaphysical conclusions on this head, drawn out as they are with an eloquence that helps us to understand Fichte's influence among his contemporaries. The general metaphysical principles of Fichte are important to us only in so far as they guided Hegel to his Dialectic. In his *Doctrine of Knowledge* (if we may so translate *Wissenschaftslehre* (1794), Fichte carries out (as he thinks) the Kantian Criticism consistently to its furthest consequences. There remains no thing-in-itself; but all begins and ends in Ego. What corresponds, however, to a thing-in-itself is the element of distinction or opposition involved in an act of Knowledge, and bringing with it a perpetual effort to overcome it and to abolish the very existence of a non-Ego. In his practical life where man is active (as distinguished from his theoretical, where he is in a sense receptive and passive), this effort to conquer the non-Ego means the endeavour to bring the world into harmony with the spirit of man; and his progress, whether in knowledge or in moral action, has three stages—thesis (assertion of the Ego), antithesis (contrasted assertion of a non-Ego), and synthesis, or a harmonizing of the two. This law of three stages seems to have helped Hegel to his idea of dialectic and development, an idea which has been of the greatest importance even for the history of Economics.

Fichte had absorbed the spirit and not simply copied the letter of Kant; and it was not therefore surprising that Fichte's Principles of Natural Law[6] should have anticipated many of Kant's thoughts on the subject, though preceding Kant's book[7] by a year. Like Kant, Fichte separates the theory of Rights from the theory of Duties. He is even more rigid than Kant, for he will not allow that the former may be deduced from the latter. He holds that the only law of Nature is the moral law (VI. 82, *French Revol.*). The notion of Duty depends on a categorical imperative; the notion of Right on a hypothetical imperative. *If* there is to be a community of free beings, then each member of it must obey the maxim, "So limit thy freedom that it does not conflict with the freedom of others" (III. 10). In the world there *may be* anarchy, and logically this is the prior condition of humanity;[8] but, if there is to be society, this maxim must be so followed that the organization of Society secures the obedience of its members (III. 108). The very notion of Law implies the possibility of action that diverges from the path pointed out by the law. The *volonté de tous* may be, as in trade, to get the better of one's neighbour; but in face of the facts it becomes the *volonté générale*, or united will that right should be done (III. 106 n., 109). Original "rights of man" in isolation there are none, though there may be property in isolation (*ib.*, 116). But there are rights of *men* in communities or societies, existing prior to any political organization.[9] The distinction between Society and State is clearly laid down.

Further, rights mean nothing except in relation to men's bodies, in the sensible world, where men are identified with their bodies. There is no "right to think," for there is no external means of preventing or compelling thought. The right of self-preservation is postulated by every act of will (III. 118, 119); and my body, as well as my neighbour's, is in society inviolable (cf. 124). A man's personality is, for social and legal relations, inseparable from his body; and therefore the bodily persons of men are to be treated as an end and never as a means (114, etc.). Bodily compulsion, even as exercised by the State in its punishments, is difficult to justify; and outside of the State it has no justification. Moreover, that part of the sensible world, which I come to know thoroughly (in the way which a hunter, for example, knows his hunting-ground), and which I convert into an instrument for my ends, becomes my *property*. The ultimate foundation of property in a thing (on which, be it noted, property may be built up anterior to Society, 116) is the subjection of it by a human being to his purposes; it results from an act of will to which bodily action has given effect (116, 117). Again, as a man's individuality is distinguishable only when he is in relation to other individual men (cf. 47, etc.), so my property is individual only in relation to other people's property; it is recognised by me as mine with an implicit abandonment of something else which I recognise as not mine but another's (131).

For a perfectly moral being, says Fichte, no rights would exist; and there is no Law of Nature outside of Society. But men are not, as it is, perfectly moral, or they would not (as now) need to be trained or educated to morality by institutions. Still, the State itself is natural; and its laws are nothing but the true rights of nature realized.[10] Hitherto all writers have started with the notion of individuals in isolation, and have then supposed them united in a union that is merely artificial and arbitrary (208). Society, however, is like any organized body of what is called the world of Nature. The simile (continues Fichte) is often used in order to describe different parts of the political system (in the narrow sense of the word political) but not, as it might fitly be, of the social union itself. As in the physical organism, every part depends for its character on its connection with the rest, so in the organism of society, where a man first receives his definite work in the world. Outside of society there might be a transient enjoyment of pleasures, but there could be no sure calculation of the future. Nature is composed of the union of all organic forces, and humanity of the union of the free wills of all men. The essence of an organized body is that no part of it contains within itself the full conditions of the fulfilment of its own destiny, and this is true also of the social organism. The isolated man takes action merely to satisfy his own wants, and unless he does so, they remain unsatisfied. But the citizen often acts, and refrains from acting, for the sake of others, as well as for himself; and his highest wants are satisfied by the help of others and without his own initiative (209).[11] Every part of the organized body is at once supporting and supported; so it is with citizens in a State. Each has only to act the part prescribed for him by his place in the whole, and in so acting he is supporting the whole (209). Rousseau speaks of the individual giving himself up when he enters into the social contract; but (says Fichte) the individual has nothing to give up, nothing he can call his own, till he is already within the social union. There is, in the strictest sense no property before society.[12]

The place of men being so conceived, what is their first end? It is simply to be able to *live*. This is the justification of property, and it involves that every one should be able to live by his own labour.[13]

The State must see to it that this is possible for him. "As soon as any man *cannot* live by his labour, that is withheld from him which was absolutely his own, and the contract is, so far as he is concerned, completely annulled. He is from that moment no longer rightfully bound to recognize any other man's property. In order that the consequent insecurity of property may not continue, the rest must, as a matter of right and of the civil contract, give him of *their* own, that he may live. From the moment when any man is in want, no one really owns such part of his property as is his needful contribution to save the sufferer from want, but it belongs of right to the one in want." The State is responsible and the poor have an absolute right to support. But not till they have proved that they have done their best to support themselves. There must be no idler, any more than any poor person, in a rational State.[14] Fichte's notion of property is in other ways more limited than the common legal notion. Property in wild animals (or indeed in anything else), whenever hurtful to others, is disallowed by him. Game laws are regarded with suspicion. He considers that the most important form of property arises from the organization of industry; and he divides the great body of workers into (1) producers in the Physiocratic sense of the term, those who raise raw materials, especially food; (2) artisans; and (3) merchants.[15] When a man has chosen and obtained his sphere of labour in any of the three branches he should have an exclusive right to it, such a right as was secured by the mediaeval guilds. This exclusive right is the most important kind of property (III. 232, 233, etc.). But, besides this, the State secures to a man immunity from interference in his own House; marriage and family life are highly valued and eloquently described by Fichte (304 to 368); these relations have a legal side but they are much more than legal, they are natural and ethical. Every man's house is and ought to be his castle (242, 243). When once a man has been paid in money for his services, in accordance with general arrangements of the political system, his domestic expenditure is his own affair. The State may not even regard how much money he may be privately amassing; and a loophole is certainly left for millionaires.[16] Money is the State's recognition that the receiver has done what was required of him and is creditor of the State for an equivalent. It is "a mere token which denotes all that is useful and serviceable in a State, without being in itself of the least use" (237 to 240).

But these economical arrangements are most fully treated in an Appendix to the treatise on Natural Law published in 1800 and entitled *The Closed Commercial State, a philosophical sketch.*[17] This book contains Fichte's Utopia, and the drift of it is described by himself in a terse prefatory note as follows: "A juridical State is formed by a body of men shut off from others, and subjected to the same laws and same supreme force. Let such a body of men have no trade except with one another, let every one who is not under the same legislative and executive power be excluded from any share in commercial traffic;—they would then form a commercial State, and a *closed* commercial State, just as at present they form a closed juridical one." (*Preliminary note on the meaning of the title.*) There should be not only a common judgment-seat but a common estate (*Vermögen*) (460). There are (he says) two extreme views of the State; according to the one it is a mans general guardian and father; according to the other it is only the keeper of the peace. The truth lies in the middle. We can no longer believe that the State is to take charge of each citizen in all his concerns, to keep him healthy wealthy and wise, and even save his soul for him. It is truer to say that the State has only to secure to every man his personal rights and property; but, on the other hand, without the State there would be no property to secure. It is the *raison d'être* of the State "to *give* to every one his own, to *place* him in his property, and then afterwards to protect him in it" (399). After giving his ideas on property, as he had already done in the book on *Natural Law*, he goes on to apply them to trade and industry in greater detail. There must be equal division of the possibilities of a comfortable life, though it must be left to every man's energy to make them actual. In States as they are, it is not so; but it will be so in the rational State of the future (403). In the second place no one will interfere with another's occupation; having chosen his work, each man must confine himself to it on the understanding that every one else is doing likewise (407, 408). The population will be assigned to the various classes in proportions determined by the character and circumstances of the country. Where agriculture is comparatively hard and unproductive, there would be more need for "producers" than for artisans. But, if circumstances change, the proportion may need to change along with them (408). Further, in order to secure to every one the means of living in the way indicated, we must have a regime of fixed prices, in contrast with that of competition and speculation, where one trader flourishes at the expense of another. The great gains of successful speculation will be among the greatest hindrances to the foundation of the rational State (510).

Comfort for all is what we want; but comfort is a relative expression, and we must find a standard for our estimates. This leads Fichte to consider the measure of Value. The value of a thing (he thinks) is to be estimated by the time during which it would enable us to live,—the value of oysters, for example, by the time a man could live on a certain quantity of oysters as compared with a similar quantity of bread (415). Bread is by universal consent the necessary of life. Take bread therefore (or rather the "product," the corn, from which it is made) as alone having an absolute value, which measures the value of all other food. A pound of meat is of more value than a pound of bread because it gives more nourishment and enables a man to live by it for a longer time. Its value will be so much bread. The value of bread needs no paraphrase. In all work that does not deal with the production of food the standard of payment will be the quantity of food that a workman would need for his support during the making of his wares, and also (if his craft is a skilled one) during the time taken to acquire the skill (416). By food we should understand the cheapest food, or that which it costs least time and labour to produce. But there is food that is not simply nourishing; it is agreeable and pleasant and prized on that account and not for its nourishing powers. "By general estimation" it may thus have a value greater than its intrinsic (its nourishing power); and this extrinsic value will be equal to that amount of the standard food which could have been produced if the time and labour devoted to the agreeable food had been devoted to the standard food instead.[18]

In a State where the agreeable food is produced as well as the standard food (the luxury as well as the necessary) it is clear there is a reserved power of production; if starvation were not some way off, all the production would be of the standard food. Clearly the State has forces to spare for what is dispensable as well as for what is indispensable. Payment of work in all cases will be measured by food; but this is not to mean that all will receive the same food or have their payments measured by the same amount of it. An agricultural worker can live on vegetables, while the brain-worker must have meat (417–418). It is true (see VI. 186) that our conception of necessaries should depend not on habit but on nature; but then nature determines that they shall be different for different people. The standard of living will vary with the occupation. What is to be paid to a man is that which will enable him to support life according to the degree of comfort his calling requires. The merchant, for example, must pay the farmer what will enable the farmer to support life as a farmer should, and the customers of the merchant must pay him what will do the same for him (III. 418). This does no wrong to our ruling principle, namely, that the well-being consulted is that of all, not as now of a few (423). All must have the possibility of leisure, that they may enter on their properly human existence as free men (418). Taxes there must be, but they will be equitably levied, and the needs of the State will be less great than now. Present States take as much as they can get; the rational State will take only what it needs (Cf. 459). Its efforts will be directed to seeing that the total supply of goods is as nearly as possible at the same figure always. The fluctuations of the harvests will be met by a calculation of averages; a man's crop in good years will be valued not by that year but by the average production say of five years. The State must form statistics for the purpose of these calculations (429).

But if prices are to be fixed and stability assured to industry, there must be no dealings with those who are not under the control of our State, and are therefore liable to introduce speculative and unstable prices; all trade with foreigners must be stopped. Commercially as well as juridically, we must be a peculiar people (419, 476, 485, etc.). Towards this end, the State must call in all gold and silver money. According to Fichte, gold and silver have been chosen merely because of their general acceptability. People accept them because they know every one else will take them in exchange for goods. There is no "intrinsic value" to justify this; and, when we say that a given quantity of gold is equivalent to a given quantity of some other commodity because they both cost the same time and labour, we are not (he says) giving any explanation of the facts. "Assuming this equality of time and labour, the unsophisticated person values another man's wares not by the labour the other has spent in it, but rather by the utility he himself hopes to draw from it; and why should the cultivator reckon the gold-miner's labour in turning out a piece of gold equal to his own in the production of a bushel of corn, and hold it equally well laid out, while the farmer's corn is necessary to the miner's life, and the miner's gold by itself leaves the cultivator where he was?" (454, 455). Public opinion and nothing else has given gold and silver their place as money, and their value fluctuates accordingly (455). Fichte, like Sir Thomas More, would allow them to be kept only by the State for its dealings with foreign States (cf. 496, 467). He would have the State introduce a peculiar currency,[19] of a valueless material, and useless abroad; and he thinks that, being isolated, the State can do so by a simple *fiat*. With the same ease it can regulate the value of the currency by simply having regard to the *quantity* of it. That the value of the currency depends on the amount in circulation, as compared with the amount of commodities circulated, is his only economic principle here. He thinks, by careful watching, the State can preserve a uniform proportion throughout the growth of national wealth. It cannot be said that he shows clearness in regard to the economic theory of this subject (431 to 439, cf. 486 *seq.*).

Besides preventing foreign trade, he would hamper foreign travel, unless it be for scientific purposes (506). The isolation of the State is to be complete. The new policy, however, is to be made easier by a compensation of those who have come to depend on foreign markets for particular articles; hitherto the State by tolerating such dependence has approved it as right; it must therefore secure to the parties in question the continued enjoyment of the same articles, by providing for their manufacture at home, and thus stimulating new industries there. In the case of what clearly could not be made at home, public warning should be given some time before the "closing" of the State, that after the said "closing" no such articles can be had (479). Fichte has in view on a complete scale what the Protectionists of his day attempted very imperfectly, the securing of national independence in industry (477, cf. 491). This is not one of the modern features of his Utopia; but marks its affinity with Greek models; and in the detailed construction of his State Fichte has much in common with Plato. The aim of the State should be the well-being of the whole nation, and it is to be secured by division of labour; the classes are to be for the sake of the whole, not *vice versâ* (422, 423). Officials like Plato's Guardians are to be chosen, to see to the production and distribution of wealth on the lines already laid down, as well as to the general government; and, as they are not themselves producers, they get their means of living out of the taxes, as a *quid pro quo* (424, 425). Fichte calls his governors by the Spartan name of Ephors. They are to have administrative powers (160). In whatever way elected (and the manner will depend on the stage of a people's development) they are responsible to the people. Distinct from them are the judges and the executive officers (171), in regard to both of whom the Ephors, like the Roman tribunes, have only a veto. The sacro-sanctity and absolute power of the Ephors (177, etc.) undoubtedly give to Fichte's State the appearance of a benevolent despotism.

The chief features of this ideal commonwealth (the three classes, the security of living with fixed prices, the prohibition of foreign trade) are deduced from the theory of Property, and stand or fall with it (440). The current view (says Fichte) regards property as a right to things, whereas it is a right to free action, applying only to things derivatively and indirectly, so far as they are the object of the action, and never (even so) applying unrestrictedly (441). The better type is the right to a course of action chosen by myself—the right to make shoes or to till the ground. The last may be indirectly a right to the ground, but it need not be absolutely so; there might be the right of another to pasture on it when I have reaped my harvest (442). Property in land, strictly speaking, does not exist; "the earth is the Lord's,"[20] and men have simply the power to make use of it (442). Elsewhere he says that the soil and its minerals under the surface are a "natural royalty" of the State (222).

But how are the really exclusive rights of property to be assigned? The answer is, by contract of all with all, whereby every man enjoys his own right on condition that all the rest enjoy theirs unmolested. It follows that a man who owns nothing has made no contract, and is not so bound (445, 446). Every citizen as such has the right to practise his craft and to live by it. The State did not give him his powers of work; but the State can secure him the exercise of them, on the one condition that the State be closed. *Quod erat demonstrandum* (446, 447). This will of itself put an end to War, and advance Science (512).

Like other Utopias, Fichte's State owes something of its interest to its reflection of current ideas. But like Sir Thomas More, he is not content with indirect comments on the world of his own time. He expressly arraigns and condemns it.[21] Thoughtless common sense (he says) thinks that to be natural and necessary, which is really accidental. The morality, customs and institutions of its own time seem to it the only possible ones. It needs a deeper reflection to see that, besides what is, there is that which may be, and that the possible state of things is more rational than the actual. Reflection suggests the question, how did the actual state of things come about? it was not always actual. The States of Europe were formed by the breaking up of an empire; and the Whole of which they were once parts still in a sense remains. Europe is commercially in many ways a single State; but it ought to be frankly so, and adopt free trade everywhere, or frankly the opposite, and resolve itself into States that are closed commercially as well as juridically. The chief end of the State being to establish every citizen securely in his property, it must be commercially closed, or else the anarchy of competitive trade will defeat that object. The claim for free trade is really an unconscious reminiscence of Imperial unity (454). Even now, so far as we have it, it involves a war of all against all, and an attempt of each individual to turn the variations in the value of money to his gain, and so make others work for him (457, 458); and this *bellum omnium in omnes* becomes the hotter the more the world becomes peopled, and arts and sciences grow, for the greater is the multiplication of the wants of men, and the conflict of buyer and seller. The buyer, to keep down prices, demands free trade and overstocked markets, the utmost competition of sellers and makers. If he succeeds, the result is the poverty, and perhaps emigration of the worker. The seller on his part tries to engross and to force high prices by causing a scarcity; or else he adulterates and deteriorates his goods. There is waste of time and strength and goods over bad work. "In short, no one has the least security for the permanence of his condition in life, for what men are at present desiring is complete liberty to ruin one another" (458).

As to the trade between different European nations, (1) it may be a trade of mutual advantage, so that in money and in intrinsic value each State is where it was, neither richer nor poorer;—or (2) one nation may produce more advantageously for the foreigner than the foreigner for it, and part with what is indispensable in exchange for what is dispensable; it then becomes progressively poorer, and, though it may increase its stock of money, it only lowers the value of it (461);—or (3), one nation may lose by giving away its money for goods, and raising the value of its stock of money, thus feeling the weight of taxation heavier, and losing its people through consequent emigration and mortality. The value of land falls, and fields go out of cultivation. The foreigner acquires the land, and government sells itself to foreign governments for subsidies (462, 463). Meanwhile the produce of the waste lands in the shape of game, etc., increases. The people who survive find subsistence, but the real victims of the growing poverty of such States have died out, so that no one can ask why they possess nothing (464). Governments suck no small advantage out of such a state of things. They direct greater efforts towards keeping up the taxes than keeping down the sufferings of the people (465). They try to increase the exports in order to bring money into the country, and to hinder the imports in order to prevent money going out, and they try to encourage the carrying trade. These expedients secure ready money, but lead to retaliation and commercial wars (466, 467). We have a nation [England] claiming supremacy in the sea, an element which ought to be open to all, like light and air, and claiming exclusive markets abroad, where she has no more concern than other nations (468). The prosperity thus secured is not permanent. Justice and wisdom both point to a different policy. Dependence on foreign trade must always involve insecurity and the risk of over-production and loss (469, 470). Imperfect exclusion (as in the present Protective Systems), is no better than free trade; the only remedy is absolute exclusion and a Closed Commercial State (472–476).

Nevertheless as men, and even societies, exist before the State, and as the moral law, which is higher than any political and legal bond, is prior to the State, so, when the best State has done its perfect work it makes itself superfluous;[22] the highest development of man is spiritual and intellectual, and when that is reached there is no need of any State or government. Fichte, like Godwin, looks forward to a purified anarchy; but it may be "myriads of myriads of years away," and meanwhile, unlike Godwin, he regards the State and the *closed* State as a necessary aid to human progress; it is a "means towards the founding of a perfect Society."

It may be asked how far he regards even his *proximate* ideal (the Closed State) as practicable in the immediate future. The answer is given, partly in his Preface to the *Closed State*, partly in the lectures on *Characteristics of the Present Age* (1804, vol. vii.). In the former (in the dedication to Struensee) he expressly claims for the political philosopher, as distinguished from the practical politician, the right of drawing out his schemes fully and freely, without regard to immediate practicability. His work is theoretical and general; and, though he believes his conclusions true and his plans ultimately realizable, he is not to be treated as if he were applying his principles to one particular State, and at the time of composition proposing to carry them out in detail. Direct political application would need to have regard to the special features of each State concerned; and any attempt to carry out the proposed "closing," for example, would meet with the obstructions of immediate self-interest, to say nothing of other difficulties (III. 389–393).

In point of fact (as he shows in the *Characteristics*) the leading States of Europe are probably in the third of the five stages of development through which the human race must necessarily pass. Those five stages can be deduced necessarily and *a priori*, not from history but quite apart from it.[23] To show that we are now in one particular stage of the five is not so easy, and cannot be done *a priori*; but the features are (he thinks) those of the third stage, the stage of Emancipation, Sceptical Indifference, Enlightenment and Criticism, in which all authorities are questioned and tested, as distinguished from the first when men lived a life of innocence, guided by instinct, and the second when their rule of life ceased to be one with themselves, but they obeyed it as an external authority (VII. 11, etc.). After the third stage comes the epoch of rational science and love of truth as the highest thing on earth. Last of all comes the epoch when men are so identified with the truth that their art reflects reason; reason becomes their second nature. From innocent instinct, through consciousness of incipient sin, to complete sinfulness, and then from incipient holiness to perfect holiness, they press towards the end of human progress. But the end is very far off; and in the fourth stage, to which we are approaching, the State, in its ideal form, will play a great part as an educator of nations. Education, moral and intellectual, must (as Fichte learned from Pestalozzi) be national and popular. But the remote end of all the progress is cosmopolitan. If it were not that Fichte regards external nature as an obstacle to be overcome rather than as itself a form of reason, he might be regarded as completely at one with Hegel in the position that what is actual is rational. "Philosophy finds all to be necessary and therefore good" (VII. 14). "What is actually there, is there from absolute necessity, and is necessarily in the shape in which it is there; it simply could not be otherwise" (VII. 129). Such passages may have suggested to Hegel his own propositions, which have been treated as more paradoxical and pretentious, only because more rigidly and logically carried out to their furthest consequences.

It appears then that (1) in Fichte the economic end is subordinated to spiritual training; (2) that a socialistic organization of the State as it is, preceded by a Society securing rights without Government, will be followed by a Society in which *de facto* there will be a securing of all rights, and of much more besides. Fichte is, in fact, a believer in a development of the human race that will lead it through Socialism into a purified Anarchy. The remoteness of his ideal tended, along with the general distrust of his metaphysical methods, to deprive his social philosophy of its influence on later generations; and his influence on Economists, even where they have been Socialists, has taken the form of a stimulus to enthusiasm rather than of intellectual guidance. Hegel owed much to Fichte: but the influence of the former has been of a more abiding sort, because more entirely due to the convincingness of his logic, and the impressive thoroughness with which he pursued it home.

Notes

1 *Works*, I. 412, 413.
2 II. 268.
3 I. 415, 416.
4 This was Kant's view, *Practical Reason* (1788), *Works*, V. 128.
5 (Cf. Spencer, *Man v. the State*, page 6.) It may be added that one evidence of the reality is the effect produced by the loss of friends, in altering our whole world.
6 *Grundlage des Naturrechts*, 1796.
7 *Rechtslehre*, 1797.
8 Priority does not mean historical priority. See VI. 127.
9 III. 112 *seq.*, cf. VI. 129 *seq.*
10 So P. E. Dove, *Elements of Pol. Science* (Edin.), 1854, p. 119, etc., says that legislation does not grant rights, but *secures* those already granted to man by nature. This is the common ground of all believers in a Law of Nature.
11 In recasting the *Rechtslehre* (1812), Fichte carried out this notion of a positive function of the State much more fully; but it was not through these afterthoughts that he influenced speculation.
12 III. 204 and n. But see *ibid.*, 116.
13 *Ibid.*, 212.
14 III. 213, 214.
15 III. 230–232. The third class is first fully treated in the *Closed Commercial State*, III. 405 *seq.*
16 III. 241, cf. 244, 255, 438.
17 *Der geschlossene Handelsstaat, ein philosophischer Entwurf als Anhang zur Rechtslehre und Probe ciner künftig zu liefernden Politik*. Dedicated to the Prussian Minister Struensee (the younger). Its thorough-going protection may be compared with that advocated by Friedrich List, *Theorie des Nationalen Systems der Pol. Oek.*, 1877.
18 III. 417.
19 Landesgeld. III. 433. The defects of paper-money, assignats, etc., have, he thinks, been due to the fact that they have always run side by side with other money; they have represented money, not goods.
20 *Die Erde ist des Herrn*, 442, cf. 218. Comp, above, p. 52.
21 See esp. *Closed State*, *Works*, III. pp. 448 *seq.*: "Vom Zustande des Handelsverkehrs in den gegenwärtigen wirklichen Staaten."
22 "Es ist der Zweck aller Regierung die Regierung überflüssig zu machen" (VI. 306).
23 See *e.g.* VII. 19, 21. The Historical Economists can hardly claim Fichte. See Schmoller, *Litteraturgeschichte der Staatswissenschaften*, 1888.

3   Krause (1781–1832)

That neither Bentham nor Kant nor Fichte had killed the notion of a Law of Nature in Germany appears from the history of that notion as treated by the philosopher Krause. That eccentric genius has hindered his own success by revelling (like Bentham in his later life) in a peculiar terminology of his own making;[1] but it is striking that his conception of natural right has been substantially adopted by such influential writers as Trendelenburg and Ahrens in Germany, Lorimer and Green in our own country, and many leading jurists in Italy and Spain.

"Everything in life," says Krause,[2] "which is unchangeable is called by us a Law; we therefore assert that Right is a Law, a universal law, valid for all rational beings." It holds for all rational life, so far as the latter is brought by freedom into conformity to Reason. Right is a "good" of human life, for it concerns freedom; and where there is no freedom there can be no good.[3] Morality, indeed, deals with a higher subject than Right, for morality relates to all that is a Good, while Right relates only to one class. Yet the doctrine of Right is not a mere branch of ethics; it must do what ethics does not do,—inquire into the objective nature of Right, just as Æsthetics must inquire into the conditions that make one thing beautiful and another ugly. To succeed in the inquiry, we must first of all recognise that the destiny of man is to perfect and realize all his powers, and be a "complete harmonious human being." He must be perfect in his inward life, in society, in relation to physical nature, and in relation to God. His rational life is thus evidently not dependent on himself alone, but on certain indispensable conditions. Right is the claim for fulfilment of these conditions; and they include, for example, food, security, education, and facilities for playing a part in life.[4] Krause had once (*Grundlage des Naturrechts*, 1803) confined the definition to "external" conditions, but in his latest writings he withdraws the limitation.[5] In his sketch of the history of the Law of Nature,[6] he allows that he stands nearer to Fichte than to any other philosopher, and praises Fichte's attempt to deduce Right from the very nature of Self. But Fichte's adherence to the Kantian conception of Right as the "law of the mutual restriction of the freedom of each that it may be consistent with the freedom of all," is condemned, partly because Fichte only allows rights to belong to a man if the man respects them in others, partly because the notion is purely negative, partly because Fichte makes right depend on the common will, instead of the common will on Right. But Fichte, Schelling and Hegel have done well to connect the ideas of Right and of the State with the Supreme Being or Absolute Essence itself.[7] "The Statute Book [of natural law] is the eternal cosmos."[8] What is organic and well-ordered is of God and good; what is chaotic is evil, which is essentially negative and exceptional.[9] Right belongs to the former category; it is nothing if not organic.

We need not follow Krause into details, but simply remark that, like so many of his predecessors, he lays stress on the cosmopolitan as well as the national application of his idea of right, and he goes beyond most of them in applying the idea of right to animals. "Where there is life there is right."[10] The State is to him the organic system of realized or developed right; and, as it itself is only a member of the larger organism Humanity, so within it there are, as members, other organic systems.[11] In other words, like Hegel, he leaves room for society as distinct from State; and, as Right is only one phase of life, the State does not include all the activities of life in any case. Religious bodies, for example, are perfectly distinct from it, co-ordinate and not subordinate.[12]

Besides the jurists, the economists came under the influence of Krause. He remarks on Good and Goods (in effect) that that is "good" which fulfils its end and is as it is meant to be; a man is good if he fulfils *his* end, and what we call "goods" or commodities are external means to man's goodness, and should not be represented as ends.[13] This led Schäfîle to his protest against the older Political Economy, which he said treated increase of goods too much as an end in itself, and forgot that man himself was the proper subject even of purely economic inquiries.[14] But the question is not whether Man can be left out or not, for even if goods are in the forefront they have no meaning except in relation to man and his wants. The question is whether the relation of man to goods (considered strictly as means and without any distinction of moral good or evil) is not a large enough subject to deserve separate study. Recent economists (especially in Austria[15]) have as a matter of fact kept goods in the forefront; and this particular aspect of economic inquiry (not wealth in the singular but commodities in the plural) has served to keep attention fixed with great advantage on the variation of wants, satisfied by different quantities as well as different kinds of goods. Indeed the whole theory of Final Utility, as distinguished from Utility in its generality, may be said to depend on the use of this category. The Final Utilitarians may (as we have seen) have erred in posing as Utilitarians, and speaking as if a commodity as such ministered only to pleasure. In this respect the analysis of Krause seems the more accurate.

The direct influence of Krause, however, is small when compared with the indirect influence of his contemporary Hegel on modern economics.

Notes

1 *E.g.* Ja-heit, Wesen-lich, Sein-heit.
2 *Das System der Rechtsphilosophie* (1826–8), ed. by K. D. A. Röder, 1874, p. 33. Compare above Note to *Nat. Rights* (Book II. ix.).
3 See below for "Goods" in the sense of Commodities.
4 *Rechtsphil., e.g.* p. 54.
5 *Ibid.,* p. 118, etc.
6 *Ibid.,* p. 109 *seq.,* 362 *seq.* He finds himself anticipated by Thomas Aquinas, p. 118, cf. 107, 384.
7 *Ibid.,* p. 145.
8 *Ibid.,* p. 193.
9 *Ibid.,* p. 220.
10 *Ibid.,* 232, 240. (Lorimer goes further still.) See *Institutes of Law,* 2nd ed. (1880), p. 218). For Cosmopolitanism, see *Rechtsphil.,* p. 348, etc. Krause declares against Capital Punishment, 152, 302, 312, 320.
11 *Ibid.,* pp. 352, 353.
12 *Rechtsphil.,* p. 353.
13 *Ibid.,* pp. 38, 173, cf. 289, 249, 216.
14 *Mensch und Gut in der Volkswirthschaft,* 1861.
15 See especially Prof. C. Menger, *Volkswirthschaftslehre* (1871), and compare Marshall, *Principles of Pol. Econ.,* II. ii. pp. 1–7.

4   Hegel (1770–1831)

To Hegel all that is is Process, which means—development by union of opposites, which again means not a mere addition of the one to the other but a blending of them in a third, as two necessary sides of the same, so that, equally *false* when apart, they are equally *true* when together. We see this on a great scale if we consider the two opposite notions without which the world would be nonsense to us—thought and nature. Thought (says Hegel), viewed abstractly or away from nature, gives us the *Logic* of abstract notions; and externality viewed by itself gives us the *Philosophy of Nature*. The truth is, however, that when we attempt to view them by themselves we are driven from the one to the other, and we reach the *Philosophy of Spirit* in which thought makes itself its own object, and thought and externality are concretely combined. The truth lies always in the concrete view; all else is abstract and half truth. But the progress of thinking begins with the half truth; it passes, from a notion that is relatively abstract, first of all to its equally abstract opposite, and thence to a notion that is relatively concrete, uniting the two abstractions. This reconciling Third is then found, itself to be abstract, and thought is driven to *its* opposite, thence, reaching a new concrete.[1]

This dialectic[2] is unlike development as ordinarily conceived; it is like Mr. Spencer's evolution by homogeneity, heterogeneity, individuation; but it is not Darwinian evolution, where the last stages of a species do not embody and include the previous. In Hegel's view of Development, the conflicting opposites are not destroyed;[3] the surviving and victorious concrete includes them. Nothing is lost. With human beings, this and other features of the Dialectic come more evidently and obviously to the front than in the case of material objects or even of plants and animals. In Hegel's *Philosophy of Spirit*, as expounded in the *Encyclopädie*, we see this happening when the stages of the "Subjective" Spirit have been passed, and when in "Psychology," looking for laws (and not simply for lists of qualities) in Nature, man brings it nearer his own rationality, general laws being transparently "thoughts." We see it more clearly when the spirit is fully "Objective" and seeks to find itself in the external world by *action*. Man is not one with himself and free till what seems external and alien and a mere limit of his action is shown to be (like the apparently external and alien limits of Knowledge) really rational and therefore not alien to him but one with him. At first his way of realizing himself is to follow his passions, as if the whole practical truth was in the particular as distinguished from the general element of his nature; but this turns out to be mere slavery to the chance desire of the moment. Nevertheless, if he goes to the opposite extreme and simply opposes to the desires his power (as a rational being) of abstracting from each and all of them, he is still not free, for he has nothing left to will. The truth lies in neither abstraction but in the recognition that the passions have a rational meaning, and are not merely particular, though they seem so. Rational beings have, no doubt, their particular desires, though even these have a wide range and deep intensity not discernible in merely animal beings; but, besides, they have a need for a permanent possibility of satisfaction, an ideal of happiness. This ideal may be simply Wealth, or the permanent power of gratifying appetite generally. In this case it involves a half concealed reference to other men, who are thought of as relatively poorer or richer than oneself. But this reference to others takes a more explicit form in the desire of procuring from others an express recognition of superiority. This is the desire of Honour, which makes us "sleep on brambles till we've killed our man." But to kill the enemy is to miss the recognition; an enemy killed is an enemy who is not there to recognise our superiority. Gain and glory are brought together when my enemy is spared and made, in slavery, a means of satisfying my desires by working to increase my wealth. Slavery, however, though historically a step towards true freedom, is not consistent with true freedom itself. The master cannot be said to "find himself" in the slave; and the slave, though disciplined by his subjection, is excluded by it from his rights as a man.[4] Hegel, therefore, in the *Philosophy of History* is quite consistent in describing the whole progress of development in history as an enlarging of the notion of freedom—from the notion that only one is free (the Emperor of China or the King of Persia), to the notion that only *some* are free (the Greeks but not the barbarians), and from that again to the notion that all men are free. The notion of Freedom is dominant in the *Philosophy of History*.

It is also dominant in the *Philosophy of Right* (1820). True freedom does not lie either in mere legal recognition of my rights as a person, or in the mere consciousness of my empire over myself as obeying an inward law of duty, but in my consciousness of my oneness with social institutions in which, while I have personal rights, I find my duties embodied. Law and Morality are opposites and abstractions which are reconciled and made concrete and true in social morality.

This is the part of Hegel's work which touches our subject most closely. The early treatise (on *Natural Right*, 1802–3, *Wks.*, vol. i.) had been largely a criticism of Fichte and Kant. The *Philosophy of Right* contains Hegel's positive teaching, which may be described as follows:—

If we would conceive true freedom (says Hegel), we must distinguish rights from duties, and therefore Law from Morality. To fulfil his personal programme, to do the work which it is in him to do, each individual must have his separate personality and "rights" recognised; he must "be a person, and respect the others as persons" (§36). His "rights" mean simply the conditions postulated for proper fulfilment of his "duties." They are therefore natural only in the sense that men are born *for* them, not that men are born in possession of them or that there is any innate perception of them.

But to assert his personality (he proceeds) man must reflect it in external objects; for the body to be free, there must be some command over "things"; a man is not fully conscious of his personality till he has embodied it in Property. To be without property is to be without a condition on which freedom depends. In this respect all men are equal; all equally have the right to hold property (*Rechtsphil.*, § 49, p. 85). The *rationale* of property is not the economic one, the satisfaction of wants, but the embodying of the Will in an external object; it involves rather the satisfaction of Ownership than the pleasure of having a larger source for supplying the appetites. In property, as distinguished from possession, the will is identified with the external object, and this makes property the object of Law. The more clearly I leave my mark on the external object the more clearly I make it my property. Even my body is more clearly mine when I acquire bodily dexterities. Land must become private property like anything else (cf. *Rechtsphil*, § 203).

I show my appropriation first positively by taking possession, then negatively by using (altering or consuming) the thing; property divorced from use or use from property is an unreal abstraction; and it is essential to property that the proprietor can dispose of it to another, exchanging, or at any rate in some way alienating it. This leads to contract. Real ownership enables me to dispose of a thing in its whole value, not simply in its single use but in its general power of satisfying human wants (§ 63, p. 79). Alienation is only possible of "things," including particular services (as in labour for wages contrasted with selling oneself into slavery) (§ 67, cf. § 66). The slave never can contract himself out of his absolute right to emancipate himself (p. 104). Contract is an agreement made by a deliberate and particular act of will between two parties, and having for its object some particular thing or service. Accordingly neither State nor Family can rest on a basis of mere contract. The State does not arise out of a "Social Contract," but is a union without which contracts are meaningless; nor is the relation of married persons one of mere parties to a contract. The notion of a common will is beginning (in Contract) to take visible shape (§ 71), but contracting persons are not, as such, in more than mere particular accidental or superficial agreement. They do not so completely "find themselves" in the matter of a contract as to escape possibility of disagreement. This disagreement brings the notion of Wrong; and mens thought is driven below the legal notions to find means of restoring unity. The disharmony may be merely a case of Civil Injury, when both parties have really willed their mutual advantage, and it is only the force of external circumstances (the irrationality of mere particulars) that has brought about the opposite. The reconciliation is not a punishment but a compensation. In

Fraud, there is no longer this harmony of wills; there is disharmony both of wills and circumstances; but there is (on the part of the defrauder) an appearance of respect for the will of the other; he keeps up the form and tries for his own benefit to produce of set purpose the collision that was in the other case produced by the chapter of accidents. He wrongs his neighbour, and *this* contradiction is only solvable by punishment. But, when he goes so far as to ignore even the appearance of coincidence between the wills, he wrongs the very essence of personality, and the whole body of persons; he commits crime. The criminal is one who cuts the branch that supports him; he sets his particular will against the universal element that showed itself in Contract, he wills an act which is contrary to the very principle of external manifestation of the will in act.[5] This is an attack on personality itself, which has now shown itself to involve more than a mere external relation and to depend on a common basis of inward worth expressed in said relation. The occurrence of Crime, whether the crime be a violation of an alienable or of an inalienable right of the wronged person, may of course simply provoke private revenge. But this does not restore the balance, for it inflicts new wrongs, the will of the avenger being to inflict wrong in his turn. Crime and vengeance are only brought to harmony by legal punishment, which treats the matter as of public not private concern; and the will operating in punishment is conceived as that of a lawgiver, identifying himself with the law and cancelling the wrong by an act that is above the passion of individuals. The crime is retorted on the criminal in punishment, because the crime was an offence against personality in the person of the criminal himself as much as in that of his victim. Thus, to procure the infliction of punishment as distinguished from revenge, we have to think of a will identical with the law.[6]

But this notion of a will that is one with the law is no other than the first aspect in which a Moral as distinguished from a Legal view of actions presents itself. Law, fully developed, leads to morality; or, in other words, the notion of freedom is shown to involve not only law but morality. The legal relations involved in personality itself take us eventually to a point where merely legal notions are inadequate. What the judge is in law in his judicial capacity, all men are in their moral relations. The result of widening this view of the judicial identity of will with law is to give us an idea of a possible *positive* direction of life and action. Law, in the narrower sense, gives nothing but prohibitions, whereas Morality is to furnish positive duties.

But to carry us beyond the mere abstraction of inward law, contrasted with the outward and legal prohibitions, more is needed than the said abstraction itself. To take as a maxim of our acts, "Be an end and law to yourself," is to get no positive direction; it is to dwell with mere generalities. Kant's recourse to the principle, "Will nothing that could not without contradiction be thought as a universal law," does not really help us out into the world of concrete duties, for the contradiction (say of Theft and Murder) does not exist unless, positively, certain other principles have been already recognised, and the contradiction declared to be with them (*e.g.* with the principle of property, and the sanctity of human life). When the individual is (1) conscious of the meaning and scope of his act, the next question is (2) as to his chief motive in it, and (3) as to the bearing of the act on the chief good, or, in other words, its absolute value (§§ 114, 152). Mere regard for an abstract generality will supply no motive. The individual must act with a view to a law that can be realized concretely by his action; and it will not even be enough for him to avoid conflict with legal rights, as if these were all of equally supreme validity and as if the violation of property were as morally wrong as the violation of life. The individual must be conscious of his responsibility and of the need of making up his own mind instead of simply obeying a superior force. If he yields, it must be from conviction. This subjective element is indispensable in a being that is to be called moral at all (§ 107, p. 146, cf. § 112, p. 150). But it must be a really higher conception of life, not simply a protest against the legal conception of it, or else it may practically mean simple lawlessness, no advance in true freedom.

We still want to know, positively, what is the nature of the acts which the individual is to make up his mind to do. Morality, when it is treated abstractly as adequate to the whole of life, disappoints the expectations raised about it. "Duty for duty's sake" is a mere formula, which does not by itself enable man to find himself in things, and realize positive freedom. It is an abstract inward law, as "Every man has a right to do what he will with his own" may be called an abstract outward law. Yet, when we leave this abstractness, we seem to pass into the region of particular feelings, impulses, and lawless desires. Is there any way in which desires will be satisfied and the law of duty fulfilled at the same time?

Kant had taught that the introduction of desire and feeling destroyed purity of motive; yet he did not show how reason could be its own motive as well as its own chief end. He supposed the motives to be capable of a gradual purification which was never actually completed and needed an immortal life for its accomplishment; and he supposed the coincidence of duty and happiness to be a postulate so necessarily contained in the "Categorical Imperative of Duty" that it warranted us in assuming the existence of a God to bring it about. To Hegel these seem the unfortunate necessities of a wrong abstraction. Desires and feelings are to him rational, as things are, and not merely as things one day may be. A motive, therefore, is not necessarily impure because it has the element of feeling and desire in it; and moral goodness does not need to wait for a miracle in order to find itself at one with its world. The institutions for which man is born—the family, civil society, and the State—are rational and yet they enlist the feelings and desires, and they minister to well-being. In them, duties and rights are present in concrete form; law and morality are reconciled. This is what Hegel calls Social or Customary Morality (*Sittlichkeit*). In opposition to the ordinance of Creon, Antigone follows "ἄγραπτα κἀσφαλῆ θεῶν νόμιμα," a law of duty which is not an abstraction but has its source in the Family. The moral law which overcame the legal ordinance was interpreted for her by the observances of the family, with which she felt herself to be so identified that in serving it she was serving herself. The family, like the State, begins, no doubt, in πρὸς τό ζήν, but is eventually πρὸς τό εὖ ζήν; it is a union in the first place to satisfy desire and provide for material existence, but it becomes an ethical institution, training the individual to habits of reverence and affection and labour for the common good. The consciousness of self is inseparable from the consciousness of union with others. Duties and rights are united. At the same time though moral education begins in the family it cannot stop there. There is not complete freedom without distinction of individuals, as of moral subjects who have each his or her own work in life to do, and who must not be simply absorbed in the family or sacrificed to it. The Family grows into the State, which at first indeed may be a mere group of families (§ 181). The members of the family must pass out of the family. Though the legal relations of "persons" are not the highest element in freedom, yet they are indispensable to it (§ 177). The death of the head and the maturity of the members provide a natural dissolution of the local ties of the family. Hegel, in his speeches at the prize-giving of the Ntirnberg Gymnasium,[7] speaks of School life as a preparation for the independent life that follows the life of the Family. In the School the individual discovers that there are interests outside his private circle and duties to others besides his parents. He is made ready for life in Civil Society. In the family he is loved, without any necessary merit of his own; in the world at large he will be valued only by what he is and achieves for himself; in the school he is trained to use his powers for himself, and his place depends partly at least on his merit. He is trained to submit to rules and shape his action in keeping with them (XVI. 171, 172): "In the family the child has to act rightly in the sense of rendering personal obedience and affection,—in the school he must do this, in the sense of doing a duty and obeying a law; and he has in the school to do and to forbear many things which, when he was an individual by himself in the family, would have been left to his choice. Instructed in company with others, he learns to guide his action by regard to others; he learns to gain trust in strangers and confidence in himself in his dealings with them; and thereby he makes a beginning in the culture and the practice of social virtues" (XVI. 172). His life is now twofold. He is no longer absorbed in the family; he has the claims of the school as well as of the family to satisfy; but if the school is rightly conducted, his will is not: thereby crushed; he is trained to real independence, and fitted to play his part in the world.

The world means in the first place Civil Society. In the sense in which Hegel uses this expression, Civil Society is distinct both from the family and from the State. It may indeed consist of separate families as competing groups (*Rechtsphil.*, § 181, p. 239), but it is more easily conceived as consisting of individuals (whether heads of families or not) who are in competition with each other for the satisfaction of their wants, and for the means of subsistence in the first place. In Law it was the Person, in Morality the Subject, so here in Civil Society it is the Citizen that is the centre of our attention (§ 190). Men become ends to themselves here, in the sense of excluding others and making others the means to their ends. Every atom seems separate, and there is a war of the private interests of all against all (§ 187); and, ever since Christianity has taught us the infinite worth of the individual (§ 185), there must always be room found for this separate and self-interested action of the individual, or else freedom will lack one constituent element. But the separate action is not so separate as in Law and Morality. In Civil Society it must always imply a positive relation to others; and more especially is this true of the pursuit of wealth.

Individualism is only possible on a social basis. Even if we conceive the only bond to be the common rule of law regulating the relations of the individuals as persons, we find, as Political Economy shows, that the advancement or depression of one is bound up with the advancement or depression of others. There is a mutual dependence.[8] There is a unity, though it is not intended or deliberately contrived. "It is not freedom but necessity" (§ 186). The endeavour to satisfy my subjective particular nature proves to depend for its success on my coincidence with others, in division of labour, and in the other ways which it has been the task of the new science, Political Economy (under Smith, Say, Ricardo)[9] to discover. The object of Political Economy is to look at "the relations and movement of masses of people in their qualitative and quantitative concreteness and complication" (§ 189). "It is a science that does honour to thought, for it finds out laws for a mass of contingencies. It is an interesting spectacle to see how all the combinations here react upon each other, and how the particular spheres form themselves into groups, and have influence on other spheres, and get help or hindrance from them. This inter-connection, which at first seems incredible, since everything seems at the mercy of the individual's caprice, is in the highest degree remarkable, and reminds us of the Planetary System, which shows to the eye only irregular movements but has its discoverable laws notwithstanding" (*ib.*).

The prominent figure, then, in Civil Society is Man as Citizen, supplying his wants. And in the case of human beings it quickly appears that wants are unlimited (§ 191). And not merely food but good food is wanted—not merely a living but "what the English call a *comfortable* living." There arises a multiplicity of wants that put the drag on any one particular desire, and (as effectually) put the individual beyond any hope of being sufficient for himself in provision for his life. Division of labour (§ 198), with its necessary social relations, comes to his aid; and by it he gets leisure for mental culture, as well as the healthy discipline of a labour that must be guided by a reference to other men's acts and wants. Even fashion and custom show the social nature of man (§ 193, § 195).[10] The very mechanical character of division of labour corrects itself by its tendency to lead to the invention of actual machines (§ 198).

Thus individuals aiming at private wealth secure the general wealth (§ 199). But the participation of any particular individual in the latter depends on two considerations, (1) whether he has capital, (2) whether he has a dexterity prized by other men. There is possibility of unequal participation from both these sides (§ 200). So men are grouped in Classes according to their property and according to their labour. The class of landowners and the class of artisans are characteristic of civil society. If the grouping of men in families is the first foundation for the State, the grouping of them economically in Classes is the second (§ 203, cf. § 201). The Agricultural class, depending more than the rest on the co-operation of physical nature, have only in our time (*sero tamen*) been penetrated by the spirit of inquiry and reflection. Their chief feature is "substantiality"; the agricultural population are wholly buried in local interests; they have little notion of any life beyond the round of their own occupations. They are themselves part and parcel of agriculture. But scientific activity has been always more or less identified with artisan labour, in which nature plays a subordinate part (§ 203). "The first origin of States is rightly ascribed to the introduction of agriculture, bringing with it the institution of Marriage, for agriculture leads to the working of the soil, and thereby to exclusive private property" (§ 203).[11] Agricultural life brings settled manners and permanent possessions. But individual independence is the growth rather of the industrial labour associated with large cities. What a man gets by this kind of labour he owes to himself. He may get it in one of three ways, either (1) by "concrete" work, as an artisan, for his own particular wants, or (2) by "abstract" joint work for the general wants, as a manufacturer, or (3) as a merchant by the work of exchanging goods by means of the thing called "money, in which the abstract value of all wares is realized" (§ 204). Money is the means of expressing, and measuring *quantitatively*, every kind of property; and thus at a later stage (in the "State") we find the citizens made to contribute (to State expenses) more equitably by money than they could ever be made to do by personal services or otherwise (§ 299).[12]

There is thirdly (in addition to the Agricultural and the Industrial classes) the class of Public Servants. Their business is to serve the general interests of society, and their private wants are supplied by the State that takes their services (§ 205). In modern Europe, as contrasted with India or China or with the Platonic State, room is left for individual energy and choice, to determine to which class a man is to belong. This element can never be wanting to full liberty. Though it is only the particular (and not the universal) side of liberty, it is a particularity which is an essential stage both in the progress of society and in that of the individual; liberty must not remain abstract, as if it were a great thing for a man to be nothing in particular, and to choose no profession for fear of limiting himself (§ 207).

This is the region of the respectable virtues of talent, industry, energy, uprightness. Each man is pushing his own way in the world, seeking to satisfy his own wants, and to obtain and retain property for himself. But, as all are doing so, there is needed a *general protection of person and property*, which is often identified with the whole work of the State, but is only its first work. Civil Society shows its limits by requiring this protection (§ 208 *seq.*). In other words, the "particularity" of the competing members of a civil society requires a "generality" as its supporting basis—the generality of the laws and their administration. On the other hand, such a system of laws can only grow up where civilization has gone so far that men have discovered how numerous their wants are, and have set themselves methodically to procure the means of satisfying them (§ 209). Not till then will social rules pass from the form of mere custom into the form of written law, which differs from custom in being (a) a defined, and (b) a general expression of what in custom was only indistinct habitual observance. The element of individual feeling, prejudice, or revenge, gives place to an endeavour after impartial logic; and (what is of great importance), the matter of the laws is thus brought within the knowledge of all, and what was before taken for granted is now formally brought out and laid down.[13] Knowledge of the laws ought not to be the monopoly of any one profession.

Since laws deal with finite matters, they are constantly found to fall short of perfect adequacy; and yet at each given time they should be made quite adequate. The conflict of this postulate of adequacy with the necessity of new laws results in what Hegel calls (in Kantian language) the "antinomy" of legislation; but in spite of it legislation is quite indispensable. We do not cease to plant trees although the leaves will need to be renewed every year (§ 216). There seems to be another contradiction in the fact that crime, by being treated as a wrong to society, and not merely to an individual, seems to be made greater, whereas the punishments of it may often be made less than they would be before or outside of civilization, say in the heroic times (§ 218). But there is no contradiction; the punishment can be safely made less because Society is conscious of greater strength than any individual revenger of injuries, and can be merciful in proportion to its strength (§ 218). Another apparent contradiction results from the fact that, where law is developed, rights can only be secured in so far as the law prescribes them, and individuals may occasionally be aggrieved at their failure to secure rights which they are convinced they possess (§222). But such is the condition on which a civil society must exist; and Courts of Equity will lessen the grievance, such as it is (§ 223).

Hegel goes on to vindicate trial by jury and publicity of proceedings. The verdict of the Jury is (as it were) the utterance of guilt or innocence of the accused out of his own mouth and heart, for in being judged by the jury he is judged by his peers (§ 227). It is his own sentence on himself, and no longer a mere external fate to him (§ 228). Civil Society thus, in spite of its "atomistic" character, has come to a consciousness of its general element.

This general element expresses itself still more unmistakeably in the formation of a corporate body for local government. The aim of a Corporation is not the mere securing of justice between man and man in accordance with the laws, but the positive advancement of the prosperity of the citizens (§ 229). The first duty of it is no doubt the enforcement of Police regulations to secure law and order and prevent cheating (by Adulteration Acts for example) (§§ 234 *seq.*). Hegel is in these matters no blind lover of *laissez-faire* (see esp. § 236). The individual has been torn from the family by civil society, and he has claims on it as he had on the family. For its own part, regarded as a unity, civil society has claims on him as standing to him in place of the family, and as itself collectively one family. Hence for example it can enforce education and vaccination (§ 239), and prevent the existence of such things as a mob or proletariate (*dass kein Pöbel entstehen soll*) even if this involves protection of the individual against himself (§ 240). And it stands towards the Poor as a father to his family (§ 241). "With the poor the General Power takes the place of the Family, coping with their immediate destitution and also with their aversion to labour, their tendency to crime, and the other vices that spring from their situation and their feeling of wrong" (§ 241). The growth of population and industry is a feature of every unhampered civil society, and the result is on the one hand wider commerce and greater production, leading to great profits and accumulation,—and on the other hand greater specializing of individual labour and greater dependence of the workers, who run the risk of losing all the higher enjoyments and intellectual benefits of civil society (§ 243). A proletariate arises in a country when any considerable numbers fall below the standard of living deemed necessary for a member of society in that country. The existence of this excessive poverty aids the concentration of excessive wealth in few hands. The proletariate have lost self-respect, and have lost the desire to make their own living; and yet they claim the right to receive their subsistence; they are full of rebellious feelings and hatred of the rich. "Against Nature no man can assert a right, but in a state of Society destitution at once wears the garb of a wrong, inflicted on a particular class" (§ 244). The question how best to help the poor is amongst the most imperative and anxious questions of modern societies. One difficulty is that to give relief without labour is contrary to the first principle of civil society, individual independence, and to give it for labour is to increase the overproduction of goods which (in conjunction with the want of corresponding productive consumers) was the very cause of the evil at first. For all its overflowing abundance of wealth, civil society seems too poor[14] to cope with the excess of poverty and the growth of the proletariate. We see that in England the Poor Rate and indiscriminate private charities undermine the body corporate itself. In Scotland, to prevent the demoralizing influence of legal relief, the extremely poor are left to resort to begging (§ 245). The dialectic, which has shown itself in this tendency to the growth of a proletariate over against great fortunes, pushes civil societies beyond their own bounds, and leads them to colonization, either sporadic or systematic, in order to find customers and subsistence (§ 246, cf 248).

As family life and *terra firma* go together, so do industry and the sea. To be afloat is to be loosed from local ties and exposed to dangers.[15] But the sea, while detaching men from their own civil society, brings them into contact with other such societies. It unites far more than it separates, and is a true civilizing agency (§ 247). The securing of the independence of colonies Hegel regards as analogous to the liberation of a slave it is the greatest advantage for the mother country, just as the slave's freedom is really so for his master (§ 248).

Corporate government, *i.e.* Civil Society as a corporate unity and as a group of corporations, has the task of caring for the general interests which have just been discussed, as well as for mere law and order; and in this care for the general weal we see the immanent social morality (as distinguished from law) beginning to show itself;—it is the universal element supervening on the particularity of competition (§ 249). The industrial classes above described, being most characteristic of civil society, most markedly show the tendency to form corporate groups (such as Guilds and Trades' Societies), caring for, and, it may be, training their members and thereby securing their means of living. In this way corporate life reinforces and strengthens family life, and the individual himself gets recognition and standing before his neighbours. In this way, too, help may be given to poverty without the degradation of the recipient. To Hegel, the sanctity of Marriage and the Sense of Honour in members of a guild, club, or association, are the two roots of a well-ordered State. The rise of trade-guilds among the industrial classes seemed to him an event comparable in importance with the introduction of agriculture and property among the rural classes (§253, cf. § 255). A man's "natural right" to practise his trade where he best can is no doubt in some degree limited by a guild. (In many German towns in Hegel's days the right to work at a trade was not conceded unless the would-be worker contributed to a benefit society.) But the workman is also in some degree saved from the reign of chance, and he is trained to labour with others for a common end (§ 254).

Such spontaneously formed associations, commercial or otherwise, Hegel considers to be essential to a perfect State (§§ 289, 303, etc.); they make Society organic throughout instead of a loose aggregate. The abolition of them in France, in 1789, seems to him therefore regrettable; and he considers that it necessarily led to centralization, for it left the masses inorganic and left all organization to come from above. The appearance of such associations is a sign of the need felt by the "particular element" to "throw down roots" into the universal (§ 289).

Still the common interest sought in the guild is not the interest of all citizens but only of a class; and the guild owes its own dignity to its place in a greater body that cares for the whole people, and this body is the State. Though last in theory, the State is first in the actual world; the family and civil society, as they now are, could only arise within the shelter of the State and on the soil of it (§ 256). In the State we have a more true individuality and more true universality than in civil society. In its best form it is a condition of the best kind of individual action.[16] It is not a mere sum of the other elements; it is "something *more*, a bringer of *new* things." It is not simply a name for the aggregate of the particular wills embraced by it; but, as Rousseau happily suggested, it is an expression of the "general will," or of the resolutions formed by the citizens as members one of another and not capable of being formed (still less carried out) without that organic union.

Hegel therefore regards the State as the "eternal and necessary" realization of the spirit of man; it is God come down to us in the likeness of men (§ 258).

No doubt in this world of chance and caprice the divine idea is marred by many imperfections; but it is still recognisable, even as in the criminal and cripple may be recognised the likeness of humanity (§ 258).

Hegel proceeds to deal with the three features of the State: its constitution and domestic legislation, its relation to other individual States (or its place in International Law), and its place in the greater world and Universal History, where the spirit of man is Judge over the contending States (§ 259).[17]

The first of these three aspects receives much the largest share of his attention. The State is the realization of concrete freedom. Modern States are immeasurably stronger and deeper than ancient because "the principle of subjectivity" is fully recognised, and brought into the service of the "substantial unity" of the State. We are to have the same religious devotion to the State as the ancient Greeks and Romans, with a fulness of independent individual life that was not allowed in Greece and Rome. The modern State is bound up with the happiness of all its members; in relation to the State, a man's rights and duties coincide absolutely "in one and the same respect." The conscious will and effort of the individuals are as essential to the State as is the State to them. The general interest becomes their own particular interest. The State is not to them a mere external Fate, or it would not be what it is, a living "organization of freedom." In ancient States the identity of the individual's will with the State's was secured only by the ignoring of any distinct individual will, whereas now the individual is to have views of his own and a will of his own, but in the good State his views and his will prove to be at one with those of the State, though distinguishable and distinct from them (§§ 260–262, cf. § 268, etc.).

Hegel illustrates his conception that "the State is an organism," not only (§ 269) by the old fable of the belly and the members, but by an original physiological analogy. In the nervous system (he says) there are two phases of feeling: there is "abstract feeling" or Sentiency, a dull feeling of internal movement and of the processes of nourishment and digestion, etc., where I keep myself to myself; and there is the phase of "difference" when the feeling passes from within me to without me in what we call Irritability. Now the Family may be represented by the sentiency, Civil Society by the irritability, while the State is represented by the nervous system as an organized whole, which is only a *living* whole so far as it includes *both* sentiency and irritability (§ 263). If the State is not built on family and civil society, "it stands in the air" (§ 265). As Hume said that "government is founded on opinion,"[18] so Hegel conceives that, though people may say in their haste it is all a matter of brute force, "what really holds things together is the profound feeling of order which all have," and their trust in the stability of political security, a trust which is second nature with them, and is really their will, whether consciously or not (§ 268).

The chief end of the State is the good of the whole community, including therefore the particular and private interests of the members. Though it is true that a constitution is not made but grows (cf. § 274), the State is above all things self-conscious and deliberate and reasoning in all its actions; and therefore Religion, which is above all things a feeling of what is the truth as distinguished from a logical and reasoned-out statement of it, must not be identified with politics either to the absorption of State in Church, or of Church in State. That "devout men need no laws" is the saying of a fanatic (§ 270).

The Church (if we may leave Hegel for a moment) shows how difficult it is for a spontaneously-formed society to remain quite spontaneous. Without an organization the best Church does not long hold together. The Quakers have felt the difficulty; and the Independents, at one time in our history so strong for assault, have found the need of a central authority like the Presbyterian Synods and Assemblies. If organization came first, the result would be as in a French colony in contrast to an English settlement; where spontaneity is not found, it is seldom created. The healthy order of development seems to be first the spontaneous union (as of the early Christians), then the deliberate organization. The first beginning would be spiritual life, which simply trusts to itself, and leaves outward organization to come of itself, the faithful meeting only when they felt so disposed. This Anarchism, whether or not it be the highest ideal, has never lasted long. No church has been ever able to dispense with definite rules of faith and order.

Hegel goes on to consider the different forms of the State's necessary activity. There is the domestic constitution, in which executive and legislative powers, distinct as they are, cannot be really separate, but must be one in the Sovereign. The Sovereign Power is best represented by a constitutional monarch. The monarch exists to put (as it were) the dot on the i; but to Hegel this seems a very necessary function; the unity of the national will must be represented by a single personality (§§ 273–280). There is truth in the old argument for hereditary monarchy, that it places the throne out of the scope of competing factions; but the deeper reason is that thereby the impression is made on the citizens that the State is above caprice and accident, and endures from age to age. Hegel thinks little of the mere grounds of expediency, or of contract between king and people, alleged by some defenders of the monarchy (§ 281). The hereditary principle in the monarchy is adequately justified by the reason explained; it is the higher and more rational form of the patriarchal principle (§ 286). Primogeniture, too, is defended as furnishing a constant element in civil society as contrasted with the variableness of the industrial classes (§ 306).

The monarch for his part must be constitutional. The kingly acts must show reason for themselves (§§ 283, 284), and "guarantees" must be found in institutions with which the monarchy must feel itself bound up, just as the general liberties are bound up with the monarchy (§ 286). The officials under the sovereign must be neither mere hirelings doing a duty mechanically, nor knights errant doing it fitfully from caprice, but men whose minds are really set on serving the general interests, and who use their own reason, and give play to their own peculiar talents in the public service (§ 294). The watchfulness of the sovereign, and of the guilds and other bodies in the State will defeat any tendencies to bureaucracy (§ 295).

These organized intermediate groups possess a consciousness of the meaning of the State such as is present nowhere else in the community. They constitute the Middle Classes, which Hegel (like many of our own writers) regards as the centre of political intelligence and stability (§ 297). But it will be noted that he does not identify them with the *bourgeoisie*. His middle class seems to consist of the whole system of organized social groups, which logically would include the working classes whenever they are organized into trades societies or other disciplined Unions.

Hegel is no more and no less democratic than Aristotle. The term, "the People," is used, he says, sometimes in the sense of "that part of the people that does not know what it wants. To know what one wants needs really much knowledge and wisdom, which 'the people' do not possess" (§ 301). Representation in Parliament is needed *not* in order to discover political truth and give true decisions on any question, and *not* in order to provide "checks" on the King, but to complete the articulate and graduated organization, reaching from above to below, and from below to above. If it were only the Monarch and officials that were organized, what is left would be a mere mob (§ 302, cf. § 314). Scope is wanted, too, for freedom in the common sense of the term; and hence publicity is essential to parliamentary deliberations (§ 314); but the members of a parliament, though they give voice to that element of liberty on behalf of particular groups or localities, are, when once elected, not mere delegates with a mandate, but beings possessed of thought and will of their own, and using them in the service, not of a section, but of the whole community (§ 308). Public opinion has been, and always must be, a great power; it represents the views of healthy common-sense as opposed to the prejudiced views of a biassed party in any question; but [as Aristotle said] the "people" can draw no fine distinctions, and unorganized public opinion has as much in it to be despised as to be respected (§ 316–319). Hegel recognises the need of liberty of the press, though with similar qualifications (§ 319). Public opinion is the counterpart of the "subjectivity" of the Monarch at the other extremity of the State. The unity of the State, made evident by the individuality of the Sovereign, implies what Hegel calls "ideality,"—an organic union of inseparable elements (§ 320). But it is not only a union; it is a unit; besides "ideality" it has individuality, a relation to other individuals whom it excludes,—in this case other States against which it asserts its independence (§§ 321, 322), and from whom it claims recognition (§ 330). In War the sacrifice of life and property for the State shows that the State's claim is higher than any of its members'; and, on the other hand, war may show that the claim of a particular State to a particular place in the world is by no means absolute (§ 323). Hegel refuses to allow that war is merely evil. With the experience of Prussia and the War of Liberation in memory, he sees many virtues in war. The merely contingent earthly life and finite property of men are sacrificed, and thus show un-mistakeably their finitude, which in peace is too easily forgotten. A perpetual peace such as Kant desired would lead to lethargy (§ 324, cf. §§ 330, 333), even were the international compact which Kant suggests not (as it is) an impossibility. The necessity of war involves the necessity of a special institution, a special class, or Standing Army, just as necessarily as other special needs lead to marriage, and to an official and trading class (§ 326). The soldier's virtue is bravery, in the sense of self-sacrifice in the public service, not in the sense of mere personal courage (§ 327). The *object* of the courage makes all the difference; and in modern times bravery appears rather in the individual's subordinating himself to the ends of that larger body of which he is a member, than in his individual initiative (§ 328).

As the individual person is not really individual till brought into relation with other persons so the State is not really a State till brought into relation with other States (§ 331, cf. 322). The others must respect it as a State, just as the other persons must respect me as a person. As between persons, so between States, there arise contracts or Treaties, of which it is the object of International Law to secure the preservation. But States, having no government over them, are to each other in a state of Nature; and there is no prætor to enforce the contracts (§ 333, cf. 339). War therefore does not seem avoidable (§ 334). Each State regards the good of the whole as supreme law, but it is the good of its own particular whole (§ 337). Hence the difficulty sometimes felt in reconciling morality and politics, morality being usually treated too narrowly, as if that were moral law between States which is so between individuals (§§ 336, 337). When a conflict arises, it must be remembered that it is between State and State, not between individual and individual; accordingly the minimum of injury should be done to individual life and property (§ 338).[19]

We said there was no praetor to enforce treaties. But in place of a prætor there is Divine Providence, or the Spirit of the World, whose development takes place through the dialectic of this very conflict among the finite spirits of the separate States. "The history of the world is the judgment of the world" (§§ 339, 340, 341). What seems to be merely might is found to be also right; the final victory has belonged to that national spirit which has represented the furthest stage of the universal spirit.[20] Human perfectibility is in this sense no phantasy. But, though the various national spirits are instruments of the supreme spirit, they are unconscious instruments (§§ 342, *seq.*); and each nation (being limited by the conditions of physical nature) can represent the supreme spirit only in one epoch (§§ 346, 347). Hegel (as Dante in the treatise *De Monarchiâ*) considers that, while that epoch lasts, its right to rule other nations is absolute. The individuals at its head, not the less really because unconsciously, are fulfilling the purpose of the divine spirit (§ 348, etc.). There have been four empires that have played this large part—the Oriental (representing "substantiality," in which individuals are lost), the Greek (in which individuality has had free and artistic scope), the Roman (in which anarchy has been reduced to rule, but an abstract universal rule), and the German (in which universality and individuality, law and liberty, are reconciled in the modern State) (§§ 352–360). The idea of the State represented by the last coincides with the idea of religion and the idea of knowledge in their modern form. There is no abstract opposition either of God and His world, or of thought and things, or of order and freedom.

The fortunes of the Hegelian philosophy, the parting of Hegel's followers into two or even three groups, will be found recorded by Erdmann in his *History of Philosophy*.[21] In relation to social questions the importance of Hegel is, that of all the abstract philosophers he was the most concrete, both in his ethics, where the truth is represented as only attainable in society, and in his philosophy of history where the true freedom worked out by history is represented as a reconciliation of man with the world. But in economics, which he treated only incidentally, his influence has naturally been indirect; and we shall find it most powerful among the "Young Hegelians," or "Hegelians of the Left."

Note

The first part of Hegel's *Philosophy of Right* has been expounded by Dr. Hutchison Stirling in his *Lectures on the Philosophy of Law* (1873). Professor Edward Caird has excelled himself in his brief account of the life and philosophy of Hegel (Blackwood's Philosophical Classics, 1883). For the second section of the *Philosophy of Right*, relating to Morality, Mr. F. H. Bradley, in his *Ethical Studies* (1876), gives many useful illustrations.

Notes

1 See other volumes of this series: *Philosophy of Fine Art*, p. 167.
2 Hegel, *passim*, e.g., *Phil, of Right*, § 31, p. 63.
3 In Mr. Bosanquet's happy pharse they are "put by."
4 *Rechtsphilosophie*, § 57; *Philosophie der Geschichte*, Part II., Sect. ii. But the locus classicus is *Phanomenologie*, Bk. IV., A. (ed. 1841), *Wks.*, vol. ii., p. 139 *seq.*
5 This reminds us of Kant's principle of universalizing the maxim. If we all so acted, nobody would find it possible to be free.
6 Cf. δικαστής as δίκαιον ἔμψυχον, Arist., *Eth.*, V. (4), 77.
7 *Wks.*, XVI. p. 157 (year 1810), *ibid.*, pp. 167, 171 (1811). Compare his Life by Rosenkranz, p. 253. There is a hint of the same perhaps in *Rechtsph.*, pp. 212, 232.
8 ἡ χρεία συνέχει ὥσπερ ἕν τι ὄν, Arist., *Eth.*, V. (5), 13; ἐν χρεία ὦσιν ἀλλήλων, *ibid.*
9 *Rechtsphil.*, § 189, p. 249.
10 Hermann has pointed out the economical *advantages* of fashions, which are less obvious than their disadvantages. See *Staatswirthschaftliche Untersuchungen*, 2nd ed., 1870, pp. 99, 100, ftn.
11 Compare Rousseau's saying that the man who first drew a line round a strip of land and said "that is mine," was the real founder of Civil Society (*Inégalité*, pt. II., p. 67).
12 The money equivalent for services is described by Hegel as "abstract services."
13 *Gesetzt*, a play on *Gesetz*, as if "law" meant what was "laid down." § 215, cf. 217.

14 He says "too poor in the sort of property (*Vermögen*) that is peculiar to it" which may mean *saleable* goods.
15 A Common idea of the Greek Philosophers.
16 Cf. Sax, *Staatswirthschaft*, pp. 13, 17.
17 See Schiller's poem, "Resignation:" "Die Weltgeschichte ist das Weltgericht."
18 Essay on *The First Principles of Government*.
19 Cf. Rousseau, *Contrat Social*, I. 4: "La guerre n'est done point une relation d'homme à homme, mais une relation d'Etat à Etat," etc.
20 Träger der gegenwärtigen Entwickelungsstufe des Weltgeistes.
21 Vol. iii. of the translation in this series pp. 5 to 106, §§ 331 to 342. Cf. also below, Book V., ch. i.

Book V

Modern Philosophy (IV) Materialistic Economics and Evolution

1 Karl Marx (1818–1883)

The later or "scientific" Socialism of Germany so magnifies the merely eco-nomical element in history and society that it seems to allow no place for Philosophy. Nevertheless it is a historical fact that the straitest sect of scien-tific socialists represented by Marx and Engels sprang from the philosophy of Hegel, and confessed its origin.

In the Postscript (dated January, 1873) to a second edition of his book on *Capital*,[1] Marx complained that his critics had failed to understand his method of exposition. The *Revue Positive* of Paris accused him of treating economics metaphysically (in the Comtist sense of the word) and then of confining himself to a mere critical analysis of the facts. German reviewers cried out against Hegelian sophistry. A Russian critic found his method of investigation to be strictly realistic, but his method of exposition to be the dialectic of German idealism.

Marx replies that investigation and exposition are bound to proceed by different methods. The former has to master the facts in detail, analyse their different complications, and trace their inward connection. Only then can the actual movement of things be adequately expounded. But in the final exposition the life of the things is reflected in ideas, and there may *seem* to the reader to be a construction, *à priori*. The method is dialectical (he adds) but the dialectic is not the Hegelian. "My dialectical method is fundamentally dif-ferent from Hegel's, and is even its direct opposite. For Hegel it is the process of thought, which (under the name Idea) he even converts into an independ-ent Subject, the Demiurgos of the actual world, which is only its outward manifestation. For me, on the contrary, ideas are only the material facts turned up and down in the human head. The mystifying look of the Hegelian dialectic was criticised by me nearly thirty years ago, when it was still in vogue. But at the time I was finishing the first volume of *Kapital*, these dreary pretentious mediocrities the Epigoni, who now have the ear of lettered circles in Germany, were treating Hegel as the good Moses Mendelssohn treated Spinoza in Lessing's time, 'like a dead dog.' I therefore openly avowed myself a disciple of that great thinker, and even coquetted here and there (in the chapter on Value)[2] with his peculiar phraseology. Dialectic certainly under-went mystification in Hegel's hands; but, for all that, it was he who first comprehensively and deliberately expounded its general movements. With him it is upside down. We have to turn it over if we would discover the rational kernel in the mystical shell. In its mystical form it became the fashion in Germany, because it seemed to explain the existing state of things. In its rational form it is a terror to the *bourgeoisie* and its *doctrinaire* spokesmen, for it not only gives explanation, positively, of the existing state of things, but also of its negation, its necessary decay; it views every form of existence in its actual process of movement, and therefore on its perishable side; it lets nothing impose on it; it is essentially critical and revolutionary."

We may add the words of Friedrich Engels, the chief prophet of the school since the death of Marx:—"Readers will be surprised to stumble on the cosmogony of Kant and Laplace, on Darwin and modern physics, on Hegel and classical German philosophy, in a sketch of the growth of socialism. But scientific socialism, once for all, is an essentially German product, and could only have come into being in the nation whose classical philosophy had kept alive the tradition of conscious dialectic, *i.e.* in Germany or among Germans. The materialistic view of history and its special application to the modern war of classes (between proletariate and *bourgeoisie*) was only possible by means of dialectic; and, if the pedagogues of German *bourgeoisie* have so drowned the memory of the great German philosophers and their dialectic in the swamps of a barren eclecticism, that we need to appeal to modern physical science to vouch for the existence of dialectic in actual facts, we German socialists are proud to trace our descent not only from St. Simon, Fourier, and Owen, but from Kant and Hegel."[3] Germany has been always revolutionary in the world of theory,—as once by her monks, so now by her philosophers.[4] Hegel's dialectic (says Engels) has converted socialism from a Utopia into a science; German socialism is no mere reproduction of Owen and Fourier, nor even is it a more logical development of their principles; it contains an entirely new element, borrowed from philosophy.

We must ask ourselves, What is the nature of this contribution made by philosophy to socialism, and how far has it been taken up by the latter in a merely eclectic fashion?

Hegel died in November, 1831. Ten years or so afterwards, while the fight for his mantle was still raging among German philosophers, his disciples in France and Russia had begun to interpret his doctrines in a revolutionary sense, and even his own countrymen were finding more than an official optimism in the *Philosophy of Right*. The spread of Hegelianism in "Young Russia" was no doubt assisted by the fact that revolutionary writings could slip through the hands of the censors if well-wadded with seemingly harmless philosophy.[5] But, if they had not actually contained a revolutionary element, these writings could hardly have stimulated, as they did, so many social and political movements on the Continent from 1840 to 1850, and still in 1883 be thought an essential part of modern socialism.

It is significant that in the passage above quoted Engels speaks of Kant and Hegel, but says nothing of the socialist Fichte. Hegel held always the first place. Marx at one time (1845) had not only projected but written with Engels, a book which was to express their common attitude to German philosophy in the form of a criticism of Hegel's successors. It was never printed; but Engels gives us the substance of it in his paper on *Ludwig Feuerbach and the Outcome of Classical German Philosophy* (Stuttgart, 1888, reprinted from *Neue Zeit*, 1886).[6] In 1844 Marx had begun in the *Deutsch-Französische Jahrbücher*, which he was editing with Ruge in Paris, a review of Hegel's *Philosophy of Right*, giving more space, however, to his own views than to his author's. In the same year he wrote with Engels the *Holy Family*, a volume full of obsolete controversy, and discreditable scurrility, directed against mediocrities now forgotten, of whom Bruno Bauer was perhaps the most notable. Incidentally the statement of the writer's own opinions lends the book some interest. It is to be noted that P. J. Proudhon[7] is mentioned with friendliness and respect; and at first sight this seems very natural, for Proudhon was the first to found a revolutionary social philosophy professedly on Hegelian lines. To understand fully the position of Marx, we must know the position of Proudhon; and the substance of his views may be here given without real digression.

Proudhon considers that Political Economy is still in his own time defective because it has been disjoined from philosophy.[8] In his *System of Economic Contradictions, or the Philosophy of Poverty* (1846), he states his belief that Hegel's formula has given us once for all the key to all science and logic. There is (he says) a political economy which possesses "absolute certainty as well as progressiveness" by being the concrete objective realization of metaphysics.[9] But the old political economy of Adam Smith and J. B. Say is a collection of mere observations, a chronicle of the most obvious customs, traditions, and practices of men in the matter of wealth, and its production and distribution. It is (shortly) "tradition," and is confronted with "socialism," which is (shortly) "Utopia."[10] Socialism is essentially criticism, and there is nothing in it which is not in the political economy criticised by it, as "nihil est in intellectu quod non prius fuerit in sensu." Proudhon opposes both of them; he would say not "il faut organiser le travail," or "il est organise," but "il s'organise."[11] Political Economy has identified itself with the old jurisprudence and principle of property; it counts as permanent and definitive what is only transitory. Malthus spoke its death sentence when he uttered his allegory of "Nature's Mighty Feast,"[12] which meant in brief "Death to him who possesses nothing." On the other hand, socialism hands us over to arbitrary creations of our own brain, *a priori* ideals of reason, which lead to despotism.[13] "Philosophy" will reject both. What is the essential truth in political economy? Value is the central doctrine. Value is "the proportional relation according to which each part of the elements of wealth forms part of the whole." Its foundation is utility, but its proportion is fixed by labour. Proudhon finds an "economic contradiction" in the fact that value in exchange and value in use are indispensable to one another,[14] and yet the result of the multiplication of "values" is to lower them.[15]

This is a fair example of Proudhon's indifferent skill in reasoning. When two phenomena, unlike in kind from each other, are yet necessarily related, so that they vary in degree inversely the one from the other, the variation is said by him to "contradict" the necessary relation. It is "antinomies" of this sort which he considers to form the essential feature of political economy. The contradiction (he conceives) is not in words only, but in deed and in truth—a real Kantian antinomy in the nature of things.[16]

With the same show of philosophy, he goes on to trace the economic evolution of humanity, in stages or "epochs" which come logically in a certain order, not always the same as the order of time.[17] It passes through an epoch of analysis (Division of Labour) to that of synthesis (Machinery), and then to the epoch of Competition. Competition (still on Hegelian principles) destroys itself and results in its own opposite, Monopoly,[18] which makes the fourth epoch. Its coming was inevitable, but lamentable, for it involves that man drains his fellows dry, and makes them mere means to his ends. An act of society, which would regulate the conditions of labour and exchange, and make all comers welcome to "Nature's mighty feast," would be a rational expression of the organic development of humanity.[19] Falling back on the ideas of his earlier (and more famous) book, *What is Property?* (1840), Proudhon declares property in every form to be monopoly, and to be in contradiction with the notion of value common to himself with the older economists,[20] which ascribes it to labour. On the other hand, socialism and communism seem to him chimerical.[21]

Property was the fourth stage. The fifth is that of Police and Taxation,[22] where monopolists pay ransom by being taxed for public purposes. But to take the substance and leave the shadow of property, is only another "contradiction"; we should do better to take the whole. As it is, the taxes often fall most heavily on the poor.[23] Religion, which teaches submission to such evils, is thereby interposing an obstacle to the removal of them. On the other hand, the new dogma taught by Rousseau, St. Simon, Fourier, and Owen, that human nature is perfect and society corrupts it, seems rather worse than the old theological dogma of a corrupt human nature. Humanity is gradually becoming better, and it will reach not indeed an infinite ideal, but an equilibrium, when it shall have destroyed its three enemies, God, the State, and Property. Proudhon is thus metaphysically and socially an anarchist.[24]

In the sixth epoch, that of the Balance of Trade, society finds internal regulation an imperfect compensation for the existence of a proletariate, and seeks help from without.[25] Here too we have a "dialectic," a movement towards free trade and a movement towards protection. The monopoly preserved at home is opposed in foreign trade![26] Proudhon attacks Bastiat, "the Achilles of Free Trade," and considers custom-houses to be as necessary to society as machines.[27] The failure of free trade to cure our evils has been practically admitted by the rise of the new enthusiasm for loan-institutions which are to make everybody a capitalist. This leads him to the seventh epoch, of Credit; credit involves "the canonization of cash."[28] But to recognise the State in the matter of credit, and refuse to admit its interference in trade, is simply another "contradiction." The State is "the caste of non-producers"; it neither produces nor possesses property and capital. Property is the feature of the eighth epoch; it implies the detachment of man from nature and society, by credit,—that is to say, by making possible such things as loans on the security of property, and enabling the monopolist to stand free of his fellow workers, and live on their labour. "It is the right to use and abuse, and therefore to be a despot."[29] At one time property was necessary, and even salutary; but it has brought disastrous consequences: "It means the depopulation of the earth." Accordingly this epoch is followed by its opposite (the ninth stage), the epoch of Community or Communism, both of which Proudhon, without allowing their distinction from each other,[30] pronounces utopias and logomachies.

He decides against communism by arguments in no way peculiar to himself, laying special stress on its incompatibility with the Family, and "the organic elements of societies" (II. 278). "Communism is the religion of poverty" (303, ft.). "Communism in science, as in nature, is synonymous with Nihilism, undividedness, immobility, night and silence" (303, top). It does not see that the economic problem is to secure the greatest possible production and consumption by the greatest possible number of men. It tries like ordinary proprietorship to get the greatest possible nett produce (II. 309). "Whoever appeals to force and to capital in order to organize labour is a liar, because the organization of labour must be the downfall of capital and force." The next (or tenth) stage is that of Population. Malthus spoke demonstrable truth about it, and to him was confided the charge of proclaiming to the world that "Pan is dead"—society is dead, killed by its eternal enemies, monopoly and utopia (II. 311–313). Proudhon, thinks he, for his part, has discovered that the dictum of Malthus (stated before by him to be demonstrable truth) is overturned by the fact that men not only suffer poverty but anticipate it, and that wealth tends to increase faster than population (II. 341, cf. 325). There is discoverable, he says, "a specific virtue which will re-establish the balance between population and production" (II. 328). What is it? Malthus would make marriage a privilege of the well-to-do (II. 351). But Proudhon thinks it possible that humanity may one day become an assemblage of saints, and that the union of the sexes will sink to its proper subordinate position with all, when a change of the conditions of labour has given to the labourer the discipline of education and of the comforts of life, as well as the ennoblement of virtue (II. 390).

Powerful as are his descriptions of the evils of present society, and keen as are his perceptions of the drift of the social movements of his day, and his criticisms both of evils and proposed remedies, it must be allowed that his own remedies are shadowed out in vague phrases, and that his *Philosophie de la Misère* is as intangible as any of the Utopias he censures. He had his fame and its nemesis, the latter in the shape of Karl Marx's most brilliant controversial pamphlet, *La Misère de la Philosophie* (Brussels, 1847). Later generations will almost wonder at the comparative moderation of this pamphlet, if they remember the utter barbarity which characterized the disputes of social reformers in those days. Their hatred of the capitalists is not expressed with more savagery than their hatred of one another; a difference of opinion as to ways and means is resented and held treason and betrayal, in spite of agreement as to the end in view. If any reader thinks these statements exaggerated, let him glance at a page or two of *Die Opposition* (Mannheim, 1846), edited by Karl Heinzen, and containing diatribes by the editor, Ruge, Oppenheim, Nauwerk, etc., against Proudhon and others, or of the same Heinzen's book on *Helden des deutschen Communismits* (Bern, 1848),[31] or of the *Heilige Familie*, by Engels and Marx (Frankfurt, 1844), written against Bruno Bauer, Faucher, Jungnitz, Edgar, etc.

Heinzen said of Marx that his function in life was to bury his friends, Proudhon among the number. Marx had once been friendly to Proudhon. He had hailed his question, "Quest ce que la Propriété?" as a worthy modern parallel to the question of Sièyes "Quest ce que le tiers état?"[32] He considers that Proudhon has once for all unmasked the inhuman character of Political Economy. Proudhon, however, sometimes spoke of history as built on an eternal foundation, a God who is guiding humanity, and who is Righteousness. "We need only apply logically the law that Proudhon himself sets up, the realizing of righteousness by means of its negation, in order to rise above this Absolute too in history. If Proudhon does not go so far, it is due to his misfortune in being born not in Germany but in France" (39, 40).

So wrote Marx in 1844; but in 1847 the tone is very different. He begins by a serious and most effective criticism of Proudhon's discussion of Value, showing that all that is sound in Proudhon on that subject is to be found in Ricardo, whom Proudhon does not take the trouble to understand. "Posterity will find it very simple-hearted in M. Proudhon to give, as a revolutionary theory of the future, a theory which Ricardo has scientifically expounded as relating to the bourgeois society of his own day, and to take as a solution of the antinomy between utility and value what Ricardo and his school have long ago presented as the scientific formula for only one factor of the antinomy, value in exchange."[33] Proudhon neglects the ruling power of demand which instead of an already constituted ratio of proportionality gives us only a continual movement towards such. In comparison with Ricardo, Proudhon is a mere rhetorician.[34] When Ricardo reduces the value of labour itself to the cost of the labourer's maintenance, the cynicism lies not in his words, but in the things he is expressing. Proudhon, by making the labourer's reward always proportional to the hours of labour, would prevent the labourer from receiving the occasional gain that comes from the fluctuations in demand.[35]

Marx shows even in this early work[36] signs of that wide (if not always accurate) acquaintance with economical literature so abundantly displayed afterwards in his *Kapital*. If he borrows from English socialists, he acknowledges the debt. Bray in particular is praised for his analysis of industrial conditions,—though Marx points out that Bray stops short of State Socialism, would allow individual accumulation, and regards common ownership of the means of production only as an ultimate and far-off end.[37]

Finally, Marx goes on to say, Proudhon has credited kings and princes with having given to the precious metals their unique position as money;— but all history shows that these potentates were themselves swayed by "economic conditions," and could do no more than give voice to them.[38] Money, like other things, has a commercial value exactly and rigorously determined. It is as vain to cry "Cursed coin," as "Cursed corn."

Marx then turns to Proudhon's metaphysics. To explain the genesis of economical categories, Proudhon has taken up the logic of Hegel, the method of position, negation, and synthesis (negation of negation). This method (says Marx) is the abstraction of *movement, i.e.* it is movement or process regarded in the light of pure reason alone, or an assertion followed by its contradictory, followed by the union of the two contradictories in a reconciling third notion. Proudhon, however, never succeeds in taking more than the first two steps; and in order to get steps or stages at all he needs to treat as successive social facts that are necessarily coexistent. He has nothing of Hegel's dialectic but the verbal phrases of it. We do not find in his pages that the categories themselves pass into their opposites, and thence into a new category; Proudhon makes the transition for them. He opposes "good" to "evil" and asks himself how to get a minimum of evil. Proudhon himself allows that this apparent logic is a scaffolding which may be removed without damage to his argument. The logical order is not, he confesses, the same as the historical. In fact Proudhon has not gone through idealism to history; he has never understood idealism at all.[39]

It hardly needed Proudhon's own later admissions[40] to convince us that Marx is right on this point. For his own part Marx himself, though he understood Hegel as well as any Hegelian is ever acknowledged by any other to understand him, played with Hegel's terms, and did not really try to convert the dialectic into an economic as well as metaphysical method.[41]

His own economic position is given in outline in the *Poverty of Philosophy*.[42] The Economists (he says) have a peculiar way of proceeding; they recognize only two kinds of institutions, those of art and those of nature. To the economists the institutions of feudalism are artificial, those of modern *bourgeoisie* natural, as, to the theologians, their own religion is from God and every other is man's invention.[43] The present arrangements by which wealth is created and productive forces utilized are "natural laws" independent of time, "eternal laws" which must always rule society. History (in their view) once existed but exists no more. It existed once because there were once feudal institutions with arrangements for production quite different from the present. Feudalism (Marx allows) had also a proletariate of its own, the serfs. It had its "good" and "bad" elements, the latter being in the end victorious, for they are the elements that create *movement* by evoking conflict. To eliminate the bad would be to kill the germ from which present civil society has grown. Once successful, the bourgeois society crushed not only all the old economic forms of feudal life, but the civic and political relations corresponding. Rightly to judge of production under feudalism, we must consider it as founded on a struggle of classes, which went on till the one class was victorious. The mode of production and the industrial system which developed through this struggle are far from being eternal laws. The changes occurring in the productive powers of men brought about changes in the industrial system; to preserve the new powers of production the traditional forms of the old must be destroyed; once these were destroyed, the class once revolutionary became conservative; thereupon a new antagonism of classes began to develope. There is a new proletariate, in conflict with the *bourgeoisie*; and the conflict flows necessarily from the new economic conditions. "From day to day it becomes more clear that the system of production under the *bourgeoisie* has a double-sided character; under the same system, in which wealth is produced, poverty is produced also; and under that in which powers of production develope there are developed also 'powers of repression.' The result is that the wealth of the middle class is only produced by the continual destruction of the wealth of its individual members and the consequent increase of the proletariate."

As the antagonism comes more clearly to light, different schools of economists begin to show themselves. We have first the Fatalists, classical and romantic. The former (as Adam Smith and Ricardo) live at a time when the struggle with feudal survivals is not yet over; their mission is simply to show how as a matter of fact wealth is acquired in the bourgeois society, to formulate the new laws and categories, and to show their relation to the old. Poverty is to them simply the pain that accompanies a new birth whether in nature or in industry. The latter belong to our own time, when the contrast of the wealthy and the proletariate is complete. They use a tone of superiority and disdain towards the working classes. "They copy the doctrines of their predecessors; and the indifference, which with their predecessors had something of *naïveté* has with them something of coquetry."

After the fatalists we have the Humanitarians, who take to heart the bad side of present arrangements, and try to alleviate the sufferings and lessen the antagonism. They advise the workers to be temperate, to work hard, and to have small families, and they advise the employers to put enthusiasm and humanity into their business. Their doctrines are full of distinctions between theory and practice, principles and conclusions, ideas and applications of them, good sides and bad sides of everything. Fully developed, the humanitarian becomes the Philanthropic school, which denies the necessity of antagonism and would make all men capitalists. The theories of these Philanthropists depend on abstraction from the unpleasant parts of the reality. They think to preserve bourgeois categories without the contrasts inseparable therefrom. They fancy themselves in opposition to the *bourgeoisie* and are really more at one with it than the other schools are.

Lastly, the Socialists and Communists are the theorists of the proletariate as the Economists are of the middle classes. Since the whole character of bourgeois production is not yet fully developed, the proletariate is not yet a compact class with a political programme; the material conditions for the emancipation of the proletariate are not yet fully formed; and the form to be taken by the new society is not yet discernible. Hence the Socialists and Communists are as yet Utopians who seek to meet the needs of the oppressed classes by improvising systems and running after schemes of social regeneration. "But, in proportion as history goes forward and with it the struggle of the proletariate becomes sharper and sharper, they need no longer look for science in their own minds; they have only to note well the movement passing before their own eyes and make themselves the organs of it." Till then they will see nothing but distress in the distress around them, without seeing in it the revolutionary side, the subversive movement which is to overturn the old society. "When science is produced by the historical movement and associates itself therewith in full consciousness of cause and effect, from that moment it ceases to be *doctrinaire* and becomes revolutionary."[44]

Even in 1847 we see that Marx had a clear view of the work before him. In his later books, the *Criticism of Political Economy* (1859), and especially *Das Kapital* (1867), he accomplished much of it. England, in which he lived during the last half of his life, was the country where the peculiarities of modern industry had most fully shown themselves; and *Das Kapital*, whatever may happen to its arguments, is likely to hold its place as a storehouse of references to the facts of English industry from the end of last century to the middle of the present. Towards the Economists, Marx is in these later books more decidedly hostile. His own economical doctrines are Ricardian and deductive; but they are presented as true only of human nature as it appears under the system of modern industry, which is now almost ready to vanish away.

In this system (he tells us) wealth means a collection of goods for sale. Goods are, indeed, in the last resort, outward objects that satisfy wants. That is their value in use; but in the system in question it is the value in exchange that is all important. Goods have, no doubt, a quality as well as a quantity; but in our modern world it is the quantitative aspect that needs and gets special attention. Now we are at once brought face to face with the question how it is that certain quantities of things so unlike each other in quality as iron and wheat become commensurable. What is the common element? If we abstract from the value in use, we find only one property left, the fact that the things exchanged are the product of labour, "abstract human labour."[45] Goods exchange according to the "average social human labour" which they need to produce them, or, more particularly, according to the time taken to make them by workmen neither exceptionally fast nor exceptionally slow, but of ordinary ability, with appliances neither ahead of the times nor behind them, but abreast of them. Cost is in fact average minimum cost. This "average social human labour" is "abstract labour" in the sense that the results of concrete weaving and tailoring, etc., are all measured for exchangeability by the quantity of working time in the abstract taken to produce them. The possibility of their translation into this form is the condition of their exchangeability, though the latter is not created by the former, still less by Money, which is only the "phenomenal form of the immanent measure of value, the working time."[46]

In all previous epochs the products of labour have been objects of use; but only in our own under the *régime* of the Capitalists is equivalence based upon value in the sense described, and goods are made for Sale and not for use, and the relation of the producers to each other is transformed into a relation of their products to each other. It is the state of things described by Hegel in the Philosophy of Right. The legal relation of persons who only realize their personality by having property, is characteristic of the Bourgeois Society.[47]

The reign of Capital begins with the world-wide trade introduced by the discoveries of the 16th century. Historically it appears in opposition to Property in Land, and in the form of Money; "No land without a lord," "Money has no master." The difference between money as capital and money as money is at first simply in the forms and formulas of their circulation. As money it stands midway—the exchange is goods for money, and then money for goods again. As capital, it is at the extremes;—the exchange is of money for goods, and then goods for money again.[48]

To explain how this process can be profitable is to explain the existence of a surplus value, a value accruing to the capitalist beyond the equivalent of the "socially necessary labour" already described. We see that competition reduces goods to cost price; yet the moneyed men get more than the cost price. How is this? The solution lies in the fact that they can purchase a commodity (labour) which has the property of producing value, more value than it itself has. The value of the labour is determined, like that of other things, by the "labour socially necessary" to produce it, in other words, necessary to produce the means of living according to the average standard of the same in the given society. This is all the average labourer will fetch; and its price is represented say by three or four hours' labour a day. If he worked only for these three or four, the employer would make nothing by him; but the employer has the upper hand, and by paying him his cost price can secure not only his work for three or four hours, but for the whole day, of eight or ten hours. For five or six hours of the day the labourer produces value over and above his own cost—a surplus value. This is the secret of the Profits of the Capitalist. He may increase this surplus value either (1) "relatively," by reducing the cost of the labourers' subsistence, or (2) "absolutely," by lengthening the time during which the labourers work. In either case, the effect is produced by increasing the unpaid labour at the expense of the paid.[49] The articles made are sold (on Ricardian principles) at their cost price, which depends on the time socially necessary to produce them, not on the wages paid to the producers. If they are made in quantities more than enough to pay the socially necessary wages, the surplus quantities are really turned out by the workers for nothing, for the workers get nothing but the said wages.

Even the friends of Marx and his theories have found a difficulty at this point. Marx himself allows that competition tends to reduce the profits of capitalists to a level; and yet undeniably the proportion which labour (or the "variable" part of capital) bears to the fixed (or "constant") part of capital differs exceedingly between one business and another. Now, profits consist of prices got for goods made by unpaid labour; and these prices (like other prices) are said to be determined by the time socially necessary to produce the goods. But, if competition reduces profits to the same margin in all businesses, the prices cannot be equally determined in all businesses by the said necessary time of production, for the profits in businesses where labour bulks largely are (it appears) lowered by the competition of capitalists, or else these businesses (having more of unpaid labour) would yield higher profits than the others. Marx says himself:—"Every one knows that a cotton spinner, with much constant and little variable capital, gets no less profit or surplus value than a baker, with relatively much variable and little constant."[50] He adds:—"For solution of this apparent contradiction many middle terms are necessary,—as in elementary algebra it needs many middle terms to make it clear that % can represent an actual quantity." He has perhaps given his explanation in the unpublished third volume of *Kapital*.[51]

Whatever we think of the theoretical economics of Marx, it is as strictly deductive as Ricardo's, and on the whole follows the same lines. It is surprising, therefore, to find Marx expressly rejecting the Malthusian doctrine of population, and ascribing to each stage of society its own "law" of population, the Malthusian being only the law of the "capitalistic" stage of production. In *present* society the increase tends to be such as in conjunction with the effects of invention provides a surplus population ready to do the work for which they are wanted by the capitalists. They are only in excess because under this industrial system the producer is separated from his product, and the production benefits only the employer and capitalist.

Apart from the phraseology of such a passage (which will seem awkward to those who feel bound to conceive a law as a generality and not as varying with the facts to which it applies),[52] there is nothing absurd in its contention that the analysis given by Ricardo and Malthus applies only to the modern world of "great industry." Marx in this differs little from Bagehot, and even less from the more moderate historical economists, who allow a place to theoretical deduction, but confine it to our own society, and exclude it from all reasonings about primitive communities and half-developed civilizations, like that of Europe in the Middle Ages. Historical economists are a genus wide enough to include theorists like Marx, and professedly pure historians like Thorold Rogers and Roscher, who introduce their deductions furtively and eclectically. The historical method and the Hegelian are not opposed; but the latter is no doubt to a greater extent *a priori* in so far as the prejudgments with which we enter on a study of the historical facts are essential and undisguised. As Marx himself retained nothing of Hegel except the "method," the prejudgments might mean no more than that in nations which have a history at all there is a movement of thought[53] with a logic in it, tending through the struggle of opposing principles towards partial solutions, that come in their turn into conflict with each other—and that this process goes on without end, the present economic society being simply one stage in it. Marx and Engels, however, have another prejudgment besides this. The process is to them always more or less obviously economical in all cases. The logic they expect to find in the changes is always that of economical facts. The economical element in history is the dominant element.

In taking this view of history,[54] the scientific socialists seem to be committing the mistake which they blame in Ricardo and the older economists. They are taking the ruling principle of their own age for the ruling principle of all times. Economical influences are probably in our time the most important of all the many forces at work in society. But before our own times it is doubtful if they were so; and it is possible that in the remote future they will lose the primacy. The ideal of Marx (if we may judge from *Das Kapital*, I. p. 56) is a society of free men with common ownership of the means of production, consciously using their individual powers of labour as a social function. All the products of individual labour will be judged by their value-in-use. The collective product of society will (*a*) be used socially to serve over again as means of production (in other words capitalized); and (*b*) it will be distributed among the members for satisfaction of their wants. The method of distribution will vary with the social organization of a people and their historical development. But the share of each member in the means of subsistence will be determined by the time of his labour. This time will play a double part (1) determining the distribution of the different classes of labourers in proportion to the different wants of society, according to a general plan, (2) acting as a measure of the individual share of the producer in the common labour, and therefore in that part of the product which is given over to individual consumption. The social relations of men to their labour and to the product of their labour will remain transparently simple both in production and distribution.

Marx being no Utopian, does not predict the exact form which regenerated society will take, even as Hegel was never weary of telling us that the philosopher can make no predictions. But philosophy is more than criticism; and, to judge by the accessible written evidence, Engels, who modestly holds himself a mere follower of Marx, has a much clearer philosophical vision than his master. There is probably no scientific socialist who has so well justified his claim to have followed the spirit of Hegel's philosophy; and for socialism at this stage of its history he has probably said the last philosophical word.

In his *Development of Socialism from a Utopia to a Science* (1882), Engels distinguishes the former from the latter in the following way. The older socialists, whether they were "enlightened" French metaphysicians of the 18th century (like Mably) or really in touch with the working classes (like Fourier and Owen), saw absolute truth and absolute justice in their own conceptions of society. All else to them was false. Their different "absolutes" rubbed each other's angles down, and the result was an eclectic or "average" socialism (p. 18). The New Socialism recognises in the first place that instead of constructing a future society we must understand the present. Starting with Hegel's principle that all is movement and change, Engels concludes (in spite of Hegel) that there is no absolute truth. The only absolute truth would be that all truth is relative. Hegel's own dialectic is inconsistent with any finality of results. In his later book, *Ludwig Feuerbach and the Outcome of Classical German Philosophy* (1888), Engels argues that the dictum "the real is the rational and the rational the real" means "what must be shall be," but also that the real has in itself a dialectic displacing it for a new real; no particular institution, though it shows its present or relative rationality by persisting to exist, is to be considered eternally rational. The Prussian constitution, because real, was rational only in the sense that "the Prussians of Hegel's time had the constitution they deserved to have"; but the movement that was changing it into something quite different was equally rational, and proved so by *its* persistence. (*Ludw. Feuerb.*, pp. 2, 3.) The famous paradox of the great Idealist might be paraphrased by Goethe's words:—

"Alles das besteht
Ist werth dass es zu Grunde geht." (p. 4.)

Here lay the Revolutionary character of the Hegelian principle. Truth lies in a process of development. The institutions of a particular time are historically necessary; but equally so is the germ they contain of their own removal and replacement by different ones. The conservatism of Hegelianism is relative; the revolutionary character of it is absolute, and the only Absolute.

"With Hegel all Philosophy ends—partly because it is he who comprehends its whole development in his system, and partly because without intending it he has pointed the way out of the labyrinth of systems to the real positive knowledge of the world" (*Feuerb.*, p. 9). There were a Hegelian Right and Hegelian Left, because the emphasis could be laid either on the relative Conservatism or upon the Dialectic. The difference showed itself strongly in Politics and Religion. The Left or Young Hegelians followed Strauss (*Leben Jesu*, 1835), and went on to the Materialism of the 18th century, quitting what Hegel himself counted essential, the idea that nature is only an external realization of thought. Feuerbach frankly raised nature to the first place (*Essence of Christianity*) but his apotheosis of Love, though a natural reaction against the apotheosis of "pure thought," led to a useless and unscientific socialism, which had broken away from Hegel before it had understood him (*Feuerb.*, p. 13). The Materialism of last century had not the notion of development which is now beginning to animate science (*ib.* 25, cf. *Dev. of Socialism*, p. 24; and Kautsky, *More*, p. 328). Then the Revolution of 1848 threw both philosophy and Feuerbach into the shade.

Engels is no Agnostic; he thinks the revival of Kantianism in Germany is "a step backwards and practically only a timid way of accepting materialism behind the scenes and rejecting it before the public" (*Feuerb.*, 19). He is frankly a materialist, even in name (which Feuerbach had declined to be, p. 21). The moving impulse of philosophers, from Descartes and Hobbes to Hegel and Feuerbach, has not (he thinks) been the "power of pure thought" but the advance of science and industry (p. 19). The materialistic view of history finally displaced the idealistic (in Engels' opinion)[55] when the middle classes and the proletariate became unmistakeably opposed to one another. Such events as the outbreak at Lyons in 1831, and the agitation of the Chartists (1838–42) made it clear that the doctrines of orthodox Economists regarding the identity of interests between capitalists and labourers and the beneficent effects of unlimited competition were untenable. "But the old idealistic view of history knew no class wars depending on material interests, in fact knew no material interests at all. Production, and in fact all economical relations, came up only incidentally as subordinate elements in the history of civilization. The new facts compelled a new examination of history; and it was then shown that *all* previous history, with exception of primitive antiquity,[56] was the history of class wars, that these conflicting classes of society result on each occasion from the relations of the production and trade,—in a word, from the *economical relations* of their epoch, that therefore the economical structure of society at the time concerned forms the real basis on which are to be explained in the last resort the whole superstructure of legal and political arrangements as well as of the religious, philosophical and other views of each historical period of time." "Idealism was driven from its last refuge—history; a materialistic view of history was established, and a way was found to explain man's consciousness by his actual existence instead of (as hitherto) his existence by his consciousness" (*Development*, p. 26). Socialism carries out this view of history by thoroughly examining the present structure of industrial society. It commits itself to no ideal of the future. It shows at once the necessity of the growth of the present arrangements and the necessity of their downfall. Their essential characteristic was first shown by Marx in his doctrine of Surplus Value. The materialistic view of history and the theory of surplus value are both of them needed to convert Socialism from a Utopia into a science; and both are the services of Marx.[57]

In 1884 Engels was able to push the materialistic view of history a step further. Relying on Lewis Morgan's *Ancient Society, or Researches in the Lines of Human Progress from Savagery through Barbarism to Civilization* (1877), he published an account of the *Origin of the Family, Private Property, and the State*.[58] He says that in writing this book he was only carrying out a design of Marx, and that he has largely used his notes. As we have already seen, Engels is never beyond suspicion of allowing his modesty to wrong him, a generous fault which might be counted a virtue if it did not hinder his critics from being sure whom they are criticising.

He accepts Morgan's main conclusions in opposition to those of Bachofen and Maclennan. Morgan finds in the Iroquois Indians the key to the family life of primitive men. He finds the earliest ascertainable form to be that in which the members of the same clan might not marry within the clan but might not marry outside of the tribe, the so-called marriage being not a permanent union, and descent being reckoned through the mother and not through the father. This early type explains many peculiarities of the *gens* or clan, in Greece and Rome and elsewhere. The gradual transition to Monogamy is explained by Engels as ultimately in all its steps due to economical causes. The establishment of Monogamy was to secure the property of the man and its accumulation beyond possibility of dispersion. As the above-mentioned tribal communism is the characteristic mark of savagery, the temporary and terminable union is the mark of barbarism, and monogamy of civilization.[59] With the first considerable division of labour (when pastoral people became separated from the rest) came exchanges and accumulation of wealth, and with these slavery, and a revolution in the family, when the woman was no longer on a footing of equality with the man. With further division of labour (the rise of artisans labour in distinction from agriculture) exchange became exchange of *goods*, and private property arose, bringing with it monogamy. Last came the growth of Merchants, and the use of money, and the State to protect those who have against those who have not. "The State is neither a force imposed on society from without nor the realization of the moral idea; it is the product of a particular stage in development, the admission that Society is in conflict with itself, from oppositions of classes which it is powerless to remove."[60] This brings us to classical Greece and the ground becomes more familiar. We hear of the three forms of slavery characteristic of the three stages of civilization: ancient slavery, serfdom, and labour for wages. Lassalle and Engels are not far apart here, though Engels mentions the former only to repudiate his non-materialistic view of the Roman testament.[61]

Economists are not exempt from the common human frailty of claiming credit for amazing originality on the part of themselves or their friends. The theory of surplus value, whether true or false, is found in other authors than Marx, some of them long his predecessors. Marx may or may not have borrowed it from Rodbertus;[62] but the theory had been more or less clearly present to the minds of socialistic economists in England[63] since the beginning of the century.

The materialistic, or at least "economical view" of history is also not peculiar to Marx. To say nothing of Harrington,[64] Ferdinand Lassalle (1825–1864) tells us in his *Workmen's Programme* (1862) that in the Middle Ages the ruling element in society was to be found in the proprietors of land, for agriculture was then the chief form of industry. From this followed serfdom, villeinage, knights and kings. The progress of industry, in the form of manufacture and commerce with large capital, overthrew the feudal Society, and in place of the feudal relations substituted middle class employers and free workmen. There was production for a cosmopolitan market instead of production for personal use or for a local market. The French Revolution did no more than give legal effect to a *de facto* revolution. The third estate became dominant; and the ruling element of this second stage of modern history declared itself to be the possession of capital, in place of the mediaeval possession of land. Active citizenship has depended on payment of taxes even in France.

The ruling element in the third stage is to be the Working Men; the disinherited are to inherit all things. Their cause is that of humanity in general, for they are not a class; they are the people.

This is the view of Lassalle in the *Arbeiter-programm*; and of course it is not identical with that of Engels in detail, nor does it involve what we might have expected not only from a student of Hegel but from an editor of Heraclitus, a general principle of development, destructive and disintegrating without limit. But Lassalle has a warmer feeling for Fichte than for Hegel (see *Die Philosophie Fichte's und die Bedeutung des deutschen Volksgeistes*, 1862). In his book on *Acquired Rights* (1861) Lassalle expressly discards the Hegelian view of the philosophy of law. There are no absolute categories, deducible from a universal and eternal notion of right and underlying historical law. The categories of the philosophy of right must be historical. The law of nature is itself so; it develops with the human spirit in history. "As the philosophy of religion is the development of the consciousness of God, so the philosophy of right is the development of the consciousness of right among men" (*System der Erworbene Rechte*, ed. 1880; I. 59, 60). The particular case which leads to his discussion of the point is that of "acquired rights." His decision about these is that legislation must not be "retro-active" in the sense of making particular acts wrong that had by existing laws been right, but may be "retrospective" where a new law alters general social conditions or arrangements that do not come under the individual will. Law may fix the age of majority as 24 instead of 21 without any regard to present "rights," because it is not by a man's voluntary act that he becomes either 21 or 24; and it may alter general rights of property so that a class of things once property may cease to be so. Custom and tradition have nothing inviolable or unalterable in them. The most impressive example of the historical development of a legal notion is that of Inheritance. Testamentary law is nothing if not Roman. Now the essence of the Roman notion of a Will was *not* that bequest was deduced from the law of property, and was simply a transmission of property; the Roman will was the Roman embodiment of the idea of Immortality.[65] The testament is meant to cause an identification of the subjective will of the heir with that of the testator, so that the former shall as it were perpetuate the existence of the latter on earth by acting as the latter willed him to act; the heir succeeds not essentially to the possessions but to the will of the testator. This triumph of "abstract inwardness" is the "direct dialectical step towards the deeper inwardness of Christianity, where the immortality was supposed to be not in this world but beyond it." (*Erw. Rechte*, ed. 1880; II. 22, 26, 186, 187, 430, etc.). In the *suits heres* the wills are already identical without acceptance of any testament by the heir, because the heir as under the *potestas* of the head of the family has his will already identified with that of the head. In Intestacy search is made by the law for such persons as have been *in potestate* of the person concerned, and the general will of the people (the spirit of the nation generally) is taken as the will of this particular person. Otherwise, acceptance (*aditio*) is necessary to make inheritance an acquired right (*ib.* 472).

It was quite otherwise in German law, where the essential idea was that there was a moral identity of members of the Family, and birth determined succession. Here too indeed an act of will is essential to the acquired right, but it is the act of begetting on the part of the father—not an act of acceptance on the part of the son (II. 482, 485).

It is clear (Lassalle thinks) that inheritance is neither a matter of mere positive institution nor a matter of unchangeable law of nature. The notion has its stages of development, of which the Roman and the German are two. The regulation of inheritance instituted by the French Convention supplanted the individualism of Roman law (which, though in perverted form, had been ruling the minds of lawyers) by the notion of family inheritance; but the Family had now become a State institution (*ib.* 499). It was really regulation by the State; and it is evident that Lassalle regards such regulation with favour. It is remarkable that, though Lassalle is on these points opposed to Hegel, he believes himself to be reasoning on Hegel's premises and with Hegel's method (*Erw. Rechte*, II. 486 n., 488).

This treatise, the most laboured and powerful of the severer works of Lassalle, was not utilized by him in his popular discourses. In the latter he advocated the supplanting of the existing forms of industrial organization by the introduction of a system of co-operative industry organized and supported by the State and not on the voluntary principles recommended by such men as Schulze Delitzsch, whom he delighted to set at naught.[66] He did not live to carry out his philosophy into his economics. Perhaps his exertions as an agitator would have prevented the achievement, though exile might possibly have become to him, as to Marx, the "bridle of Theages."[67]

Features common to Lassalle, Engels, and Marx are the economical view of history and the belief that the working classes are now the tools of the other classes and yet worth all the rest. Both these positions well deserve discussion. Socialism owes its strength to them far more than to particular economic theories such as that of the Iron Law of Wages or that of Surplus Value, which have been unable to stand criticism.

Note

Of the numerous books on Socialism Mr. John Rae's *Contemporary Socialism* 2nd ed., 1891, and Mr. W. H. Dawson's *German Socialism and Ferdinand Lassalle*, 1888, stand very high, the former for its economics, the latter for its history. They have a judicial tone which is wanting in nearly all the German writings on the subject.

Notes

1 P. 818 (1872). The edition bears this date (1872), though evidently not published till the beginning of 1873.
2 Not only there (he might have added) but in such passages as *Kapital*, I. 793 (2nd German ed., 1872): "The capitalistic mode of production and capitalistic property are the first negation of the individual property founded on a man's own labour," etc., etc.
3 *Development of Socialism from a Utopia to a Science*, 3rd ed., 1883. Preface (dated 1882). Engels was born in 1820 and is happily still living.
4 Marx in *Deutsch-Französische Jahrbücher*, p. 79, 1844.
5 For the influence of Hegelianism on Young Russia, see the articles of G. Plechanoff on N. G. Tschernischewsky in *Neue Zeit* (Stuttgart) Aug. & Sept., 1890.
6 See his Preface there; and compare Marx, *Kritik der Polit. Oekon.*, 1859, Preface.
7 Born 1809; died 1865.
8 *Contrad.* (popular edition), II. 395, 396.
9 *Contrad.*, I., 35, 36; II., 172, 173.
10 *Ib.*, I. 37, cf. 254.
11 *Ib.*, I. 45.
12 *Ib.*, I. 38, cf. 532.
13 *Ib.*, I. 41, 55.
14 *Ib.*, I. 74, 82. Compare, as regards the stress on proportionality, Jevons, *Pol. Ec.*, ch. iv.
15 In *Contrad.* I. 60 (cf. II. 254), he says, "Exchangeable value is given by a kind of reflection of value in use, as the theologians teach that in the Trinity the Father, contemplating Himself from all eternity begets the Son,"—a profane analogy which reappears in Marx's *Kapital*.
16 *Contract.* I. 67.
17 *Ib.*, II. 252.
18 *Ib.*, I. 179, 229, etc.
19 *Ib.*, I. 248, 249.
20 The paradox of Brissot, "Property is Theft," has become identified with Proudhon. The notion that capital is accumulated labour (*Contrad.*, I. 274, etc.) may be traced to English economists.
21 *Ib.*, I. ch. vi., cf. ch. xi.
22 *Ib.*, I., ch. vii., 276, cf. 281, 282.
23 *Contract.*, I., ch. viii., especially 320–335, 368.
24 *Ib.*, II, ch. ix.
25 *Ib.*, II. 13, cf. 49.
26 *Ib.*, II. 47, 54, cf. 71.
27 *Ib.*, II. 92, 95–97.
28 *Ib.*, II., ch. xi.
29 Dr. Diehl (*P. J. Proudhon, seine Lehre und sein Leben*, Halle, 1888) has well pointed out that the correct interpretation of the definition in the *Pandects* of "jus utendi et abutendi" is "right to use and to use *up*,"—a very different thing from "abuse" in most cases.
30 *Contrad.*, II. 261. It must be allowed that the "Communistic Manifesto" of Marx and Engels (1848) shows by its title that its authors did not recognise any hard and fast distinction. Engels says elsewhere (see Heinzen, *Helden des deutschen Communismus*, p. 53) that Communism is not a doctrine, but a movement.
31 *Ex pede Herculem*. In this latter book he compares Marx by turns to an ape and to a mouse (p. 68).
32 *Heilige Familie*, 36. By an odd slip he puts Say for Sièyes. The question, however, was not new; and the answer, "Property is Theft," had been given by Brissot "*La Propriété et le Vol*," 1780.

33 *Mis. de la Phil.*, pp. 20, 21, cf. 44.
34 *Ibid.*, pp. 25, 27.
35 *Ibid.*, p. 90.
36 *E.g. Mis. de la Phil.*, pp. 49, 50, he quotes Atkinson, Bray, Edmonds, *Hopkins*, Thompson. He meant *Hodgskin*. See Prof. Anton Menger, *Rechtauf den vollen Arbeitsertrag* (2nd ed. 1891), p. 52n.
37 *Mis. de la Phil.*, pp. 50–58. The book cited is, *Labour's Wrongs and Labour's Remedy, or the Age of Might and the Age of Right*, by J. F. Bray (Leeds), 1839.
38 *Mis. de la Phil.*, pp. 50, 67, 71; cf. Emerson's lines: "Things are in the saddle and ride mankind."
39 *Mis. de. la Phil.*, pp. 97, 98, 100 to 103, 104 to 106.
40 *Théorie de la Propriété* (1865), quoted by Diehl, *P. J. Proudhon* (1888), p. 91.
41 See above quoted Postscript to *Kapital*, I.
42 Pp. 113 *seq.*
43 Compare *Kapital*, I. 59 n.
44 *Misère de la Phil.*, p. 119.
45 It is as when we put articles on the scales, and, however different their qualities, judge purely their *weights*. I. 32.
46 *Das Kapital*, I. 72, cf. 48.
47 *Das Kapital*, I., chap. ii.
48 *Ib.*, p. 128, 129. In usury it is simply of money for money without the middle term. p. 138.
49 "Absolute" and "relative" are often used in this loose way by Marx. By the very definition this "absolute" is a relative.
50 *Kapital*, I. 312 (3rd ed., 303).
51 The Second was published posthumously in 1885.
52 Engels (*Ursprung der Familie*, 4th ed., p. 184) speaks of "laws" dwelling in apparent chance and asserting themselves with rigorous necessity.
53 Or, as Marx would have said, "of *facts*, whereof thoughts are simply the expression."
54 For further criticism see below (ch. ii.).
55 *Entwickelung des Socialismus*, p. 25,
56 Even this exception is now denied by Engels. See *Ursprung der Familie*.
57 *Entwick.*, p. 27.
58 *Ursprung der Familie*, etc. The book has been translated into several languages, of which English as yet is not one. The edition quoted here is the 4ᵗʰ (1892).
59 *Ursprung der Fam.*, p. 37.
60 *Urspr. d. Fam.*, pp. 177–8, cf. 181.
61 *Ibid.*, p. 186.
62 See Engel's Pref. to vol. ii. of *Kapital*.
63 Bray, Read, and especially William Thompson.
64 "A noted author has made property the foundation of all government, and most of our political writers seem inclined to follow him in that particular." Hume, *Essays*, 1741. (Of the first principles of Government.)
65 Leibnitz, the most individualistic of philosophers, had propounded a theory of which this was a feature. (*Nova Methodus Jurisprudentice, pars specialis*, § 20. See *Lassalle, Er. R.*, II. 501.)
66 Esp. in his *Bastiat-Schulze* (1864).
67 He had planned a treatise on *The Systematic Development of the Philosophy of Spirit. Erw. Rechte*, II. 486.

2   Epilogue

Relation of Economics to the Theory or Evolution

We have finally to consider whether the theory of Evolution, either in its philosophical or in its Darwinian form, is an argument for Socialism, and whether the positions of the Socialists, apart from the theory of evolution, have any measure of truth.

The discussion will seem to many economists to be outside the range of their subject, as the work of economics is mainly analytic and relates to "social statics." But a purely analytical and statical inquiry seems impossible. We can never find all the truth about the present condition of industry in the present itself; and, when we try to do so, we find ourselves altering the meaning of the word "present" at every step. We cannot understand the nature of Work for Wages, for example, without looking backwards to the formation of the capital that made its first payment possible and forwards to the profitable sale of the product which is the condition of its continued payment. The "present" comes to mean a day or a year, a generation or a century, as may suit the purpose of the particular analysis on hand. We may abstract from all causes except the economical; but, if our method led us to abstract from all economical sequences and look only at economical facts without any dynamical or causal connection, it could not lead us to any truth. Economical progress (or at least process) is the object of our inquiry even when we are trying to study what we call the facts of our own time. Whether such economical movement takes place according to the principles of Evolution is therefore not a question beyond the range of economics.

When "evolution" occurs in popular language and when it is said (for example) that all must take place by "the law of evolution," little more is usually meant than that changes must be continuous and there must be no sudden break; there is seldom, if ever, any idea of the priority of the whole to the parts, or any conception of development as a change in which the later outcome may be said to determine the earlier stages more truly than the latter the former. Yet, judging the theory of development by its best exponents, we find this deeper idea present.

The principle of evolution or development is perhaps best illustrated to the philosophical reader by a reference to Aristotle's distinction of power or possibility (δύναμις) from act or realization (ἐνέργεια). In the life of each ordinary human being manhood may be taken as the realization of what is present in childhood as a power or possibility. The steps from the latter to the former are stages in a development or evolution. In all life, human or not, this distinction is present. There is a germ which grows into the mature plant or the mature animal. There is first a promise or potency, and afterwards a fulfilment or realization. Development is not simply change. It implies that there is something gained, but gained in greater or less measure from within, not simply imposed from without on the subject of the development. The changes that have taken place leave the identity of the subject of the changes unimpaired. In becoming what he is, the man remains in a sense what he was as a child. If he were not the same, the case would not be one of growth and development, but simply of the addition of another unit to the total number of men or the substitution of a new unit for an old. But the past is preserved while the form is altered. In pronouncing a change to be a development we are mentally conjoining and comparing the past and the present, and pronouncing them conjoined in fact.

This notion of development is not abandoned when we speak of the growth of a nation. The identity of the human being remains though every part of his body has changed in the course of his growth from boy to manhood or else it is not *he* who has grown. The identity of a nation has been preserved through its changes, or else it is not *it* that has grown. On the other hand the growth of a nation does not depend on the continued existence of particular individuals composings the nation, but on the continuous preservation of a common consciousness in the members existing through successive times. The unity is that of the nation.

Such is development in general theory. The evolution of Humanity carries the analogy one step farther. The growth of the human race is indifferent to the fate of particular nations, but not to the common consciousness of men regarded as one great organic body developing together to maturity. The past is always thought as conjoined with the present; what is now actually present was in the past potentially so.

This at least is the philosophical notion of development as presented by Hegel.[1] There is therefore no justification for the view that Hegel's Method is merely negative and destructive or can be so regarded without the abandonment of Hegel's general position. When Engels tries to deduce from Hegel's own logic that the Hegelian Idealism must give place to Materialism, he is no doubt well aware of the retort which any tyro in Hegelianism could at once make that the *next* step in development would overthrow the said materialism and replace it by a truth that conciliated the two opposites, idealism and materialism, with one another. Whether the resulting Pantheism would be Hegel's own philosophy or not, we need not here discuss.

Darwinism is a particular form of the general theory that there is an evolution of life in the world. It differs from the Hegelian theory of development in its application to cases where preservation of identity is not possible, and where even the continuity of growth exists only *for us* and in retrospect.[2] Darwin[3] explains "the origin of species," both in the animal and the vegetable world, by supposing with Malthus in all living things a tendency to rapid multiplication, leading necessarily to a struggle for existence, and (second) by supposing that in each living thing produced by this power of propagation there is some slight difference from its fellows, such variations giving an advantage in the struggle to some over others, the result being a "natural selection," "a survival of the fittest."[4] Malthus had seen that there must be a struggle for room and food. Darwin showed that in all plants and animals, and in man in his early stage, the victory in the struggle must go to those to whom nature had given some slight peculiarity that proved a help to them and was wanting to their rivals.

The result in successive generations is so great an alteration of the living creature that it seems to belong to a new species. But what we call a new species is simply the old sifted and resifted by "natural selection." "Species have been modified during a long course of descent. This has been effected chiefly through the natural selection of numerous successive, slight, favourable variations, aided in an important manner by the inherited effects of the use and disuse of parts, and in an unimportant manner (that is, in relation to adaptive structures whether past or present) by the direct action of external conditions, and by variations, which seem to us in our ignorance to arise spontaneously."[5] "These elaborately constructed forms [the birds, plants, insects, worms of the 'tangled bank'] have all been produced by laws acting around us. These laws, taken in the largest sense, being Growth with Reproduction, Inheritance which is almost implied by reproduction, Variability from the indirect and direct action of the conditions of life, and from use and disuse, a Ratio of Increase so high as to lead to a Struggle for Life, and as a consequence to Natural Selection, entailing Divergence of Character and the Extinction of less improved forms. Thus, from the war of nature, from famine and death, the most exalted object which we are capable of conceiving, namely the production of the higher animals, directly follows" (*Origin of Sp.*, chap. xv., pop. ed. 1885, p. 429).

Darwin may have conceded too much or too little to other causes than natural selection. *Adhuc sub judice lis est.* About the importance of natural selection itself as a main cause of the origin of species there seems to be a general agreement amongst those best qualified to judge. It is confessed on the other hand that the tendency to vary is assumed, like the tendency to multiply, simply as a given fact.[6] "Selection" implies choice of what is there, but not origination of the matter of choice. We may add that selection gives us only difference, and not development as above defined. What survives at least in the lower forms of the struggle is not the same as what went before it; there is no identity or consciousness of such. There is no pretence made by Darwinians that survival means fitness in any moral sense; the morally worse men may only be the more fit to survive in the sense that they are best able to suck advantage from their surroundings; and that is all that is claimed by the theorists.[7] It is no more than the fitness which enables the holders of the worse coins to get advantage over the holders of the finer under "Gresham's law" of the currency. The worse coinage survived because it was the fitter; it was the fitter because, being the worse and yet accepted, it was the more economical. It is not fair to describe the saying, "The fittest survive" as an analytical judgment (containing nothing in its predicate that was not contained in its subject), for "fittest" must be understood in the sense intended by the introducers of the phrase, "those having the most favourable variations," with the further conception that they are few who survive. There is a huge squandering of individuals in order that a favoured few may maintain their lives and propagate their race.

It might seem that Darwinism, instead of favouring equality and Communism, is essentially bound up with a hypothesis of difference; without spontaneous *variations* there is no scope for natural selection. But natural selection must not be judged by its harshest form, the form which it takes in the lowest circles of life, any more than the law of population. It is often the case that a generalization broadly true is stated by its first exponents as universally true. As Malthus qualified his first account of the principle of population, Darwin modified his first statements of the principle of natural selection (cautious as they were) by bringing in the agency of sexual selection; and his followers have introduced further modifications, when applying the theory to human institutions. The adaptation of population to food takes place by very different checks among savages and among civilized men. In Tierra del Fuego as in England there is an equilibrium between population and food; but there is an important difference between the ways in which the equilibrium is produced in the two cases. So natural selection (they say) works by very different means in the lower and in the higher circles of life. Moreover, if the struggle for existence is transferred from individuals to solid *groups* of men,[8] the individuals within the groups are lifted out of the struggle in the sense in which the parts of an organic body are dispensed from struggling with each other, though not from aiding or hindering the whole body in its struggle with other bodies.[9] In the same way inheritance in the groups or transmission through successive periods of time in them means more than in the individuals. It is doubted by most biologists if acquired as distinguished from spontaneous variations can be transmitted by inheritance from individual to individual; but ideas at least, existing as they do in the social environment and common consciousness, whether in clear consciousness or as habits, may be preserved from age to age. The spiritual environment is preserved by the individuals as a group, and it outlasts the individuals. In the "natural selection" of moral ideals there is not within the group any necessity that the vanquished in the struggle be slain or let die, but simply that they be converted.[10]

When Darwinism is thus stated, it becomes a theory of development very closely akin to the philosophical, for it really involves the conservation of the past and instead of the preservation of mere life the object of the struggle is the attainment, deliberately conceived, of a better life. By adopting this view, however, we are not brought directly nearer to the adoption of any Socialistic ideal. The most direct analogy of which socialists could avail themselves would be the experimental or tentative character of any development taking place on purely "Darwinian" principles, that is (we are to understand) on the principles of Darwinism as exhibited in the lower forms of life. It might be argued that socialistic government ought to be tried like any other, and if it proves the stronger its victory will be enough for its justification,—and further, that on Darwinian principles, whether we wish it or not, this is precisely what must happen: the experiment must be tried, and the fitness of that form of government will appear in Its survival. But the theoretical *arguments* for socialism would then rest on general grounds; and indeed it seems clear from the want of unanimity among Darwinians in matters of Sociology and Politics that the principles of the Master are perfectly neutral on such questions.[11] This is precisely what we should expect. Natural selection explains how but not why certain occurrences have taken place. It leaves the subject-matter of all our problems unaffected. If we take up the three leading classes of economical questions in the order we have previously chosen—as relating (1) to the notion of Wealth, (2) to Production and Distribution, and (3) to Society and the State, we shall perhaps find further reasons for this conclusion.

(1) The notion of wealth, comfort, and standard of living must include all the various elements of man's nature, physical and spiritual. This necessity is now recognised largely by means of the recorded expansion or development of human wants in the past. It could hardly have become a generally accepted axiom if history had not shown an approximate realization of it in times past among the "favoured races." In Plato it is a novelty rather than an axiom, and even to him it was a postulate for a few men, not for all. Without the notion of an expansion of wants, modern political economy would lose much of its motive power. Economy in supply of one want is practised for the sake of the supply of another; and the constancy in the volume of human desires has, as above noticed, been with more or less accuracy set down as an element of economical reckoning. But so far as it goes this feature of humanity tells most in the latest stages where the struggle for bare life becomes the endeavour after well-being in a larger sense. There is development but not necessarily Darwinism.

(2) In production and distribution, development takes the Darwinian form far more conspicuously. Almost the first form of economy in a human society, however small, is division of labour leading to separation of employments. There is an analogy here, which has been most fully worked out by Mr. Herbert Spencer, with the formation of separate organs in the living body.[12] Differentiation of function leads to differentiation of structure, and the unity of the body instead of being impaired is made stronger. It would seem no doubt that what in animals leads to a natural selection at the expense of the unfit leads in men rather to a distribution of tasks in which variations prove severally of co-ordinate advantage. But it is the society that adopts

this division of labour, which is the unit to be considered; and natural selection may quite well be the agency that gives this type of society the victory over a simpler type, where the unity more resembles what Hegel called "a unity identical with itself," than an integration of differences. This may be regarded as Darwinism in its higher form, where absolute extinction of the unfit is not a necessary consequence of natural selection, and where variations, whether spontaneous or artificial, may be transmitted from one generation to another. What has been frequently called in these pages "*sponte acta*" can from the nature of the case be never purely spontaneous. As the education of a child is never left to itself even when its guardians (on the principles of Rousseau's *Emile*) desire so to leave it, in the same way the utmost spontaneity of the individual cannot imply his total detachment from the influences of society. The thoughts and actions of every individual within the social group are never those of the single individual unit as if he were a new creation, but are those of a member inheriting the ideas and feelings of the group. What Locke says of generation[13] may be taken of industrial production with an equally profound significance. To produce is not to create, but simply to occasion. The tentative character of industrial improvement brings it under the Darwinian formula; and it is a character attested by all experience. Whether an invention be a happy accident or deliberately planned and endowed with every presumption of usefulness, we still count it wise to say no more of it than "it must have a fair trial"; and we wait to see whether it works well or ill, and whether it displaces rivals. It may lie unused for reasons either economically sound or the reverse. As a rule such a "variation" as an invention, if it adds economical strength, will enjoy economical survival. But the dependence of some nations more than others on the immediate present will cause that to be to them economically unfit which to another with larger resources and powers of waiting would be true economy. The growth and distribution of wealth and capital are thus an element in the question; and, so far as these are affected by laws and institutions, it might be argued that economical fitness depends partly on political causes.

Whatever be the causes that help or hinder success, the success itself is worked out in the minds and habits of the members of a society by a tentative sifting analogous to "natural selection." This was the gradual improvement of complicated tools and machines, which Marx had in mind, when he desired to "Darwinize" industrial history.[14] After saying (*Kap.*, I. 352) that "the Manufacturing period simplifies, improves, and multiplies the working tools by adapting them to the exclusive special functions of sub-divided work," he quotes in a note what Darwin says of the natural organs of plants and animals: "As long as the same part has to perform diversified work, we can perhaps see why it should remain variable, that is, why natural selection should not have preserved or rejected each little deviation of form so carefully as when the part has to serve for some one special purpose; in the same way that a knife which has to cut all sorts of things may be of almost any shape, whilst a tool for some particular purpose must be of some particular shape" (*Origin of Species*, chap. v. pp. 118, 119, pop. ed.). In a later note (*Kap.*, I. 385) Marx goes on to say: "Darwin has awakened interest in the history of natural technology, *i.e.* the growth of the organs of plants and animals as instruments of production for the life of plants and animals. Does not the history of the growth of the productive organs of men in society, *i.e.* the material basis of every separate social organization, not deserve the same attention? And would this not be more easily furnished since, as Vico says, human history is distinguished from natural history by *our* having made the one, and not having made the other? Technology displays the active relations of man to nature, the direct movement of production that goes on in his life, and therewith the movement that goes on in the social relations of his life and in the ideas derived from them. Even the history of religion when it abstracts from this material basis is uncritical. It is in fact much easier to find by analysis the earthly kernel of the religious nebulosities than conversely to develope the sublimated forms out of the corresponding conditions of actual life. But the latter is the only materialistic and therefore the only scientific method. The weak points of the materialism of abstract physical science when it excludes the historical movement may be seen in the abstract and ideological conceptions of its spokesmen, whenever they venture beyond their special study." Without adopting this materialistic view of history, we may recognize that industrial development on its mechanical side has been largely Darwinian. The question whether invention is more often due to the actual workers or to onlookers is still debated. But, whether inventions are accidental or contrived variations, occurring casually to the workmen or excogitated by an "inventor," they are submitted to the ordeal of selection by practice; and it is through the results of this selection that progress is made. But industrial development implies inheritance of ideas by successive generations in the social group concerned; and this inheritance may at once preserve an invention and hinder its further improvement. A plough and a ship may differ little now from their Homeric counterparts, for the sound technical reason that the conditions do not admit wide variation. In regard to most implements the success of a variation is hindered by mere custom, if there be no struggle, even of commercial competition, or none sufficiently keen to turn every little advantage into a great one. In the case of one tool, money, the tool of exchange, the greatest part of the efficiency of the tool depends on custom itself; and the variation whether from religious, æsthetic, or political causes must never be so great as to break the continuity of custom, which determines the power of coins to pass current among all classes of the people. It has been shown[15] that no descendants so demonstrably resemble their remote ancestors and have so slowly adopted their actual variations from these, as is the case with coins.

It may be allowed then that in Production Darwinism has an indisputable place. There is on the whole continuous change by means of the selection (through competition) of variations, however much this process may be arrested or delayed by special causes in special cases. The same may be said of Distribution.

In regard to the third (Society and State) the question is less easily answered. The early development of societies before the existence of the State, in the sense of a central administrative government, was in all probability Darwinian; and after the formation of States the struggle of States against States was (and to some extent still is) Darwinian. But it is open to any philosopher to attempt to go below the fact of variation to a supposed "inner logic" which would explain the variation itself.[16]

The question too still remains—is all favourable variation (that gives one State victory over another) economical variation, and is all history a record of the effects of economical causes? If it were so, then, as the tendency of industrial development seems to be towards centralization, the aim of political reformers would seem naturally to be to give conscious political expression to that industrial tendency, and (more than that) to make the whole work of the State economical. The latter is actually the claim of some socialists, and it seems to be logically implied in the proposition that the only potent cause of historical charge is the economical—in other words, all causes but this are superficial.

The position has some resemblance to that of Buckle in regard to morals. All progress, he said, was intellectual; there were no discoveries in ethics. Among the intellectual discoveries Buckle ranked those of certain economists as of high importance. Material progress and the intellectual aids to it seemed to him to be civilization itself—all else being superficial. But some socialists speak as if the intellectual elements were created by the economical, going thus a step beyond Buckle. The very Reformation is ascribed to an economical cause; Peter's pence proved too oppressive.[17] The Thirty Years' War owed its length to the existence of a country proletariate in Germany which supplied troops without limit.[18] The Crusades were largely due to the "land hunger" of the barons.[19] The Jesuits formed a great commercial company, and their State in Paraguay was simply an organization of the non-producing classes.[20] Marx himself connects the Animal Psychology of Descartes with the growth of the Manufacturing system; "animals are machines" could not have occurred to a mediaeval writer.[21] Engels by the aid of Lewis Morgan's *Ancient Society* proves to his own satisfaction that the growth of the family both in prehistoric and historic times is essentially due to economic causes (*Urspr. der Fam.*, etc., 4th ed. 1892).

It would be very nearly as easy to prove that every historical event (whatever else on the surface) was essentially due to religious and moral causes; this was, roughly speaking, the view of Carlyle. Historical economists in Germany and in England, instead of saying that all history is economical, maintain that all economics is in essence historical, relative, and subordinate. In point of fact, historians have shown the presence, in all events, of economical, religious, artistic, and political elements. The question which of them all is at any given time the most potent efficient cause cannot be settled *a priori* by any dogma, laying down absolutely that one is always or invariably the most potent cause. The historians try to tell us how the various causes act on each other and with each other. In prehistoric or very early historic times and among savages the economical cause will usually be dominant; the struggle for bare subsistence will be in full force. At some epochs (as in the Crusades or the spread of Mohammedanism) religious enthusiasm and military strength seem paramount; though they had economical effects, they were not due to economical causes. In recent centuries economical causes seem to become more powerful in relation to the rest. Yet the political ideas of the French Revolutionary writers were more powerful both in America and in Europe than any economical causes of which France at least could in that time show the results. The intellectual and generally speaking the spiritual elements of well-being have come to bulk far more largely in the public mind than ever before. A greater extension of physical comfort is desired for the avowed reason that it gives leisure and opportunities for the acquisition of spiritual good. This is the contention too (to their credit be it spoken) of many of the very socialists who would persuade us that the materialistic view of history is the only true one.

The materialistic view seems to be a reaction against a view of history which saw in it if not a record of battles a record of political events, occurring through the agency of sovereigns and statesmen. In the last hundred years it has been becoming more and more impossible to overlook the influence of the people and their industrial condition; and the distribution of property has become a more burning question than the assertion of political rights. Whether the economical element in national life has been always and alone the ruling element or not, it is an element of the first importance now even in the view of politicians. Apart from the peculiar and ultra-Ricardian view of Value with which Marx and Engels have identified their form of socialism, the socialistic statement of the position and claims of the working class, and more particularly the proletariate, are worthy of careful attention.

The strength of the employer is that he has property, and the weakness of the isolated workman is that he has none. It is urged that in order to prevent the existence of a dependent class of working people we should make the State the proprietor, if not of all goods, at least of the means and materials of production.

Now it is fair to recognise that this act of centralization is conceivable without the destruction of all and every kind of private property. The notion of Hegel that without property personality does not become real has had its influence on the followers of the Young Hegelians. Their desire seems to be that, in order that as many as possible may acquire property, a *particular kind* of property should be taken from private hands and acquired by the State. Absolute communism is probably not a view held by any of the leaders of the school of socialists now under consideration. From the nature of the material world, possession must be exclusive. Value itself involves individual possession, whether it be value in exchange or value in use. Value involves limitation and the limitation of possession; and property is simply the legal extension of this possession, *inter alia* beyond present to future goods, and beyond goods made to the sources and materials and instruments of their making. The revolt is against the degree and extent of the limitation not against the limitation itself. There is no form of society that could realize the entire absence of appropriation, for what one man uses another cannot use at the same time and in the same respect.

On the other hand, it might be argued that all so-called property, owing to human mortality, is simply at the most possession for a life-time. The rights of bequest and inheritance might be conceivably altered without any attempt to abolish private property. Lassalle's criticisms of Hegel, that he represented transitory historical phases of the law of property as flowing from the philosophical notion of property itself, seem to be justified. What alterations in laws of bequest and inheritance would tend to produce greater equality in wealth and opportunities among the citizens of a State, cannot be decided without regard to the time, place, and people concerned. The same must be said of the centralization of the means of production. If history is to be our only court of appeal, we might appeal to it for record of the fact that human nature has made its most solid progress slowly and tentatively. The only deadly sin would be to rest content with things as they are. Socialists have done good service by drawing attention to the frequent absence of real liberty, and the presence of very great inequality.

The proletariate have not much more liberty in the choice of their work than the poor suitor in the days when Lord Eldon said "The law is open to all," and was answered (by Horne Tooke) "So is the Freemasons' Tavern." On the other hand, because unskilled labourers are now at the bottom of the scale, it does not seem necessary for the better ordering of the commonwealth that they should be raised to the top. English economists of past generations have no doubt unfairly favoured the predominance of the Middle Classes in the conduct of the affairs of the nation. But we need not pass from one extreme to another. Men who work with their hands for wages are of the same flesh and blood as any other members of society, and are no more free from weak and evil passions than any others. The wiser socialists speak rather of a removal of classes, which would mean of the social distinction of classes, the econonomic distinction of classes being probably irremoveable because being, so far as can be seen, indispensable to efficient work. Under the most extensively centralized government of industry it is hard to believe that in the hands of human beings, as they are now known to us (and to speak of them otherwise is Utopian), industry could create an adequate quantity of products without the old aids of divided labour and separate employments, leading necessarily to different mental and bodily habits, as well as flowing naturally from different capacities of mind and body. The utilising of such "variations" seems essential to economical progress, and indeed to progress of any kind in an age when extreme specialisation is demanded for excellence in any branch of science as well as of industry.

A change in the method of distribution is not so difficult to conceive. The abolition of production for sale and a return to production for use have seemed an attractive prospect even to men who have no keen sympathy with the philanthropic side of socialism. The attraction of the "Social Revolution" for such men as Richard Wagner the composer, has lain largely in this feature of it. Wagner thinks that money-making has been the curse of music as of other arts in these latter days; the social revolution would rejuvenate music by making it to be studied for its own sake; there would be hope then for the Music of the Future; and it would take the form of the musical drama, the highest form of art, because conjoining all the arts in one, but the latest product of time, because never perfectly to be realized without the enthusiasm of a united free and enlightened democracy. But at present the poets or poetasters are paid to write words for music already composed, and composed for hire, whereas the theme should beget its own music in the mind of one poet-musician, or in the mind of poets and musicians who are of one heart and soul, and feel one common inspiration.[22]

There is certainly nothing so prosaic as money-making; but to abolish our usual standard of value and means of exchange we need something more than descriptions of the artistic and even of the political and social defects of things as they are. As was before said, economic progress has been in time past largely if not wholly due to "natural selection"; and, if we would change our system of industrial rewards and punishments, we should need to proceed tentatively. If it be answered that socialism as such cannot be realized piecemeal or experimentally, but must be all together or not at all, then it is difficult to believe that socialism in the hands of its scientific expounders has ceased after all to be a Utopia; it is the prophecy of a change in human nature to be effected suddenly by a change of the laws of the land. But this doctrine of "all or nothing" is not essential to socialism; and tentative efforts to carry out the idea of collective property and collective manufacture, whether in parishes, cities, or counties, will, by their success or failure, throw light on the possibilities of the future, and need rouse no fiery passions.

A revolution so gradually prepared may be truly described as the aim of the majority of socialists in this country now. It was not the aim of Marx and Engels, still less of the majority of their followers. A sudden cataclysm was on their lips if not in their thoughts. Evil conditions would wax worse and worse, till they reached a point beyond all endurance; then the suffering people would rise and overthrow the "capitalistic system." The Hegelian method, it may be admitted, was consistent with sudden revolution; but, as must also be admitted, it would carry us to a point beyond the cataclysm. Hegelian development never takes us back to an original simplicity of relations, but includes the conflicting elements while reconciling them. It would lead us not to the conclusion that "capitalistic" production will "pass away with a great noise," but that the old opposition between employer and labourer will give place to a system in which the labourer will be his own employer. Yet (to proceed in the spirit of Hegel) this does not mean a return to independent individual labour or domestic industry. It might mean the formation of social groups, in which the capitalists are the members, and the work is undertaken by and for the groups, the place of the employer being taken by a hired manager of the group, while the workmen are at once hired and hirers. Lassalle had this in view; but he thought capital was inaccessible to the workmen without the aid of the State. If this aid were given, the result would be to unite employer and employed, but still to leave the capitalist outside.

There seems to be nothing in the theory of Development to point us clearly to any centralization of all industrial organization in the State. It has yet to be shown in practice that beyond a certain limit centralization would not be fatal to the spontaneous organization which has as yet been the main source of all industrial progress. Co-operative industry could be carried on by such a closely federated union, that practically it would be as centralized as the Land League or the Roman Catholic Church, as an *imperium in imperio*. But it could also be, like Protestantism, a multiplication of separate societies, with no closer external bond than that of separate trades societies that have their common interests and also their points of divergence. No philosophical theory can show which of these two forms will be taken eventually by co-operative industry. There is nothing in the theory of development to show whether the future hides in it socialism established and maintained by the State or Anarchism such as Fichte conceived it, lying beyond socialism when the latter had had its perfect work. But if history, as Hegel conceived, is a record of the development of freedom, we might expect that the future form of government will at least leave room for individual liberty, "variation," and even caprice. We may be at ease on this head; men will never sell their liberty to purchase a compulsory equality and fraternity; and, if socialism became a tyranny, it would have a short life.

The analogy of the education of the individual may perhaps apply to the education of a nation. There was a dispute[23] (not yet obsolete) between those who viewed the former as properly a discipline, or subjugation of the passions, those who viewed it as instruction or the acquisition of knowledge, and a third group of theorists who, like the Greeks, regarded it as properly the development or awaking of the faculties. In a complete education all three have their place, discipline, knowledge, and development of powers. In a nation too there must be order and law; there must be science; and there must be freedom to show special powers. If it be said that the distinction of nations is arbitrary, yet humanity as a whole has learned these lessons when it was so divided; and the lessons must be remembered, if civilization is not to vanish away with the outward forms in which it has grown up.

Notes

1 *Passim, e.g., Philos, of Hist.* (Engl, tr.), pp. 57, 58, (German) pp. 67–69.
2 Continuity is implied in the sense above stated, that there be no *saltus*. See Darwin, *Origin of Species*, chap. vi. p. 156 (pop. ed. 1885): "Why should Nature not take a leap from structure to structure? On the theory of natural selection we can clearly understand why she should not," etc., cf. 234.

3 Darwin, *Origin of Species, passim, e.g., Introd.*, p. 5, and pp. 50, 413, 429 (pop. ed.). See above (*Malthus*), Book III., ch. i.
4 This statement is taken in substance from Mr. A. R. Wallace's *Darwinism*, pp. 10, *seq.*
5 *Origin of Species*, conclus., p. 421, pop. ed. The 1st ed. was published 1859. Mr. A. R. Wallace had published the same view at the same time and in complete independence of Darwin.
6 Metaphysically Leibnitz might have deduced the former from the "identity of indiscernibles"; but that principle is itself in need of proof. It might also be considered that a simple difference in time and in place would be itself a difference in environment.
7 Even this fitness is always *relative* to the powers of the other competitors. See *Origin of Species*, chap. vi. p. 163 (pop. ed.).
8 For the formation of the groups, see Bagehot, *Physics and Politics*.
9 But see a curious passage in Roux quoted by Wallace in *Darwinism*, p. 416 note. Roux thinks that a "struggle of the parts *in* the organism" may sometimes account for the disappearance of organs.
10 Mr. S. Alexander has brought out this point very fully. *Moral Order and Progress*, p. 354 *seq.* The drift of Prof. Pulszky's *Theory of Law and Civil Society*, 1889, seems to be similar, pp. 58 *seq.* (in relation to the conflict of what he calls "societies" within the State). Compare also Mr. J. H. Muirhead, *Elements of Ethics* (1892), pp. 226 *seq.*
11 To realize the extent of these divergencies, see Prof. O. Schmidt, "*Darwinismus und Socialdemokratie*" (*Deutsche Rundschau*, v. 2), and Mr. D. G. Ritchie, *Darwinism and Politics*, pp. 1–11. Cf. papers in *Neue Zeit* (1890).
12 See Sociology, ch, xiv. P. 335.
13 "Can any man say he formed the parts that are necessary to the life of his child? Or can he suppose himself to give the life, and yet not know what subject is fit to receive it nor what actions or organs are necessary for its reception or preservation?" ... "If any one thinks himself an artist in this, let him number up the parts of his child's body which he hath made, tell me their uses and operations, and when the living and rational soul began to inhabit this curious structure." ... "Those who desire and design children are but the occasions of their being," etc. *Civil Govt.*, §§ 52–54. Compare above, page 249.
14 It is to be observed that Marx accepts Darwin while he rejects Malthus on whom Darwin has built.
15 By Mr. C. F. Keary, "Morphology of Coins," in *Numismatic Chronicle*, V. (3rd series) 165–198, VI. 41–95.
16 Such an "inner logic" was attempted by Hegel; development in his sense would explain not only the selection but the variation.
17 Kautsky, *More und seine Utoftie* (1888), p. 41 *seq.*, 66, etc., cf. 76.
18 *Ibid.*, p. 32 note.
19 *Ibid.*, 56.
20 *Ibid.*, p. 91 note.
21 *Das Kapital*, I. p. 406. For remarks on this passage and generally on the view now discussed, see *Dr.* Paul Barth, *Geschichts-philosophie Hegel's*, etc. (1890).
22 Wagner, *Oper und Drama* (1851). *Die Kunst und die Revolution* (1849). *Kunstwerk der Zukunft* (1850). *The Music of the Future* (1860), translated by Dannreuther, 1873.
23 See F. D. Maurice, *Lectures on National Education* (1839). The various elements of a modern state are comprehensively treated by Mr. J. S. Mackenzie, *Introduction to Social Philosophy* (1890).

3   Summary

The results of the foregoing inquiry may now be briefly reviewed. The treatment of economic ideas in Ancient and a great part of Modern Philosophy is affected by the fact that economics did not until modern times exist as a separate study. Accordingly the philosophers of the earlier periods devoted more space in their philosophical books to economic discussions than the philosophers of the later, who were free to hand over all such discussion to the economists. Plato's treatment of economical subjects is for this reason much more ample than Hegel's.

But, if direct economic discussion tends rather to assume a less than a greater place in philosophical works, the consideration of the philosophical roots of ideas which economists take for granted, tends to take a greater place. This appears not only in regard to the theory of the foundation of property, family, society, and State,[1] but in regard to the psychology of the feelings, desires, and volitions connected with the pursuit of subsistence and wealth. The time when political economy became a distinct study in the hands of the Physiocrats and the Scottish philosophers was also the time when the motives of an ordinary human life were investigated with the greatest curiosity.

Recurring to Ancient Philosophy, we find that Plato conceives wealth sometimes as the necessaries of life, sometimes as life's superfluities. He would prefer that men should content themselves with the former, to be interpreted ascetically, as the simplest style of living that is consistent with living and working at all. But he practically admits that neither this simple living nor the correspondingly simple society and State will be adopted by men as they are. Aristotle for his part would not insist on ascetic living, but assumes that for human beings who are not only to live, but to live well, and develop all their powers, a comfortable life and fair opportunities are necessary. The impossibility of making certain of such favourable outward conditions, especially for political activity, helped to lead the Stoics and Epicureans to fall back on the notion of individual independence, by which was meant an independence of outward comfort as well as of political circumstances. This was also the ideal of Christianity, although detachment from the world, once the world had become generally Christian, became a duty of which laymen were allowed to relieve themselves. The theory of Christianity, even more than that of

Stoicism, was inconsistent with Slavery, and prepared the way for the claim of all human beings to the outward opportunities claimed by Aristotle for the Greeks.

In regard to the production and distribution of wealth, the work of Ancient Philosophy, so far as it went, was accepted with fewer modifications. The Platonic principle of division of labour was applied by its author to trade and industry, as well as to the relations of the powers of the human spirit and the departments of the State to each other; and he observes (though he is not always consistent) that industrial division of labour seems spontaneously to create a society, anterior to any State, while, after a certain point, it leads to the establishment of a State. The economical principle of division of labour was by Plato once for all founded on its philosophical basis.

Yet he attaches more importance to its artistic than to its economic effects; the analogy of the fine arts is applied by him not only to moral action but to industrial; he thinks more of the increased power of the producer to turn out a result good in itself than to turn out larger supplies of useful articles. He would like to keep money-making out of the business altogether, and has not Aristotle's clear notion of money, while he thinks that artisans' labour at the best is unfit for a Greek citizen, as marring both body and mind. Aristotle, on the other hand, pointed out some obvious differences between art and morality, and between art and industry. Morality relates to action in the sense of conduct, the fine arts to a production where the product is an end in Itself, industry to production where the product is only a means to an end. In describing tools and means of production Aristotle comes near to the notion of Capital, and he recognises the function of Money. But Interest to him seems contrary to "nature," and money-making, though apparently inevitable, is in a great measure unnatural also. Trade as distinguished from industry is a form of cheating; the gain of one man is the loss of another. Money-making, except as subsidiary to the support of the household, is pronounced inconsistent with the rational nature of man; wealth should always be treated as a means and not an end. As against Plato he refuses to simplify society artificially. Man is by nature a social and political being, and the intercourse of man with man in trade, as in all his other proceedings within the State, is a relation to which differences are as essential as a common basis of union. Aristotle gives us the first analysis of an actual political society as distinguished from an ideal one. He does not, however, clearly distinguish Society from State, and does not clearly recognize some of the most important elements in human nature (appearing in industry and trade perhaps more remarkably than elsewhere) which tend to organize society as it were from below, and apart from the action of a governing body. Yet both in Plato (especially in the *Laws*) and in Aristotle there is clear recognition that every practicable government must rest on the traditional morality and customs of the people governed. In both philosophers there is a tendency to ratify, as permanently valid, institutions (like Slavery) which were only transitional. Plato rose above this prejudice in the case of women, but not in the case of artisans.

Finally, in regard to the possibility either of socialism or of communism, Aristotle has no doubt given the weightiest criticisms ever arrayed by a philosopher against these doctrines; but they are felt to be inconclusive inasmuch as the industrial element in society played a humbler part then than it does now, and even that humble part received scanty attention. Aristotle has given us a classical politics but not a classical economics, even for the days before individualism.

For individualism, the philosophical basis was laid by the Lesser Socratics, Stoics, and Epicureans. It takes at first the false form of independence through restriction of wants. Even the State (in the idea of most of these philosophers) is unnecessary to me if my wants are few and small enough. This is the *reductio ad absurdum* of asceticism. In Stoicism the independence has a more positive meaning; the individual is strong enough by himself because he is a member of a body much larger and more sublime and potent than any earthly State. In Christianity, too, as his citizenship is in heaven, the individual is not dependent on terrestrial governments, and he sees their terrestrial limitations; they put barriers between man and man where God has made all of one blood. The notion of a common humanity, leading, as it did eventually, to a claim of equal rights for all, was thus spread in civilized Europe.

The notion of Natural Law (which led later to the claim of natural rights) as revived and new-defined by Stoicism exerted great influence on Roman Law under the Empire, but lost its power with the decline and fall of the latter. Political philosophy, when it went back at the Renaissance (as in Machiavelli) to ancient models, did not at first move strongly in the old direction of natural law, while it remained in the narrow sense political.

In More's *Utopia* we have the revival of the Platonic Republic with additions that make the scheme entirely modern. Improvement of the outward conditions, not only of the few but of all, is declared to be essential to a good State; and the economical element in the social body receives for the first time its proper rank as of the highest moment for public welfare. Even Bodin, who deals more with practical politics, has learned this lesson, and lays stress at least on the importance of the middle class and the industrial and commercial members of the community. The aggrandisement of particular States, under the rule of an Absolute Monarch, was the aim of most writers immediately after him, when they wrote on political economy. Montchrétien's book, the first to bear the title *Economie politique* (1615) is of this nature. The "Mercantile System" was tainted with this narrowness, whatever allowance we may make for misrepresentation.

It was the apparently abstract theories of Grotius and his successors that were to set in motion the current of ideas leading to the foundation and upbuilding of a separate study of general Economics. Grotius substituted for the decisions of the Popes and the rules of the Church, the law of Nature, as yielding both a morality and an international arbiter. The morality is not due to deliberate will, but the law of nations in a sense is so. Particular institutions and proceedings are deliberately instituted; but our conduct towards them, once they are there, is determined for us by natural laws. So, if nations go to war, they are bound by natural laws to treat each other in a particular way. If private property is instituted, it must be respected in virtue of natural laws. The State is founded by a contract, which gives effect to the laws of Nature in a particular way, and no longer leaves men the absolute licence of the *primævus naturæ status*, the state of nature. Without troubling himself like Aristotle and the Stoics about the metaphysics of the subject, and "Nature" in the larger sense, Grotius deduced the political contract founding the State, and with it all contracts within the State, from human nature and its laws.

Hobbes brings out the notion of a political contract more fully. It implies (he says) that the original state of men is a state of isolation; they are separate atoms; and their union in the view of Hobbes is not a natural but a purely artificial one. In the state of nature every man's hand is against every man, and every man's hand against him. Men are equal in their boundless desires and unlimited claims, and equal also in their helplessness. Their weakness drives them into an agreement to give up their liberty for the sake of life and peace. Thus are nations made; and (whatever Grotius may say) towards each other these nations themselves are in a state of unqualified hostility. Selfishness rules between nations as it once ruled between individuals till their weakness tempered it with wisdom.

Such a theory, which was in later times to be held true of matters economical, is applied by Hobbes to economical matters only by way of corollary. He gives nearly a complete economics, embedded in his political philosophy, and (if we may say so) feeling quite at home there, for what branch of activity should be "concluded all under" selfishness if not the world of business?

Of the opponents of Hobbes, Harrington at least is well aware of the importance of the economical element in the body politic. His *Commonwealth of Oceana* is based on an Agrarian law. Political power (says Harrington) depends on possession of land, and the amount of land to be owned by one individual must be limited by law.

Though more practicable than More's *Utopia*, the republic *Oceana* was still not at that time within the range of practical politics. Utopias had less influence than an apparently more abstract political philosophy, with a directly practicable concrete application. In reply to writers, who attributed to Adam and King James a divine patriarchal right to rule over a subject people, Locke maintains that "by nature" all men are free and equal, not in Hobbes' illusory sense, but both before and after the foundation of the State. So far from being necessarily at enmity with each other, they may form a civil society even before the existence of the State, and in that civil society make their natural rights more secure than before by agreeing to respect each other's property, which means each other's labour. Within civil society, too, economic institutions, including the use of money, may grow up by mutual consent of men without any political contract. Even after the State is founded, economical phenomena are regulated by principles of their own.

We have thus three important features in Locke's political philosophy, (1) the claim of "natural rights" of liberty and equality, (2) the clear distinction of Society from State with the inclusion of economical phenomena in the former, and (3) the foundation of property on labour. Locke has here presented three aspects of the subject which were to be fully treated by later writers through the next two centuries. They had never been so adequately treated before him, inadequate as his own discussion certainly is. Hume, while accepting the distinction of Society and State, with his keen criticism brought out the difficulties in the way of theories that appeal to "nature" and a social contract, as well as the objections to labour as a title to property. Hume's own works bear witness to the growing interest in the psychology of these questions. The writings of Shaftesbury, Mandeville, and especially Hutcheson, had made searching investigation into the motives of action, the possibility of disinterestedness, the relation of morality and selfishness. Mandeville in particular, when professing to contend that private vices are public benefits, had taken economical facts for his chief illustrations;—each man consulted his own pleasure and interest, but the result of the separate selfish actions of individuals was the maintenance of a social machinery which was of greater collective benefit than if it had been deliberately framed for unselfish ends. Hume meets Mandeville's paradox by arguing, as a Utilitarian, that an action is virtuous not vicious if its consequence is public benefit. The "passions" as such are not evil, for reason cannot lead to action without them. Avarice and luxury are necessary and desirable for national progress; human wants are constantly multiplying. No doubt (he adds), while objectively moral action is what tends to public advantage, subjectively it springs from the reflected pleasure called sympathy; what would give me pleasure, if I saw another do it, is an action which it is morally right for me to do.

There are here two difficulties. The first is to establish on Hume's principles any objective end of action at all. Neither the public advantage nor even the general interest of the individual himself can easily if at all be resolved into pleasure or built up out of it. Yet for Economics, the idea of wealth, a collection of the means of possible satisfaction, and not simply the feeling of an isolated actual satisfaction, is indispensable. Hume indeed distinguishes happiness from wealth if not from pleasure, and thinks (like Hutcheson and Adam Smith) that the first is much more equally distributed on the earth than the second. But happiness too is relatively permanent and objective. If it is a "sum," its relation to its units must be determined. Hume does not determine it, though he sees *inter alia* how in the estimates of advantage or interest the element of time figures very differently for a State and for an individual;—he takes his fixed points for granted without deciding how they are fixed.

The second difficulty is for a writer who has rejected the ordinary view of causality to get a foundation for a science of human nature, including a political philosophy. But Hume passes over this difficulty, and lays great stress on the need for scientific treatment of these subjects. "It is the chief business of philosophers to regard the general course of things," and in regard to matters of trade and commerce, amongst others, the actions of large numbers can be reduced to "general principles," while the actions of a few individuals cannot be explained scientifically. Hume has thus prepared the way for a systematic study of general economic principles such as is found in the French Economists and in Adam Smith; and Hume has also drawn the distinction between principles that are permanently true of all societies, and principles that are true only in particular societies and times.

His philosophy in fact has two voices. In his analysis of causation we hear the voice of the sceptic; in his pleadings for permanently true general principles we hear the voice of the scientific investigator, who cannot avoid assuming that there is a permanent truth discoverable. In ethical and economical reasoning he is the scientific investigator. The permanent principles of the virtues both moral and intellectual are sympathy and utility, the former being a disguised form of the latter, and hardly discernible at all in one most important virtue, the virtue of justice. Justice (to Hume as to Plato) is not the interest of the stronger, but the community of sentiment without which even a band of robbers (still less a State) would not hold together. It implies a recognition of common humanity, and it leads to the establishment of such an order as will save the community from starvation and want. This order would include certain institutions inevitable and permanent, but also institutions peculiar and transitory, to be explained as history and Montesquieu explain them.

Adam Smith may be regarded as following Hume's footsteps in his *Moral Sentiments*; but in his *Wealth of Nations* he is on the track of Quesnay, Mercier, Gournay, and the French Economists generally. Like them he contends against the economic policy of the Mercantile System, which would increase exports and manufactures to the prejudice of imports and agriculture in order to fill the treasury of the sovereign. The mercantile theory (of the 16th and 17th centuries) was more political than economical; it depended on the assumption that commercial independence is as desirable as political and can be as plainly secured. There was no "school" of mercantile teachers. But the Economists of France in the middle of the 18th century were certainly a school, perhaps the first school of economists strictly so called, and probably the most compact that has ever existed. Their economics and their political philosophy were in close connection. In economics they were on the whole the spokesmen of the capitalist farmers, as in later times Ricardo was spokesman of the capitalist manufacturers. The only net produce was to them the produce of agriculture and the extractive industries; and agriculture itself depended for its productiveness on the "advances" made by the farmers whether in the shape of wages or in the shape of material appliances. In a well-ordered state these facts would be recognised; taxation would be laid where in any event it must ultimately fall—on the landholding class, and not on the manufacturing and trading classes, who produce no surplus and can therefore give up none, and whose maintenance depends on the farming class. Complete liberty of trading both at home and with foreign nations should be allowed, in order that the agriculturists may get their wants supplied cheaply and thus have their powers of productive labour strengthened. This "natural order" of society is the basis of "natural rights," the condition under which these are exercised. These rights include right of property in labour or freedom to work where a man will, and right of property in the outward objects in which labour is embodied. The natural order secures to every man the fruits of his labour; and the appropriation of land is allowed, in order to furnish the motive for careful cultivation. This revival of the theories of Locke contributed to the growth of that popular political philosophy associated with the French Revolution.

Adam Smith, who was lending his aid to a similar if more sober movement of thought in England, had in his mind the plan of a complete social philosophy, of which the *Inquiry into the Nature and Causes of the Wealth of Nations* gives us one branch, the *Moral Sentiments* and the *Essays* giving us an idea of what the others might have been if the author had been able to finish his labours. Philosophy to him is "the science of the connecting principles of nature." The connecting principle is in ethics sympathy, in economics commercial ambition.

Both in ethics and economics he assumes that men are, and have been, substantially the same all the world over, and also that nature made the individuals, while groups or associations of individuals are artificial. Regard for society is very secondary and derivative. But without other individuals in which to see himself the character of a man could not develope, and he would have no moral sentiments. Direct sympathy is the origin of all virtues, including even Justice, in which Hume saw primarily utility. Adam Smith, feeling the power of Greek philosophy more than Hume, comes nearer than Hume to the idea of duty for duty's sake. He has also an even more optimistic belief in the equal diffusion of happiness; and, as a theist, he sees "an invisible hand" disposing human actions towards the general good, in spite of the shortcomings of the agents. He fully admits the need of improvement in the condition of the poor, as well as in political arrangements affecting all ranks of the people. But he thinks that improvement is usually spontaneous, and is better secured by the removal of obstacles than by deliberate attempts to advance the general welfare. The commercial ambition of men aiming purely at private interest secures the public benefit. In accordance with the principle of the division of labour, an organization of society, which he calls "the simple system of natural liberty," establishes itself of its own accord, even if the obstacles are not removed. So, like the French Economists, he advocates free trade at home and abroad, and he considers that men have a natural right to dispose of their labour and its product wherever and in whatever way they individually think best. The State exists mainly for defence of life and property and for the administration of justice, though it must also undertake public works, that would be left undone without its aid.

The doctrines of Political Economy are not fully considered in detail. The distinction of luxuries and necessaries, which had been brought into prominence by Mandeville and Hume, is recognised; but it was left to Malthus to show its bearing on the increase of the numbers of the people. The doctrine of value is sketched after the French Economists without the application to rent made by Adam Smith's successors. But there is no part of the subject that is not presented in some part or other of the *Wealth of Nations*, and one part at least (on taxation) not only in detail but systematically. In point of comprehensiveness, even Steuart's large treatise is inferior to his compatriot's. Adam Smith has exercised as momentous an influence on political economy as his friend Hume on metaphysics; and it is striking that the philosophy, which was by and by to grow out of a critical study of Hume, was destined at a later date to affect the political economy which grew out of a study of Adam Smith.

The next step in political economy was taken in face of a new Utopia of political philosophy, a proposal to do without the State altogether. The idea of following nature and dispensing with institutions, proposed ironically by Burke in his *Vindication of Natural Society*, is carried out seriously by William Godwin in his *Political Justice*. Society, as the spontaneous growth of Nature, is to stand alone without the State. Governments have injured not only trade, but every branch of human activity. The ideal is a simple society without government. The progress of enlightenment and the victory of truth will slowly but surely lead to a happy world, where plain living and high thinking will prevail, and there will be deliverance from passion and a sufficiency of leisure and comfort for all born into the world.

Malthus interposed with the criticism that there was no sign in men of such a disappearance of the passions and complete supremacy of reason. One passion in particular, the desire of marriage, would lead to consequences fatal to Godwin's society. When pressed, Malthus admitted that reason could be so far victorious as to put a "moral restraint" on this passion, deferring the satisfaction of it to save the standard of comfort. But it seemed to him that this restraint itself would be better fostered by the usual inequality of civilized men than by the equality of Godwin's ideal society.

Malthus brought into political economy that Utilitarian emphasis on consequences which has played a great part in it ever since. He also associated political economy with laws that were laws of nature, not in the lawyers' sense, but in the sense of the physical sciences. In the third place, he discredited the reference to natural rights, including the right to live and the right to labour. He showed that physical nature and human nature stood more seriously in the way of progress than human institutions, political and otherwise. Yet by throwing men back on their responsibility as individuals, he is more at one with Godwin and the French philosophers of the 18th century than he ever himself acknowledged. The same is true even of Bentham. Yet Bentham's criticism of natural rights and law of nature, as they were conceived at the end of the 18th century, was so searching that, in England at least, it has stood in the way of any such revival of these ideas as has taken place in Germany.

In place of them, Bentham introduced "the greatest happiness of the greatest number" as the test not only of good morals but of good legislation. He was supported by James Mill and Ricardo among economists, and the Utilitarian doctrine, as he held it, gave colour to economical writing for the next half century. The points of contact were the predominance of self-interest in the sense of regard for material prosperity, both in abstract economics and in the Utilitarianism of Bentham—the political individualism of both, the common assumption that human action is due to deliberate calculation, the common assumption of the boundlessness and indefinite expansion of human wants, the common use of a calculus of pains and pleasures, and the common assumption of the infallibility of the individual where the individual's interests are concerned. It can perhaps be shown that these are not necessary assumptions even of an abstract political economy; but the Utilitarian philosophy of Bentham was forced into union with economics and applied to politics by a group of men who strongly impressed their generation. James Mill, in applying these principles to the theory of government, argued that the end of government was to bring about such a distribution of the "materials for happiness" as would ensure the greatest sum thereof to its subjects, and it can best do this by increasing the inducements to labour, for without labour niggardly nature will yield us little or nothing. Now, the best inducement to labour (he says) is the securing of the fruits of it to the labourer; government therefore exists for the protection of the labourer against spoliation; in other words, it exists to protect property. Under such a government men following purely their own interests will further the public interest. James Mill allows that in international law we have to appeal to other motives, and trust to the respect men have for the praise or blame of their fellows; and he ought to have allowed for this element in the relation of subjects to sovereigns as well as of nation to nation,—while, as his son saw, he ought to have paid more regard to the "rights of minorities." The tendency of economists to confide in large numbers and averages, and to appeal (under cross-examination) to what will happen "in the long run" has been fortified by the old formula of Bentham. But Utilitarian political philosophy, in claiming Greatest Happiness for the majority, aided political reform in the direction of equality, and introduced a rough working test by which existing institutions must stand or fall.

John Stuart Mill, on whom fell his father's mantle, ceased to be a follower of Bentham and yet remained (in his own opinion) Utilitarian. But in ethics he admitted a difference in quality between pleasures, and therewith a nonutilitarian standard. In political philosophy he was led by the influence of French writers to recognise the impossibility of treating societies and States as if their component units were everywhere alike and all equally modifiable by legislation and argument. In his economics a similar concession is made, though the provisional necessity of an abstract method is firmly reasserted. Political economy (he says) deals with the "laws of such of the phenomena of society" as relate to wealth so far as those phenomena are not affected by other motives than the pursuit of wealth. But in reality he has two conceptions

284 Modern Philosophy: Materialistic Economics

of economic laws; there are the laws of production which are analogous to physical facts, and the laws of distribution which are of human institution, and therefore modifiable and in a sense arbitrary. The latter include such laws as necessarily follow from institutions once established (such as private property), even if the actual establishment of them be nowise necessary or always desirable. The laws of value and prices for example are thus hypothetically true for all societies. On the other hand, Mill has much to say on behalf of the contentions even of the Utopian socialists and communists. He refuses to put limits to the future possibilities of social union and communion; in this sense he is no adherent of Cobden and the Manchester School of political writers. None the less he is careful to protest that whatever action is taken by the State the personal liberty of the individual must be jealously maintained; and he considers that the individual is even now too much under the coercion of society, to say nothing of the State; —prejudice, for example, has maintained the "subjection of women." In claiming for women the same opportunities as for men, Mill has helped to widen our ideas of social progress, and made not only political but economical problems wear a new aspect.

In the up-building of economic theory Mill's work is less important. There is some ground for the charge that he is an eclectic, as well as for the charge that he is a formulator. The next step in economic theory was (in England at least) taken by economists who remained Utilitarians and based a theory of value as determined by Final Utility on Bentham's calculus of pleasures and pains. Mill, like Ricardo, excluded consumption from economics, and had no distinct glimpse of the new doctrine of Value. He thought that Ricardo had said the last word on the subject. Ricardo indeed has been the Spinoza of economic theory. Yet value, as a central economic doctrine relating to a central social problem, that of distribution, demanded the most searching investigation, and could not receive it except in connection with consumption.

In such an investigation twenty years ago or so, German and English economics found their point of convergence. After the common impulse given to both by Adam Smith and Ricardo, Germans and English had seemed to follow separate paths, as they have so often done in philosophy. In both countries, the phase of economics now reached has been largely even if indirectly affected by the philosophy.

German metaphysics made a new departure with Kant's *Critique of Pure Reason* in 1781, and German Ethics with the *Metaphysic of Ethics*, 1786, and *Critique of Practical Reason*, 1788. But political philosophy was not so well served by the Konigsberg philosopher. In his *Rechtslehre* (1796) Kant teaches that Civil Society exists to secure the outward freedom, not the happiness of its members. The rational (though not necessarily the historical) basis of the State, is an original contract by which all give up their natural liberty to secure civil liberty and are bound to give absolute submission to the ruler they have chosen. Kant's notion of the State is not very different from Adam Smith's; it is to be keeper of the peace and protector of property. Law is separated by him from Morality as, in Adam Smith and Hume, Justice is deemed unlike any of the other virtues. Kant looks forward to a Universal Peace, and thinks that trade will be a chief means of introducing it. "Nature," by a mechanism which is non-moral, will thus bring about a result demanded by the moral law. The individual looks after himself; nature provides for the race; and nature will one day secure that all human capacities shall be developed, in a cosmopolitan civil society. The development of the race in history will be slow and sure.

This notion of Development was expanded by Fichte, and still more by Hegel.

Fichte, agreeing with Kant in the severance of law from morality, goes far beyond him both in politics and in economics. He has two ideals, a National and a Cosmopolitan. The National Ideal is a State shut off from its neighbours industrially, as European Staces were then shut off politically; and this closed State was to be organized on socialistic principles to prevent the evils rampant (even a century ago) in the production and distribution of wealth. The Cosmopolitan Ideal is (like Godwin's) the absence of all States; when national States are perfect, they will make themselves superfluous, for they will present the world with an educated, purified, and elevated humanity that is able to order its conversation aright without any aid from them.

It might fairly be contended that Fichte's contemporary, Krause, has been a greater power than Fichte in economical speculation; he has certainly been so in the philosophy of law. The idea that natural right is a claim for the conditions that make a rational human life possible is first clearly taught by Krause, and it is found now not only among Krause's professed followers in Germany but in philosophers otherwise so divergent as T. H. Green[2] and Mr. Herbert Spencer, as well as in Lorimer.[3] It may indeed be described as the conception now dominant in the policy of all civilized governments, at least towards their own subjects. Since Grotius, and in spite of Hobbes, the idea that might is right has been discredited.

Both of Fichte's ideals were Utopias, and, like other Utopias, have lost their influence with the changes of time. His metaphysical doctrines have been really more potent, though seemingly more remote from everyday life. The conception of development as a progress through opposites was Fichte's contribution to Hegel's more ambitious and more logical system. Hegel finds that whatever is is composed of two opposite elements in process of becoming united in a third which reconciles them. His logic or "dialectic" is not (he says) simply in men's thoughts but in things themselves, for things and thought are one world. Hegel counts himself the most concrete of thinkers, for the opposite elements which other philosophers have regarded abstractly as necessarily separate he regards concretely as necessarily united. The process of development takes place by virtue of this conflict and union; the reconciling third element, held abstractly, awakes an opposite element of its own, and the two are then reconciled in a new concrete. The development involves that the past is not lost or destroyed but is "laid by" in the present. In human beings this process comes to light more clearly than elsewhere. For example, rational freedom arises out of the nullity of the abstractions of mere caprice and mere passion; it is the truth that was in them both. The philosophy of history traces the development of the idea of freedom from stage to stage. The philosophy of law, morals, society, and the State gives us a view of the same development, statically. True freedom does not (as some might fancy) lie in mere recognition of the individual's rights as a person, though the recognition of such rights is indeed indispensable to it; nor does freedom lie (as others might think) in mere consciousness of empire over oneself in obedience to a merely inward law of duty; it lies in a man's oneness with social institutions, where, while he has rights, he finds his duties also embodied. Law and morality are thus opposites which are reconciled and made concrete in the family, civil society, and the State. On Hegel's principles of development the last includes all the foregoing as its elements; and it seems to follow that there must always exist in the world of men, whatever the progress of the race, rights and duties, families and associations, all under the one State, which is as imperishable as they. Hegel gives an assured place to Civil Society as distinguished from the body politic; and it is in civil society that the "laws" of economics have their special sphere of action. But, though spontaneously formed, civil society (in his conception) passes necessarily into organized groups; and, the more numerous and the better organized the groups, the stronger and more nearly perfect is the State in which they grow. The strength of a State must on occasion be asserted outwardly, in conflict with other States; and the absolute cessation of such struggles (in negotiations or even in wars) cannot be expected, and is not to be desired. There is no outward force to bring the various States to one mind; but the indwelling and controlling power of Providence secures victory to that State which represents the general march of intellect at its farthest point. Such a State may be said to conquer by divine right; and so in history we find in successive epochs the Oriental, the Greek, the Roman, and finally the German spirit holding the field. The last includes and represents all the truth that was in the three former and something more. Even the Prussian Monarchy is to Hegel for this reason substantially rational. "What is real is rational."

Even before the death of Hegel in November, 1831, his followers had begun to break up into a Left, a Right, and a Centre. The Hegelian idea of development might be taken up (as it was by the Right), with an emphasis on its conservation of the past and its relative justification of the present;—or it might be taken up (as by the Left) with an emphasis on the ceaselessness of change, and the inevitableness of revolution;—or finally, by moderate men (of the Centre) the balancing of the two might be kept in the forefront, as it was by Hegel himself. It was the "Young Hegelians," or Hegelians of the Left, who passed from philosophy to economics, and applied the Hegelian notion of development to economic history. Strictly speaking, Marx and Engels applied it to all history, for they regard all history as ultimately the product of economic causes. The certain economic revolution brings with it in their view the certain political revolution.

The first elaborate attempt to apply the logic of Hegel to economics was made by the Anarchist P. J. Proudhon in 1846; but the phraseology of Hegel was employed by Proudhon without any thorough appreciation of its spirit, and the ideas of classical economists were handled with a fallacious if not sophistical perversion of their meaning. Proudhon's way of escape from a labyrinth of his own constructing is in the end an unintelligible compromise in the guise of a Hegelian reconciliation of opposites. Marx, in exposing Proudhon, states his own position. He rejects the current view that property and the institutions that concern the protection of property and the production and distribution of wealth are "natural" and permanent. They belong, he says, to a stage in history beyond which development will certainly carry us. As the antagonism of the aristocracy and the middle classes under feudalism has landed us in our present social and political institutions, so the present antagonism of the middle classes and the working classes will carry us into a completely different system of society. But to understand and co-operate with this change we need to understand the economic situation as it is. The inquiry thus foreshadowed in 1847 was carried out in 1859 and 1867. The book of Marx on *Capital* took Ricardo and his theory of value in earnest. In the present state of industry, goods and services are exchanged according to "the average social human labour" needed to produce them. Goods are made for sale, not for use; and, as competition reduces the value to the average cost, they only yield a profit to the employer when he forces his "hands" to work a certain portion of their day for nothing. The possession of property by the employer makes this feat possible; and with its accomplishment the growth of capital goes on, and its reign is more and more firmly established. Not so firmly however that it will not sooner or later give place to a system under which the instruments of production will be held by the State for all, instead of by the few for themselves. When the struggle of the classes reaches its keenest intensity, the end is at hand, the revolution will come.

The view that all history is economical seems to be as abstract as Ricardos economics, on which Marx founds his own political economy. Historical Economists have pointed in the opposite direction; they have reasoned "from particular to particular"; they have tended to explain all economics by the other elements in history rather than all history by its economical element. Yet Engels, who gives the most recent exposition of the "scientific socialism" of Marx, retains the "materialistic" view of history, and even pushes it beyond written history to the history of primitive man. Lassalle had applied the same view to the development of legal forms.

But neither the Materialistic view of history nor the Ricardian economics can be said to be so essential to modern socialism that its claims disappear when either is refuted. Its strength lies in its appeal to the principle that there is a right of all human beings to the opportunities of developing what is in them, and in its powerful demonstration that such a right is not now realized.

But, though the materialism of socialists is irrelevant to the issues, the notion of development is not. The object, even of economical inquiry, is not merely facts but their connection and sequence. This is even more true of political philosophy generally. We must therefore ask ourselves what meaning the theory of development or evolution is to receive and what follows from the acceptance of it.

The popular notion of evolution is that of continuous change. The philosophical conception of it, long ago presented by Greek and perfected by German philosophy, is that of a change where the past is not abolished but preserved, and the subject which has experienced the development remains identical throughout the changes, that which was in it in germ at the beginning reaching its maturity at the end. Hegel would add that the development proceeds by a conflict of opposite principles.

The Darwinian theory is a particular form of the theory of development. It is a theory of continuous change, where in the struggle for existence natural selection secures the survival of the fittest. It is applied especially to the origin of species among living things. By the principle of Malthus, which Darwin accepts, nature causes an indefinitely great propagation of individuals, each of which, though very like every other, has some small point of difference. As they cannot all find room and food, those only will live and breed which have such points of difference as will help them to succeed in the struggle for existence. The result of centuries of accumulated variations is seen in groups of living creatures differing from each other, the one group from the other, so widely as to seem absolutely different species; but all have come from a common ancestral pair; and the differences are due to the different circumstances of the struggle, and to the accumulated peculiarities that enabled particular individuals to live and breed where the less fortunate failed. Naturalists are now agreed that natural selection has been at least one very potent cause of the origin of species, though the extent of the influence of the subsidiary causes is not so undisputed. But the Darwinian theory assumes, without explaining, the variations of individuals; and it provides us with no means of pronouncing a judgment as to the quality of the results of this evolution. There is no identity of Subject throughout the changes, and there is nothing in the theory to show that the last winners are "better," by any other standard than that of successful survival. There are many instances of Darwinian development in economic phenomena; and economics, like Darwinism, gives us by itself no means of judging the results. But the struggle for existence means, by ordinary standards of judgment, something less savage when it is between societies than when it is between individual men; and even the Darwinian notion of development can be applied, like the Malthusian theory of population, in a form which betokens improvement as well as mere survival. It is not the bare doctrine that might is right. Within civilized nations the contest becomes a struggle not for mere living but for a better life; and the vanquished are converted, in spite of themselves, not slain or allowed to die. To apply the theory in this way to societies, however, we need to found our standard of judgment not on the Darwinian but on the philosophical notion of development.

It is not obvious that Darwinism would favour socialism, or indeed any particular plan of social reform. It explains how, but not why, certain occurrences have taken place, and leaves us still to deal with our old problems by the aid of conceptions outside of Darwinism itself. Darwinism is in keeping with the view that the industrial improvement and organization surrounding us have in great part grown up spontaneously, or tentatively, and that *laissez-faire* does not necessarily mean chaos. The development of the individual members of society is the chief end of society itself, and of the State which is its articulate representative head. To secure this end, the necessary outward conditions must be assured to each member of society; and, as long as human nature remains as it has been in all history, so long there will be need for a State to do this work. But, as each individual must himself use the opportunities, so assured to him, in his own way, there must be (in no narrow sense of the word) individual liberty secured to him. The future may bring with it changes in the statute laws of property, in order to bring it within reach of every one, as a condition of development. As long as there is room kept open for personal and moral freedom, originality, and every kind of individual variation, the world of mankind will not be losers.

Notes

1 *E.g.*, in the writings of Wagner and Cohn, Cossa and Loria.
2 As early as 1881. *Liberal Legislation and Freedom of Contract*, p. 10. See also *Works*, vol. ii. 450, 476, 477, 479, and especially p. 341 note, though Krause's early view is there treated as his final.
3 See above, p. 196. Compare Pulszky *Theory of Law and Civil Society* (Engl, transl.), 1888, pp. 342, etc.

Index

Debasement of currency: (Bodin) 52, (Hobbes) 63.

Debts (Public): the ruin of nations (Hume) 79.

Definitions: 9, 74, 114, 163, 184. See Abstract Method.

DEGRASLIN: 142 n.

Democracy: (Machiavelli) 15, 48–49, (Harrington) 43n7, 69 (Rousseau) 272 (Hegel and Aristotle) 256, democracy and music, 272.

DEMOCRITUS: 18.

DESCARTES (René): 154, 256, 269.

De TOCQUEVILLE (A.): 181.

Development: ix, x, 11, 21, 20, Book V. ch. ii *passim*, of faculties 20, not in Mill 159, (Kant) 238, (Fichte) 245 (Hegel) Book IV. ch. IV *passim*, development and Darwinism xiii.

DIDEROT (Denys): 100. See Encyclopedists.

DIEHL (Dr. K.): 260n29, 261n40.

DIETRICH (K.) 208n35.

Distribution: (Plato) xii, 4, 9, 14, (Aristotle) 25, (More) 49, 51, 52, (Hobbes) 62, (Harrington) of land, 69, 71, (Hume) 87, 90, (Ad. Smith) 159, 172, laws of—23n31, 59n6, 284, (Godwin) 285, (Malthus) 159, (James Mill) 172, (J. S. Mill) 159, 172, (Darwin) 268, in distant future 85.

Division of labour: (Plato) 4, 11–13, 15, 18, 20, (Aristotle) 26, 29 (Xenophon) 22n17, (More) 77, (Grotius) 104, 139, (Locke 281, (Hume) 116, (Ad. Smith) 154 *seq.*, 161, (Godwin) 156, (Fichte) 212–13, (in relation to Government) 230, (Proudhon) epoch of—246, primitive 154, 203 physiological 116, a permanent fact 19.

Domains: (Hobbes) 62.

DOVE (P. E.): 220n10.

DUMONT (Etienne): 177n46.

DUNBAR (Prof. C. F.): 108n39.

DUPONT DE NEMOURS: 106, 108n31.

Duties as divine commandments: 132 Note.

DWIGHT (T. W.): 69n13.

Economy: relation of means and ends 168, relation of past, present, future 85, economy and waste 82, 106, 115.

Economics: in sense of Domestic Economy 25, 52, 182.

Economical element predominant: viii.

Economical Categories and Legal (or Historical): 13, 55, 141, 189, 202, 211, 213, 228.

Economists, schools of: (Marx) 250.

EDMONDS (T. R.): 261n36.

Education: (Plato) 11, 18, 20 (Harrington) 69, Physiocrats 100, 101, (Ad. Smith) 138 (Rousseau) 131, (J. S. Mill) 159, (Fichte) 219, (Krause) 222, (Hegel) 166, 211, (Proudhon) 247, (Maurice) 274n23, in view of Development 224.

ELSTER (Prof. L.): 34n43.

EMERSON (R. W.): 261n38.

Emigration: (J. S. Mill) 217, 218, (Fichte) 209, 210 (Hegel) 224.

Encyclopedists: 131, 138.

ENDEMANN (W): 43n8.

ENGELS (Friedrich): Book V. ch. i., also 244.

Ephors: (in Fichte) 216.

EPICURUS: 37, 126, 202, (Hume's "Epicurean") 37.

Equality: (Aristotle) 52, (Bodin) 52, (Hobbes) 173, (Locke) 72, 73, (Hume) 92 (Physiocrats) 114, equal distribution of happiness 91, (Ad. Smith) 48, 73, (Rousseau) 118, 131, (Godwin) 151, (Condorcet) 154, (Malthus) 79, 154, (Bentham) 82, (J. S. Mill) 145, (Christianity) 51, 57, (Darwin) 160, 161.

ERDMANN (Prof. J. E.): 3, 5n2, 22n19, 23n64, 34n43, 239.

ERYXIAS: (pseudo-Platonic) 22.

ESPINAS (Prof. A.): 5, 54n25, 107n6.

Ethics: relation to economics, etc. 82, 86, (Plato) 4, 9, (Aristotle) 27, (Christianity) 58, (More) 177n30, (Grotius) 55, 58, (Hobbes) 71, (Mandeville) 47, (Ad. Smith) 202, (Godwin) 154, (Malthus) 157, 158, (Bentham) 196, relation to legislation 235, (J. S. Mill) 186, (Kant) 201, (Fichte) 211, (Krause) 222, (Hegel) 228.

EUCKEN (Prof. Rudolf): 146n17, 208n30.

Evolution: the word 158 n. See Development.

OWEN (Robert): 86, 158. 197n4, 244, 246, 254.

PAINE (Thomas): xii, 141, 143, 146n6, 193.
PALEY (Archdeacon): 79.
PALGRAVE (R. H. I.): xi, 34n43, 43n8, 176n5, n9.
PANTALEONI (M.): 176n15.
Papacy as international mediator, 55.
PARADOL (Prévost): 24n81.
Paraguay: Jesuits in 190 (cf. 29).
Parliamentary representation: (J. S. Mill) 194, (Hegel) 237.
PATTEN (Prof. S. N.): 162n33.
Penal laws: 10, 104.
Perfectibility (Fichte) 210, (Hegel) 238, (Proudhon) 247. See also Condorcet, Godwin.
PERRY (Prof. A. L.): 161n12.
Personality: (Stoics) 38, in relation to property (Hegel) 122, to the body (Fichte) 213.
PESTALOZZI (J. H.): 219.
PETTY (William): 110.
Philosophy: described xvii, relation to economics etc. 275, science of connecting principles (Ad. Smith) 112, systems like machines 112, philosophy and sciences (J. S. Mill) 145.
Philosophical Radicals: 141.
Physiocrats: viii, xii, 5, 98–107, 108n35.
Physiology: 4, 135n46, 183.
Piecework: 120.
PITT (Wm., the Younger): 134n12, 151, 163.
Plagiarisms: 106 n.
PLATO: origin of State 90, 231, two ideals in Republic 285, ideal in Laws 285, (Aristotle on) 245, Christian counterparts to Guardians 11–13. compared with More 80, 85, 87 "*sponte acta*" 90, government 90, 231, division of labour 115, City of Pigs 11, 13, 130, philosopher kings pseudo-temperance 206, pleasures differing in kind 26, xii, 4, 10, 11, 145
Pleasure and desire: xvii.
PLECHANOFF (G.): 260n5.
Political Economy: described vii, distinct study 275, relation to cognate studies 57, modern

begins with taxation 75, described by Hume 282, concerned in metaphysical controversy 249, dealing with things "limited in supply" (Jones etc.) 57, 88, touching philosophy 190, the name P. E. 220n10, branch of philosophy (Ad. Smith) 113, narrow and wide sense 120, including theory of population 183, defined (J. S. Mill) 165, schools of (Marx) xii, concerned with development 205. See also Economy, Classical Economists.
Population: (Aristotle) 33 (cf. 64), (More) 52, (Bodin) 52, (Hobbes) 173, English in 17th century 175, 251, encouragements to (Harrington and Locke) 99, 157 (Berkeley) 79, (Mercantile theory) 47, 53, (Physiocrats) 99, (Ad. Smith) 157, relation to natural rights 139, (Godwin) 153, (Condorcet) 204, (Malthus) 155 (J. S. Mill) 183, (Hegel) 231, (Proudhon) 247, (Marx) 253, (Darwin) 158, 161.
POSTE (E.): 24n80, 35n57.
Primogeniture: (Hegel) 236.
PRIOR (Matthew): 146.
Production: (Plato) xii, (Aristotle) 25, (More) 49, (Locke) 243 (Hume) 267, productive class (Physiocrats) 103, (Ad. Smith) 94n2, 134n29, (J. S. Mill) 202, (Kant) 204, (Fichte) 215, (Proudhon) 331, 334, (Marx) 249, for sale and for use 42, 271 feudal 250.
Productive labour 118–9, 281
Profits: (Marx) 253. See also Interest, Usury.
Proletariate: Book V. 270.
Property: (Plato) 11, (Aristotle) 26, (canon law) 4, 41, 43n8, (More) 52, (Grotius) 55, (Hobbes) 53, (Harrington) 93, (Locke) 92, relation to value 165, (Hume) 284, (Physiocrats) 114 (Ad. Smith) 138–9, (Rousseau) 153, (Godwin) 282, (Bentham) 283, (James Mill) 283, (J. S. Mill) 185, (Kant) 246, (Fichte) 222, 225, (Hegel) 255, (Proudhon) 246, laws modifiable in future 284.
Protection: (J. S. Mill) 202, (Fichte) 213.